How to do *just about* anything on a

COMPUTER

Microsoft® Windows®

xp
edition

READER'S DIGEST

How to anything

do *just about*
on a
COMPUTER

Microsoft® Windows®
xp
edition

Published by The Reader's Digest Association Limited
LONDON • NEW YORK • SYDNEY • MONTREAL

Contents

PRACTICAL HOME PROJECTS

TROUBLESHOOTING

How to use this book

Find out how this book will help you make the most of your PC

With easy step-by-step tuition, expert advice and inspirational ideas, How To Do Just About Anything On A Computer *will help you put your computer to the best use*

Unlike most other computer books, *How To Do Just About Anything On A Computer* assumes that you are more interested in, say, creating a letterhead than you are in becoming an expert on electronics. For this reason, the book is organised into projects – all the things you are likely to want to do with your PC. These projects are designed to be of real, practical benefit to you and your family.

Learning to use your computer is more fun when approached in this way. You'll see why the programs work the way they do, and so you can apply these skills to other tasks.

Each project is set out into easy-to-follow, step-by-step procedures. The steps are accompanied by pictures that show you what you'll see on your screen. This means you'll never be left wondering 'Where's the menu they are telling me to click?' because you'll see a snapshot that shows exactly where the arrow should be when you click it.

Before you explore the full potential of your PC, you need to set it up, learn some housekeeping and get to know Microsoft® Windows®, the ringmaster of your PC's programs. This is covered in the first part of the book: 'You and Your Computer'.

Today's computers are increasingly reliable. But if glitches occur, turn to the Troubleshooting section. In most cases, you'll find what you need to get your PC running smoothly again.

All the rest is down to you: we hope you enjoy the countless tasks you can achieve on your PC.

Getting around the book

How To Do Just About Anything On A Computer contains four sections, taking you from the initial set-up, to connecting to the Internet, applying your skills practically and solving problems. Each follows a similar step-by-step format with snapshots of what should be on your screen at any given stage of a process.

You and Your Computer

This section guides you through setting up your PC, understanding the roles of hardware and software, and learning the basics of key programs. Find out how to care for your computer and how to maximise its efficiency.

The Internet

Learn how to connect to the Internet. Find out how to send and receive electronic mail (e-mail), and access information through the World Wide Web quickly and safely. You can even learn how to create your own web page for other users to access.

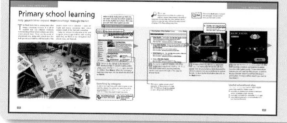

Practical Home Projects

Choose from 40 practical projects that take you through the steps involved in creating a range of documents, including a recipe database, kitchen plan, illustrated stationery, home accounts spreadsheet, greetings cards and posters.

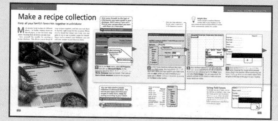

Troubleshooting

Your computer and its related hardware and software can behave unexpectedly at times. If this happens to you, don't panic. This section helps ease your concerns and offers a wide range of easy-to-follow solutions to common problems.

Special features

The book also offers the opportunity to apply your skills to real-life projects.

Make your PC skills work for you

The book contains larger undertakings that require you to draw on the skills you have developed as you try your hand at individual projects. Use your word-processing skills, your spreadsheet know-how and your graphics experience to take the stress and drudgery out of moving house, running a club, or organising a family celebration.

Glossary and Index

Found a word you don't understand? Turn to the back of the book to find clear, concise definitions of the most commonly used terms and phrases. You'll also find a comprehensive index to guide you around the book.

Which software?

This book assumes that readers are operating PCs that run Microsoft® Windows® XP Home Edition. Windows XP is a great advance over earlier versions, such as Windows ME and 98, and in places is significantly different from its predecessors. Even so, much of the advice given in this book applies to older systems, and most of the home projects are possible using earlier versions.

With the exception of a few projects that use specialist software, most projects use either Microsoft® Office® XP (Standard Edition) or Microsoft® Works® 6.0. Any instructions regarding, say, Microsoft Word (the Word Processing program within Office) will also apply to the Works Word Processor unless otherwise stated.

Where necessary, the book will also refer to other programs you can buy that work in a similar way.

And which hardware?

You do not need a top-of-the-range computer to get the most out of this book. The minimum specifications for your PC are a 300Mhz or faster Intel Celeron/Pentium or AMD K6/Athlon/Duron processor, 64MB of memory (although 128MB makes everything work much faster) and a CD-ROM or DVD Drive. Any PC bought new in the last two years is likely to be at least this powerful.

Finding your way around the page

You are guided through every project in this book by means of a series of illustrated steps and a range of visual features. Here are the key features you should look for on the page.

Before you start
Projects begin with a Before You Start box. This outlines points to consider, documentation to collect, and tasks to do before beginning the project.

Extra help
Above and below the steps you will find hints, tips and warnings of common pitfalls.

Step-by-step
Projects are set out in easy-to-follow steps, from the first mouse click to the last. You get instructions on what keyboard and mouse commands to give, and what programs, folders and menus to access to complete the project.

Other programs
This tells you which other programs can be used to complete the project, and how to access them.

Templates on CD-ROM
This lets you know that you can access predesigned templates for the project on the accompanying CD-ROM.

Magnifications
Snapshots of the PC screen that require special attention are magnified so that you can see them more clearly.

Additional information
Below the steps you will find explanations of the more complicated aspects of the project, as well as tips and variations.

Snapshots
Pictures of the PC screen – snapshots – show you what you should be seeing on your screen at the point they appear in the project.

Bold type
Anything written in bold type indicates a command that you need to carry out. It could be a menu, menu option, dialogue box tab or button. It might also be a toolbar button that you need to click on with your mouse, or a key on your keyboard that you need to press. You will also find words in quotation marks which are either the exact words you will see on screen, or those that you must type in as part of a step.

PRACTICAL HOME PROJECTS

Hints and tips

You will find additional information to help you complete the task in hand and to improve your understanding of the workings of your PC.

Close-up
These offer an insight into the complicated workings of your computer, allowing you to get an idea of what happens 'behind the scenes'.

Key word
Important words or phrases are defined in order to increase your understanding of the process being addressed on the page.

Short cut
Look for this symbol for guidance on increasing your efficiency by learning quick and easy ways to complete common tasks.

Watch out
These warn you about problems that you may encounter, or mistakes you might easily make, as you use your computer.

Bright idea
These are suggestions for variations or additions you can make to a project which can help you adapt it to your specific needs.

Talking to your computer

Your PC is always ready to carry out your orders. You can communicate with it in any of the following ways.

Menus

In most programs you will see a menu bar sitting across the top of the program window. On it will be a File menu through which you can select options to save a document and print. There will also be an Edit menu, through which you can cut (remove) text or images and paste (insert) them elsewhere.

To access a menu, click on the menu name. The contents of the menu will appear in a drop-down list. Click on the command you want your PC to perform.

Toolbars

Toolbars feature a series of buttons that can be clicked to access frequently used commands – the command for saving a document, for example. They offer a quick alternative to going through the drop-down menus. The toolbar or toolbars (some programs have several) are located at the top of the program window just below the menu bar. To find out what a toolbar button does, place your mouse pointer over it – in most programs a description pops up.

Dialogue boxes

If your computer needs you to make a decision or give it additional information (this often happens when you enter a command through a menu or the toolbar), a box will pop up on your screen and ask you to confirm or alter the program's default settings (these are standard settings which you can alter to your own liking).

Do so by clicking in the relevant parts of the box, by selecting choices from lists, or by typing in information. Some dialogue boxes contain identification tabs, much like those used in a filing cabinet, which you click on to access other windows through which you enter related information. In Excel's Format Cells dialogue box, for example (below left), there are tabs for Number, Alignment, Font, Border, Pattern and Protection. If you click on the Font tab (below), you can then select a font, font style, size and colour for your text.

Mouse instructions

You will often be asked to use the buttons on your mouse. These are the terms used:

Click Press and release your left mouse button once.
Double-click Press and release your left mouse button twice in quick succession.
Right-click Press and release your right mouse button once (a pop-up menu will often appear).
Drag Press your left mouse button and, keeping it pressed down, move your mouse so that your cursor 'drags' across the screen (this is used to highlight text or reshape an object).

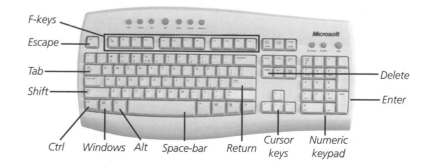

Keyboard help

Use your keyboard to take short cuts to commonly used commands (see page 74 for details). If you are advised to use one of the special 'hot-keys' (shown right), you will often find a picture of the recommended key, such as the one shown left.

F-keys
Escape
Tab
Shift
Ctrl   Windows   Alt   Space-bar   Return   Cursor keys   Numeric keypad
Delete
Enter

YOU AND YOUR

The better you **understand** your PC, the more you will get out of it. Knowing what each element of the PC does, and how to **set it up** properly, will get you up and running. And good **housekeeping** practices will ensure that your PC functions **efficiently**. Once you master the basics, you will have laid the **foundations** for successful computing.

COMPUTER

Setting up your computer

Your new PC has arrived. Start off on the right foot by setting up your work area properly

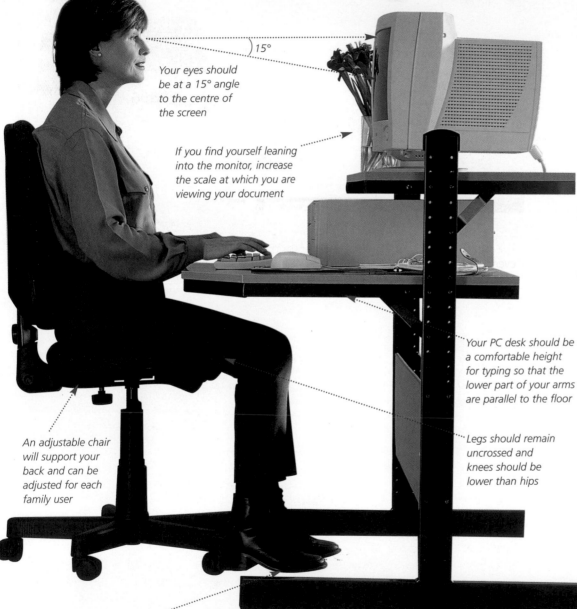

15°

Your eyes should be at a 15° angle to the centre of the screen

If you find yourself leaning into the monitor, increase the scale at which you are viewing your document

Your PC desk should be a comfortable height for typing so that the lower part of your arms are parallel to the floor

An adjustable chair will support your back and can be adjusted for each family user

Legs should remain uncrossed and knees should be lower than hips

Feet should rest flat on the floor

Your computer will be a valuable tool for all the family, so it's worth taking time to plan your computer space and system well, to ensure it is both easy and safe to use.

Ideally, it would be best to convert a small room, or a corner of a larger one, into an office, so all the family can use the computer without being disturbed. When selecting an area, check that there is adequate space and several mains sockets, not just for your equipment but for a desk lamp, too. You will also need to be near a telephone socket, so that you can connect to the internet or send and receive faxes.

Set aside some time – 3 to 4 hours – to set up your computer properly. Think carefully about how to arrange your area, as a poorly laid out system will be irritating and may even prevent you from using your computer to the full.

It's a good idea to spend some time reading those manuals, too. You need to know where to plug in the cables!

● *Invest in a proper computer desk. This allows you to alter the height of the monitor and keyboard, and tuck the keyboard away when not in use.*
● *Buy an adjustable chair, which all the family can adjust for good posture and maximum support.*
● *If your feet don't rest comfortably on the ground, buy a footrest.*

COMPUTER FURNITURE

Naming and placing the parts of your computer

Your PC's hardware comprises all the parts that you can actually see and handle. Knowing exactly where to place each of these elements will ensure a safe and efficient work area.

Monitor
This houses the computer screen. Position your monitor to avoid reflections, but avoid facing a bright window yourself as this may lead to eyestrain.

System unit
This is the part of your computer that connects everything together. Leave space so that you can plug in the cables easily. Don't leave cables trailing.

External speakers
For the best sound quality, speakers should be well spaced apart at desk level or higher, not just pushed under the desk. Ensure that the computer is situated so that others are not disturbed by computer games or alert sounds.

Mouse
Place the mouse to the left or right of your keyboard to minimise arm movement. Use a mouse mat to create the correct amount of friction for the mouse, and be sure there is room to move the mouse back and forth.

Keyboard
Make sure the keyboard is on a stable and level surface within easy reach. Leave enough space in front for hands and wrists. Ensure that the desk is at the correct height.

Printer
Position your printer near the system unit. Make sure there is sufficient space around it for loading the paper trays.

⚠ Watch out
Repetitive Strain Injury (RSI) is muscle strain due to repeated actions. Home PC users are unlikely to experience problems but a good posture and typing technique is still essential. When working at your PC, stand up, stretch and move about regularly.

Hardware and software

Understanding how these operate is key to success

Hardware and software work together to allow you to perform the wide variety of functions possible on your PC.

Hardware is the actual 'body' of the computer system, comprising the system unit and all the elements that you can plug into it, such as the keyboard. Your computer's hardware determines which type of operating system you can use. PCs made with Intel processors, for example, cannot run the Apple Macintosh operating system.

Software is the thinking part, or mind, of your computer, putting all the hardware to work. The most important piece of software on your computer is the operating system. By translating your instructions into a language the hardware can understand, the operating system lets you communicate with various computer parts and control how the computer and its accessories work. Microsoft® Windows® is the most popular operating system for PCs. An operating system is so important to the workings of a computer that, without one, you cannot open any files, use a printer or see anything on the screen.

However, in order to perform specific functions, such as editing a report, playing a computer game or keeping a check on your household spending, your computer also needs to use specialised software, called programs. There are thousands of programs available, each designed to perform different kinds of tasks. Programs enable you to do anything, from writing formal letters and compiling spreadsheets, to editing digital imagery and even making your own films.

Other types of computer

Apple Macintosh computers, or Macs, work in a similar way to PCs in that you access documents through a desktop. Although some programs, such a Microsoft® Word, are available for both Macs and PCs the two versions are different and cannot be run on the other operating system.

Swapping files between PCs and Macs can sometimes be difficult, not least because modern Macs do not have floppy disk drives.

Introducing your software

Understanding what software does will help you to get the most out of your PC. This introduction describes the operating system and the different types of program available.

The operating system

The operating system allows you to interact with the computer's hardware. It manages the saving of files on the hard disk, translates commands given through the keyboard and mouse, and sends data to the screen or printer. It also interacts with other programs you may be running, allowing them to communicate with the hardware.

Any software packages you use rely on the operating system to provide this basic level of communication with the hardware. Most new PCs are supplied with Windows XP as their operating system. Earlier versions include Windows 98 and Windows Me.

Which program?

FINANCIAL PROGRAM

For calculating household expenditure, use a financial program. This will enable you to keep a check on your domestic bills, monitor your outgoings and work out your overall balance, enabling you to manage your money effectively.

WORD PROCESSING PROGRAM

To write letters, reports and any other documents that are mainly text-based, use a word processing program or the word processing tool in software suites. Most include a range of fonts and style features and allow you to insert pictures in the text.

GRAPHICS PROGRAM

To work with pictures use a graphics program. This will help you to create greetings cards, invitations, posters and personal stationery. You can use the graphic galleries available on your PC or from CD-ROM galleries. You can even use your own photographs.

DATABASE PROGRAM

To make address lists, or lists of contact details, use a database program. Software suites often have a database tool, or you can use a separate database program for more complex work.

SPREADSHEET PROGRAM

For making complex budget calculations and carrying out financial analysis you can use a spreadsheet program. These programs can also show figures as a chart or graph.

GAMES PROGRAM

Playing with games is an entertaining way of becoming more adept on the computer. You usually have to buy each game program separately, although some systems come with some simple games included.

Key word

Software suite *A software suite incorporates the basic aspects of several programs in one package. While their components may not be as powerful or as versatile as individual programs, low-cost suites such as Microsoft Works offer value for money and let you perform many useful tasks.*

Storing software on your hard disk

All software, whether it be the operating system or programs, uses storage space on your hard disk. This space is measured in terms of 'bits' and 'bytes'.

A bit is the smallest unit of computer storage. A combination of eight bits makes up a byte.

A kilobyte (KB) is 1,024 bytes; a megabyte (MB) is 1,024 KB; and a gigabyte (GB) is 1,024 MB.

A typical home computer will have as much as 60 GB of hard disk space. This space is soon used up – the Microsoft Office suite alone can use several hundred megabytes of disk space, and the Microsoft Works suite uses around 40MB.

Making the most of hardware

Get the most out of your PC by understanding the purpose of each part

Once you have unpacked your PC and set up the different hardware elements, it's worth taking the time to get to know exactly what each part does.

All personal computers have the same basic elements. Knowing how they fit together and operate as a unit – and understanding where you fit into the picture – will help you and your family to get the most out of home computing.

Your computer is simply a tool that, given the correct instructions and data, will make your day-to-day life easier and more enjoyable. You enter instructions and information into the computer via the mouse and keyboard. The results can be seen on your monitor's screen and printed out on your printer. The most important part of the computer – the system unit – links all these elements together.

Whatever make of computer you have, it will have these same key components that allow you to use it. Although most computers look similar, there are variations between models, so always check instructions in the computer manual to make sure you're using your equipment correctly.

The mouse

A mouse is used to select items on screen and move the text cursor (a flashing line that identifies where new text appears). You move the mouse around with your hand and a mouse pointer moves around on the screen, allowing you to select menus and click on commands.

The monitor

Your monitor is home to the computer screen, which shows you what your computer is doing. Monitor screens come in different sizes and, in the interests of preventing eyestrain, the bigger the better. LCD (liquid crystal display) flat screens take up less space and can give much sharper pictures than older CRT (cathode ray tube) designs.

The keyboard

The keyboard is used for typing in data and commands, and has the familiar typewriter keys plus a number of extra ones. On the right is a separate numeric keypad, plus navigation keys (with arrows) that help you to move around the screen. There is also a series of function keys along the top that allow you to give special commands.

⚠ Watch out

Always use the Shut Down command from the Start menu before turning the power switch off. Never turn the power switch off when Windows is running. Some newer PCs automatically switch off power when shutting down.

💡 Bright idea

If environmental issues are a concern for you, look out for 'green' hardware. Some manufacturers have used plastics and packaging in their computer systems that can be recycled.

The system unit

This is where all the cables plug in. Whether your system unit is on its side (a desktop unit), or its end (a tower unit), it acts in the same way. The system unit also contains disk drives (a floppy disk drive and a CD-ROM drive).

Power switch
This is used to turn your PC on and, on older PCs, to turn it off.

Optical drive
Your PC has either a CD-ROM or a DVD-ROM. Use it to install new software, and play music CDs or DVD movies. You may also have a CD-RW for saving files.

Power-in socket
This is used to connect the PC to the mains supply.

PC expansion cards
The sockets here let you connect other devices, such as speakers and monitors, to expansion cards fitted inside the PC.

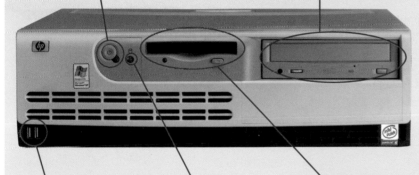

USB sockets
Sockets on the front of a PC make it easier to connect devices.

Hard disk light
This light flickers when the hard disk is being used by the computer.

Floppy disk drive
This allows you to store or transfer files to your PC on a floppy disk.

Mouse and keyboard sockets
Serial ports used to connect the mouse and keyboard to the PC.

Serial port
Used to connect the PC to an external modem. PCs with internal modems will have a modem telephone socket. You may be able to plug a mouse in here.

Printer port
This connects the PC to the printer. It is also called the parallel port.

USB Sockets
Use these sockets to connect items like music players, scanners, cameras or joysticks. There may also be convenient extra sockets on the front of your PC. You may also be able to connect your mouse and keyboard this way.

Printers

You need a printer to put your work on paper. Almost all home printers are ink-jets. Even cheap versions can print in colour at near photo quality. More expensive versions print each page more quickly and on larger paper sizes.

If you will be printing lots of pages, a a more expensive laser printer may be a better idea. It will produce better quality black and white print-outs and most likely have a faster printing speed.

Laptop computers

All the components of a laptop computer are in a single unit. The screen is smaller and not as bright as on a desktop computer. The keyboard is smaller and does not have the extra keys. The mouse is built-in, as a tiny joystick or touchpad.

Laptops can be powered from the mains or by a rechargeable battery, but don't expect more than 4 hours use from a single charge.

Starting up your computer

You've set it all up – now switch on and begin using your PC

Once your computer's been set up properly, you're ready to get going – so remember to make sure it's turned on at the mains.

Turn on the computer via the power switch on the system unit. You also need to turn on the monitor. The Windows XP logo appears above a set of three scrolling green 'lights', showing that the computer is checking itself over. After a few moments you will see the Logon screen. Click on your username (you will need to enter a password if you use one). After a few moments you'll see a colour screen that Windows calls the Desktop. Small pictures, or icons, will appear on the Desktop, and you may also see a message asking if you would like to find out about new features in XP.

The Desktop icons

Through the Desktop icons you can access important utilities and all your work. To open an icon place your mouse pointer over the top of it and double-click with the left mouse button.

 In Windows XP, click on the Start button to see the **Start Menu**. This contains links to all of your programs, your files, photographs and music, and to system utilities and help text.

The programs and files you use most often have their own links. Despite its name, the Start menu is also the place to go if you want to turn your computer off, or switch to another user.

My Computer shows you all your computer's disks (hard drive, floppy disk and CD-ROM drive).

My Documents leads to a folder that you can use to store any files you create.

 My Network Places allows you to access and view other computers connected to your own.

 Recycle Bin is where files go after deletion. These can then be deleted completely or retrieved if you have made a mistake.

Running along the bottom of your screen is the **Taskbar**. It always contains the Start button and usually a clock. There may also be other program buttons visible, such as Microsoft Internet Explorer. As you open new windows, they will appear as buttons on the Taskbar, so you can always see what's open, even when other windows cover them up.

Basic window features

Programs and files are displayed inside a window, and your computer can display several windows at once. This key will help you find your way around.

Menu bar
This contains drop-down menus through which you issue commands.

Minimise button
This reduces the window to an icon on the Taskbar.

Maximise button
This enlarges the window to fill the screen. Click on it again to return it to its original size.

Title bar
This displays the name of the window. To move the window, click on the Title bar and, with the left mouse button pressed down, move the mouse pointer across the computer screen. This is called 'dragging'.

Close button
This closes the window.

Scroll bars
To view any hidden contents of a window, click on the arrows at the ends of the scroll bar or click on and drag the slide bar.

Toolbar
Toolbar buttons provide shortcuts to common commands.

Window borders
To resize windows, place the mouse pointer over the window's border. When the pointer changes to a double-headed arrow, hold down the left mouse button and drag the window into the size you want.

Address bar
This shows you where you are, and also allows you access to other files and folders.

Status bar
This gives information about the contents of the window.

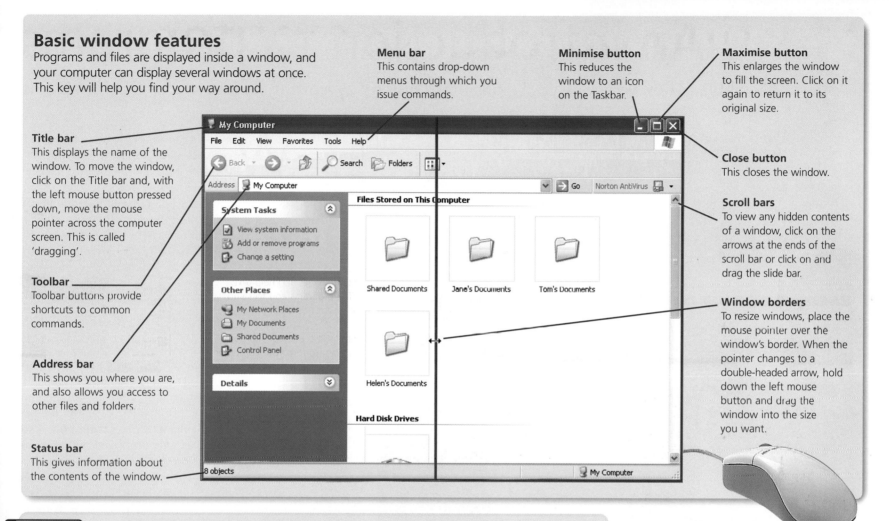

In older Windows versions...

Windows ME and 98 have much smaller Start menus than XP, but most of the same features are present or appear on the Desktop instead. For example, **My Computer** appears in the top left hand corner of the screen. You can customise Windows XP so that its Start menu works in the same way.

Settings Lets you customise your computer.

Run... Provides another way to launch your computer's programs.

Find Searches for files and information.

Log Off... Used when several people share the same computer.

Help Displays 'help' files about Windows.

Shut Down... Turns off or restarts the PC.

Using the mouse

Once your computer's switched on, you can really see how the mouse works. Moving the mouse on your desk moves the mouse pointer on screen.

Place your mouse pointer over an icon and a box will appear telling you what the icon does. When you want to look 'inside' an icon, press the left mouse button twice quickly. This is known as 'double-clicking'. The double-click principle applies to the opening of programs or files.

An introduction to programs

Improve your skills **more** quickly **by** getting to know your PC's programs

Windows, the operating system, helps connect each element of your PC together but it can't perform practical tasks such as letter writing and calculating your bills. For these jobs you need to use additional software – called applications, or programs – which is designed to carry out specific tasks.

Most personal computers come with a varied package of programs (known as bundled software or software suites) already installed. Two of the most popular packages are Microsoft® Works and Microsoft® Office.

Your package explained

Works, a package of 'mini-programs' grouped together, offers you tools to perform most of the tasks you might want to carry out on a home computer, and it also includes many pre-set documents, called Wizards, that you can customise for your own purposes (you are given step-by-step guidance on how to do this).

Office comprises several individual programs (Word, Outlook®, PowerPoint® and Excel). The more sophisticated capabilities of each of these programs, compared to their equivalent in Works, means that they can be used to produce a wider range of documents. Because they are more advanced, together they use up more of your hard disk space than Works. You will find Wizards in both Office and Works.

Works Suite is an expanded version of Works. It uses Word as its word processor, and contains extra useful programs, such as an encyclopedia.

Understanding your bundled software

Knowing what each program in your bundled software can do will help you decide which will be the most appropriate for the tasks you want to perform.

Microsoft Office

Word is an extremely powerful word processor which is able to produce 'written' documents of all kinds, including letters, memos, newsletters and posters. You have the option to create documents from scratch or, for many types of document, to use one of the program's Wizards or templates. The Wizards let you choose the content and how the document looks, while the templates have a preset layout.

Excel is a spreadsheet program, used for organising and calculating numerical data. It is ideal for keeping track of all types of budgets and accounts. Like all spreadsheets, it takes the form of a grid containing 'cells' into which you input figures and formulas to make calculations. Excel allows you to have several spreadsheets, or 'worksheets', within the same document, and enter calculations using figures from each of the worksheets. This is particularly useful when organising, say, a major event that comprises mini-projects. Once data is entered, you can then select, or 'filter', specific information to analyse.

Excel can also produce a range of charts and graphs that can be used to illustrate trends in your spreadsheet figures. These are particularly useful as they simplify complicated numerical information, presenting it in a clear, easily understandable manner.

Outlook is a Desktop 'information management' program. It contains an address book into which you can enter contact details for friends, family and business associates. It also has a diary and calendar that will help you to keep track of your current schedule and forthcoming appointments. Outlook can also be used to send and receive e-mails through the Internet or through an internal company network.

PowerPoint is most often used in business. It enables you to create presentations for conferences, company meetings and marketing projects. It gives you the means to structure information efficiently and incorporate graphics within your text. It even offers animation effects to maximise the impact of your presentation. You can create notes for your own use in addition to handouts for your audience.

Although a useful business tool, PowerPoint can also be used at home to make a computerised 'slide' show for your friends and family .

Microsoft Works

Word Processor. This program allows you to create a range of word-based documents, and has many Wizards to help you design pages. It is similar to Microsoft Word, but slightly less sophisticated – Word allows you to add colours and borders to text boxes needed to create business cards.

Calendar. This feature lets you keep track of appointments, important dates, birthdays and anniversaries. It integrates with the Works **Address Book**, so that you can be reminded automatically about a friend's birthday, for example.

Spreadsheet. This program allows you to monitor and analyse numerical data. It also offers a number of Wizards for common documents such as household bills, invoices and accounts, which you can customise and use.

Database. This program is ideal for recording details about related items. For example, you can record details of your household contents. Using its ReportCreator function you can sort and group selected information (say, to update your household insurance), perform calculations and add some explanatory notes.

Accessory programs

Accessories are small programs within Windows that perform specific tasks. Your computer will almost certainly contain a calculator, a drawing program (Paint), simple games and a basic word processing program (WordPad).

To open an accessory program, go to the **Start** menu and click on **All Programs** then **Accessories**. Click on the program you want to use.

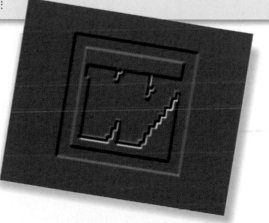

Getting around a document

Learn how to open a program and navigate around the screen

Opening a program and creating a new document will be among the first things you do on your computer. The process is similar in most programs. The steps are the same whether you are using a spreadsheet, database or word-processing program.

All programs can be accessed by clicking on the **Start** button on the Taskbar that runs along the bottom of the screen, then clicking on **All Programs** in the menu that pops up. Another menu appears listing all the programs on your system. Click on the program you wish to open. The program opens and a blank document appears. You can now start typing.

Before you do this, it's useful to understand the different parts of the window. The window shown is from the Microsoft Word word-processing program (Microsoft Works is very similar).

Inputting commands

Whichever program you are using, you input commands using your mouse and keyboard. These commands might relate to the look of the document or to the material it contains.

The mouse

The mouse is the best way to access the command options available through your document's menus and toolbars (see opposite). To activate items on screen (menus, shortcut icons, and so on), use the mouse to move the cursor over them and press your left mouse button down then release it (this process is known as 'clicking').

If you are asked to 'click', press and release the left mouse button once; to 'double-click', press and release the left mouse button twice in quick succession.

If you are asked to 'drag' (you will do this to move items on the screen or to select text), press the left mouse button and, holding it down, move your mouse. As you do so, a section of text will become highlighted, or the on-screen item you clicked on will also move. When the relevant text is selected, or the item has moved to the correct position, release the mouse button.

'Right-clicking' – that is, clicking with the right mouse button – anywhere on screen will activate a pop-up menu offering formatting functions and other options. Click on an option to activate or open it.

The keyboard

The most obvious use of the keyboard is for typing in text and data, but it is also possible to issue commands by using special combinations of keys (these keyboard commands are discussed on page 74).

It is also possible to use the arrow keys at the bottom of your keyboard to move your cursor around within a document. Most people find this more laborious than using the mouse.

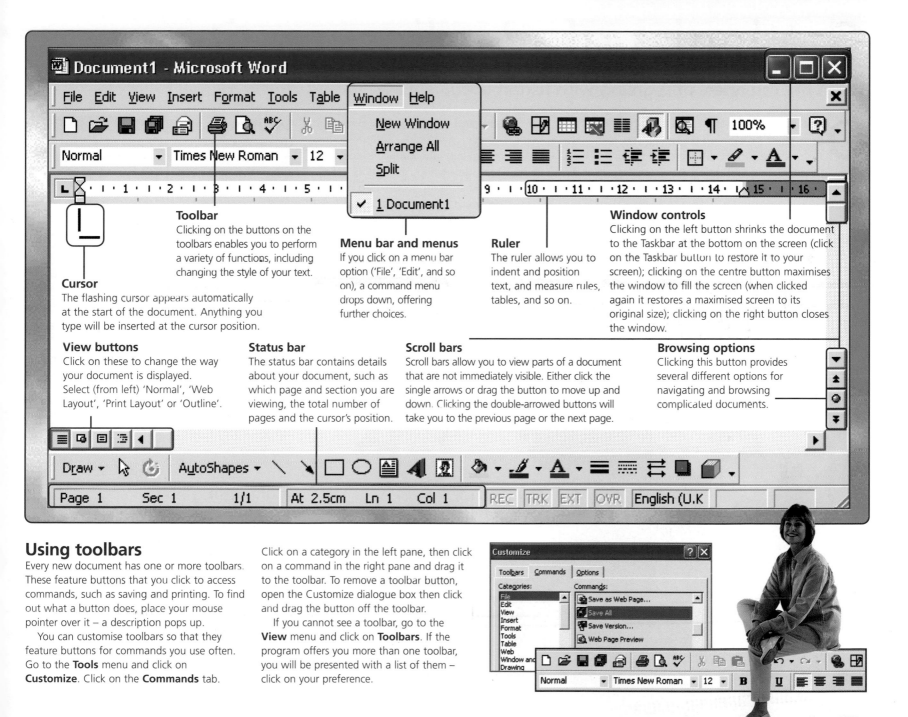

Document1 - Microsoft Word

File　Edit　View　Insert　Format　Tools　Table　Window　Help

New Window

Arrange All

Split

✔ 1 Document1

Normal ▾ Times New Roman ▾ 12 ▾ 100%

Toolbar
Clicking on the buttons on the toolbars enables you to perform a variety of functions, including changing the style of your text.

Cursor
The flashing cursor appears automatically at the start of the document. Anything you type will be inserted at the cursor position.

Menu bar and menus
If you click on a menu bar option ('File', 'Edit', and so on), a command menu drops down, offering further choices.

Ruler
The ruler allows you to indent and position text, and measure rules, tables, and so on.

Window controls
Clicking on the left button shrinks the document to the Taskbar at the bottom on the screen (click on the Taskbar button to restore it to your screen); clicking on the centre button maximises the window to fill the screen (when clicked again it restores a maximised screen to its original size); clicking on the right button closes the window.

View buttons
Click on these to change the way your document is displayed. Select (from left) 'Normal', 'Web Layout', 'Print Layout' or 'Outline'.

Status bar
The status bar contains details about your document, such as which page and section you are viewing, the total number of pages and the cursor's position.

Scroll bars
Scroll bars allow you to view parts of a document that are not immediately visible. Either click the single arrows or drag the button to move up and down. Clicking the double-arrowed buttons will take you to the previous page or the next page.

Browsing options
Clicking this button provides several different options for navigating and browsing complicated documents.

Draw ▾　AutoShapes ▾

Page 1　　Sec 1　　1/1　　At 2.5cm　Ln 1　Col 1　　REC　TRK　EXT　OVR　English (U.K

Using toolbars

Every new document has one or more toolbars. These feature buttons that you click to access commands, such as saving and printing. To find out what a button does, place your mouse pointer over it – a description pops up.

You can customise toolbars so that they feature buttons for commands you use often. Go to the **Tools** menu and click on **Customize**. Click on the **Commands** tab.

Click on a category in the left pane, then click on a command in the right pane and drag it to the toolbar. To remove a toolbar button, open the Customize dialogue box then click and drag the button off the toolbar.

If you cannot see a toolbar, go to the **View** menu and click on **Toolbars**. If the program offers you more than one toolbar, you will be presented with a list of them – click on your preference.

Customize

Toolbars | Commands | Options

Categories:
File
Edit
View
Insert
Format
Tools
Table
Web
Window and
Drawing

Commands:
Save as Web Page...
Save All
Save Version...
Web Page Preview

Normal ▾ Times New Roman ▾ 12 ▾ B U

The basics of word processing

Learn the essentials of working with text in documents

O nce you have opened a new document in a word processing program, you can start typing in text. The great advantage that word-processing computers have over typewriters is that they allow you to revise and refine your text as much as you wish. You can also adjust the appearance of your text, its size, shape, colour and position on the page, and the spacing between individual letters, words and lines. You can even add special effects such as shadows. This is known as 'formatting'.

Becoming familiar with the terms used in word processing, and the basics of working with text, will enable you to create and modify documents with ease.

Setting up your document

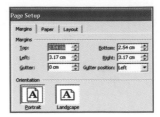

Before you start typing you should first specify the orientation of the document, the size of the paper you want to print on and the size of its margins. To do this, go to the **File** menu and click on **Page Setup**. Click in the margin boxes and enter your settings, then click **OK**. (Your program will have default settings that you may not need to change.)

Typing in text

> I would like to raise several points:
> • Seventy people have confirmed that they are
> • Twenty people have confirmed that they are :
> • Four people have yet to respond

To enter text, just type on the keyboard. As you type, the words will appear at the cursor position on your screen. When you reach the end of a line, the text will automatically flow on to the next line. To start typing on a new line before reaching the end of the current one, press the **Return** key on your keyboard and continue to type.

Highlighting text

To format a section of text you first need to select, or 'highlight', it. To do this, place your cursor just before the relevant section and press and release your left mouse button once (this is called 'clicking'). Press the mouse button again and, keeping it pressed down, move the mouse to the right (this is called 'dragging'). As you do this the text appears as white in a black bar. Release the mouse button once the relevant text is highlighted.

To highlight all the text in a document, press the **Ctrl** key and, keeping it pressed down, press the '**A**' key.

Formatting the text

Once text is highlighted it is ready to format, or style. Go to the **Format** menu and click on **Font**. A dialogue box appears offering formatting options. The Word dialogue box is shown here (fewer options are available in Works).

Fonts

Your word processing program offers a range of fonts (particular styles of type). To view the list of fonts, click on the arrows (this is called 'scrolling'). Click on your choice of font (it becomes highlighted).

Colour

To alter the colour of text, click on the arrow next to the Font color box, scroll through the colours and click on your choice.

Remember that too many colours on one page can be overpowering.

Effects

You will be presented with a number of special effects that you can apply to text. To choose one, click in the relevant box (a tick will appear). Click the box again to remove the effect.

Font style

Once you have chosen a font, select a font style for it. Typically, you can choose whether your text appears in a regular format, or in italics or bold. To select a font style, click on your choice from the Font style box.

Size

The size of text is measured in 'points' (pts). The greater the point size, the larger the text. However, point sizes are not uniform across all fonts, which means that 10pt text in one font may be taller than, say, 12pt text in another font. To alter a point size, scroll through and click on your choice in the Size box. A good rule of thumb is not to use text smaller than 8pt or 9pt, as it becomes difficult to read.

Underline

You can underline text in a number of ways. Click on the arrow next to the Underline style box, scroll through the options and click on your choice. If you do not want text to be underlined ensure **None** is selected.

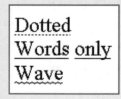

Preview

The Preview pane shows you how your choices of font, size, and effects will look.

OK

Click **OK** to apply your formatting changes to the highlighted text.

Using the toolbar

Most of the styling options shown above also appear on the Formatting toolbar near the top of your window. If the toolbar isn't there (you may accidentally remove it), go to the **View** menu, select **Toolbars** then **Formatting**.

Toolbars appear along the top of your window but can be dragged to anywhere on your document. To move the position of your toolbar, click on it (make sure you do not click on one of its buttons), then drag it to its new location. It appears with a Title bar bearing the name of the toolbar. To alter the shape of your repositioned toolbar, click on one of its edges and drag accordingly.

After highlighting your text click on the appropriate toolbar buttons. (To see what a toolbar button does, place your mouse pointer over the button – a small box describing its function pops up.)

Laying out your document

Your word processing program allows you to adjust the structure of your documents, making them easier to read and drawing attention to important information.

Adding borders

To add a border around a section of text, to give it definition, highlight the relevant text (here, the company address) then click on the arrow beside the **Border** button on the toolbar. You will be offered a choice of styles. Click on your preference.

Paragraph indents

A simple way to distinguish where each new paragraph begins is to indent its first line. Click in the paragraph, go to the **Format** menu and click on **Paragraph**. In the Indentation section, click on the arrow beside the Special box and select **First line**. In the By box set the space required then click **OK**. (In Works, set the space in the First line box then click **OK**.)

You can also indent entire paragraphs by highlighting them and clicking the **Increase indent** button on the toolbar.

Adding numbers and bullet points

To make lists easier to read, add a number or bullet point before each item. Highlight the list then click on the **Numbering** or **Bullets** button on the toolbar. The Numbering button automatically numbers points sequentially.

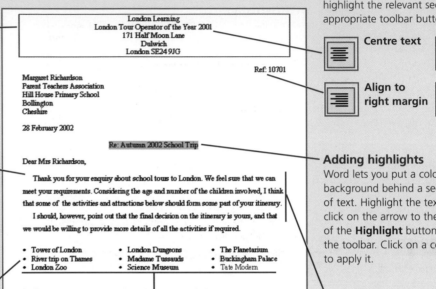

London Learning
London Tour Operator of the Year 2001
171 Half Moon Lane
Dulwich
London SE24 9JG

Ref: 10701

Margaret Richardson
Parent Teachers Association
Hill House Primary School
Bollington
Cheshire

28 February 2002

Re: Autumn 2002 School Trip

Dear Mrs Richardson,

Thank you for your enquiry about school tours to London. We feel sure that we can meet your requirements. Considering the age and number of the children involved, I think that some of the activities and attractions below should form some part of your itinerary.

I should, however, point out that the final decision on the itinerary is yours, and that we would be willing to provide more details of all the activities if required.

- Tower of London
- River trip on Thames
- London Zoo
- London Dungeons
- Madame Tussauds
- Science Museum
- The Planetarium
- Buckingham Palace
- Tate Modern

I will be in contact again soon to discuss these suggestions further.

Yours sincerely

Aligning paragraphs

To position, or align, text in your document, highlight the relevant section then click on the appropriate toolbar button.

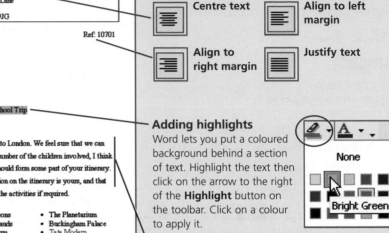

Centre text

Align to left margin

Align to right margin

Justify text

Adding highlights

Word lets you put a coloured background behind a section of text. Highlight the text then click on the arrow to the right of the **Highlight** button on the toolbar. Click on a colour to apply it.

Using columns

To place text in columns, highlight the section, click the **Columns** button on the toolbar and select an option from the drop-down panel. (In Works you cannot place individual sections of text into columns.)

Line spacing

To adjust the space between each line of text (this may make your document easier to read), highlight the relevant section, go to the **Format** menu and click on **Paragraph**. In the Spacing section (in Works, first click on the **Spacing** tab), click on the arrow beside the Line spacing box, click on your choice then **OK**. (You can click on several options to see them in the Preview pane first.)

What if I make a mistake?

If you make a mistake, click on the **Undo** button on the Standard toolbar. (If the toolbar isn't there, go to the **View** menu, select **Toolbars** then **Standard**.) You can continue to click on it to undo previous commands. If you undo an action you then want to redo, click on the **Redo** toolbar button.

(In Works, you can undo the 100 previous commands. Go to the **Edit** menu and click on **Undo** or **Redo**.)

Moving or copying text

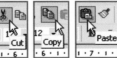

To move a section of text, highlight it and click on the **Cut** toolbar button. The text will disappear. Position the cursor where you want the text to reappear, click once, then click on the **Paste** button – the text will reappear in your document.

To copy a section of text so that it appears more than once in a document (you can also copy text from one document to another), highlight it then click on the **Copy** toolbar button. Position the cursor and click where you want the text to appear, then click on the **Paste** toolbar button.

You can also perform these functions by highlighting text then going to the **Edit** menu and clicking on an option.

Finishing touches

Once you have finished formatting and laying out your document, it's a good idea to check it for spelling and grammatical errors. Also, you can now add extra features, such as headers and footers.

Spelling and grammar check

When you type in text, some words may appear with a wavy red or green line underneath. A red line indicates a possible spelling error; a green line

Vennison Stew with Orange

Preparation Time: 20 mins plus
Cooking time: 1 hour

indicates a possible grammatical error. When you have finished typing your document, go to the **Tools** menu

and click on **Spelling and Grammar**, or press the **F7** key.

Your PC scans your document, selecting the underlined words for you to check and suggesting how to correct the 'error'. If you don't agree with any of the suggested changes click on **Ignore**; if you do agree, click on the relevant suggestion then on **Change**.

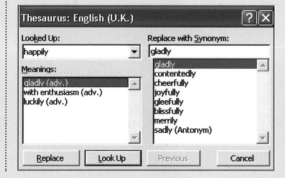

Thesaurus

To ensure your document reads well, open the Thesaurus function to find alternatives to repeated words, and suggestions for more suitable words.

To do this, highlight the word you would like to find an alternative for, go to the **Tools** menu and click on **Language** then **Thesaurus** (in Works, click directly on **Thesaurus**). Or, press the **Shift** key and, keeping it pressed down, the **F7** key.

The Thesaurus dialogue box will show a list of alternatives. Click on the appropriate meaning of the word in the Meanings pane, then on your choice of replacement word in the Replace with Synonym pane. Click on **Replace**. If you don't think the alternatives are any better, click on **Cancel**.

Headers and footers

Word processing documents can include a section at the top and bottom of each page – known as headers and footers, respectively. Any text entered into these sections automatically appears on each new page of your document. This is useful if you want to include a title for your document at the top of each page, and the date or page number at the bottom.

To add text to these sections, go to the **View** menu and click on **Header and Footer**. The cursor now appears in the Header section. Type in your text and style it. Then scroll down the document, click in the Footer section and do likewise.

To add a page number to the Footer in Works, click in the Footer, go to the **Insert** menu and select **Page Numbers**. In Word, go to **Insert AutoText** and **Page**. A dialogue box asks how you want the page number to be aligned, and whether you want it to appear on the first page or not. Only a figure is entered – you may want to type in 'Page' before it. In Works, the symbol *page* appears in the footer. In both programs, the page number updates itself on each new page.

To return to normal view in Word, click **Close** on the Header and Footer toolbar. In Works, simply double-click on the main part of your document.

Counting your words

If you are writing a long article or essay, it can be useful to know how many words you have written. Go to the **Tools** menu and click on **Word Count**. Word will also count the pages, paragraphs and even characters used. (In Works, you are given a total word count for your document, including footnotes, headers and footers.)

Word Count

Statistics:

Pages	1
Words	843
Characters (no spaces)	3,387
Characters (with spaces)	4,222
Paragraphs	10
Lines	47

Figuring out spreadsheets

Learn how to use spreadsheets for financial planning and budgeting

Of all the computer functions, spreadsheets are the hardest to get to grips with. But a small investment of time and effort will soon pay dividends, because once you have the hang of them, spreadsheets can perform very complex financial calculations. You can, for example, set up a spreadsheet to work out the true cost of running your car, including such invisible outlay as depreciation and wear and tear. All you have to do is 'explain' the task to the program once: it will do all the arithmetic for you, month after month, year on year.

Opening a new spreadsheet

This book deals with the two most widely used spreadsheet programs: Microsoft Excel and the spreadsheet tool in Microsoft Works. To open a document in either program, go to the **Start** menu and select **All Programs** then **Microsoft Excel** or **Microsoft Works**.

If you open Excel, a new blank document will automatically appear on screen. If you open Works, the Works Task Launcher will open. Click on the **Programs** tab, then on **Works Spreadsheet** button, then on **Start a blank Spreadsheet**.

Saving your document

After opening a new document, go to the **File** menu and click on **Save As**. The Save As dialogue box appears. Click on the arrow at the side of the 'Save in' box and scroll down to select a folder in which to save your document. Enter a file name, then click **Save**.

Another popular spreadsheet program is Lotus 1-2-3. The principles of using spreadsheets – as given here for Excel and Works – can also be applied to 1-2-3.

OTHER PROGRAMS

Finding your way around

Identifying the various elements of your spreadsheet document will help you to navigate around it more easily, and so use it more effectively. Most elements are the same for all spreadsheet programs.

Understanding spreadsheets

A spreadsheet is a grid of 'cells'. The columns are like the columns in a ledger – you can use them to make lists of figures and perform calculations. Each column is identified by a letter of the alphabet, and each row by a number. So every cell has its own unique address, comprising the letter of the column and the number of the row it is in (A1, A2, and so on). You can type numbers, text or formulas into these cells. The formulas make it possible to get the program to do all the complicated and laborious arithmetic for you.

Using the Formula bar to input data

When you first open a spreadsheet, cell A1 is automatically selected as the 'active cell' – indicated by a thick black line around the cell – and you can type directly into it. To make entries into other cells, click on them first. As you make entries, they will appear in the Formula bar located below the toolbars. You can view and edit the contents of a cell in the Formula bar.

To the left of the Formula bar are two buttons (marked '**X**' and '**✔**') that only appear after you type something in. If you make a mistake in your entry, click on the **X** button to cancel it; if it is correct, click on the **✔** button to enter it (or press the **Enter** or **Tab** keys).

What you can see

Spreadsheets look quite complicated. But once you understand how they work and how to find your way around them, they are easy to use. The documents displayed here are from Microsoft Excel. The main difference between these and Works documents is that there are fewer toolbar options in Works.

When using spreadsheets, the mouse pointer becomes a thick white cross, rather than the normal arrow head you will see elsewhere.

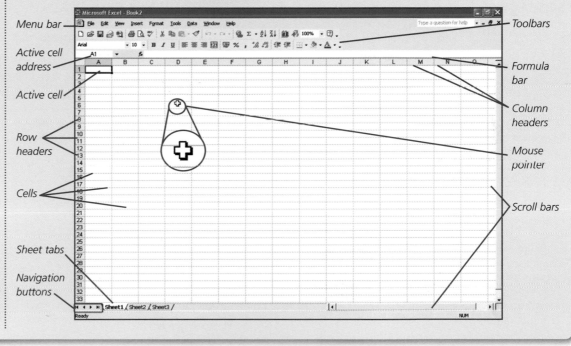

Menu bar · Active cell address · Active cell · Row headers · Cells · Sheet tabs · Navigation buttons · Toolbars · Formula bar · Column headers · Mouse pointer · Scroll bars

=B3*C3

Moving around a spreadsheet

You can move from one cell to the next in several ways. You can either click on the next cell using your mouse, navigate to the cell you want using the four arrow keys on your keyboard, or press the **Tab** key. To move to a previous cell, press the **Shift** key and, keeping it pressed down, the **Tab** key.

In Excel, unless you want to move to a new row, do not press the **Return** key, as this will activate the cell below the one you are currently in.

Selecting cells

You can select cells for styling, cutting and copying in several ways. To select a column or row of cells, click on the grey column or row header. To select cells that are adjacent to each other, click on the first cell and, keeping the left mouse button pressed down, drag the cursor across or down the screen until the entire range of cells is selected, then release the mouse button.

If the cells you want to select are not adjacent, but are dotted throughout the spreadsheet, press the **Ctrl** key on your keyboard and, keeping it pressed down, click on each of the cells in turn.

Tips for using spreadsheets effectively

When you are dealing with numbers, it pays to give some thought to how to lay out the spreadsheet. When you type in information, be as careful as possible.

Adding titles and headings

To make it easier to identify your spreadsheet and navigate around it, it is helpful to enter a title at the top of the sheet, and to give separate headings to columns and rows. To do this, click on a cell and type in your text.

Adjusting column widths

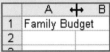

If an entry is too long for its cell, adjust the width of the column. Place your mouse pointer over the right-hand edge of the grey column header. When it becomes a double-headed arrow press the left mouse button and, keeping it pressed down, drag it to the desired width. Release the mouse button. You can make the column automatically adjust to include the widest entry in any of its cells by placing the mouse pointer in the same position and double-clicking.

Locking row and column headings

Often, column and row headings can disappear off screen when you scroll through large spreadsheets, making it difficult to keep track of which figures relate to what. To keep the headings viewable at all times, drag the small button at the top of the scroll bar down. This splits the worksheet into two independent panes, one to house the headings, one for the rest of the spreadsheet.

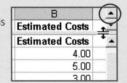

Enter identical data in multiple cells

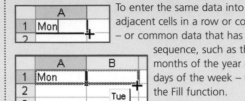

To enter the same data into adjacent cells in a row or column – or common data that has a set sequence, such as the months of the year or days of the week – use the Fill function.

Type an entry into the first cell. Place the mouse pointer in the lower right-hand corner of the cell. When it becomes a small black cross, press the left mouse button, keep it pressed and drag it over the cells you'd like filled. Release the mouse button.

To enter the same number into several columns and rows at once, select the cells, type in the number then press the **Ctrl** key and, keeping it pressed down, the **Enter** key.

Moving and coping data

To move data in a spreadsheet, use the Cut, Copy and Paste commands. Select the cells you want to place elsewhere (the source range). To remove the source range, click the **Cut** toolbar button. The cells become selected. To leave the source range in its position and copy it, click the **Copy** toolbar button instead. Now click on the cell that you wish to be the top left-hand cell of the position where you want the moved information to appear (the target range). Click the **Paste** toolbar button.

Insert and delete columns and rows

Your spreadsheet design can be easily edited according to your changing needs. For example, you can insert a new column or row. To do this in Excel, click on the grey column or row header (these contain either a letter or number) where you'd like your new one to be placed. Go to the **Insert** menu and select **Rows** or **Columns**. A new row/column appears before the one where your cursor is positioned. To delete a row or column, click on its header, go to the **Edit** menu and select **Delete**.

In Works, all four commands – Insert Row, Delete Row, Insert Column and Delete Column – are found in the Insert menu.

Sorting by rows

Spreadsheet entries can easily be sorted, or prioritised. You can, for example, have items appear in order of expense. To do this, select the column(s) to be sorted. In Excel, go to the **Data** menu and click on **Sort**. In Works, go to the **Tools** menu and click on **Sort**. Both Excel and Works allow you to choose which column or columns you want to sort, up to a maximum of three. You can also choose whether you want to list the results in ascending (A-Z) or descending (Z-A) order. Make your choices then click on **OK**.

Formatting cells

Changing the style of the text or figures in your spreadsheet is a good way to help you to distinguish information quickly. Select the cell or cells to be formatted, go to the **Format** menu and click on **Cells**. In the Format Cells dialogue box click on the **Font** tab. Select a font, style, size and colour as desired, then click **OK**. Alternatively, select the cells then click on the relevant buttons on the toolbar.

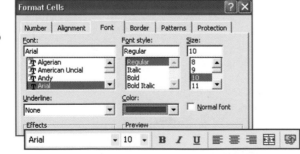

Performing calculations

It is the ability of spreadsheets to perform complex calculations which makes them such a powerful tool. It is worth the effort to learn how to use formulas correctly.

Adding figures

In Excel you can add together the contents of columns, rows or any combination of selected cells. Select the cells and their total is displayed on the Status bar at the bottom of the screen.

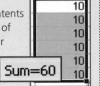

Using the AutoSum function

Both Excel and Works have an AutoSum toolbar button to calculate figures. But they work in slightly differing ways.

In Excel, to add figures in adjacent cells in a column or a row, select the relevant cells then click the **AutoSum** button. The total will be displayed in the next cell of the column or row.

In Works, you must click on a blank cell in the column or row you want calculated, then click the **AutoSum** button. The cell references, or addresses, for the cells will appear in a formula. If they are correct, press **Enter**; if not, type in the correct cell references. The total will appear in your selected cell.

`=SUM(C2,D3,D2,E3)`

In Excel, to add up figures in cells that are not adjacent to each other, click on an empty cell, then on the **AutoSum** button. The selected cell will display the legend '=SUM()'. Enter the cell references of the cells to be calculated. You can do this manually or by clicking on them, inserting a comma between each one. Each co-ordinate will be added to the formula automatically. Press the **Enter** key.

To add up figures in cells that are not adjacent to each other in Works, click on an empty cell then press the '=' key on your keyboard. Works now knows you want to enter a formula. Enter the cell references of the cells to be calculated, either manually or by clicking on them, inserting a '+' sign between each one. Press **Enter**.

To delete a formula in a cell press the **Delete** key.

Further functions in Excel

There are a number of preset functions in Excel that can take the effort out of spreadsheet calculations. Click on an empty cell to make it active and type in '='. Click on the arrow button between the Active cell address box and the Cancel button near the top

of the window. A drop-down menu will appear. Click on an option and a dialogue box will appear, giving a brief description of the function it performs, such as the average value of selected cells, or depreciation of an asset (for example, a car) over a specified time period.

Further functions in Works

For other calculation functions in Works, click the **Easy Calc** button on the toolbar. A dialogue box appears, listing

common calculations and more specialised ones. Click on the **Other** button at the bottom of the box for a scrollable menu of the program's 76 preset functions with more detailed descriptions.

More complex equations in Excel and Works

You're not restricted to simple sums – you can create formulas for any type of calculation. Click on an empty cell and press the '=' key. Then type in the cell references of the cells to be calculated in your formula, separating them by the relevant 'operators' – the symbols for addition (+), subtraction (-), multiplication (*) and division (/). Press the **Enter** key.

Item	Units ordered	Price per unit	Total	Disco
Gloss Paint	6	9.99	59.94	
Brushes	4	5.99	=B3*C3	
Sandpaper	3	6.99		
Roller	7	4.5		

Spreadsheet programs automatically process some operators before others (for example, multiplication and division before addition or subtraction) so, to ensure that one part of the equation

Final Total	=(D2-E2)*(D3-E3)

is calculated before the rest, enclose it in brackets.

Setting number formats

To help to prevent the accidental calculation of inappropriate data in Excel, it is advisable to format cells for currency, dates, percentages, times, and so on. Select your cell(s) then go to the **Format** menu and click on **Cells**. In the Format Cells dialogue box click on the **Number** tab. Choose from the scrollable menu of options, select the number of decimal places and, if a negative number, a style, then click **OK**. Works offers fewer options: go to the **Format** menu and choose **Number**.

An introduction to databases

Learn how to use database programs to keep records that you can sort

Databases are used for storing and organising large amounts of data about related topics. For example, you can create a database to catalogue your recipe collection and then search it to find all the lamb dishes or all the dishes using coriander.

A database's ability to organise and prioritise data in different ways also makes it suitable for storing names, addresses and contact details. If you forget someone's surname, you can search the database by first name only, by telephone code or by address.

But databases are more than just deposit boxes for information. They also make calculations. You can, for instance, enter the value of each item of your household contents, then add up the total value to provide a guide to how much you should insure your possessions for.

Working with fields

The building blocks of a database are fields. Each field represents a category of information. In an address database, they might be surname, first name, address, telephone number, and so on. To build a database, you must first create fields for it.

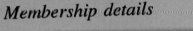

Membership No.	First Name	Surname	Street Address	Town

Creating records

Once the fields have been created you can begin to make your entries – each entry is known as a record. For each record, you fill in the fields. The database allows you to organise the records in a number of ways – for example, you can list them in alphabetical order or by date. You can also browse through the records, search for a particular entry and print out selected aspects.

First name: Gillian
Surname: Foster
Street address: 12 Hambley Garde
Town or city: London
Postcode: N24 7YT

Opening a new database

In the **Start** menu select **All Programs** then Microsoft Works. The Works Task Launcher will appear. Click the **Programs** tab, then **Works Database**. Click on **Start a blank database**. The Create Database dialogue box appears.

Membership details

Membership details

Membership details

Record No:	0001
Surname:	Coady
First names:	Emma
Date of birth	26/05/68
Registration:	03/02/85

Address: Flat 6, Sherbourne Drive, Putney, London (previously Flat 3, Warholl Mansion Block, Bern Street, Putney, London)

Telephone No: 0181 879 7865 (work 0171 354 7689)

Occupation: Nurse

Club rating: 5

Notes: Took out yearly membership, due to be renewed on 4/10/2000. Has had several lessons which have improved her game considerably. Could do with doing additional training during the week.

Microsoft Works Task Launcher

Home | Tasks | Programs | History | Customize | ? Help

PROGRAMS
Type your question and click Search, or click a program.

Search

Works Word Processor
Works Spreadsheet
Works Database
Works Calendar
Address Book
Works Portfolio

Works Database

Organize and track household information. The Database stores t enables you to create reports showing only the information you need.
Works Database on the Web.

Start a blank database
CD and tape inventory
Home inventory worksheet
Recipe book
Works Web site

Start a blank database
CD and tape inventory

Building a database

When you open a new database, the Create Database dialogue box appears, in which you specify fields. Don't worry if you miss one out, or enter them in the wrong order, as you can edit your database later.

Setting up fields

As you enter field names you are given a chance to format them and choose a style for them.

Field name

Type your field name into this box. Field names should not be more than 15 characters long (this includes spaces between words). The more fields you create, the greater the flexibility of your database. It is sensible, for example, to create separate fields for first and surnames so you can search by either category.

Try to enter field names in the order that you wish them to appear in your database. It's good practice to be as organised as possible at this stage.

Format

You have a choice of formats for your field names. These relate to the type of information you are entering. The date field, for example, is automatically set up for the day, month and year. Select an option by clicking it. A small black dot indicates that the Format is active.

Choose the following formats for the appropriate information:

General This is the default setting for all field names. Text entries are aligned to the left, and numbers to the right.

Number This lets you specify the way that numbers are displayed. For example, you can select the number of decimal places, or whether negative numbers appear in red.

Date Select this to specify how dates are displayed – by month only, with or without the year, or with the month as text rather than a number.

Time Select either 'AM' or 'PM', and whether to include seconds as well as hours and minutes.

Text Use this if you want to display numbers as text rather than figures, or if you wish to include dashes or spaces (these are particularly useful when entering telephone numbers).

Fraction If you want to store fractions – 2¾, for example – choose this format. When entering data, type a space between the whole number (2) and the fraction (3/4) to let Works tell them apart. The decimal equivalent appears in the Entry bar when the cell containing a fraction is selected.

Serialized Choose this format to get Works to automatically add a serial number to each record. This unique number is useful if you need to sort records into the order in which they were entered.

Appearance

You will be given style choices for how you want your number, date, time, fraction and serialised formats to appear. For example, you may want to include decimal values in your numbers, and to have months written out in full in dates. Scroll through the lists and click on your choice.

Add/Cancel

After you have created a field and selected a format and appearance for it, click on the **Add** button to confirm your selection and move to another field. When you have created all your database fields click on **Exit**. Your database will appear in List View, with your field names as headings at the top of columns.

✔		Membership No.	First Name	Surname	Street
☐	1				
☐	2				
☐	3				

Database programs

Microsoft Works includes a database tool. It also contains a selection of database Task Wizards (these are predesigned documents that you open and use as they are, or customise to your liking).

The Standard edition of Microsoft Office does not include a specific database program, but its spreadsheet program, Microsoft Excel, can perform many of the same tasks (see page 35).

Saving your database

When your database appears for the first time in List View, it is called 'Unsaved Database'. You should save it immediately with an appropriate name.

Click on the **Save** toolbar button or go to the **File** menu and click on **Save As**. A dialogue box appears. In the 'File name' box type in a name for your database. Click on the arrow beside the 'Save in' box to see the destinations to which you can save your file. Select a folder then click on **Save**. For more detailed information on saving documents, see page 36.

Getting around your database

Your new database appears in List View, which looks similar to a spreadsheet. There are three other ways to view your database, too. Become familiar with them before entering any records.

Different points of view

You can view your database in four different ways, each of which lends itself best to a particular use. All the views can be accessed via the View menu, or by clicking on the appropriate buttons on the toolbar.

List View

Immediately after you create your fields, your database is displayed in List View. This view allows you to see a number of records at the same time. It is useful when you simply want to browse your records, move data (copy and paste) from one record to another, or when entering a series of numbers or dates.

You can enter information into your database in List View by first clicking on a cell then typing your entry (it also appears in the Entry bar at the top of the window). List View is also used to display the results of any searches that you run (see opposite).

Surname	Street Address	Town or city	Postcode	Registration
Foster	12 Hambley Gan	London	N24 7YT	08/09/1999
Ianni	Flat 4, 7 Frith St	London	WC1R 6XX	08/09/1999
Knighton	233 Bedminster	Bridge Road	1YY	09/09/1999
Davidowicz	25 Ellesmer Roa	Birmingham	B24 56T	11/09/1999
James	773 Long Lane	Glasgow	G12 7GT	11/09/1999
Adams	12 Kings Road	Farnham	GU8 9TT	15/09/1999

Form View

Each record can be viewed separately using Form View. Most people prefer to enter information using this view – it means you can see the entries for all the other fields as you enter new data into the database.

Membership No.:   00001

First Name: Gillian

Surname: Foster

Street Address: 12 Hambley Gardens

Town or city: London

Form Design

In Form Design you structure the look of Form View. You can rearrange fields and their adjoining field boxes. You can also add text colours, select different fonts, and add borders and Clip Art images.

To move field names around the page, click on them and drag them into place.

To adjust the size of a field box, first click on the right or bottom edge, or the bottom right-hand corner of the field box, and then, with the left mouse button pressed down, drag it until all the information you want to include fits in the box.

Report View

A good database allows you to extract data. Through Report View you can design and print out a report that organises your information by related subjects. It also lets you perform calculations on fields, such as the total of subscription fees club members have paid to date.

Membership No.	Surname	Fees Paid/Owed
00006	Adams	-£15.04
00005	James	-£33.72
00003	Knighton	-£37.30
00002	Ianni	-£46.20
00001	Foster	-£52.50
00004	Davidowicz	-£62.50
	SUM	-£247.26

Inputting your records

You can enter data into your database in either List View or Form View.

In List View, click on the relevant cell and type into it. To move to the next cell, either click in it using your mouse, or press the **Tab** key on your keyboard. (To return to a previous field, or cell, press **Shift** and **Tab**.) Unlike spreadsheet programs, pressing the Return key will not move your cursor to the next cell or row in a database.

In Form View, click the field box adjoining the field name and type your data. Press the **Tab** key to move to the next field (or the next record when you come to the end of the current one), and the **Shift** and **Tab** keys to return to a previous field, or record.

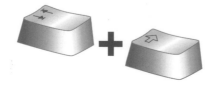

Navigating through forms

In Form View and Form Design you can view other records by clicking on the appropriate arrows displayed on each side of the current record name at the bottom of the window.

The arrows immediately to the left and right of the current record name take you to the previous and next records respectively. The arrows to the outside of these take you straight to the first and last records.

Finding information and sorting your records

Databases allow you to prioritise and organise your information as you please, and to search for specific entries quickly and easily.

Finding information

A single database in Microsoft Works can store up to 32,000 records. To locate a record quickly, you can initiate a search. In List View go to the **Edit** menu and click on **Find**. The Find dialogue box appears on screen. In the 'Find what' box type in a key word or words (be as specific as possible), select the **All Records** option then click **OK**. The records containing your key word will appear in a list. To return to your full list of records, go to the **Record** menu, select **Show** then **All Records**.

You can search in Form View in the same way but the records are displayed one at a time. To move between them, click the arrows at the foot of the screen.

Find

Find what: James

Match
- ○ Next record
- ● All records

Membership No.	First Name	Surname	Street Addres
00005	Peter	James	773 Long Lane
00003	James	Knighton	233 Bedminst

Membership

First Name: Peter   Surname: James

Street Address: 773 Long Lane

Sorting records in your database

You can use the Sort function in Works to re-order your database. Go to the **Record** menu and click on **Sort Records**. In the Sort Records dialogue box you can choose to have your records prioritised by up to three fields. For example, by first sorting by 'Date of birth' in ascending order, the oldest person in your database will appear at the top of the list, and the youngest person last. If you then sort by 'Surname' in ascending order, those who share the same date of birth will then be listed alphabetically. Sort a third time by town in ascending order, those who share the same birthday and name will be listed alphabetically by town.

Sort Records

Sort by: Date of Birth — ● Ascending ○ Descending   OK / Cancel

Then by: Surname — ● Ascending ○ Descending

Then by: Town or city — ● Ascending ○ Descending

Choose the fields in the order you want them sorted. For example: Last Name, First Name

Click on the arrows beside each Sort box, scroll through the lists and select your choice of field. You have the option of sorting records in Ascending or Descending order (Ascending lists entries A to Z, or 1, 2, 3...; Descending lists entries Z to A, or 10, 9, 8...).

Editing your database

After you have created a database, you can add and delete information, and perform calculations.

Inserting new records

To insert a new record between existing records, click on the row number where you want to insert it in List View. Go to the **Record** menu and select **Insert Record**. To delete a row, click on the row number, go to the **Record** menu and select **Delete Record**.

Adding and moving fields

To add a new field, click the field heading where you'd like it to appear in List View. Go to the **Record** menu and select **Insert Field**. Choose to insert it before or after the selected one. A dialogue box appears in which you give the new field a name. Click **OK**. To delete a field, click its heading then go to the **Record** menu and select **Delete Field**.

First Name	Surnam
Gillian	Foster
Paolo	Ianni
James	Knighto
Ursula	Davidow

To move a field, click on the field heading in List View. Move the mouse pointer to the edge of a highlighted cell. When it changes to a 'drag' pointer, drag the field to its new location. To move a record, click on the row heading and do the same. In each case you must be able to see the intended destination in the window.

Calculating data

You can perform calculations on values

		=Price-Deposit
Price	Deposit	Total Due
£1,500.00	£500.00	£1,000.00

in two or more fields and display the results in another. If you have fields for 'Price' and 'Deposit', create a third called 'Total Due'. Click its heading and type '=Price-Deposit' in the Entry bar to show the balance.

Microsoft Excel as a database

Microsoft Excel can be used to perform database functions. Instead of entering field names, headings are typed into the spreadsheet, in cells along the same row. Records are entered into the rows below. (Records must be numbered manually, so create a heading for 'Record No'.)

Fees Paid/Owed
(All)
(Top 10...)
(Custom...)
-62.5
-52.5
-46.2

To look at a sub-set of your data, use AutoFilter. Go to the **Data** menu and select **Filter** then **AutoFilter**. Each column appears with a menu arrow on the right. Click the arrow on the menu

you want to filter, then select **Custom** from the drop-down menu. Now set your criteria. For example, in a 'Fees paid/owed' column, you can select records to see only those people who owe money. In the Custom AutoFilter dialogue box specify records for which the fees paid/owed are less than '0', then click **OK**. To return to the full database, go to the **Data** menu and select **Filter** then **Show All**.

Custom AutoFilter

Show rows where:
Fees Paid/Owed
is less than — -30

Fees Paid/Owed
-33.72
-37.3
-46.2
-52.5
-62.5

Membership details

Record No: 0001

Surname: Coady

First names: Emma

Date of birth: 26/05/68

Registration: 03/02/85

Address: Flat 6, Sherbourne Drive, Putney, London (previously Flat 3, Warholl Mansion Block, Bern Street, Putney, London)

Telephone No: 020 8879 7865 (work 020 7354 7689)

Occupation: Nurse

Saving and printing

Transform your work into printed documents

Your computer stores work in much the same way as a conventional filing system. The documents that you create on your PC are kept in folders. Within the folders are sub-folders that help you organise the different areas of your work. For example, if you create a folder for office work, you could then create sub-folders for business correspondence and accounts. As with any filing system, it's vital to organise it well right from the start.

Windows XP helps by automatically creating folders for different types of files. You can easily set up each family member as a new user of the computer, each with his own set of files and folders. A well-ordered system makes it easy to save and retrieve your work – far easier, in fact, than with a traditional paper-filled filing cabinet.

Printing is easy

Printing your PC files (these are the documents you create, rather than the folders in which you store them) is one of the most useful skills you can master on your computer. Depending on the type of printer you have, you can print on a variety of paper sizes and weights (thicknesses). You can print out sticky address labels and even print directly onto envelopes.

By using the many font styles, colours and graphics available on your PC, it's possible to produce printed work that looks professional.

As soon as you create a new document, save it. Continue to save it as you work. This way, should your PC crash, your work will not be lost.

▶ SAVING YOUR WORK

Save As

Save in: 🖵 Desktop

📁 My Documents
🖳 My Computer
🖳 My Network Places

File name: Letter to Liz

Save as type: Works Document (*.wps)

1 To save a file, click on the **Save** toolbar button or go to the **File** menu and click on **Save As**. A dialogue box appears. In the 'File name' box type in the file's name. Click on the arrow to the right of the 'Save in' box to see the destinations to which you can save your file.

Auto saving

The more often you save files, the less work you risk losing if your computer crashes. You can set some programs, including Word, to save files automatically at regular intervals. Go to the **Tools** menu and click on **Options**. Click on the **Save** tab. Click next to 'Save AutoRecover info every:' and set a time interval. Finally, click **OK**.

☑ Save AutoRecover info every: `10` ⬍ minutes
☑ Embed smart tags
☐ Save smart tags as XML properties in Web pages

*If a sub-folder is selected but you wish to return to the main folder (moving up one level), click on the **Up One Level** button. To return to a main drive, click on the arrow beside the 'Save in' box, scroll through the list that appears and click on the drive.*

Up One Level

Create New Folder

Bright idea
*You can print multiple copies of a long document and have the pages collated in order. In the Print dialogue box click on the box beside Collate. Enter the number of copies you want then click **OK**.*

The procedure for printing documents is more or less the same, irrespective of which program you are working in. Here, a Word document is printed.

PRINTING YOUR WORK

Print (HP LaserJet 4V)

2 To create a sub-folder within, say, the My Documents folder found on your Desktop, click on the **Create New Folder** toolbar button. In the New Folder dialogue box type in a name for the folder then click **OK**.

3 Your sub-folder appears in the main folder. Double-click on it, and it appears in 'Save in' box. Now, click on **Save** to save your document into it. The document name now appears on the file's Title bar, and an icon for the Word file appears in the new sub-folder.

Go to the **File** menu and click on **Print**. In the dialogue box you are offered several options, such as printing multiple copies and printing a range of pages. Click **OK**. To print without seeing the dialogue box, click on the **Print** toolbar button.

Setting your page
You can adjust how your document prints out. Go to the **File** menu and click on **Page Setup**. Click on the **Paper** tab. Scroll through the 'Paper size' box and click on your choice. Click **OK**. If you do not want your document to print out as Portrait, select the Landscape option in the **Margins** tab. Click **OK**.

Print preview
To check how your document looks before printing, click on the **Print Preview** toolbar button or go to the **File** menu and click on **Print Preview**. To return to your original document layout, click **Close**.

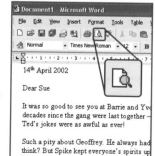

How your computer works

Discover what happens inside your PC when you switch it on

When you switch on the system unit of your PC it has to complete several automatic operations before it is able to process the commands you will subsequently input via your keyboard and mouse.

To ensure that the operating conditions are as they should be, all your hardware components, such as your memory and keyboard, are checked to make sure that they are undamaged and are able to communicate with each other and with your software.

This process is called 'booting up'. It takes only a minute, but it's the most important minute of your PC's working day. Unless the hardware and software don't communicate properly, nothing else on your PC will work.

Your computer's memory

The basic functions of your computer are governed by different types of 'memory'.

RAM

Random Access Memory (RAM) is the memory used by your computer temporarily to store the files and programs you are working on. It can process your commands extremely quickly. This type of memory only works when the computer is switched on; when it is turned off, anything left in RAM is lost.

ROM

Read Only Memory (ROM) holds basic details about the computer and a small, self-test program that runs every time you switch the computer on. ROM is part of your computer's 'identity', and is retained when your PC is turned off. You can't change or remove what's stored in the ROM, which is why it's called 'read only'.

CMOS

Complementary Metal Oxide Semiconductor (CMOS) memory stores your computer's settings, such as which type of hard disk it uses. The CMOS also remembers the date and time. It is powered by a small battery that recharges itself when the computer is switched on (switch it on at least once a month for an hour or two).

BIOS

The Basic Input/Output System (BIOS) memory controls your computer hardware. The BIOS tells the operating system which hardware to expect to come into operation and how it is arranged. It is as if your computer were a chef, and the BIOS his assistant, checking he has all the necessary ingredients. The BIOS is stored within the ROM.

⚠ Watch out

If your PC was not shut down properly the last time you used it, a message will flash up the next time you switch it on. If this happens, allow your PC to boot up, then restart it immediately. This ensures that the shut-down mistake has no lingering after-effects.

🔍 Close-up

In addition to switching on your system unit, you may also have to turn on your monitor, and any other peripheral units, such as a scanner or printer, if they have separate power sources.

When you switch on...

The first two minutes after you switch on are vital to the performance of your computer. Here's what happens after you press the power button.

Start up your computer

The first sound you will hear is the whirr of the fans. These regulate the temperature inside the system unit and operate for as long as the computer is switched on. Be careful not to cover any of the air vents on your PC as this will cause overheating. A modern computer can have as many as three fans blowing air over critical components, such as the graphics card.

Roll call

The first task your computer performs is the POST (Power On Self Test). This checks that the most important components such as the hard disk are present and working correctly. While your PC is going through this test you should see lights flickering on and off as the computer tests the CD drive, hard drive, floppy drive and keyboard. During these initial tests, the computer also checks the CD or DVD drive for a start-up disk – this allows you to make repairs in case of a major problem with your hard disk.

Once the POST is complete, Windows XP starts to load. You'll see a black screen with the Windows XP logo and three green lights scrolling from left to right (see left). These show that Windows is loading all the information it needs to co-ordinate the various

To begin, click your user name

Helen
Jane
Tom

components of your computer system. The tasks it performs at this stage include loading drivers – special programs that enable components like video cards to work – into memory; looking for new devices that may have been added to the computer since it was last switched on; and detecting any network that your computer may be attached to.

When this process is complete you will see the Windows XP Welcome screen (left, below). Click on your user name (if you use a password, type it in and then hit return or click on the green arrow). Windows will play a sound and load your personal configuration – your choice of desktop pattern and icons on it and in the start menu, as well as your personal set of folders including My Documents, My Pictures and My Music.

A quicker start

If you have used PCs with older versions of Windows, you will notice that XP starts up more quickly than its predecessors, and doesn't show pages of forbidden numbers and letters before it starts to load. One of the reasons for the quicker start is that XP can stop the computer from doing certain time-consuming tests before starting to load Windows. Also, once the operating system begins to load it does so in a much more efficient way, so that booting up can take as little as 30 seconds.

The hard disk

The hard disk is a series of magnetised metal disk platters. They are read by a small arm that passes over them – a little like an old-style record player. However, the arm never touches the disks – it skims thousandths of a millimetre above the platters, which you can hear spinning.

Ready and waiting

After your computer has checked through your hardware and software, you will be presented with the basic Desktop that tells you the computer is ready for use. Icons displayed on the Desktop may include shortcuts to Internet software, documents or folders and the Recycle Bin.

My Documents

My Computer

How software works

Learn how the operating system, programs and your PC's hardware interact

No matter how powerful your PC, it is an inert box of chips and wires until it is told what to do and think. Computers function only when they are given instructions. Software is the electronic 'brain' that gives your PC these instructions. The most fundamental piece of software on your computer is the operating system. The operating system on most PCs is Windows. Just as your brain coordinates your thoughts with your movements, so Windows controls all the actions that you ask your PC to do, from printing a page to closing a window.

From DOS to Windows

The original operating system for PCs was DOS (Disk Operating System). To use this system you needed to know the language, and you typed in commands one by one. These commands were quite complicated, and meant that DOS was difficult for most beginners to use.

In Windows XP, the DOS system is still accessible as a program called Command Prompt. If there is a fault with Windows, computer specialists can use this facility to execute text-based DOS commands to control the way the computer works at the most basic level.

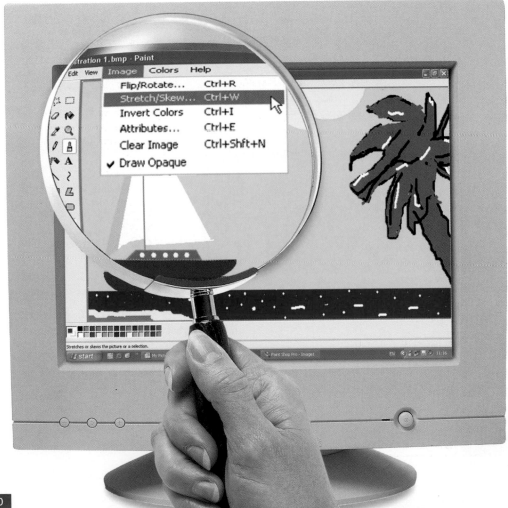

```
Command Prompt

Microsoft Windows XP [Version 5.1.2600]
(C) Copyright 1985-2001 Microsoft Corp.

C:\Documents and Settings\Tom Ruppel>
```

Using Windows requires no knowledge of computer languages. It has a Graphical User Interface (GUI – pronounced 'gooey') that allows you to operate your PC by moving your mouse pointer around the screen and clicking on buttons, menus and images. All Windows-compatible programs and additional hardware can be accessed through the Windows system.

Windows gets updated regularly and contains new features and improvements with each upgrade. The most recent version is Windows XP, which offers a completely updated look and lots of new features. Significantly, XP promises to be much more stable than previous versions of Windows for home users.

Bright idea
*Before buying a new program
check the packaging to see how
much RAM it needs, and make sure that your
computer has memory to spare (see below).*

*The Taskbar that runs along the bottom
of your Desktop shows you which
programs you have open – each is
displayed as a separate button. In this
Taskbar, Outlook Express, Excel, Word
and Paint Shop Pro are open.*

How does Windows work with other programs?

Understanding what happens when you open a program within
Windows will help you operate your computer more effectively.

The role Windows plays

Application programs
(so-called because they're
designed to be applied to a specific task)
rely on Windows to communicate at a
basic level with the computer's hardware.
This 'middleman' role does away with
the need to duplicate the same basic
features into every application.
Programmers are able to concentrate on
making sure each program performs its
specialist tasks as well as possible.

So, for example, when you save files
and the Save As dialogue box appears on
screen, this is an element of Windows,
not of the program you are using.

What happens when you switch your PC on?

When you switch your computer on,
Windows starts automatically. Its
program code is read from the hard
disk then loaded into the computer's
RAM memory.

If no software other than Windows is
loaded, all you can do on your PC is see
which files are on your hard disk, adjust
your PC's settings and run some very
basic programs. For most other tasks,
you have to call on application programs.

Even Windows accessories, such as
Internet Explorer, Paint and WordPad, are
separate programs dedicated to their
own jobs of Web browsing, painting
small pictures, and simple word
processing, respectively. (For more
information on specific programs you are
likely to use, see page 20.)

Opening programs in Windows

When you open programs they too are
loaded into the computer's RAM
memory. They then draw on Windows'
facilities to communicate with your
computer's hardware.

Windows allows you to run several
programs at once, and to move easily
between them. For example, if you
wanted to edit then insert a picture into
a Microsoft Word document you were
working on, you could open the Paint
program, edit the picture, then insert it
into the Word document. At the same
time, you could be researching the
subject of the document on the Internet
using the Internet Explorer program.

The importance of memory

As each new program is opened it loads
up into the computer's RAM memory,
alongside the other software already
running. This is why it's important that
your computer has enough RAM (at least
64MB, although 128MB will make your
computer run much better). If you don't
have enough to run a particular program,
your computer stores the excess data on
its hard disk. However, this makes all the
programs you have open run much more
slowly. (To find out how to add more RAM
to your PC, see page 344.)

When you have finished working with
a program you should close or exit it. The
program then unloads from the RAM,
freeing it up for use by other programs.
This may also speed up the operation of
the other programs that remain open.

Checking your RAM

To find out how much RAM you have on your PC, right-
click on **My Computer** and click on **Properties** from
the pop-up menu.

The General tab gives you basic information your
computer: which version of Windows you are using
and who it is registered to; what model of processor is
in your computer (a 300Mhz Pentium or equivalent is
the minimum recommended); and the total amount of
RAM installed. The other tabs allow you to discover
more detailed information about your machine.

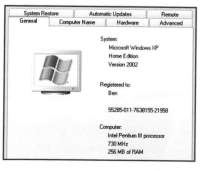

Storing all your data

How to make space for everything you need

Your computer's hard disk is where all your programs and documents are stored. The more programs and documents you have, the less disk space there is in which to store them. As the hard disk fills up, your computer will slow down. Disposing of unwanted documents in the Recycle Bin, and uninstalling software that you no longer use, will help to conserve hard disk space (for more details, see pages 54-55). However, eventually you may need to use extra storage devices.

Your first choices

Most computers contain a floppy disk drive, located in the system unit. Floppy disks can store about 1.44MB of data each – that's equivalent to about 60 one-page letters or one digital image scanned in at a low resolution.

Although floppy disks are still a popular way of moving files – between home and office, for instance – their lack of storage capacity makes them a poor way of storing data. It's also worth noting that shared floppy disks are the most common source of viruses, so storing valuable data on them can be risky (this doesn't apply if you are using new disks).

If your computer is relatively new, it will most likely have a CD-RW drive. This is like an ordinary CD-ROM drive in that it can read music and data CDs. It can also 'write' information onto special blank CDs. As much as 700MB of data can be stored on each disk, and Windows XP makes it simple to store data this way. If you don't have a CD-RW drive already, it's easy and cheap to add one on.

Which storage device?

These devices are all suitable for storing large quantities of information. If you need to transfer data to other PCs, make sure each PC has the same type of drive.

DVD-R

Many PCs have DVD-ROM drives, which can read high capacity DVD disks as well as ordinary CD-ROMs. It is now possible to buy DVD writers, the DVD equivalent of CD burners. These drives offer huge amounts of storage – as much as 4.5GB per disk – but can be expensive, as are the special disks used for recording.

Zip disks

These are one of the most popular storage devices available, with each disk able to hold 100MB or 250MB of data, depending on the version. Because of their popularity and widespread use, Zips disks provide a great way of sharing files with other PC users.

Super disks

Super disks look like floppy disks but can hold almost 200 times more data. The Imation LS120 SuperDisk was the original version with 120MB of storage. A newer verson, the LS240, has double the capacity. Super disk drives can also read normal floppy disks.

CD-Rewritable Disks

The most cost-effective form of storage for your PC is a CD-RW drive. This will write to CD-R disks, which cannot be erased, or to CD-RW disks that can be overwritten.

Tape drives

This is the oldest form of technology for storing large computer files. Nowadays, they are used mainly for creating back-up files of your work in case you lose the originals. They are too slow for everyday use, and the wide variety of different types available makes them unsuitable for exchanging files.

Connecting a drive

The storage devices described on this page are separate, external items that need to be connected to your system unit in order to function as data storage devices.

Almost all devices of this type will connect to your PC using a USB socket. Some of the most recent drives use USB 2.0 interfaces, which allow for very fast transfers – as long as your PC is similarly equipped.

Supplementary hardware

Extend your computer's capabilities with added devices

Once your computer knowledge and confidence grows, you will be eager to expand your PC's capabilities. A wide range of devices is available that will make working with your computer even more interesting and enjoyable.

If you like to use images in your work, a scanner is a surprisingly cheap way to get high-resolution images into your computer.

With added hardware, you can really make the most of your computer, turning it into a complete home office and entertainment centre

Not all images need to be scanned. Digital cameras will allow you to take photos and transfer them to your PC, no scanner required.

It's also possible to buy video cameras that attach to your computer. As well as being fun, you can hold video conferences with colleagues who have cameras. Making home movies is possible when you attach a digital camcorder to your PC.

Hardware can also be bought to make the most of existing on-screen entertainments. The new generation of joysticks, for instance, really take game playing to a new dimension.

These extras can be built up over time. You need not buy everything on the same shopping trip.

Modems

Almost all home computers sold in the last 4 years have an internal modem that allows you to connect to the Internet using a phone line. If your computer doesn't have an internal modem, it's easy to add an external model, which can also act as a fax and answering machine. To take advantage of an always-on, high-speed internet connection, you'll need either a cable modem or an ADSL model (above), depending on the telephone service you subscribe to.

 Bright idea
Most computers come with a built-in standard modem these days. However, they can go wrong and often aren't worth the cost of repair. Instead buy a new external modem, which attaches to your computer by a USB cable.

Scanners

A scanner will transform your paper images and photo prints into graphic files that you can then edit and use on your PC. The most versatile kind of scanners are 'flatbed' scanners. They can scan not only individual sheets of paper, but also pages from books without damaging the binding.

Picture quality is described in terms of resolution, measured in dots per inch (dpi). The more dots that make up an image, the higher the resolution and the better the quality of the image. Buy a scanner with a resolution capability of at least 600dpi.

Digital cameras

Digital cameras take photographs without using any film. You transfer pictures directly to your computer through a connection lead or digital memory card reader. The best digital cameras are quite expensive, but medium-priced ones still offer good quality: especially when you take into account that you won't need to buy film and get it developed, or buy a scanner.

Joysticks

If you're a fan of computer games, a joystick is essential. Many home PCs come with their own joystick, but you can also buy joysticks with extra feature buttons and better grips. They plug into a port in your system unit. The best joysticks are those that also provide feedback – recoiling as you fire guns, or shaking as you drive over rocks – but these 'force feedback' devices only work with games software that supports them. It's also possible to buy steering wheels and pedals for driving games.

Video cameras

If you mount a small video camera on the top of your computer you can conduct video conferences. These small cameras are also used for the WebCam sites on the Internet. Bear in mind that video conferencing requires a powerful PC, and without special high-speed phone lines, the picture can be jerky and the sound can stutter.

Microphones

Most microphones are fine for common uses – recording a narration, for instance – but you can also use a microphone with speech-recognition software, so you don't have to type: you just speak your thoughts, and the words appear in your document. This software is being continually refined, but you still may have to spend a long time teaching it to recognise your voice to get the best results.

Installing drivers

Additional hardware usually needs extra software. At the very least, you will need a driver – software that allows Windows to control the added hardware.

In the simplest cases Windows XP does the work for you. It recognises many pieces of hardware as soon as they are added to your PC, and connects to the web to search a Microsoft database for a suitable driver. Sometimes you may need to run the set-up program provided on a CD with the hardware.

Always check, when buying a new peripheral, that it will work with Windows XP and that suitable drivers are included or can be downloaded from the Internet.

45

More software for your PC

Extend the uses of your computer with extra programs

When you bought your PC, a selection of software will have been included. Common packages include Microsoft® Works Suite, Microsoft® Office XP, Lotus® SmartSuite® and StarOffice™. Each of these contains a number of programs that allow you to perform a range of functions such as word processing and spreadsheet work. The software that comes with your computer is known as bundled software.

Although this bundled software allows you to perform many different tasks on your PC, you're bound eventually to want to use more specialised or advanced software. If music is a hobby, for instance, you may be interested in a particular composing package; and if you have children, you may want a selection of games to play. You will also want to use virus-checking software to be sure your computer is kept free from viruses.

Checking the requirements

Before you buy a new piece of software, check the information on the packaging to ensure it runs on your version of Windows. You should also find out how much memory (RAM) and hard-disk storage space it requires.

To see how much disk space you have available, go to the **Start** menu, click on **My Computer**, and right-click on the C: drive and select **Properties** from the pop-up menu. To see how much RAM is built into your PC, go to the **Start** menu, click on **Control Panel**, then **Performance and Maintenance**. Finally click on **System** to see detailed information about your PC.

Close-up
When buying goods by mail order through a magazine advertisement, check that the magazine operates the Mail Order Protection Scheme (MOPS). This offers consumers protection if the software doesn't perform the tasks claimed of it.

Watch out
Copying programs from friends is not obtaining software for free – it's stealing. Unless you have purchased a licence, you are breaking copyright laws and could be prosecuted.

'Free' software

You don't always have to buy new software for your PC. Some of it can be obtained free, if only for a limited period.

Jasc Software — the power to create®

company info | product info | free downloads | how to buy | s

What is an Evaluation Version?

Evaluation versions provide a way of obtaining and evaluating software to try a program on their own computer before buying it.

While evaluation versions are copyrighted, and the copyright holder specifically grants a user the right to freely evaluate and distribute the

After using the evaluation version for the defined trial period, the user or remove the evaluation version from their system.

Freeware, shareware and evaluation software

Freeware describes software that's available completely free. Most of the programs have been written by PC enthusiasts and are of good quality.

Shareware and evaluation software are offered free for a limited period (usually 30 days), after which you will not be able to operate the program.

If you want to continue to use a shareware program you must pay a fee (usually much lower than the price of similar, shop-bought packages). To continue using evaluation software, you must purchase a full copy.

Sources of software

Specialist PC stores and electrical shops are good places to start, but the other sources outlined below may save you money.

Downloading programs

It's possible to download shareware, freeware and evaluation software from the Internet. Locate a dedicated Web site (see box below), then follow the on-screen instructions on the site.

Your PC will tell you how long the download will take – a big program can take hours on a dial-up connection. Once it has downloaded, you will need to install the program before running it.

PC magazines

Look out for free, cover-mounted CD-ROMS on PC magazines. Some CDs will hold 'full product' or complete programs, while others will offer demonstration or shareware versions.

Buying mail order

Mail order or 'direct' software vendors offer competitive pricing over high street retailers. Look at the adverts in PC magazines to compare prices. Software can be downloaded from the Internet or dispatched by post.

Where for wares?

TUCOWS (www.tucows.com) is a website that lists most shareware and freeware programs available for download. Here we've searched for Gardening programs and chose to try a program that lets you care for a virtual plant on your PC desktop.

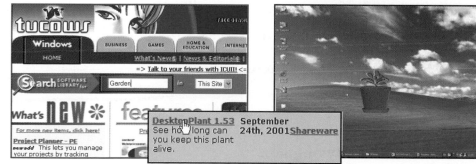

Filing your work

Learn how to name and save your files,
and to organise your work efficiently

It can be far easier to locate your work in a well-organised filing system on your computer than it is in a normal paper filing system

Your computer is an electronic filing cabinet. Each piece of work is stored in folders (as are all the programs you use). Folders can be stored in other folders which are like the drawers in the cabinet. It is tempting to keep all your files on your computer Desktop where you can see them but, as with a real desk, it makes life easier if you tidy things away before the clutter gets out of hand.

Filing made easy

Don't worry that you will forget where you put files, because Windows makes it easy to find them. It is like having an efficient personal assistant – or it is as if your filing cabinet could tell you exactly what is in all its drawers.

You can access your computer's filing system through a handy facility called Windows Explorer. Through it you can move folders and files around, make new folders and even copy, or duplicate, folders and documents.

There are several ways to create folders. The method you use will depend on how you save your work.

▶ CREATING FOLDERS

1 To create a folder in Windows Explorer, go to the **Start** menu, select **All Programs** then **Accessories** and click on **Windows Explorer**. In the left pane click on the drive or folder in which you want to create the new folder.

Naming your files

Always name your files logically so that, should you misplace one and not remember its full name, you can still activate a search for it. If several members of the family are using the computer, create separate folders in which each person can store work. Use your name or initials when naming documents so that you don't get confused as to whose 'Personal Accounts' are whose.

Bright idea
*To rename a file or folder, click on it in Windows Explorer, go to the **File** menu and select **Rename**. Type in the new name over the highlighted old name.*

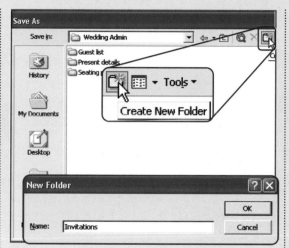

2 Go to the **File** menu and select **New** then **Folder**. In the right pane a new folder appears, with its name highlighted. The default name, 'New Folder', will be replaced as soon as you begin typing in the new name.

You can create folders in which to store work as you save documents. In the Save As dialogue box click on the **Create New Folder** button. In the New Folder dialogue box give the folder a name then click **OK**. Now double-click on your named folder and click on **Save**.

It is possible to create new folders by using your right mouse button. When you need to create a new folder click the right mouse button, select **New** then select **Folder**. The default name on the folder that appears will be replaced as you type in the new name.

Finding lost files

To find work you have misplaced, go to the **Start** menu, select **Search** then choose one of the search options. Clicking on **All Files and Folders** brings up a dialogue box where you can type the file name, or as much of it as you can remember. Choose other options as appropriate, then click on **Search** to begin looking.

Search by any or all of the criteria below.

All or part of the file name:
Party planner

A word or phrase in the file:

[Search]

Look in:
Local Hard Drives (C:;D:)

Copying and moving files

Keep your documents in order

There will be occasions when you need to copy or move files. You may want to make a back-up of a document (a duplicate copy of a file to use in case your other one becomes damaged or lost), or transfer a file to another computer to work on. Perhaps you need to copy work onto a floppy disk, or you would simply like to store a file in a more appropriate folder on your computer. Whatever you want to do, Windows makes it easy.

To copy to a floppy disk, first insert the disk into the floppy disk drive.

BEFORE YOU START

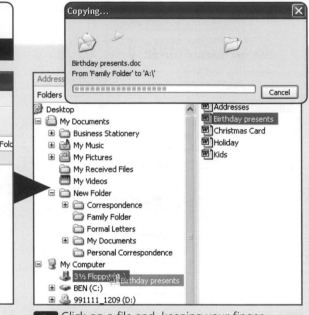

1 Go to the **Start** menu, highlight **All Programs** then Accessories and click on **Windows Explorer**. By clicking on the folders in the left pane of the window you can locate the file you wish to copy in the right pane.

2 Click on a file and, keeping your finger pressed down on the mouse button, drag the file over to the 3½ Floppy [A:] drive icon in the left pane. When the drive icon becomes highlighted release the button. A dialogue box shows the copy operation in progress.

⚠ Watch out

Remember that dragging a file from one drive to another results in two copies of that file: the original on the source drive and a copy on the destination drive.

If you drag a file to another location on the same drive, the file will simply move to the new location, without a copy being made. To create two copies of a file within a drive, use the Copy and Paste commands in the Edit menu.

Bright idea
*Save yourself time by copying or moving several files at the same time. Press the **Ctrl** key and, keeping it pressed down, click on each of the files or folders. Release the **Ctrl** key and move or copy them as usual.*

*To copy a file onto your hard disk open **Windows Explorer** from the **Start** menu (see previous Step 1).*

▶ BEFORE YOU START

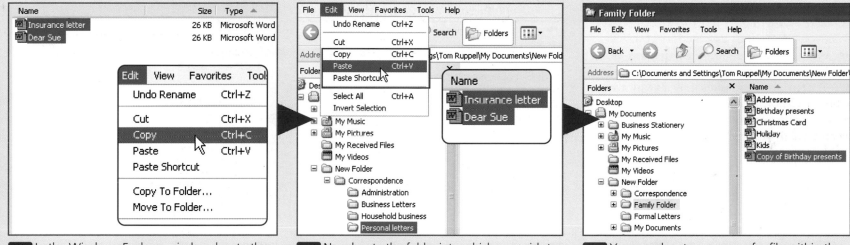

1 In the Windows Explorer window, locate the file or files you wish to copy. Click on the file. (To select several files at once, press the **Ctrl** key on your keyboard and, keeping it pressed down, click on each of the files.) Go to the **Edit** menu and select **Copy**.

2 Now locate the folder into which you wish to copy the selected file or files. Click on it then go to the **Edit** menu and select **Paste**. The copied files now appear in the right pane of the window, alongside any files that were already in the folder.

3 You can also store a copy of a file within the same folder as the original. Click on the relevant file, go to the **Edit** menu and select **Copy** then **Paste**. To distinguish the copy from the original, Windows names the copy as 'Copy of …'.

Relocating files

Just as with a conventional paper filing system, it will often be necessary to move your files and folders to more suitable locations. Windows Explorer helps you do this. Click on the file or folder then, keeping your finger pressed down on the mouse button, drag the file or folder over to its new location. When the destination folder is highlighted, release the mouse button. The file or folder will then move.

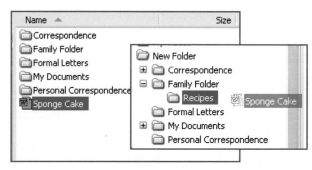

Maximising disk space

How to make the most of the space on your computer

Watch out

If you intend to delete (or restore) a folder from the Recycle Bin, remember that Windows will delete (or restore) the entire contents of the folder, not just the file you are interested in. Be sure you want to do this before proceeding.

E nsuring that your computer works efficiently means organising your folders and files effectively and using the available storage space properly.

As you create files and folders you will use more and more hard-disk space. This won't be a problem initially but, as the hard disk fills up, your computer may slow down as it searches for the correct file or folder, or performs a task. You will also find it more difficult to install new programs.

Deleting out-of-date folders and files, and uninstalling old software, will free up disk space, allowing your PC to run smoothly.

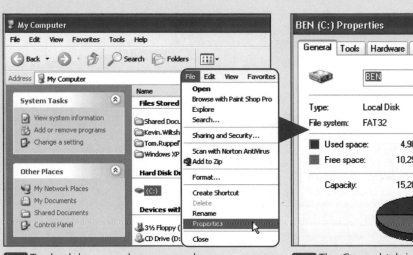

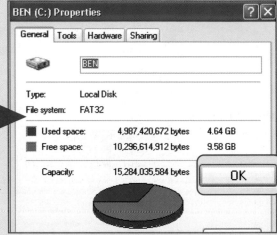

1 To check how much space you have on your hard disk, double-click on the **My Computer** icon on the Desktop. In the My Computer dialogue box click on the **[C:]** drive icon, then go to the **File** menu and click on **Properties**.

2 The General tab in the Properties dialogue box is selected. You can see the amount of Used and Free space, as well as hard-disk capacity. A diagram gives an instant overview. Click on **OK** or **Cancel** to close the window.

How much space do I need?

To keep your computer working efficiently, it's important that you keep a minimum of 100 MB of hard-disk space free. If you want to install new software, check how much disk space the software requires.

To do this, insert the software CD, set up the installation and look for the screen that lets you know how much space is required. If you don't have enough space available, quit the installation by following the on-screen instructions.

To delete files or folders, go to the **Start** menu, select **All Programs,** then **Accessories** and click on **Windows Explorer.**

DELETING FILES

If you send a file to the Recycle Bin by mistake, Windows allows you to restore it to its original location.

RESTORING FILES

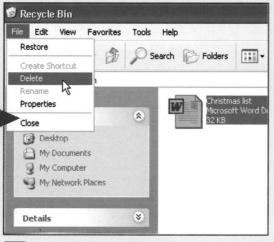

1 Click on the file or folder you wish to delete. Go to the **File** menu and select **Delete**, or press the **Delete** key. A prompt box asks you to confirm your command. Click **No** to cancel or **Yes** to send the files or folders to the Recycle Bin on your Desktop.

2 Files in the Recycle Bin continue to take up space until the Bin is emptied. To completely remove an item from your computer, double-click on the **Recycle Bin**, click on the file, go to the **File** menu and select **Delete**. You will be asked to confirm your choice.

The Recycle Bin has a useful safety net if you make a mistake in deleting an item. To rescue a file from the bin, double-click on the **Recycle Bin** Desktop icon, click on the file you want to rescue, go to the **File** menu and select **Restore**. The item is then sent back to its original location.

Empty your bin

If you want to empty the Recycle Bin completely, double-click on its desktop icon. A window will open showing the contents.

Select **Empty Recycle Bin** from the last of tasks in the left-hand pane. Confirm the command at the prompt.

Bright idea
To remove program files, use the special Uninstalling function described on page 54. Do not drag them into the Recycle Bin.

Tidying your hard disk

Learn how to uninstall software to create space on your PC

Over time, your PC's hard disk may become clogged up with programs you no longer use. Removing them is often the best way to create space and ensure that your computer continues to run smoothly.

It is essential that programs are removed completely. Simply dropping them into the Recycle Bin is like pulling up a weed and leaving the roots behind.

Get it right

To ensure effective removal, programs may have their own uninstall facilities, found in each program's folder. For the many that do not, use the Add or Remove Programs function in Windows.

The steps here are a guide only, as each uninstalling process is unique.

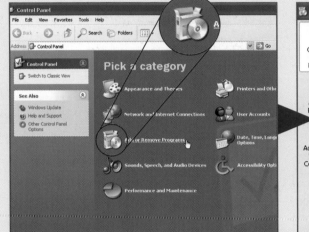

1 Windows XP has a built-in utility that helps you to remove unwanted programs properly. In the **Start** menu, click on Control Panel, then on **Add or Remove Programs**.

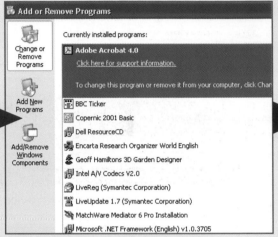

2 The Add or Remove Programs window appears, with the Change or Remove programs option selected. A list of all the programs that can be removed using this process is shown in a panel. Scroll through and click on the one you want to remove.

⚠ Watch out

Before uninstalling any programs, check that no-one else in the family wants to keep them. Then close down all active programs before starting the uninstall process.

Specialist uninstalling software

Some programs do not come with an uninstall option which means Windows will not put them into its Add/Remove Programs list. Other programs may be listed but then throw up problems while you are trying to uninstall them. To deal with these programs, consider buying some of the specialist uninstalling software available. Most of this software is inexpensive and can sometimes be obtained as shareware (software distributed free with magazines for a trial period).

Bright idea
Before you uninstall any software, back up any related data that you wish to keep, and ensure that you still have the original installation disks or CD in case you want to reinstall the program later.

When you uninstall a program the Add/Remove facility may not remove shortcuts you have made to it in the Start menu. You can do this separately yourself.

▶ Removing shortcuts

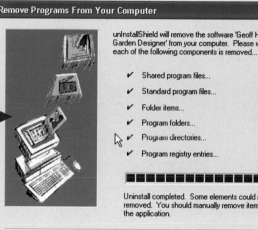

3 Click on the **Change/Remove** button (some programs may have a separate Remove button). Your PC will open an uninstalling program designed for the software you have chosen. It will ask you to confirm your decision to uninstall. Check that you have selected the right program, then click on the **Yes** button.

4 Your PC will now uninstall all relevant files. A dialogue box will show you the operation in progress. (If some program files are shared with other programs, you will be asked whether you want to remove them. To be safe, choose **No**.)

5 The removed program might still appear in the list of your most often used programs in the Start menu. To clear the list, click on **Start**, right-click in a clear area and choose **Properties**. From the Start Menu tab, click on the **Customize** button. In the General tab, click on **Clear List**.

Deleting other shortcuts
You may have placed a shortcut to the program you have removed on your desktop. To remove it, minimise all your windows to get to your desktop. You can do this by holding down the **Windows** key and down pressing '**M**' at the same time. Right click on the shortcut icon that you want to remove and choose **Delete** from the pop-up menu.

Understanding computer viruses

Take the right precautions to keep your computer healthy

Vigilance pays when it comes to viruses. Make sure you install an anti-virus program on your computer and run it regularly

Viruses are computer programs that are designed to cause harm rather than good. Once inside your PC they can cause all sorts of problems, from making unwanted messages appear on your screen, to causing programs to crash, or your printer to stop working. In very rare cases, they can even delete all the data on your hard disk.

There are several ways a virus can infiltrate your computer. When they first appeared, viruses were most often passed on via floppy disks. But nowadays the biggest danger is from the Internet. Most often viruses are 'caught' by downloading infected files attached to innocent-seeming e-mail messages.

Anti-virus software

But no matter how your computer catches a virus, you probably won't be aware of it until something goes wrong and damage has been done. However, you can take precautions and limit the risk of catching a virus.

The first step is to buy an anti-virus program, such as McAfee's VirusScan. It is also sensible to subscribe to an update service, so that your PC will be protected against new viruses. This is often free for a year or so.

Then it's a matter of using your common sense. Treat all e-mail attachments with extreme caution. And set up a weekly routine for checking your hard disk.

How viruses infect your PC

Identifying the different sorts of virus, and knowing how they spread from one computer to another, will help you keep your PC infection-free.

TYPES OF VIRUSES

File virus

A file virus infects program files. Once the affected program is running, it can infect other programs on your hard drive or on a floppy disk inserted in the A: drive.

	Microsoft Access Shortcut 3 KB		Microsoft Excel Shortcut 3 KB
	Microsoft Outlook Shortcut 3 KB		Microsoft Word Shortcut 3 KB
	Microsoft PowerPoint Shortcut 3 KB		Microsoft Works Shortcut 3 KB

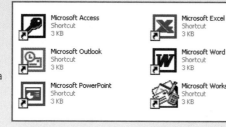

Macro virus

A macro virus infects individual documents. It affects files created in programs that use macro programming language, such as Microsoft Office's Word and Excel programs. One way to protect against this family of viruses is to set a high level of Macro Security. In the **Tools** menu choose **Options** and click on the **Security** tab. The **Macro Security** button is near the bottom.

	A	B	C
1			
2			
3	**January Bills**		
4			
5	Mortgage	£ 633.85	
6	Loan	£ 145.95	
7	Phone	£ 35.45	
8	Gas	£ 23.50	
9	Electricity	£ 36.74	
10			

Boot and partition sector viruses

Boot and partition sector viruses infect the system software; that is, the special parts of the hard disk that enable your computer to start, or 'boot' up. These viruses may prevent you getting your computer working at all. They work by removing your PC's start-up instructions and replacing them with their own set of instructions. You may need specialist help if your computer catches this type of virus.

THE WAYS VIRUSES ARE SPREAD

Floppy disk

Always be wary of floppy disks as they are made to move files or programs between computers. The more machines that a disk is used on, the greater the chances of the disk picking up a virus and passing it on. Jaz and Zip disks can carry viruses in the same way as a floppy disk.

3½ Floppy (A:)

E-mail

However, some e-mail programs can catch viruses simply by opening an infected e-mail message. You should also be wary of opening a file attached to an e-mail as the file itself may carry a virus. As a general rule, do not open up files attached to unsolicited e-mail.

CD-ROM

You are safe with a CD-ROM (except in the extremely unlikely event that it was made with a virus). 'ROM' stands for Read Only Memory, which means it will not accept viruses – or, indeed, any other kind of information. However, with recordable or rewritable CDs you need to take the same precautions as with a floppy disk.

Wksstecd4 (D:)

Internet

Internet Explorer

Don't download software of dubious origin from the Internet. Use a reputable company, such as Corel, Norton, Microsoft or McAfee.

> ⚠️ **Watch out**
> Be careful when buying software on a disk. Ensure it comes from a reputable source and that the packaging has not been tampered with. If the disk has been used there is a chance that it carries a virus. Remember, pirated software is illegal and greatly increases the chances of catching viruses.

> 🔑 **Key word**
> **Computer bug** A computer bug is different to a virus in that bugs are accidents or mistakes in programming, rather than programs specifically designed to cause harm.

Keeping up to date

Update Windows so it stays stable and secure

Microsoft Windows XP is a major advance over previous versions of the operating system, such as Windows 98 and ME. But even a system as stable as Windows XP occasionally needs minor revisions. These are made available as Windows Updates, and the easiest way to get them is over the Internet (see page 88 for how to get on-line).

The Microsoft website can check out your system and prompt it to download any recommended updates. You can even set up your machine to do the checking automatically, so that it alerts you when a new update has been released.

Updates can fix minor problems in the ways that Windows operates – nine times out of ten you won't even have noticed that there was a problem – but most often are made to improve the security of your computer. Security updates are almost inevitable, as no manufacturer can think of every way that a malicious mind might try to break down their product, so that obscure security lapses are only discovered after a product has been released to the general public.

Whenever an update to Windows is released, Microsoft publishes information on its Web site about what is being updated and the problem that it is correcting. Using this information, you can decide whether or not you need to update your system – often the problems addressed on the Web site aren't relevant to home users.

Microsoft also occasionally releases 'Service Packs' – collected packages of updates and improvements that can be downloaded from the Microsoft website or ordered on CD-ROM.

You need an Internet connection to use Windows Update (see page 88). Make sure your modem is plugged into a phone socket.

(see page 88)

Bright Idea
Office Update works in a similar way to Windows Update to keep Microsoft Office, if you have it, fully up to date.

BEFORE YOU START

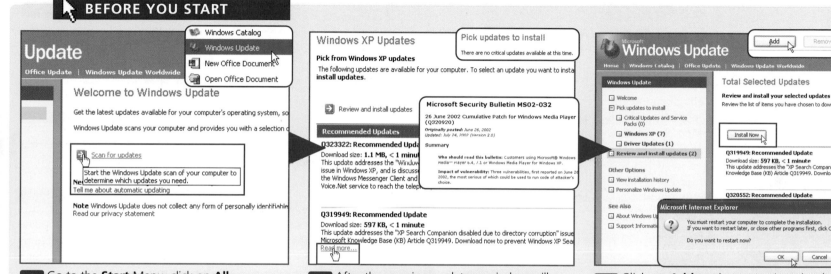

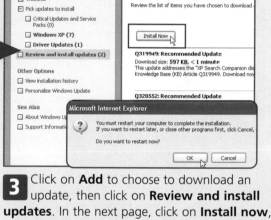

1 Go to the **Start** Menu, click on **All Programs**, then on **Windows Update**. You will be asked to connect to the Internet. An Internet Explorer Window will open with the Windows Update Welcome page. Click on **Scan for Updates** to start checking your system, a process that may take some time.

2 After the scan is complete, a window will open listing any critical updates that are needed. There may be none. Other, less important updates can be viewed by clicking on the links in the left hand column. Each update has a 'Read more' link that takes you to web pages explaining more about how the update works.

3 Click on **Add** to choose to download an update, then click on **Review and install updates**. In the next page, click on **Install now**, Read and accept the license agreement if there is one and watch as the download starts. Once it is complete you may need to restart your PC.

Auto updating

Your PC can automatically check for updates when you are online. The process can be slow, so this option makes most sense if you have a fast connection. For Automatic updates, go to the **Start** menu, right-click on **My Computer**, then on **Properties**. In the System Properties dialogue box, click on the **Automatic Updates** tab. Make sure there is a tick in the box next 'Keep my computer up to date'. You can choose whether to be notified of new updates or have them downloaded and installed automatically. When an update is available you will see a message on your desktop.

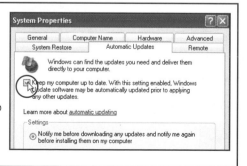

Defragmenting and scanning the hard disk

How to help your computer to perform at its best

Taking care of your computer means ensuring that the hard disk is working at its optimum level. Defragmenting and scanning the hard disk on a regular basis will help. Defragmenting makes sure large files can be stored in such a way that access to them is as easy and quick as possible. Scanning checks the hard disk and floppy disks for errors.

Windows XP has two useful tools – Disk Defragmenter and Check Disk – that carry out these tasks. You need to use them regularly to maintain the smooth running of your PC.

Defragmenting is particularly important if you use your PC for editing video, as this puts large amounts of data onto your hard drive.

It can take half an hour or more to defragment your hard disk. Don't set the process in motion if you haven't got this time to spare.

DISK DEFRAGMENTING

1 Go to the **Start** menu, select **All Programs**, then **Accessories**, then **System Tools**, then click on **Disk Defragmenter**. Note that Disk Cleanup and Scheduled Tasks are also in this location.

Close-up
When you save a large file, your computer will often split it up into fragments and store it in different locations on the hard disk. Your computer can still find the file but it takes longer to do so. Disk Defragmenter rearranges the fragments of a large file so that they are stored next to each other. This makes it easier and quicker for your computer to access files.

Use Check Disk to check your floppy disks for errors too. The process takes a minute or two.

► CHECK DISK

⚠ **Watch out**
Never cut short a disk defragmentation run – you could damage system and other files. Let the program run its course.

2 In the Disk Defragmenter dialogue box click on and highlight the drive you want to defragment (unless you have fitted an extra hard drive to your PC there will only be one choice). Click **Defragment** to start the process. You can view the progress of the operation on screen.

1 Go to the **Start** Menu, click **My Computer**, and then right-click your hard disk drive, normally **C**. Click **Properties**, and then click on **Tools**. Under **Error-checking**, click **Check Now**.

2 Click next to 'Automatically fix file system errors' and 'Scan for and attempt recovery of bad sectors', then click on **Start**. The utility will ask if you wish to schedule the examination – click on **Yes**. Then restart.

Vital for video

For most relatively new computers, hard disks are so large and they access data so quickly that the effects of defragmenting can be negligible. However, certain application programs do place huge amounts of data onto your hard disk and work best if they can read the data back in a steady stream. A good example is digital video. If you use your computer to edit your home videos, you will regularly be placing many Gigabytes of data onto your hard disk. Even a large disk can fill up quickly and become badly fragmented, so it's a good idea to regularly defragment a disk drive used for this purpose.

Caring for your equipment

Cleaning hardware regularly will prevent problems in the future

Your computer needs simple but regular maintenance to stay in good condition. Problems such as your mouse seizing up, or the keys on your keyboard becoming stuck, can be easily avoided if you clean your equipment regularly. And keeping your work space clean and tidy will create a more pleasant environment for everyone to work in.

Simple measures include making a rule that you don't drink or eat at or near your PC, and that you protect it with a suitable dust cover when not in use. When cleaning, spare a few minutes to check that those 'spaghetti' wires are out of harm's way, too.

Kit yourself out

Have a cleaning routine that you carry out once a month. As with any type of cleaning, ensure that you have the correct materials for the job. Computer stockists offer a variety of cleaning products, but a multipurpose cleaning kit is probably the best choice for the home user. A typical kit comprises PC wipes, PC buds, cleaning cloths, cleaning fluid and a cleaning card. You should also consider buying a dust spray.

Before you start cleaning, make sure you've turned your equipment off at the wall socket – it is never safe to use fluids with electricity.

Dust and stains on your screen can make it more difficult to read

Watch out
Never use ordinary household spray polish or liquid spray cleaners on your keyboard. If liquid gets between or under the keys, it can damage the mechanism.

Bright idea
Before cleaning your keyboard, turn it upside down over a bin and shake it gently. Much of the debris that has slipped between and under the keys will fall out.

Cleaning your hardware

A few minutes of light maintenance every month is all that's required to keep your machine running at peak performance and in showroom condition.

The keyboard

Because your keyboard is an exposed component of your computer, dirt will inevitably accumulate between and under its keys. To remove it, wipe the keys with special cleaning buds or use dust spray to blow away dust. If you have them, work cleaning cards dipped in cleaning solution between the keys.

The printer

Check the paper paths of your printer to ensure they are clean and free from ink or toner. Use wipes to remove any spillage, but be careful not to get toner on your hands or clothes as it is difficult to remove. Don't touch the printing mechanism itself unless the print manual gives cleaning advice on this. Perform a print test (consult your print manual for instructions) to check on the ink or toner level. Replace print cartridges or toner as required.

Floppy and CD drives

Keeping your floppy disk and CD-ROM drives clean ensures that programs and files can be accessed smoothly and are less prone to data loss.

Specialist floppy and CD cleaning disks are available from computer stockists. Simply insert the appropriate cleaning disk and follow the on-screen instructions.

The monitor

It is important that you keep your monitor screen in pristine condition. Using a dirty, stained screen leads to unnecessary eyestrain. Use a PC wipe to keep the screen clean, clear and safe – the non-smear varieties are best for the job.

The mouse

Follow this simple routine to keep your mouse running smoothly and trouble-free.
1 Turn your mouse upside down and wipe the base firmly with a special PC wipe.
2 Twist the mouse-ball cover so that it opens and the ball falls out into your hand.

3 Clean the mouse ball by wiping it with a lint-free cloth. Dab it with sticky tape to pick up any dust or dirt particles that have accumulated on it.

4 Using a PC bud or your fingernail, remove dust and fluff from inside the mouse ball socket, concentrating on the three rollers that make contact with the ball.
5 Finally, return the ball to its socket and twist the mouse ball cover back into place.

Welcome to the world of Windows

Fast and flexible – your PC's operating system lets you use your PC with confidence

To drive your car you don't need to know the intimate workings of an engine. It helps should you break down, but it's not essential. So it is with Windows. You don't need to know the layers of code that make it run, you just need to know the best way to drive it, while getting the most benefit.

Windows gets its name from the fact that every program – word processor, database, spreadsheet – operates inside its own window on your PC's Desktop.

Keeping your house in order

Windows is an 'operating system', the set of instructions which make sure your computer runs smoothly. It acts as a housekeeper, by keeping files in order, and allows your PC to perform basic jobs, such as printing.

You can personalise Windows to suit your needs by, for example, giving your computer its own background (a picture or pattern that covers your Desktop).

Windows XP has a choice of dramatic images to decorate your Desktop

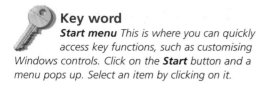

Key word
Start menu *This is where you can quickly access key functions, such as customising Windows controls. Click on the **Start** button and a menu pops up. Select an item by clicking on it.*

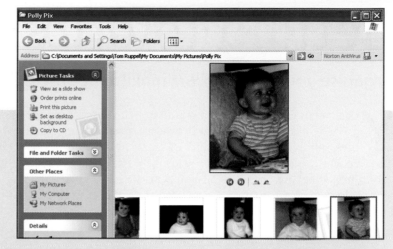

Advances in Windows
Since Windows first appeared, it has been updated to keep pace with new technology. Windows XP is the latest version but Windows 98 and ME are still widely used.

XP has an updated look but contains many familiar features – a desktop with a Recycle bin, a Start button and Taskbar. Like earlier versions, XP can only run software compliant with Windows.

XP has a much larger Start menu, and dedicated folders for music, pictures and other types of file. It integrates with the internet very closely and is much more stable than earlier versions of Windows.

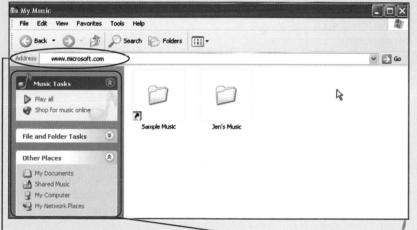

Windows XP lets you connect to Internet sites by typing a Web address into the Address box. You have to be connected to do this.

XP puts links to tasks relevant to the folder being looked at in the left-hand pane of a window. In My Music, for example, there is the option to Play all.

Changing face of PCs
In the days of DOS – the PC operating system before Windows – the way to print a file, say, was by typing in intricate commands in computer language (below).

```
Command Prompt
Microsoft Windows XP [Version 5.1.2600]
(C) Copyright 1985-2001 Microsoft Corp.
```

The birth of Windows 3.1, then Windows 95 and 98, literally changed the face of PCs. The visual nature of Windows lets you see exactly what you are doing on your PC's Desktop.

The mouse became the new steering wheel. It allows you to move and organise files by picking them up and dropping them into the folders that you have created and named.

The Start button and Taskbar introduced in Windows 95 meant that you could find files, open programs and use Windows' many tools in just a few moves of the mouse. Windows XP has many new features including a dedicated My Pictures folder, which allows you to view its contents as a filmstrip and to order prints online.

Bright idea
*Help is always at hand. Click the **Start** button and select **Help and Support** from the menu, or use the Help drop-down menus at the top of almost every window. Alternatively, simply press the **F1** key on your keyboard to get assistance relevant to the program you are using.*

Getting to grips with windows

Organise your Desktop for maximum efficiency and ease of use

Your computer's Desktop is much like a conventional desk in that it holds files, folders, documents and tools. These are all represented on your PC by icons.

By double-clicking on any icon you will open it. The opened icon – whatever it represents – will appear as a separate window on your Desktop, and its size, shape and position can all be set by you.

Having several windows open on your Desktop at once can be just as confusing as having a pile of papers scattered all over your desk. But there are ways to keep your work area tidy and boost your efficiency.

Controlling the size of windows

The buttons in the top right-hand corner of a window help control its appearance.

The Minimise button

Click on the **Minimise** button to shrink the window to a button on the Taskbar. Clicking on the Taskbar button will restore the window to the Desktop.

The Maximise button

Click on the **Maximise** button to expand the window to fill the whole screen. When a window is maximised, the button changes to a Restore button. Click on this to restore the window to its original size.

The Close button

Click on the **Close** button to close a window or program.

Scroll bars

Often, you won't be able to see all the contents of a window. When this happens, scroll bars appear to the right of, and/or bottom of, the window.

To view the window's contents, click on the arrows at each end of the scroll bar, or click on the slider itself and, keeping your finger pressed down on the mouse button, drag it along.

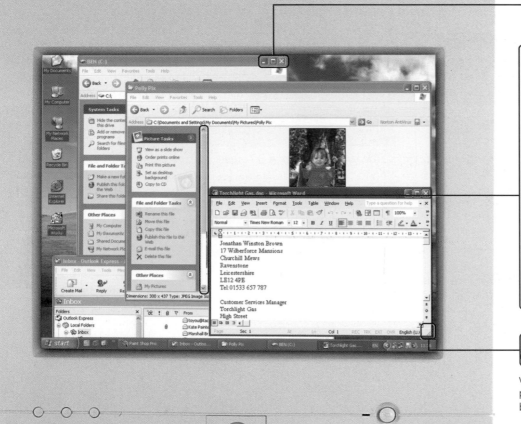

Resizing windows

To adjust the height or width of a window, click on any of the window's edges (the mouse pointer will change to a double-headed arrow when you are in position). Keeping your finger pressed down on the mouse button, drag the window in or out.

To resize the width and height at the same time, click on the window's corner and drag it diagonally.

Short cut
You may find it easier and quicker to maximise windows by double-clicking on the Title bar that runs across the top of them.

Bright idea
*If several windows are open and you need to see your Desktop, right-click on the **Taskbar** and click on **Show the Desktop** from the pop-up menu. To restore the windows to your screen, click on **Show Open Windows**.*

Arranging windows on your Desktop

Windows is extremely flexible when it comes to organising open folders and documents.

Working with windows

Ideally, it is best to have just one or two windows open on your screen at any one time. This not only keeps your Desktop tidy, but also makes it less likely that you will file documents in the wrong place.

Tiling your windows

You can arrange your windows so that you can see the contents of each one at the same time. Individual windows can be 'tiled' – that is, arranged in squares across your screen so that every open window is visible on the Desktop. (Think of a tiled wall or floor.)

Right-click on the **Taskbar** and select **Tile Windows Vertically** or **Horizontally**. This arranges all your folders and open programs in a neat 'tiled' layout. To revert back to your former screen, right-click on the **Taskbar** and select **Undo Tile**.

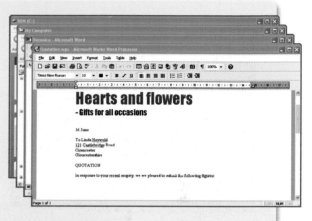

Cascading windows

Another handy option is Cascade Windows, which arranges windows so that each one overlaps the one before, diagonally, from the top left-hand corner of your screen. This is useful if you have several windows open, as you will still be able to see the name of each one filed behind the other. Clicking on a cascaded window will bring it to the front of your stack.

To operate this function, right-click on the **Taskbar** then click on **Cascade Windows** from the pop-up menu. To revert back to your former screen, right-click on the **Taskbar** and select **Undo Cascade**.

Exploring with Windows

Windows can quickly build-up on screen. To save you wading through a mass of folders to find a file, use Windows Explorer (go to the **Start** menu, select **All Programs** then **Accessories** and click on **Windows Explorer**).

This allows you to access all the contents of your PC from one window. The drives and folders appear in the left pane, while the contents of a selected folder or drive appear in the right pane. To select a folder, click on it.

Close-up
*To see what's behind a maximised window, press the **Alt** key and keep it pressed down. Now press the **Tab** key. Open windows appear as icons in a beige panel in the middle of your screen. Move along the icons by pressing the **Tab** key. When you release the keys the icon with the border around it opens up on screen.*

Personalising your Desktop

Decorate your PC to make it feel like part of the furniture

We all like to add individual touches to our houses. The colour that we paint our front door and the layout of our front gardens make us feel that our home truly belongs to us. It is just as easy to put a personal stamp on Windows.

If, for instance, you don't particularly like the background colour or pattern of your Desktop you can change it by selecting a different background from Windows' library. Options include landscape scenes, flowers, shapes and bubbles. You can easily change your background again if you get bored with it.

| Arrange Icons By ▸ |
| Refresh |
| Paste |
| Paste Shortcut |
| New ▸ |
| Properties |

Background design

To change the background on your Desktop, right-click anywhere on the Desktop and select **Properties** from the pop-up menu. In the Display Properties dialogue box click the **Desktop** tab. The Background section lets you choose from a list of different background styles.

Scroll through the list, clicking on the different styles to view them in the preview window. In the 'Position' box choose from Center, Stretch or Tile. Center places the image in the middle of the screen, Stretch fills the screen with the image and Tile repeats the image to fill the screen. Different backgrounds have a different position as their default setting, depending on the image. Click **Apply** to see the image on the Desktop and once you have found one you like, click **OK**.

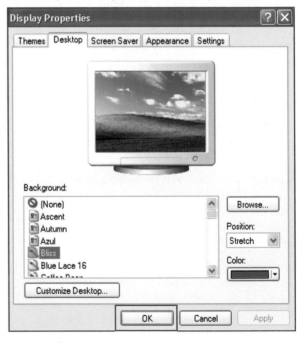

Key word
*Properties Nearly everything you see in Windows
has its own properties, which give valuable
information about your PC's resources and allow you to vary
its settings. To see an item's properties, right-click on the
object and select* **Properties** *from the pop-up menu.*

Bright idea
*To remind yourself of an important or amusing
message or slogan, select the* **Marquee**
*screen saver. Type in your text and select a font, colour
and style for it, along with the speed at which you wish
it to travel across your screen.*

While you were away...

Screen savers appear when your PC is on but not in use. They can be fun and also protect work from prying eyes. To select a screen saver, right-click anywhere on the Desktop and select **Properties** from the pop-up menu. Click on the **Screen Saver** tab. Scroll through and select an option in the 'Screen saver' box. It then appears in the preview window. (In Windows XP you can choose **My Pictures Slideshow** to display the images in your My Pictures folder as your screen saver.) Set the length of time your PC waits before activating the screen saver in the 'Wait' box, then click **OK**.

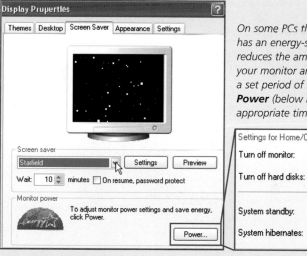

*On some PCs the Screen Saver tab
has an energy-saving option that
reduces the amount of power to
your monitor and/or hard disk after
a set period of inactivity. Click on
Power (below left) and select
appropriate timescales from the list.*

More than just a Desktop

Themes allow you to change your background, sounds and colour schemes, and are an optional extra with Windows XP. A selection is available with the Microsoft®Plus! package, which provides a number of other options for personalising your computer. To apply a theme, click the **Start** button, then click on **Control Panel**. Select **Appearance and Themes**, then **Change the computer's theme**. Scroll through and select a theme from the drop-down list. Click **Apply** or **OK** to change the theme.

Setting passwords for users

If your PC has more than one user, each can have a personalised version of Windows XP. They can access the PC without interfering with other users' settings. Each has their own background, folders and Start menus.

Users with administrator rights can set up accounts. Go to the **Start** menu, click on **Control Panel** then click on **User Accounts**. Select **Create a new account**. Enter a user name and account type, then click on **Create Account**. The account appears in the User Accounts window, click on it and select **Create a password**.

Customising Windows controls

Tailor your computer's settings to make it work the way you want

When you are using your PC it's helpful to know that you can tailor Windows controls to suit your needs. For example, you can change the speed at which your mouse double-clicks, alter the size and shape of the mouse pointer, and change the appearance of your screen. Left-handed users can even swap the role of the mouse buttons.

Mouse settings

To customise your mouse settings, go to the **Start** menu, select **Control Panel**, then **Printers and Other Hardware**, then **Mouse**. There are five tabs at the top of the Mouse Properties dialogue box – Buttons, Pointers, Pointer Options, Wheel and Hardware.

Buttons allows left-handed users to swap the role of the mouse buttons; Pointers lets you choose a 'scheme', or style, for your on-screen pointer; in Pointer Options you can alter the speed at which your mouse pointer moves, and in Wheel you can adjust how far your mouse wheel scrolls down the page.

If you are visually impaired, changing the shape and size of your mouse pointer will help you see it more clearly on screen

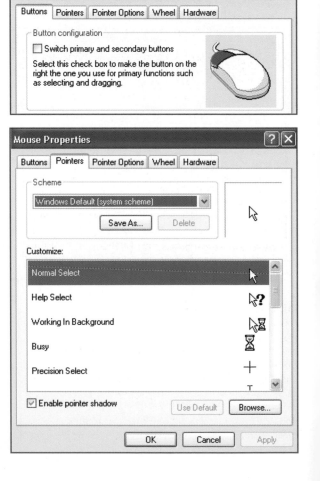

Bright idea
*Windows is aware of British Summer Time and can change the clock in spring and autumn. In the Date/Time Properties dialogue box click the **Time Zone** tab, then click in the 'Automatically adjust clock for daylight saving changes' box. Click **OK**.*

*To prevent pressing the Caps Lock key accidentally and typing in capital letters, use ToggleKeys, which will alert you with a warning sound. In the Accessibility Options dialogue box select the **Keyboard** tab and tick the Use ToggleKeys option. Finally, click **OK**.*

Date and time
The current time is displayed on the right-hand side of the Taskbar. To see the current date, place your mouse pointer over the time display. The date will pop up in a second.

To set the date or time, double-click on the Taskbar Clock. In the Date & Time tab of the dialogue box, click on the relevant arrows to adjust the settings.

To set the time zone for your location, click the **Time Zone** tab in the Date and Time Properties box, click on the arrow, scroll through and select your zone. Click **OK**.

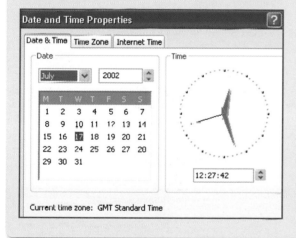

Disability options in Windows
Windows offers help to users with disabilities. Go to the **Start** menu, select **Control Panel**, then **Accessibility Options.** Click again on **Accessibility Options** in the next window. These are some of the options available:
● If you are hard of hearing, set your PC to send out visual warnings. Click on the **Sound** tab then click in the Use SoundSentry box. Scroll down and select a setting from the 'Choose the visual warning' box. Click **OK**.
● If you have trouble moving your mouse, clicking on the **Mouse** tab, then on the Use MouseKeys box, lets you use the numeric keypad on the right-hand side of your keyboard to move your mouse pointer.

● If you are visually impaired, select the high-contrast viewing mode (above). Click on the **Display** tab, then click in the 'Use High Contrast' box. Click **OK**.
● Users with slight visual impairments can also use the Magnifier. In the See Also section of the Accessibility Options window, click on **Magnifier**. Click **OK** to clear the first window. Magnifier creates a separate window at the top of the screen that displays a magnified portion of the screen. Set the magnification level and tracking options. Click on **Exit** to end magnification.

Setting sounds
If your PC has a sound card you can configure Windows to play a number of built-in sounds.

Go to the **Start** menu, select **Control Panel**, then **Sounds, Speech and Audio Devices**, then click on **Change the Sound Scheme**. In the Sounds tab, scroll through and click on an event from the 'Program events' box. Now click on the arrow to the right of the 'Sounds' box, scroll through and click on your preferred sound (or None for no sound). To preview sounds, click on **Browse**, select a sound from the list and click the play arrow (right) to hear it.

Close-up
*Windows XP lets you decide how you open folders on your Desktop (with one click or two), and whether folders open within the same window or separate windows. Go to the **Start** menu, click on **Control Panel**, then **Appearance and Themes**, then **Folder Options**. In the General tab of the dialogue box, click besides the setting you want and click **OK**. Click on the **Advanced** tab for further options.*

Create your own shortcuts

Fine-tune the way you work on your PC, and save yourself time and energy

Once you are familiar with the basic workings of Windows and you have a reasonable understanding of which programs and commands you use most often, you can begin using shortcuts to help you launch or activate them quickly.

You can create simple shortcuts to folders, documents and to almost anything else, including a printer, program and a drive. These can then be activated directly from the Desktop or Start button. You can also arrange for programs to launch when you start up Windows.

The Start menu

The Start menu in Windows XP watches how you use your computer and changes its contents accordingly. For example, the lower part of the left hand column will gradually fill up with a list of programs that you use most often – there's no need to tell Windows to do this.

Like almost everything in XP, the Start menu is fully customisable. You can choose how many programs it displays and whether it shows a list of the 10 documents that you most recently worked on. If you choose, you can also have the Start menu show links to the documents you have opened most frequently.

You don't have to rely on Windows XP to put programs in the Start menu for you. You can also choose to 'Pin' a program to the menu so that it's always quickly available for you to start up. Click on **Start** to open the Start menu, click on **All Programs** and choose the program you wish to add to the menu. Right-click on it, and choose **Pin to Start menu**. The Program's icon will now appear in the upper left-hand part of your Start menu.

Bright idea
No more arguments! Windows XP allows each user of a computer to set up the Start menu, taskbar and desktop to suit his or her preferences. When you log in to the computer, your desktop and menus will appear, just the way you like them.

Customise the Start menu to suit the way you work

You can change the Start menu to suit how you use your computer. Choose whether you want to view items in new windows or as further menus – you're the boss.

Viewing folders as menus
It can sometimes be quicker to be able to view commonly used items, like the Control Panel, as a menu attached to the side of the Start menu, rather than cluttering up the screen with a new window.

To view the Control Panel as a sub-menu, right-click anywhere on the task bar at the bottom of the screen. In the pop-up menu select **Properties** then click on the **Start Menu** tab. Click on **Customize**, then on the **Advanced** tab. In the list in the centre of the window choose the **Display as a menu** option for the Control Panel. Click **OK**, then **Apply**, then **OK** again to close the Start menu properties Dialogue box.

Now when you open the Start menu and roll over Control Panel, a list of all your Control Panel items will open to the right. You can choose to view other Start menu items such as My Computer, My Pictures and My Music in a similar way.

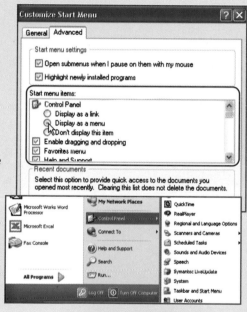

Show on desktop
It often helps to be able to reach your most commonly used items from the desktop.

To place an icon for My Documents on the desktop, click on **Start** to open the Start menu. Right-click on **My Documents**, and choose **Show on Desktop** from the drop-down menu. A My Documents icon will appear on your desktop.

You can send a shortcut link for any file or folder to the desktop. Open the folder that contains the file, folder or program you want. Right-click on the item, choose **Send To** from the drop-down menu, then **Desktop (create shortcut)** from the sub-menu of options that appears.

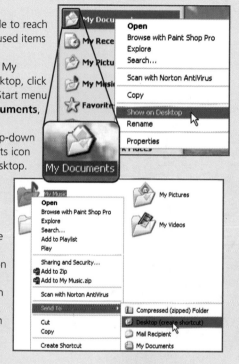

The ultimate time-saver…

You can arrange for an often-used program to launch whenever Windows starts. Go to the **Start** menu, Click on **All Programs** and navigate through the pop-up menus to find the program you want. Right-click on it and choose **Copy**. Click **Start** and then **All Programs** again and double-click on **Startup**. The Startup items folder will open. Right-click in it and choose **Paste Shortcut**. A Shortcut icon for the program you have chosen will now appear in the Startup items folder. When you next restart your computer and log in, your chosen program will start automatically.

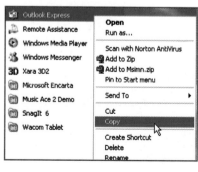

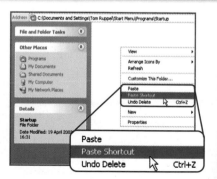

Quick keyboard commands

Save yourself time by using 'hot-keys' instead of your mouse

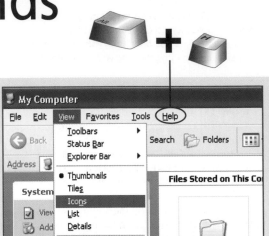

Nearly all the actions or commands you perform with your mouse can also be done by pressing 'hot-keys' – these are single keys or a combination of keys on your keyboard. For example, in Microsoft Word you can access the spelling and grammar facility by pressing one of the 'F', or function, keys at the top of your keyboard, or print by pressing the Ctrl and 'P' keys at the same time.

Using the hot-keys is quicker than using your mouse, especially if you do a lot of work from the keyboard, such as word-processing.

Selecting main menu options

The main menu bars in Windows and programs such as Word and Works look very similar. They contain common menus such as File, Edit and View. If you look carefully at the menu names you'll notice that one letter is underlined. These underlined letters indicate the keyboard shortcut that can be used to open the menus.

Instead of moving your mouse pointer over the menu name and clicking on it to open it, press the **Alt** key (immediately to the left of the Space-bar on the keyboard) and the underlined letter simultaneously.

In the My Computer window (see above) pressing **Alt** and '**F**' will open the **File** menu; **Alt** and '**E**' will open the **Edit** menu; and **Alt** and '**V**' the **View** menu.

Short cut
*Most keyboards have a Windows key – found between the Ctrl and Alt keys. Press it to open the Start menu and use the cursor keys to move around the menu items. Press the **Enter** key to open a highlighted option or program.*

Watch out
*When you use a key combination that involves the Ctrl or Alt keys with a letter or function key, press the **Ctrl** or **Alt** key first. Otherwise, you may issue the wrong command.*

Key word

***Keyboard shortcut** This describes a key combination that replaces a mouse command. It can take the form of pressing just one key, such as a function key, or several keys, such as **Ctrl + F4**.*

How to select menu bar options
To select a menu from the menu bar in Windows or in a program, press the **F10** key. The first menu button – File – will become depressed. To move along the menu bar to access other menus, press the 'right' arrow key (one of four arrow, or cursor, keys at the bottom of your keyboard). The menu buttons will become depressed as you move through them.

To open a menu, select the menu name then press the 'down' arrow key. When the menu opens press the 'down' key again to move through the menu items. As you do so, each item becomes highlighted. Press **Enter** to select a highlighted item.

Using the function keys
The function keys along the top of your keyboard perform pre-assigned duties, or functions.

Press **F1** to access a program's Help facility. This helps you to solve software problems.

From the Window's Desktop, press **F3** to access the Find: All Files dialogue box (above). This allows you to search your hard disk to find a file. You can use function keys in combination with other keys. To close a window or program, for example, press the **Alt** key and the **F4** key at the same time.

Moving around the Desktop
You can use keyboard shortcuts to move around your Desktop. For example, click on the **My Computer** icon then press the arrow keys to move around your various Desktop items. They become highlighted when selected. (Against the default Windows XP Desktop this is very subtle in appearance.) Press **Enter** to open a selected icon, try this on your My Documents folder.

The same principle applies inside the folders. In My Documents, use the arrow keys to move around the folder's contents. Press **Enter** to open a file or folder.

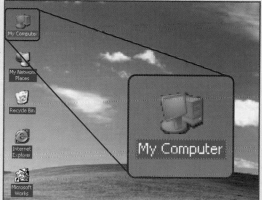

Important command keys

F-keys
Escape
Tab
Shift
Ctrl Windows Alt Space-bar Return Cursor keys Numeric keypad
Delete
Enter

Becoming a dab hand
If you have more than one window open, you can bring each one to the front of your Desktop using the **Alt** + **Tab** keys. Press **Alt** then **Tab** and a bar will appear with icons representing all the windows you have open. The uppermost window's icon will have an outline around it. To move to the next icon, press the **Tab** key. To bring that window to the front of your Desktop release the **Alt** key.

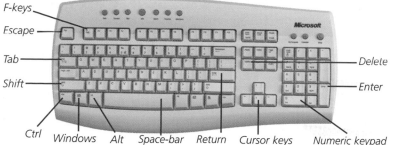

Windows built-in programs

Learn about these mini-applications and they'll soon become indispensable

Windows comes with a number of programs, known as Accessories. These are really useful and – even better – they don't cost a penny extra.

If you need to open a text document created in a program you don't have, you can use the Notepad text editor. If you have bought a scanner and want to 'touch up' or repair old photographs, you can experiment with Paint. Once you familiarise yourself with Windows' accessory programs, you will be surprised how often you use them.

Where to find accessory programs

To find Windows' accessory programs, go to the **Start** menu, select **All Programs** then **Accessories**. A menu with the accessory programs will drop down.

These include a calculator, Paint for image editing, Movie Maker for assembling videos and Notepad for basic word processing.

The Accessories menu contains other useful tools. There are multimedia facilities to help you play and record sound and video, and a powerful wizard for adding a scanner or digital camera to your computer.

Bright idea

Windows Media Player can 'rip', or extract music data from your CDs and store it on your hard drive. To save hard disk space, the music is stored in a special read-only format called WMP, which stands for Windows Media Player.

Close-up
*Notepad will only let you work in one font and font size per document. Go to the **Edit** menu and click on **Set Font**. Select a font and size. These will then be applied to the whole document.*

Everything you need from a word processor

WordPad is an effective word processor that has many features in common with Word. It includes a toolbar that lets you do tasks quickly, has a good selection of fonts and font sizes and even lets you format text. The only important function it lacks is a spellchecker.

Notepad is far more basic. Referred to as a text editor, rather than word processor, it creates only plain text files. That is, files that lack formatting, such as bullet points or a mixture of fonts. Notepad is the program to use if you need your document to be readable on any type of computer.

For your entertainment

Windows Media Player is one of the most exciting things about Windows XP. It allows you to play many different kinds of audio and video files, as well as extract audio from CDs to store and play back from your hard drive (see below left). You can can have psychedelic images swirling on screen while your songs play, and choose from a number of offbeat 'skins' that change the complete look of the program – from ultra-modern to plain surreal!

Working with photographs and other images

Paint is a simple drawing package that lets you create your own images. You can also use it to edit pictures you have on your computer. For example, you may want to restore an old photograph by removing creases or you may want to completely remove a small item.

The zoom feature makes it easy to edit your image in fine detail, pixel by pixel. Paint also makes it easy to create and install personal background designs for your computer's desktop. When you are happy with your design, go to the **File** menu and select either **Set As Background (Tiled)** or **Set As Background (Centered)**. The Tiled option fills the screen by repeating the image in a tiled effect. The Centered option fills the screen with one large image.

Making all your sums add up

Calculator carries out basic addition, subtraction, multiplication and division.

To use it, click on **Calculator** in the **Accessories** menu. Then, either click the on-screen calculator keys using your mouse, or use the numeric keypad on the right-hand side of your keyboard.

The Copy and Paste options in the Edit menu let you transfer numbers to other programs. If you want advanced functions, go to the **View** menu and click on **Scientific**.

Make the right connection

Speed costs – how fast do you want to go?

Today's computers are designed to communicate with each other, and the wider world, using the Internet. It's rare to find a new PC that doesn't come complete with a modem designed to use ordinary phone lines. Your PC will probably have a built-in 56K modem, able to download data from the Internet at a rate of 56,000 bits each second. Windows XP's Internet connection wizard makes it a simple job to get on-line using that modem and an Internet Service Provider.

Many users will be happy with this kind of Internet connection, known as a 'dial up' connection. However, if you use the Internet for more than a few hours each day, or need to send and receive large files, you may want to consider other ways to connect.

Broadband connection

You can now surf with cheap, high-speed Internet access, known as 'broadband', using either ADSL or Cable technologies. Broadband is available in most towns and cities, and can give you access to the Internet at up to ten times the speed of a normal dial-up connection. The connection is 'always on', so you don't have to wait for a modem to dial up and log on before you get your mail and files. Most broadband providers are also ISPs, and their connections are also unmetered – that means you pay a flat monthly fee – so no more unexpectedly high phone bills!

On-line radio

Broadband doesn't just give you faster downloads, it vastly improves the quality of many Internet technologies, fundamentally changing what your PC can do. For instance, you might find yourself using your computer where once you would have used a radio. With thousands of radio stations around the world sending CD quality sound to your desktop, traditional radio is hard-pushed to compete.

Picking a broadband connection

Broadband costs have plummeted, but it's worth
considering your requirements before you sign up.

ADSL

Using an ADSL modem connected to your computer, and
another in your local telephone exchange, a huge amount
of data can be squeezed down an ordinary telephone
line. The technology has quickly become popular, proving
stable and easy to use.

To use ADSL on your PC you will need software to
drive your new modem, and you will also need to
configure some system settings – in most cases the
software CD supplied by your ADSL provider will take
care of that for you.

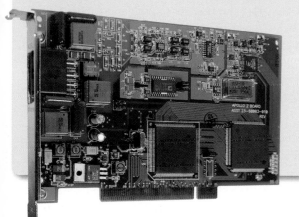

In the UK, most ADSL connections offer download speeds
of 512Kps and upload speeds of 256Kps – business users
can pay for even faster connections, but the standard
package should suit most home users.

However, ADSL is not available everywhere – your local
exchange needs to have been converted. Also the rate at
which data can be transmitted decreases dramatically
with distance. So if you live more than a few miles from
your nearest phone exchange, ADSL may not be available
to you. You can check availability at these Web sites:
'www.btopenworld.com' or 'www.demon.net'.

Cable

If you live in an area where Cable TV is available, you may
find that the company can also offer you high-speed
Internet access over the same connection. However, this
will only be true if the cable network in your area is
digital – many areas still have the older analogue version.
But for the lucky few with suitable networks in their area,
cable offers a fast and cheap alternative to ADSL.

Like ADSL you will need a special modem, and again
you will need to install the software supplied.

Some cable operators offer a low-price 128Kps service
that may fulfil your needs. While it doesn't offer the pace
of ADSL, it is an 'always on' service that provides
surprisingly rapid downloads. However, if you aim to use
your broadband connection mostly for large video or
audio downloads then this slower kind of service is
probably not the best option.

Satellite

Two way satellite broadband can give even higher
download rates than ADSL or cable, with none of the
geographic restrictions of those technologies. Satellite
broadband is available to any location in the UK with a
view of the southern sky, and works well in all but the
worst thunderstorms.

The equipment needed and monthly fees for a satellite
link are much more expensive than ADSL or Cable,
although government grants may be available for small
businesses in isolated areas. And the technology is not
ideal for 'live' connections such as making video calls to
friends or relatives overseas, due to the lag from the
50,000 mile round trip from Earth to a satellite and back.
This is similar to the delay experienced on a transatlantic
phone call, and in the order of tenths of a second, so it
will not affect the quality of other
activities such as downloading large
audio and video files.

The mobile Internet

Laptop users can now choose from an array of wireless
cards for genuinely mobile Internet access.

The latest technologies are WiFi, which connects users
when they are in small 'hotspots' such as specially
equipped coffee bars, airport lounges and hotels, and 3G,
the next generation mobile phone technology offering
very high connection speeds. WiFi ties users to an area in
the vicinity of a particular base-station. 3G, like other
mobile phone systems, allows users to wander from place
to place. However, 3G networks are only in place in a few

areas around the globe, and the
costs of using the system may
remain high for some years.

GPRS, an older phone system,
offers much lower data rates of
around 28.8Kps, but works almost
anywhere that there is an
ordinary mobile phone network,
and is ideal for checking e-mails
on the move.

Making the most of broadband

Connect your whole family with a home network

Many households these days have more than one computer, each in a different room. It can make sense to join these computers up in a home network, so that they can all share a single printer or scanner. And, with the rapid adoption of broadband Internet connections, it also makes sense to allow all the computers in a household to share fast internet access.

There are many different ways to join PCs together in a network – the simplest involves using a serial cable to join 2 PCs together. However, if there are more than 2 computers in the house, or if you are likely to be moving computers around (most likely if you have a notebook computer), a wireless network is probably the best solution. This sort of network uses a hub, a device that communicates via radio waves with terminals fitted to all the PCs around the home. The terminals can be cards fitted inside computers or devices attached to the PC by a USB connector. Such a setup can cost surprisingly little, and does not involve any messy wiring and installation of sockets.

Wireless networks most often use a standard called 802.11b, often known as the much friendlier 'WiFi'. With a WiFi network you'll be able to surf the web in bed or in the garden, and add new computers to your set-up with little problem. Although the standard range from network hub to PC is around 25 metres, some enthusiasts have extended this to many miles, using aerials made from old tin cans!

Your WiFi network connects to a broadband internet connection using a separate device called a router. As well as directing internet traffic to the different computers on the network, most routers also work as firewalls, protecting your network from unwanted intrusions via the internet.

Building a wireless network
Connect computers and share fast internet access
without any messy drilling.

The hardware set up
The heart of your network is a combined router, firewall
and wireless hub. These unobtrusive boxes are best
mounted on a wall for maximum range, and will need to
be located as near to the centre of your home as
possible, to ensure that the signal is strong throughout
your property.

Detailed instructions for the set up and configuration
of your router will depend on the particular model and
manufacturer you choose. However, networks like this
are becoming increasingly popular, so suppliers produce
extremely user-friendly devices. They are generally
configured using set up 'wizards' just like those used to
set up other hardware in Windows.

Security issues
A wireless network
lets you surf the net
from your garden. But
it will also let anyone
else in the vicinity of your
house to do the same unless
you choose the best security options
your set-up wizard suggests. At the very least,
ensure that all users log-in with a password;
better still, use additional security built-in to the WiFi
standard, such as Wired Equivalent Privacy (below left).
This will prevent any passing hackers or mischievous
neighbours from using your network and Internet
connection or reading your files.

The physical side of things is simple – there are just
two cables to plug in to the box; a power lead, and
the connection to your ADSL line.

The final touches
Once the router is connected and working, you will
need to attach USB terminals to each of your desktop
computers, and fit cards inside each of your laptops,
together with the appropriate drivers for each device.
All the software you need will come with the
hardware, and this is a simple task that you will

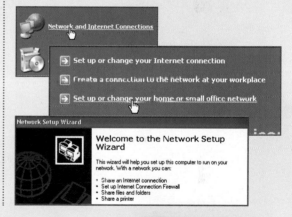

carry out only once. Then run **Network Setup Wizard**
on one of your computers to configure your network. In
the **Start** menu, click **Control Panel**, then **Network
and Internet Connections**, and then click **Set up
or change your home or small office network**.

Make sure you have a blank floppy disc loaded
when you run the progam and it will automatically
copy all your network settings onto that disc. Then
simply load the disc into your other PCs in turn. Go to
the **Start** menu, click on **Run** and type 'A:\netsetup.exe'
and your network settings will be configured instantly.

Wireless and safe
All WiFi standard equipment should be able to
broadcast and receive using something called Wired
Equivalent Privacy. This is a method of encrypting the
data that passes between PCs and the hub so that it
cannot be intercepted by a hacker. There are stronger
forms of protection available if your data is particularly
sensitive, but the standard version is more than safe
enough for most home users.

Using your PC as a fax machine

With the right connection, your computer can send and receive faxes

If you have a modem that can cope with sending and receiving faxes (and most modems can), Windows allows you to use your PC as a fax machine. This is a great benefit as it means you save both space around your desk and, best of all, the money you would otherwise have spent on a separate fax machine.

Once Windows is set up for faxing, you will see that it's as easy as printing a document. When you send a fax your computer stores the data as an uneditable image file. After the modem dials the destination number, it sends the fax image down the telephone line to the fax machine or computer at the other end.

Similarly, faxes you receive are images, made up of thousands of dots. You can view these fax images on your computer screen and print them out. You can also buy software that turns these dot-based images into text. You can then edit faxes that have been sent to you.

Remember that anything that can be printed can also be faxed, including pictures and spreadsheets, but only in black and white.

Install Windows' fax software

Windows XP does not install fax software by default, so you will need install it yourself. Go to **Start**, click on **Control Panel**, then **Add or Remove Programs**. In the left-hand column click on **Add/Remove Windows Components**. Click in the box next to 'Fax Service', then click on **Next**. The file installation will begin, and you will most likely be asked to insert your Windows XP installer disk (if the installer disk opens its own installation application click on **Exit** to return to the Add/Remove Windows Components Wizard). Once the new files have installed simply click on **Finish**.

Configure your fax software

Once you have installed your software it can be accessed from **Start**, **All Programs**, **Accessories**, **Communications**, **Fax**, **Fax Console**. The first time you use it the **Fax Configuration Wizard** will open. Follow its easy steps, completing each panel as it appears to store your name, numbers and personal details. Make sure you select your modem when asked.

When you have completed the configuration, the **Fax Console** will open, ready to send your first fax.

⚠ Watch out
Always make sure that your modem is connected to the phone line when using your fax. When you are receiving a fax, your fax software will detect the call. It will either pick it up automatically or leave it for you to pick up, depending on the set-up you have chosen (see below).

💡 Bright idea

Windows XP's fax software is fairly basic. If you want to send faxes to lots of people at the same time – for instance to distribute a community newsletter – you might prefer more advanced software, such as WinFax Pro from www.symantec.com.

Faxing direct

To send simple text faxes in Windows, go to the **Start** menu, click on **All Programs**, then **Accessories**, then **Communications**, then **Fax** and click on **Send a Fax**. The **Send Fax Wizard** runs (below right) to help you.

Click **Next**, then fill in the name and number of the person you want to send the fax to. Make sure you put their area code in the box provided, and also click **Use dialing rules** if you have already set these up – you may have already instructed your modem to dial 9 for an outside line for instance. Then click **Add** if you are sending the fax to more than one person; otherwise click **Next**. You'll then be asked what kind of fax cover sheet you would like (this contains your contact details and space for a brief message). Select whichever you prefer, then add a heading for your

fax in the **Subject** line, type your message in the **Note** section, and click on **Next**.

You can then choose when to send your fax – if you are sending lengthy faxes you may choose to send them late at night to save money on call charges and ensure the recipient's fax isn't busy receiving other messages.

Finally you have the option of previewing your fax, before clicking **Finish** to send it.

Sending faxes from programs

You can fax anything that can be printed, although naturally print quality will be poorer via fax, and of course all colours revert to black and white. But essentially the process inside Windows XP is exactly the same.

First produce your document in the normal way – here we used Microsoft Works, but Office XP is very similar. If you do not already have a letterhead you can use one of the program's existing templates. Go to **File**, **New** and choose an appropriate template. Then either type in your message, or paste it from an earlier document, and carefully check

your document – you may want to print it out in order to proofread it, or use a spellcheck – before going to **File**, then **Print**. Choose **Fax** in the drop down 'Printer name' menu, rather than your usual printer, and click **OK**.

The **Send Fax Wizard** will open. Follow its instructions just as for faxing direct (left). You might want to dispense with the fax cover sheet, in which case make sure the box next to **Select a cover page template with the following information** is unchecked.

Incoming faxes

If you wish to to receive faxes on your PC, open the **Fax Console** via the Start menu as described above. Go to **Tools**, then down to **Configure Fax** to open the **Fax Configuration Wizard** again. On the **Select Device for Sending and Receiving Faxes** panel, check the box next to **Enable Receive**.

If you share the same phone line for voice and fax calls it's probably a good idea to choose **Manual answer**. When you receive a call a dialogue box will appear, asking whether you want to pick up the call. Click **Yes**. The fax will appear in the Fax Console inbox. Just double click it to open the file.

CONNECTING TO

The **Internet** and the **World Wide Web** (the collection of Web sites created by businesses, societies and individuals) is expanding at a staggering rate. Users can now find **information** on almost any subject. The Internet also allows users, for the price of a local telephone call, to send messages in the form of **e-mail** (electronic mail) across the world. Find out how to **connect** to the Net, then go and **explore** this vast storehouse of information.

THE INTERNET

Welcome to the Internet

A meeting place, shopping centre, travel agent and library in one

The Internet is made up of a network of millions of computers throughout the world that allow people to access a wide range of information and services. It comprises the World Wide Web, through which people access this information, and facilities such as electronic mail (e-mail), chat areas, forums and newsgroups.

E-mail is a major feature of the Internet. Messages are typed into a computer then sent via a phone line to other e-mail users thousands of miles away – all for the cost of a local phone call. If you have a particular interest, forums and newsgroups provide an opportunity to exchange opinions and ideas. Many Internet Service Providers (the companies that provide connection to the Internet) set up discussion areas in which you can comment on issues of interest to you.

A spider's web of information

The World Wide Web (WWW or Web) is the public face of the Internet. It is a vast conglomeration of Web sites, made up of Web pages. The text and images you see on the Internet are part of a Web page.

Web pages are written in a computer language called HTML, or HyperText Markup Language, that allows pages to be linked together. A collection of linked pages forms a Web site, which in turn can be linked to other sites around the world, forming a global spider's web of connected sites.

All Web sites have unique addresses. These act like phone numbers, connecting your computer to the computer that holds the Web page you want to view.

To find your way around the huge tangle of Web sites – or 'surf the Net' – you need a Web browser. This is a program that allows you to view pages and move around the Web. The two main Web browsers are Microsoft Internet Explorer, usually installed with Windows XP and Netscape Navigator. Both are free of charge.

Once you are on-line, the Web is your oyster. You can use it to buy goods, including books, CDs, food and clothes, to book holidays, to research any subject, and even to play computer games. For key areas you can explore on the Web, see opposite.

All you need to connect to the Internet is a modem and an account with an Internet Service Provider

The world at your fingertips

Once connected to the Net, you are ready to explore the potential of the World Wide Web. This is made up of a collection of Web sites that promote a multitude of subjects and interests.

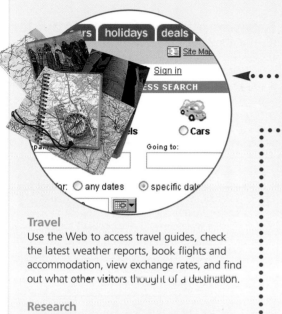

Travel

Use the Web to access travel guides, check the latest weather reports, book flights and accommodation, view exchange rates, and find out what other visitors thought of a destination.

Research

Whether you are studying for a qualification or pursuing a personal interest, there are Web sites to help you. You will even find on-line encyclopedias. (See pages 120, 124 and 130 for research projects on the Internet.)

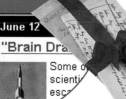

Health and medicine

The Web is an invaluable resource when it comes to health matters (but it is not a substitute for going to the doctor). You can find out about medical conditions, research treatment options and even get on-line advice – but not a diagnosis – from doctors and other health experts.

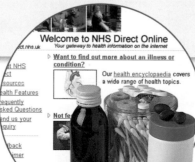

The media

The Web allows you to access the latest news from newspapers, magazines and broadcasting companies. Many of these services are free. With the correct software you can watch live television broadcasts from the other side of the world. You can get news of events before they reach the TV news bulletins or the papers.

Shopping

You can buy virtually anything on the Internet – from new shirts to a new home. The Internet also has on-line shopping malls designed to bring together Web sites for shoppers in one place. (To find out how to shop on the Internet, see page 106.)

What you need to get on-line

To surf the Net you must have a PC, a modem and an Internet Service Provider

Getting connected to the Internet is very easy and usually inexpensive. To begin with, you need a modem or other connecting device (see opposite). This provides your link to the Net. Then you need to arrange an account with an Internet Service Provider (ISP). The ISP you choose is your gateway to the Internet. It allows you to browse the World Wide Web and to send and receive e-mail. Your ISP is also the place where any Web pages you have created are stored. It makes them available to other users of the Internet.

An ISP could be a large organisation, such as BT, Microsoft's 'msn' service and America Online (AOL), or a small, independent operation that might only serve the area in which you live. Finding an ISP to suit your needs is the most important aspect of getting on-line.

Types of Internet Service Provider

The term ISP is used to describe all the companies that provide you with access to the Internet. However, these companies offer differing levels of service.

● Internet Access Providers (IAPs) offer a very basic package. These companies give you a connection and Web-browsing software, such as Internet Explorer, and an e-mail program, and provide technical help over the telephone. An example of an IAP is Freeserve (below).

● Online Service Providers (OSPs), like IAPs, provide a gateway to the Internet and e-mail handling. They differ in that they offer an extra level of service – or 'content' – including special news, information and entertainment channels, shopping services, chat rooms and topic-based newsgroups or forums. OSPs often have a home page designed to make using the Internet accessible to newcomers. AOL (America Online) is one of the best-known OSPs (below).

Key word

Web browser *This is a piece of software that acts as your window on the Internet. Your ISP will provide you with this in its start-up pack. Microsoft Internet Explorer and Netscape Navigator are two popular browsers.*

Questions to ask about ISPs

There are many different ways to go on-line nowadays. The type of connection you choose will depend on how much you will be using the Internet. If you already have a phone line, the simplest way to connect to the Internet is via a dial-up account using a modem. If you are a very heavy user of the Internet you might also consider a fast, always-on broadband connection (see below).

Ways to pay

Dial-up connections come in two main varieties:

• **Flat rate** You pay a monthly charge that gives you 'unlimited' time on the Internet (although round the clock usage is usually discouraged). You pay nothing extra for the calls you make to your ISP.

• **Pay-as-you-go** You pay no monthly fee, but instead pay the cost of each phone call your modem makes to your ISP. The longer you spend online, the more you pay. For a light internet user, pay-as-you-go services offer the best value. You can install the **rdplus.net** ISP, a pay-as-you-go service, from the CD-ROM with this book.

Flat Rate offers are becoming cheaper, however, and eliminate the chance of a nasty shock when the phone bill arrives.

Do you get any added extras?

If you want added content, in the form of business pages, chat rooms, shopping services and so on, make sure that the content you get suits your needs.

Find out how many e-mail addresses you can have on one account. Having more than one means that each family member can have their own address and send and receive e-mail from the same computer. Or, if you work from home, you could have one e-mail address for personal mail and another for business use.

Find out whether you are allocated any Web space on which to set up your own Web site. If so, how much space do you get and is it free?

Ask whether your telephone calls to the support helpline are free or charged at the local call rate. Some ISPs that offer 'free' services charge premium rates for support calls. Some ISPs offer 24-hour-a-day support.

Above all, ask if technical support is available when you are most likely to need it – when first connecting up. Check on the ISP's reliability: will you get through at the first try or will the line be engaged?

Get a real feel with a free trial

Many ISPs offer a free trial of their services, usually for thirty days. If you take up a trial offer make sure that all sections of the service are user-friendly. Are you impressed with the standard of content? And how easy is it to send and receive e-mail through the ISP? (See page 90 for more details on sending and receiving e-mail.)

Dial-up, ADSL or Cable?

A modem and dial-up connection is still the most popular way of accessing the Internet from home. A modem sends information to, and receives information from, the Internet. But modems work slowly – connecting at maximum of 56 Kbps (kilobits per second).

If you are heavy user of the Internet you may consider an always-on, broadband connection, via either **ADSL** or **Cable**. ADSL stands for Asynchronous Digital Subscriber Line, and is

a technology that allows very fast connections to be made using ordinary phone lines. The availability of the service depends on your telephone provider and your distance from the local exchange. ADSL subscribers generally pay an installation charge on top of a monthly fee.

Cable TV companies also offer fast Internet services in some areas, through the same cable as the TV signal. Both ADSL and cable connections require special modems, normally provided as part of the package by the ISP.

Send and receive e-mail

Using your PC to revolutionise the way you keep in touch

In addition to the World Wide Web and all its resources, the Internet also provides electronic mail, or e-mail. Many people find that e-mail is the single most useful feature of the Internet.

E-mail functions at a staggering speed. A message can reach a computer on the other side of the world in minutes, and all it costs is the price of a quick local phone call. And because it's operated from your Desktop, it's extremely convenient, too.

Every e-mail program has its own look, but all operate in a similar way. Here, we take Microsoft Outlook Express as an example.

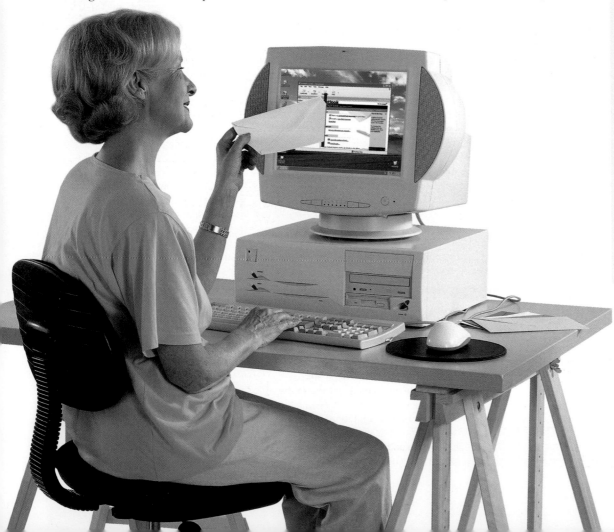

1 Click on **Start** then on the **Outlook Express** icon. A dialogue box will appear inviting you to connect to the internet. Click **Cancel** – composing your message off-line reduces the amount of time and money you spend on-line.

Choosing your email program

Windows XP reserves a space in the Start menu for your choice of e-mail program, so it's always easy to find. To set Outlook Express as your chosen e-mail program, click on **Start**, then right-click in a clear space. Click on **Properties**, then **Customize**. The section at the bottom of the dialogue box lets you choose which programs you want to appear in the Start menu as your e-mail program and web browser.

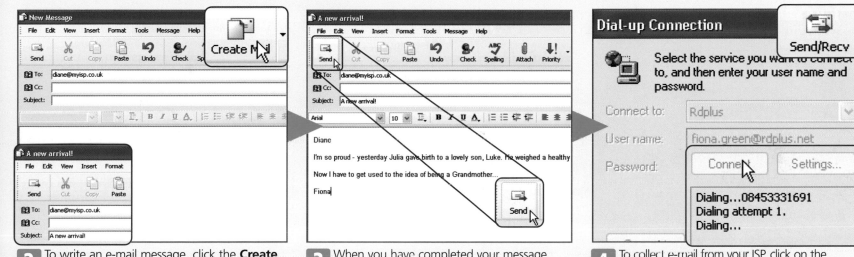

2 To write an e-mail message, click the **Create Mail** button. A blank message appears. Type your recipient's e-mail address in the 'To' box, a title for your message in the 'Subject' box and the message itself in the main panel.

3 When you have completed your message, click on the button marked **Send** (or similar). Your e-mail program then asks whether you want to connect to the Internet. Click **Connect** to activate your modem, connect to the Internet and send your message.

4 To collect e-mail from your ISP, click on the **Send/Recv** button. Your PC will dial up to the Internet and look for messages. If there are any, it delivers them to your Inbox. To read a message, click on it. To reply, click on the **Reply** button, then follow steps 2 and 3.

Sending attachments

You can send pictures and other documents with e-mails. To add an attachment to a message in Outlook Express, go to the **Insert** menu and click on **File Attachment**. A dialogue box will open. Navigate to the folder containing the file you wish to send, click once on the file, then on the **Attach** button. The file will be added to the message.

Address books

Outlook Express stores your contacts' details in its Address Book. To send a message to someone in your address book, go to the **Tools** menu and choose **Address Book**, or click on the **Addresses** button in the main Outlook window. Click on your recipient's name, then go **Tools**, click on **Action** and then on **Send Mail** in the pop-up menu that appears.

Starting out on-line

Set up your Web browser and you are ready to surf the Net

Many people are daunted by the idea of venturing onto the Internet. But, in fact, going on-line for the first time is a simple matter. It is no more difficult than installing a new piece of software.

To connect to the Internet you will need an Internet Service Provider (ISP) and a modem or ADSL – see pages 88 and 89 respectively. You also need a Web browser. This is a piece of software that opens the door through which you enter the world of the Web. Once your browser is set up, you can explore the fascinating world

Understanding Web browsers

A Web browser is a piece of software that allows you to access Web sites and navigate between them. All Web browsers are the same in principle. They contain an address box, in which you type a Web address, and an area in which Web pages are displayed.

Two of the most popular browsers are Microsoft Internet Explorer and Netscape Navigator. Internet Explorer will almost certainly have come preinstalled on your system, and is installed when you install Microsoft Works, Works Suite or Office. It's a good idea to keep your web browser up to date so that you are able to view new types of content on the internet.

Whether or not your PC came with its own browser, your ISP may also provide you with one in its start-up kit. This could be Microsoft Internet Explorer or Netscape Navigator, but some ISPs, such as AOL, provide you with their own specially designed Web browser. You can have more than one Web browser, just as you can have more than one word processor or spreadsheet program.

When your ISP software first loads, look for a button that says 'Internet', 'Browse the Internet', 'Explore' or something similar. Clicking on this will start up the browser.

Internet
Internet Explorer

Many ISPs offer CD-ROMs that make it simple to set up an Internet connection. You can also set one up using the New Connection Wizard in Windows XP.

▶ GETTING ON-LINE

Get to know your way around your Web browser

Your browser gives the Internet a face and allows you to view all its resources. Learning to use it effectively will make surfing the Net more enjoyable and rewarding.

Most browsers have a main menu, similar to that found in Microsoft Word or Works. Through the menus you can print Web pages, configure your ISP settings and access help facilities.

Use the Back and Forward buttons to navigate backwards or forwards through downloaded pages. Some browsers clearly label them Back and Forward.

The Address box is where you type Web addresses. Click on **Go** (or press the **Return** or **Enter** keys) to download the Web page.

Many sites list the main areas of their content in a 'navigation panel'. Each word is a link - click on it to see the relevant page.

The toolbar in Microsoft Internet Explorer has buttons that launch other useful programs, such as Outlook Express for e-mail, and Windows Messenger, which allows you to 'chat' with friends over the internet.

Most browsers include some form of search facility to help you find information. Type a key word or words into the search box then click on **Find** (or press the **Return** or **Enter** keys).

This is the main viewing area, into which Web pages are downloaded and displayed.

Use the scroll buttons to see all the information on a long web page. A mouse with a scroll wheel makes this easy.

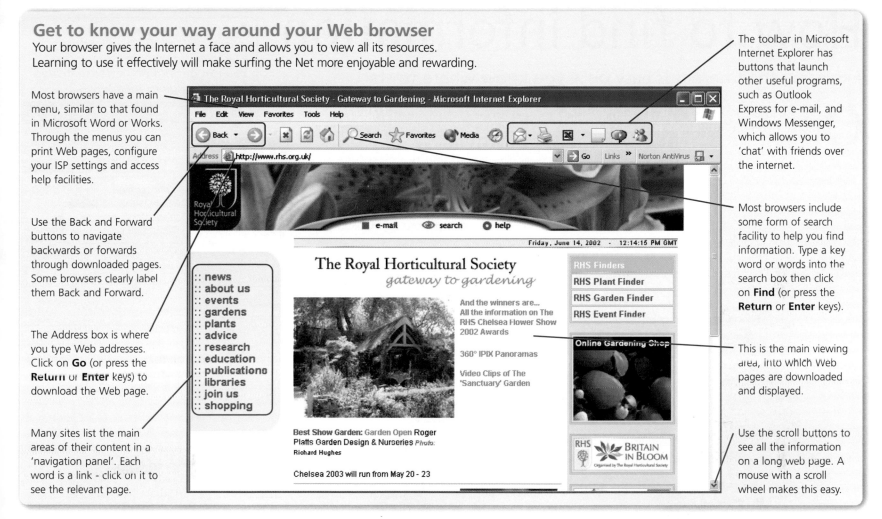

Web addresses explained

Every Web address is unique, in the same way that your telephone number is. In fact, it's helpful to think of a Web address as a telephone number, whereby you 'dial' the site's address to view it.

The 'www' in a Web address tells you that the site belongs to the World Wide Web. After the 'www' you are told the domain name (this 'points' to the computer that holds the Web site) and where that computer is located

('.uk', for the UK; '.au' for Australia; and so on).

Addresses do not always end in the country of origin. If you see '.com' at the end, for example, this indicates that the site is commercial. If you see '.gov', the Web site is a government agency.

For many pages, extra text appears after the domain name. This shows the location of the pages within the Web site.

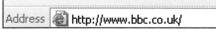

How to find information

Exploring the Internet is easy once you know where to start

Once your Internet connection is up and running you are ready to explore the World Wide Web. The quickest way to find information is to type the Web address of a relevant site into your browser's address box and press the Return key on your keyboard. The site's first page (known as the home page) will appear on screen.

If you do not know the address you can track down information using a search engine, which will search for key words or categories that you select, then present you with a list of sites to visit. The key to effective use of the Internet is knowing how to narrow your searches so that the number of sites yielded is manageable. Remember, the time you spend on-line costs money, so it pays to be efficient in your searching.

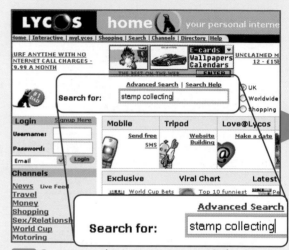

Be as specific as you can in your search and tell the search engine exactly what you are looking for. You can get tips on better searching from the engines themselves.

USING A SEARCH ENGINE

1 Connect to the Internet. In your Web browser's address box type the address of a search engine (here, www.lycos.co.uk). Click on **Go**. The site's home page will appear in a few seconds. Type your key words into the search box and press **Enter** or click on **Go Get It!**.

Which search engine?

The Web site at www.searchenginewatch.com explains how the main search engines work and how efficient they are. Here are the addresses of some popular search engines:

- www.altavista.com
- www.excite.com
- hotbot.lycos.com
- www.lycos.co.uk
- www.northernlight.com
- www.yahoo.co.uk

Your Internet Service Provider might also have its own search facility (see page 88).

Most text that is underlined within a site is a link to another part of the same site or to a new site. Click on the underlined text to activate the link.

Watch out

Do not type a Web address into a word search box. You will not be taken to the Web site. Type only key words for your search.

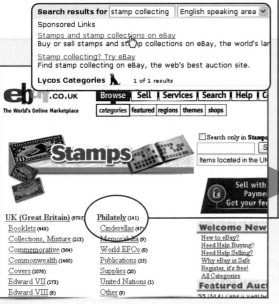

2 A list of related Web sites will appear. (Some engines tell you how many sites have been found.) Use the scroll bar to the right of the page to view the list. To view a site, click on its underlined title. Use your browser's back button to return to previous pages.

3 Some engines, including Yahoo (www.yahoo.co.uk), allow you to search by category. Click on a category (they will be underlined) and you will be presented with sub-divisions to narrow your search. Continue to click on sub-divisions until a list of sites appears.

4 For example, to find information on scuba diving, click on the **Outdoors** section of the **Recreation & Sport** category on the Yahoo home page. Then click on **Scuba**. This reveals a list of sites, resources and chat areas. Click on a site to open it.

Search by batch

Most search engines present their list of sites in batches (usually of 10). When you reach the bottom of the first batch in Google, click on **2** for the next batch, and so on.

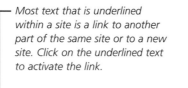

Information collected for you

Some Web sites hold databases of information that make searching easy. For example, Bigfoot (www.bigfoot.com) lists individual e-mail addresses, and Deja (www.deja.com) indexes all the messages sent to newsgroups.

Deja has its own search engine that will find topics of discussion for you. Type, say, 'apple pie recipe', into the search box and press **Return**. The search results will list messages from discussion groups about your search topic.

Your PC can use more than one search engine at a time. Copernic is a program that collects results from many search engines. Download it free of charge from the Internet.

SERIOUS SEARCHING

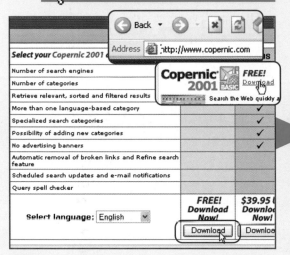

Watch out

Make sure your Internet connection is running before you double-click on the Copernic icon. Otherwise, you will not be able to use it.

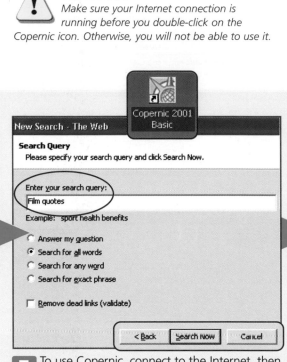

5 Type www. copernic.com into your browser's address box and click on **Go**. Click on **Downloadable Software** on the home page. In the next window click on **Copernic 2001 Basic Free Download** . Then click on **Download Now!**. In the next window click the **Download** button.

6 The File Download dialogue box appears. Click on **Save** to save the program to your hard disk. Then specify which folder to save it to. Once the file has downloaded, double-click on it to initiate its installation. Follow the on-screen instructions.

7 To use Copernic, connect to the Internet, then double-click on its Desktop icon. (You may need to register – follow the advice.) To find Web data, click on **The Web** category. Type a key word into the box that appears then click the **Search Now** button.

Bookmarking Web pages

Browsers allow you to record the addresses of favourite Web sites you have visited, which saves you having to remember the addresses and means you don't have to spend time on-line searching for the sites again. As long as you are connected to the Internet, a click on a bookmarked address will open up the site.

The process of bookmarking Web sites is similar in all browsers (look out for a facility called 'Bookmarks', 'Favorites' or 'Favorite

Places' on your browser's toolbar). To bookmark a site when you are on the Internet, first open the site, then go to the **Favorites** menu and click on **Add to Favorites**. The Add Favorite dialogue box appears with the address of the site you are visiting. Click **OK**.

To access this site again, click on the **Favorites** icon on the toolbar. A list of your bookmarked addresses appears in a column on the right. Click on the relevant address to load the site (you must be connected, of course).

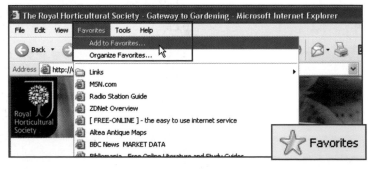

Search Progress - Film quotes

AltaVista	
ePilot	
FAST Search (allthe...	
FindWhat	
HotBot	
Lycos	
Mamma.com	

COPERNIC 2001 SEARCH RESULTS

Search: **Film quotes** (All words)

Found: **57 document(s) on The Web**

1. **FILM & TV QUOTES**
   ... Limit 1 per customer only. Cost is S&H of $6.95 Click Here
   Found by: AltaVista, FAST Search (alltheweb.com), HotBot, MSN Web Sear...
   ☐ http://www.filmquotes.com/ | 92% | Translate

2. **Greatest Quotes from Great Films**
   Famous quotes and great lines of dialogue from 75 years of so...
   more examples of the most memorable movi...
   Found by: AltaVista, FAST Search (alltheweb.com), HotBot, MSN Web Sear...
   ☐ http://www.filmsite.org/moments0.html | 91% | Translate

3. **Film To DVD Transfer Service**
   Transfer of 8mm, super8 and 16mm film home movies to DVD.
   Found by: Mamma.com
   ☐ http://mmp.miva.com/click.cgi | 85% | Translate

4. **Film Secrets - Movie Sound Quotes**

Categories
- 🌐 The Web
- 🌐 The Web - UK
- 📰 Newsgroups
- 📧 E-mail Add...
- 📕 Buy Books
- 💾 Buy Hardware
- 💾 Buy Software

Search for information...

New Search - Newsgroups

Search Query
Please specify your search query and click Search Now.

Enter your search query:
Gardening tips roses

Example: sport health benefits

○ Answer my question
◉ Search for all words
○ Search for any word
○ Search for exact phrase

☐ Remove dead links (validate)

Search Progress - Gardening tips roses

CNET Help.com	
Google Usenet service	
Topica	

Advanced Search

☑ Title	Address
☐ <<<...101 GARDENING TIPS...>>>	http://groups.go

<<<...101 GARDENING TIPS...>> Dear fellow gardener, As a ga publication. 101 Gardening Tips: You ...

☐ Housenet Regional Gardening Tips   http://groups.go
... to your area of the country, check out the National Gardenin http://www.housenet.com/lg/vf.asp?idex=/lg ...

☐ Wayside gardening tips :-)   http://groups.go
Wayside's Gardening Tip of the Month Welcome to March at ... in should be pruned in early spring only to ...

☐ HANDS On (ROSES) experiences: SanFrancis... http://groups.go
... in roses & gardening fruit trees??... PLEASE STOP HERE if you your gardening tips OVER THE PHONE ...

☐ INFO: Rose Resource - Gardening, landscapi... http://groups.go
... roses and discover everything you need to know - from gard

From: CuteFish2 (cutefish2@aol.com)
Subject: HANDS On (ROSES) experiences: SanFrancisco! Sha
Newsgroups: rec.gardens roses
Date: 1998/04/24   View: (This

I wasted 8 years plus searching for BLUE rose plants eve
ROSES in flower shows at Golden GATE Park...NO LUCK yet
anywhere!!.I did find purple/lavender roses! (it took me
hem!)

I need to ask over 1000 questions about roses & gardenin
problems leaving your phone# in SAN Francisco-San Mateo
HERE!! thanks

i scan my eyes/email for PHONE# of the Nursery in SFO ar
any public pay phone near SFO airport .... I DON'T read
email...Life is TOO short to type/read email...!

JUST PHONE contact for quick/efficient communication
:YOUR secrets for growing roses without APHIDS???>

8 Copernic now searches through a variety of search engines. It collates the findings and downloads them into your Web browser, ready for you to view. Click on a link to open the Web page. (Your search key words are highlighted in yellow.)

9 Copernic searches newsgroup and e-mail address databases in the same way. Select a category, such as Newsgroups, type in your key word and click on **Search Now**. Copernic will then search three Web sites that monitor messages posted to newsgroups.

10 The results of the search are listed in your browser, with key words highlighted in yellow. Click on a link to investigate it. Once you have opened the link, it appears blue in the list so that you know you have viewed it.

🔍 **Close-up**
Don't forget to use links to track down information. Links are a key part of the World Wide Web. They appear as underlined text on a Web page and let you jump directly from one site or page to another. Most Web sites have links to other similar sites, so you may find the information you want browsing from one to the next.

Security on the Internet

How to ensure users of your PC are protected when on-line

Internet newcomers are naturally concerned about security. They worry about whether it's safe to send credit card details over the Internet, or whether children will come across undesirable material. Concerns over the privacy of e-mail and the unauthorised issue of e-mail addresses are also common.

All these concerns are valid, but there are measures you can take to guarantee the integrity of the sites your family visits, and that your own personal details are kept confidential.

Keeping it safe and sound

Whether shopping, browsing or e-mailing, there are ways to guarantee your security on the Internet.

Shopping and security

If a shopping Web site states that it uses 'encryption' technology to transfer credit card details (a complex almost unbreakable scrambling system), there should be no security problem. However, a good Web site will also offer alternative methods of payment, such as issuing an invoice, offering to call you and take details over the phone, or faxing or posting an order form.

amazon.co.uk

VIEW B.

WELCOME | BOOKS | MUSIC | DVD | VIDEO | ELECTRONICS | SOFTWARE | PC & VIDEO GAMES
▶ INTERNATIONAL   ▶ HOW TO ORDER   ▶ WINE   ▶ SELL YOUR STU

Help > Security & Privacy > Security Guarantee

Security Guarantee

None of our customers has reported fraudulent use of a credit or debit card as a result of confident about the transaction security we offer on our site that we back every purchase

1. Our secure-server software encrypts all your personal information including credit or d address. The encryption process takes the characters you enter and converts them into b transmitted over the Internet

2. In the event of unauthorised use of your credit or debit card, most banks and card issu limit your liability to just £50.00.

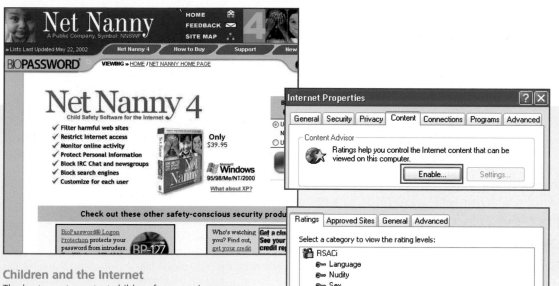

Children and the Internet

The best way to protect children from coming across undesirable material on the Internet is to use special software. Programs, such as Cyber Patrol and Net Nanny, block access to sites known to have unsavoury content.

You can also get software that creates a log of all the sites that have been visited from your PC, and so keep a check on what your children have seen. You can also use the History button on your Web browser to do a similar job (see below).

In Windows XP you can set up a 'Content Advisor' ratings system to control how much of Web sites a person can view according to its levels of language, nudity, sex and violence. To do this, click on the **Start** button, then **Control Panel**. Click **Network and Internet Connections**, then **Internet Options**. Click the **Content**

tab and the **Enable** button. In the Content Advisor dialogue box, with the Ratings tab selected, click on each category then adjust the slider to set a rating level. Setting all categories at 'Level 1' effectively bars all access to the Web, apart from the most child-friendly sites. Click **OK** when you have finished and you will be prompted to set a supervisor password. You must type it in every time you change the Content Advisor settings, so don't lose it.

Viruses and the Internet

Computer viruses can seriously damage your PC. The best way to avoid getting a virus from the Internet, or from any other source, is to use an anti-virus utility.

There is also a risk of infection from 'macro viruses' that enter your PC via e-mail attachments. You can set a high level of Macro Virus protection in any Microsoft Office program (Word, Excel, Powerpoint or Outlook). Go to the **Tools** menu and click on **Options**. Click on the **Security** tab and then on **Macro Security**. Choose a level of Macro security in the dialogue box, then click **OK**.

A computer on an 'always-on' broadband connection to the Internet can be open to malicious attack. To protect against this, Windows XP includes a 'firewall' – software that prevents unauthorised access to your machine.

Safeguard your e-mail address

Sometimes, your e-mail address is obtained by companies or individuals who send you junk e-mail, known as 'spam'. You can try to avoid this by omitting your e-mail address from forms that you fill in by hand or on the Internet.

Only give your e-mail address to individuals of your choice. Good Internet trading companies should give you the option of withholding your address, even to reputable, third-party vendors. Never reply to an unsolicited e-mail, this confirms yours is an active address.

History button

A simple way to keep an eye on the Web sites that have been visited from your PC is to use the History button that comes with Internet Explorer. When you press it, a log of all sites that have been accessed will appear to the left of the Explorer window.

To set the number of days that the History button monitors, in Internet Explorer go to the **Tools** menu, click on **Internet Options**. With the General tab selected, go to the 'Days to keep pages in history' box and input the number of days that suits you. You can also choose to clear the History folder.

Explore the world of multimedia

Watch video and animations, play games and listen to the radio on your PC

The term multimedia describes the capability of modern computers to deliver many different kinds of information at once: the elements of multimedia are pictures, text, animations, sounds and video. For example, you might find a short clip to accompany a film review, or a live radio feed at a news site. The quality of what you experience depends on the speed of your Internet connection: if you have a fast, broadband Internet connection, you will able to download and view long video pieces and animations, take part in interactive games and listen to high-quality music files.

Sights and sounds on the Internet

In order to enjoy the extra dimension of multimedia, you may need to add extra features to your browser.

Bring your Web browser up to speed

Almost all Web browsers, including Microsoft Internet Explorer and Netscape Navigator, can handle basic forms of multimedia. However, to view video clips and animation on some sites you need mini-programs called plug-ins. These vary in sophistication but the best, such as Shockwave, can play animations, video and interactive games.

The most popular plug-ins are Flash™ and Shockwave® both from Macromedia, Inc., and Realplayer® from RealNetworks®. Flash uses ingenious programming to pack complicated animations, games and interfaces into small files that download quickly. Shockwave allows more complicated games and interactivity to be displayed within your browser, fully integrated with video images.

Realplayer is the most popular plug-in for 'streaming' audio or video content to your PC. Streaming means that you can start listening to or watching a file before it is completely downloaded – the file plays while the download continues in the background, saving you a long wait. The quality of the streamed sound and pictures depends on the speed of your connection: the faster the better.

Key word

Plug-in *This is a piece of software that adds new features to your Web browser. After a plug-in has been installed, your browser will use it automatically whenever necessary.*

Watch out

If you have a pay-as-you-go dial-up connection, listening to Internet radio stations can become expensive. But if you have a flat-fee connection, or a broadband one, you can listen for as long as you like.

Downloading a plug-in

This section tells you how to download the RealOne™ plugin from RealNetworks. The procedure for downloading other plug-ins is similar.

Connect to the Internet and launch your browser program. In the address bar, type 'www.real.com' and hit the return key.

You will be taken to the homepage of RealNetworks, publishers of the RealOne plug-in.

Click on the Free RealOne Player link (or similar – the website changes often). The next page asks where you want to download the files from. Choose the closest location. A link to the software will appear in a separate window. Click on it, and choose a location to save the installer program.

Install the plug-in

Once the download is complete, open the folder that you saved the installer in and double-click on it.

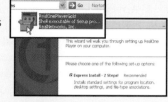

The RealOne Install Wizard will open. Choose the Express Install option. Read the License agreement and click on Accept. The RealOne player will install on your PC. When all the files have been copied, click on the Finish button.

The RealOne player will launch automatically to complete the last few stages of the set-up process.

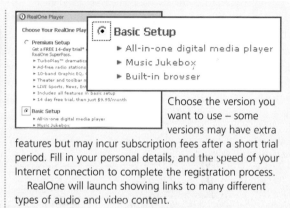

Choose the version you want to use – some versions may have extra features but may incur subscription fees after a short trial period. Fill in your personal details, and the speed of your Internet connection to complete the registration process.

RealOne will launch showing links to many different types of audio and video content.

Using the plug-in

You will most likely use the player for RealMedia clips on other websites. Here we show examples of audio and video material on the BBC website (www.bbc.co.uk).

Turn off to speed up

Multimedia files can often be very large, which means that a Web page with lots of multimedia elements in it can take a long time to open. If you would rather not have these elements present when you are using the Web, you can instruct your browser not to download them.

Go to the **Start** menu and right-click on **Internet**. Click on the **Internet**

Properties then on the **Advanced** tab. Use the scroll bars to move down to the Multimedia section.

Note that some items have ticked boxes beside them. Choose the features you would like to keep and those you would like to disable. To get rid of the ticks, click in the boxes. Click **Apply**, then **OK**. Next time you access a Web page, it will appear without sound or images.

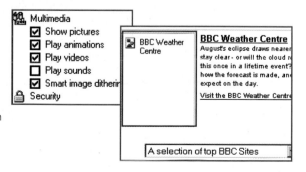

Chat to others on-line

Use the World Wide Web to make new friends and contacts

One of the most exciting things about the Internet is that it brings people together. People who share similar interests can keep in touch via e-mail by subscribing to mailing lists; others who want to chat in 'real time' (messages appear on the other person's computer screen as you type them), can use instant messenger programs to 'talk'. A growing section of the Internet, called Usenet, is made up of thousands of discussion groups. Here, people post messages that can be replied to, thereby initiating a discussion. Obtain a list of the main discussion groups from your Internet Service Provider (ISP).

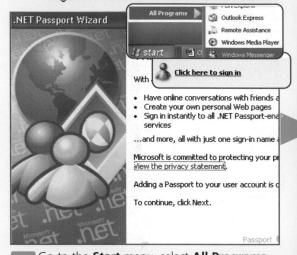

Find out which of your friends are regularly on-line and use MSN Messenger. Gather their e-mail addresses ready to add to your Messenger 'buddies'.

▶ **BEFORE YOU START**

1 Go to the **Start** menu, select **All Programs**, then **Windows Messenger**. The first time you do this, the .NET Passport Wizard will launch automatically. Click **Next** to begin following the Wizard step by step (see below right). The next time you open Windows Messenger, click on **Click here to sign in** to begin chatting.

There are other instant messenger programs available, such as Yahoo Messenger and AOL Messenger. You can also search the Internet for sites such as www.tucows.com, from which you can download messenger software that is compatible with MSN, Yahoo and AOL.

▶ **OTHER PROGRAMS**

*If your contact doesn't already have Messenger, you can send them an e-mail with detailed instructions on how to install it. You can add your own message to this e-mail. Click the **Send E-mail** button, type your message in the top box then click **Next**.*

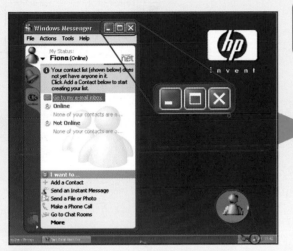

2 Once Messenger is set up, your Messenger window appears on screen. To close the window, make it larger or minimise it, use the buttons on the top right-hand corner. To open the window, double click on the Messenger icon at the bottom right of your screen.

3 To add messenger buddies, click on **Add a Contact**. If you have your contact's details, select 'By e-mail address or sign in name' and click on **Next**. Type in the e-mail address and click **Next**. Your contact will receive a message and if they accept you will be connected.

4 To send a message, double-click on your contact. A conversation window opens. Type your message in the bottom section and click **Send**. Leave the window open and the reply appears under your message. Close the window and the reply pops up at the bottom right of your computer screen – click on it to continue your chat.

The Messenger Wizard

Follow the Wizard, step by step, filling in the required details. You can set up Messenger to work with an existing e-mail address or create a new one. When all the steps are complete, a 'You're done!' message appears. Click on **Finish**. If you are using an existing e-mail address that isn't MSN or Hotmail, you will need to follow several further steps to verify your e-mail before continuing (see right).

Keyword

Emoticons These are small pictures or icons, which can be added into messages to show emotions, such as laughter. In the conversation window, click on **Emoticons** and then click on an emoticon in the drop down menu.

5 To have a three-way conversation, click on **Invite someone to this conversation**. Chose and click on a Messenger buddy in the next dialogue box, then click **OK**. When you finish chatting simply close the window. Messenger is still running; just double click the bottom-right icon when you want to chat to someone new.

6 You can also talk to others on-line in discussion groups. But unlike chat, they do not operate in 'real time'. You post a message and check back to see if anyone posts a response. To find a group, type http://groups.google.com into your web browser's address box and hit **Return**, then click on **Browse complete list of groups**.

7 To find UK groups, click on the arrow at the side of the drop down menu that starts with '1..astercity'. Select 'ucla ..vatech', then click **Go**. Click on **UK**. Next, select a category from the list of UK groups, (here **uk d-i-y**). A list of 'thread' subjects is now listed. To start a new discussion, click on **Post a new message to uk d-i-y**.

Sending photos by Messenger

In MSN Messenger, you can send your Messenger buddies files or photographs without having to open an e-mail program and attach them to an e-mail. In the 'I want to..' section of the Messenger window, click on **Send a File or Photo**. Select the contact to whom you are sending the file and click **OK**. In the next dialogue box, locate your file and double-click on it to begin sending it to your buddy. A series of messages will then appear in a conversation window showing you the progress of your action.

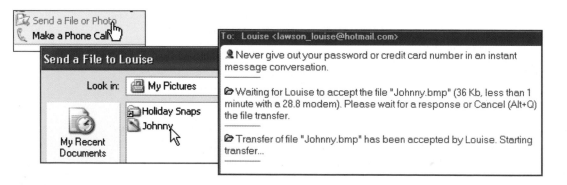

Watch out

When you are communicating with others over the Internet never divulge personal information such as your address and phone number to anyone unless you know them or feel sure you can trust them.

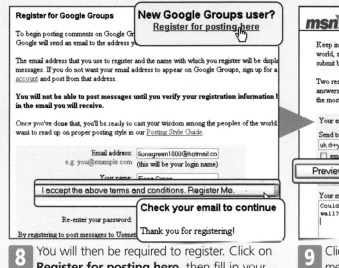

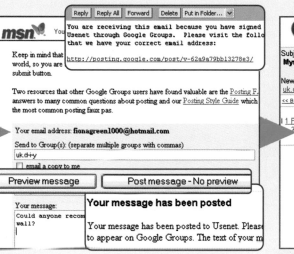

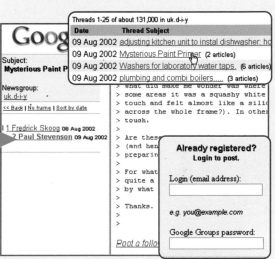

8 You will then be required to register. Click on **Register for posting here**, then fill in your name, e-mail address and a password, and read the terms and conditions. Then click on **I accept the above terms and conditions. Register me**. An e-mail will be sent to you.

9 Click on the link in the e-mail and type your message in the window that appears. You can immediately post your message or preview it beforehand. Once you have clicked **Post message**, you may have to wait several hours before it appears on the site. Keep checking back to see when your message and replies to it appear.

10 To reply to a posting, click on it. In the next window, all the additional messages that have been added to the thread are displayed on the left. Click on them to read them, then add your own message by clicking on **Post a follow up to this message**. You then have to log-in to post.

Posting style guide

Whenever people communicate on the Internet in organised discussion groups, there are often conventions and rules to follow to ensure the experience is a good one for all users. Before posting your message, click on the link to the **Posting Style Guide** and read the tips to help you use the forums more easily. You can also click on **Posting FAQ** to see the most frequently asked questions, or **Usenet Glossary** for a list of definitions of some of the more common words you'll see while using Usenet.

Shopping on the Internet

Buying what you want is just a question of point and click

On-line shopping is now becoming an everyday idea. Users have access to a far wider range of goods than can be bought in local shops. Many people prefer on-line shopping because of the convenience – no parking or queues, 'shops' open 24 hours a day, seven days a week, and goods are delivered to the door.

The prices of goods offered over the Internet are extremely competitive. Even after paying for delivery they can work out cheaper than shopping by conventional means.

In this project we show you how to buy a book and a piece of computer hardware. Use the steps as a general guide to buying any goods on-line.

Have a good idea of what you want to buy before you go on-line – it is easy to get distracted and buy things you don't need.

BEFORE YOU START

1 Connect to the Internet. In your Web browser's address box type in the address of an Internet shopping Web site (in this case, www.amazon.co.uk). Click on **Go** (or press the **Enter** or **Return** key) then wait for the site's home page to appear on screen.

Popular shopping sites

Addresses for popular shopping sites include:
- www.amazon.co.uk (books and music)
- www.cdnow.com (music)
- www.jungle.com (computer equipment)
- www.interflora.com (flowers)
- www.lastminute.com (tickets and travel)
- www.tesco.com (supermarket)

Bright idea
When you buy over the Internet make a note of information such as the date of purchase, item, cost, contact phone number or e-mail address. This makes follow-up queries easy.

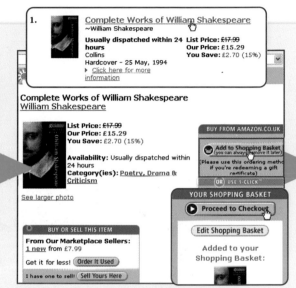

*When you click on the **Add to Shopping Basket** button you are not committed to buy at this point. You are simply collecting items.*

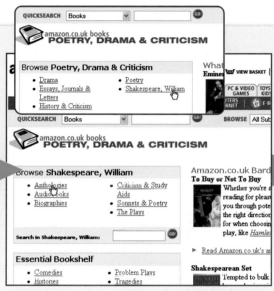

2 Navigate through to the type of product you are looking for, such as a book. Amazon's books page lists many different categories. Choose the one you want, click on it, then wait for the new page to appear. To explore the category click on a subject.

3 The most commonly sought after titles and types of book are listed at the top of each category. As with other major authors, there are hundreds of titles available to do with Shakespeare – the most popular kinds of books are grouped together to make searching easier.

4 For information on any book, such as reviews or its price, click on the title. To begin a purchase, click the title then the **Add to Shopping Basket** button. Choose as many items as you want, then to complete the purchase, click on **Proceed to Checkout**.

Making a quick search
On the Amazon home page you will see a search box near the top-left of the page. Type in the author, title, or subject of the book and click on **Go!**. A list of relevant books appears, which you can browse or buy.

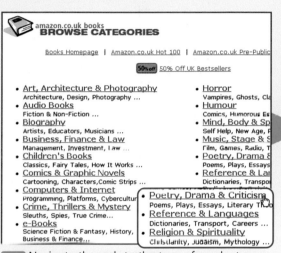

Quick browsing
The Shopping Basket lists all the books you've selected to buy, and the number of copies of each. If you decide not to buy a book you have selected, change the number in the quantity box to zero.

To continue browsing, click on the **Amazon.co.uk Home** button, or click on the browser's **Back** button to return to previous pages.

Using the Internet to buy computer hardware can save you money. We used the Lycos search engine, at www.lycos.co.uk.

COMPUTER HARDWARE

Amazon.co.uk Safe Shopping Guarantee
We guarantee that every transaction you make at Amazon.co.uk will be 100% safe. This means you pay nothing

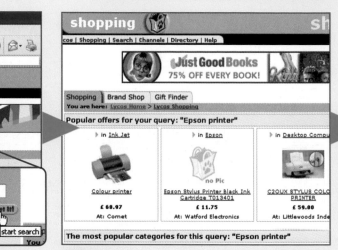

5 A page appears listing security details. Follow the on-screen instructions to complete your purchase. You can cancel the transaction up to the last minute. After completing your purchase, simply wait for delivery. It may take just a few days.

6 For other items type www.lycos.co.uk in your Web browser's address box, then press **Enter**. When the page appears, click on Shopping in the menu on the left. In the Shopping page enter a description of the item you are looking for and the maximum price that you want to pay.

7 Lycos will list all the products it can find that match your description and preferred price. If nothing suitable appears try your search again, perhaps with a higher maximum price. When you see an item that interests you, click on the link below the picture to visit the on-line shop selling it.

Bright idea
If you are reluctant to send financial details over the Internet, look for an option to fax, telephone or post your order.

Secure shopping

Never give out your credit or debit card details on the Internet unless the on-line shop you are dealing with uses a secure server for its payment pages. In Internet Explorer, the easiest way to tell this is to look for a padlock symbol in the status bar at the bottom of the page. (If you cannot see the status bar go to the **Tools** menu and click on **Status bar**.) The padlock shows that the information passing between your computer and the shop's server will be encrypted or scrambled as it travels across the Internet, ensuring only the intended recipient can read it.

Order Summary	
Subtotal of Items:	£22.81
Giftwrap:	£0.00
Postage & Packing:	£3.34
Promotional Certificates:	-£0.00
Total Before VAT:	£26.15
VAT:	£0.00
Total:	£26.15
Gift Certificates:	-£0.00
Total:	£26.15

Watch out

The internet makes it easy to buy things from overseas. Electrical goods can seem cheaper in the United States. However, they may not work – the US mains voltage is different to that in Europe. Also, duties and delivery charges can eat away any apparent savings.

Quantity	Price	
1	£ 68.97	REMOVE
1	£ 3.25	
	£ 72.22	**Total**

CONTINUE WITH ORDER
MAKE FURTHER SELECTIONS

8 Check the details and specifications carefully to make sure that the product is the one you want. If everything seems right, click on **Buy Now** (some web sites have Add to basket).

9 Once you have added all that you need to your shopping basket, click on **Continue With Order** (often this is termed Go to checkout). Depending on the shop, you may be asked to register so that your details will be automatically filled in for you the next time you use the on-line store.

10 The final step is where you enter your card details. Be certain that the vendor is using encryption – technology that scrambles your card number while it is being sent over the Internet), and press the **Submit Order** button. You will receive confirmation. Then simply wait for your goods to be delivered.

Compare Prices

There's no need to visit lots of web sites to be sure that you're getting good value. Comparison shopping sites automatically do the legwork for you, checking the price of an item at many different on-line shops. The best ones also include tax and shipping costs, so you know that you are seeing a true comparison.

Find and buy an antique

Use the Internet to seek out new items for your collection

The Internet is an excellent source of information for collectors of almost anything, from records and model cars to paintings and antiques.

For keen collectors of antiques the World Wide Web opens up a completely new way of shopping and dealing, and many auction houses now run 'virtual auctions' on-line. Collectors can also find a wealth of detail on their favourite craftsmen and women, designers and painters. And they can share information with other enthusiasts, arrange sales and purchases, and simply enjoy chatting about their hobby.

Make a list of the categories or key words to search by. If one search doesn't yield many sites you can search again without wasting time.

BEFORE YOU START

1 Connect to the Internet. In your Web browser's address box, type in the address of a search engine and press the **Return** key. Either type a key word in the search engine's search box (here, 'antiques') and click on **Search**, or click on a relevant category.

Popular search engines

The addresses for popular search engines are:

- www.altavista.com
- www.lycos.co.uk
- www.yahoo.co.uk
- www.excite.com
- www.northernlight.com
- hotbot.lycos.com

Bright idea

If you are bidding on-line in a foreign currency, make sure you know what the exchange rate is. You will usually pay at the rate on the closing date for bids. Check with the auctioneer.

Close-up

With Internet Explorer you can search and browse for Web sites within a single window. When you display the search Explorer Bar, the frame to the left displays the search engine and search results. Click on a site listed on the left and it will appear in the right frame.

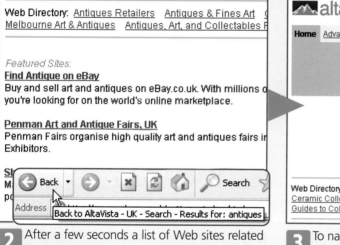

2 After a few seconds a list of Web sites related to antiques will appear. Each Web site comes with a brief description of what it offers. To view a Web site click on its name. To return to the list of sites found by the search engine click on your Web browser's **Back** button.

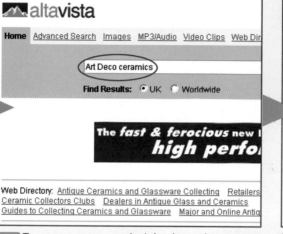

3 To narrow your search right down, be more specific in your choice of key words. Typing in 'Art Deco ceramics' will reduce the number of relevant Web sites considerably. The sites on offer include book publishers, dealers, dedicated enthusiasts and experts.

4 One of the sites listed is that of a well-known auction house, which now offers bidders the opportunity to view items on-line. You can even bid on-line for certain selected items.

Virtual auctions

On-line auctions such as www.ebay.com operate along similar lines to traditional auctions. A seller places an item on the site, often with a photograph. Bidding continues up to a set closing time. When bidding closes, the highest bidder wins. Winning bidder and seller then contact each other to arrange payment and delivery.

Fraud is rare, but 'Buyer beware' applies. Watch a few auctions before bidding yourself. Also check the feedback that Ebay users can give on each other – this is a quick way to discover if someone has a bad reputation.

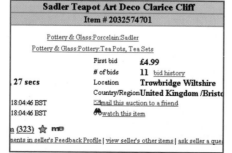

Surfing the Internet

You can browse Web sites – or 'surf the Net' – in several ways. You can open any site by typing its address in the browser's address box and pressing **Return**, or clicking on its underlined link in another site. Alternatively, you can use the browser's toolbar buttons to move backward and forward through pages and sites.

Watch out
If you join in an on-line discussion, never give your home telephone number or home address to others in the group, and always follow forum rules.

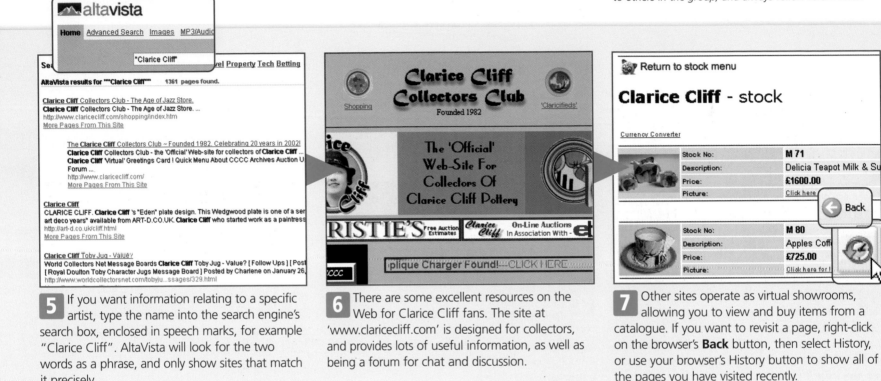

5 If you want information relating to a specific artist, type the name into the search engine's search box, enclosed in speech marks, for example "Clarice Cliff". AltaVista will look for the two words as a phrase, and only show sites that match it precisely.

6 There are some excellent resources on the Web for Clarice Cliff fans. The site at 'www.claricecliff.com' is designed for collectors, and provides lots of useful information, as well as being a forum for chat and discussion.

7 Other sites operate as virtual showrooms, allowing you to view and buy items from a catalogue. If you want to revisit a page, right-click on the browser's **Back** button, then select History, or use your browser's History button to show all of the pages you have visited recently.

Picture search

Google is one of the most popular search engines because of its speed and high success rate. You can also use Google to search for images.

Select the Images tab, then in the search box type key words to describe what you are looking for. Google will return a page of thumbnail images – click on one to see an enlarged view.

Short cut
*You can access the Internet from the Taskbar in Windows XP. Right-click on the Taskbar, select **Toolbars** from the pop-up menu, followed by **Address**. Type in a Web address (URL) in the address box that appears then press **Enter**.*

To add or reply to a message, you must register or login first!
login: fiona_green   password: ●●●●●●   LOGIN

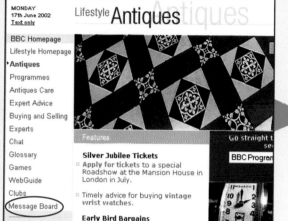

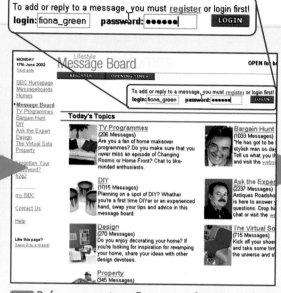

Topic - Ask the Expert
Antiques Roadshow expert, Eric Knowles will be popping into the board each week questions and queries. So keep them coming.

START NEW DISCUSSION   SEE ALL DISCU

Discussion Title   **Started By**

Small Pottery Item   Leo Doyle
I have a small piece of very colurful pottery. It stands approx 1 1/2 inches tall and is approx 1 1/2 inches at its widest point. It is bulb shaped ...
                                                    more >

FISHING REELS   Eric Atherto
Ihave 2 fishing reels which i may be intrested in selling as i seen some the same on B/H the other day Ist is a FLYREEL type Its made by ...
                                                    more >

help stoppers stuck   PHIL jones
Can any one tell me how to remove a stopper from a decanter,its been stuck for over ten years.I tried soaking it using various cleaning products,but to no a

MIRRORS
has anyone had any

Type your message:
I am a keen collector of Clarice CLiff pottery and would like to know if there are any specialist restorers of her Art Deco work. Some of my best-

8 There are many sites that you can use to 'talk' to other collectors. The most popular have their own discussion areas. For antiques, go to 'www.bbc.co.uk/antiques'. This is the home page for the BBC Antiques site. Click on **Message Board** to visit the chat areas.

9 Before you enter a Forum you have to register by filling in your e-mail address and a password in the box provided and clicking on the **Login** button. Now click on your choice of topic from the list in the main part of the page.

10 You will see messages displayed on screen. To see a message in full, click on **More**. To begin a discussion, click on the **Start New Discussion** button, then type your note in the box that appears.

Using search engines well

Each search engine has its own way of allowing you to narrow or broaden your searches for information. Look for pointers to special help sections on a search engine's home page that will teach you about searching successfully.

Google Advanced Search

Find results	with **all** of the words	Art Deco
	with the **exact phrase**	Clarice Cliff
	with **at least one** of the words	
	without the words	
Language	Return pages written in	
File Format	Only ▾ return results of the file format	

Set up a family Web site

You can make your personal mark on the World Wide Web

One of the most exciting Internet projects you can do is to create your own Web site. It is a great chance to send a message to an audience of millions.

A well-planned personal Web site can be used to promote a club or society, or to communicate with people of similar interests.

You can design your site while working off-line using Word. Then, in a matter of minutes, you can connect to the Internet and publish the pages using simple tools contained within Windows XP.

When you sign up with an ISP you usually get a certain amount of webspace – certainly enough for a simple family site. Some ISPs even let you choose the address for your site.

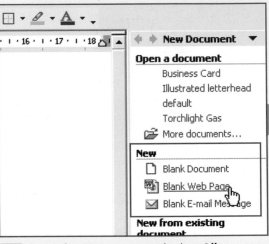

1 Go to the **Start** menu and select **All Programs** then **Microsoft Word**. In Word, go to the File menu and select **New**. A column appears down the right-hand side of screen. Click on **Blank Web Page** in this column. A new document then opens.

New XP Wizard

Windows XP differs from earlier versions of the operating system in the way that its Web Publishing Wizard works. Whereas before you could use the Wizard to transmit web pages and images from your computer to any ISP, the Wizard now limits you to Microsoft's own services, Xdrive plus or MSN Groups. To publish to the web space reserved for you by your ISP, you'll need to use other tools, accessible from within Microsoft Word, as described above.

Watch out
Some of the dialogue boxes and options shown may differ from those on your PC. This can be caused by the options chosen while installing Windows or Office, or by software updates received over the Net. This will not affect your ability to complete the project.

Key word
***Home page** This refers to the page that provides the point of entry to a collection of linked pages in a Web site. However, a home page can also stand alone, without links.*

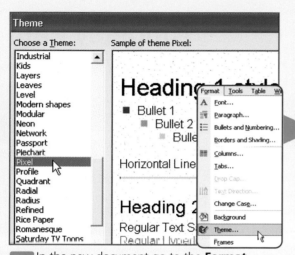

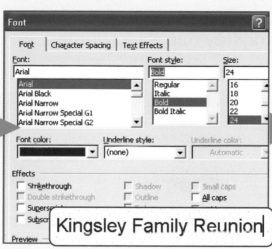

2 In the new document go to the **Format** menu and select **Theme**. Select a visual style for your pages in the Theme dialogue box. Click on your choice (here, **Pixel**), then click on **OK**. A blank Web page appears. Name and save it (see below).

3 Type your headline and any other introductory text you wish to appear at the top of the Web page. To style your text, highlight a word or words, go to the **Format** menu and select **Font**. Select a font, style, size, colour and effect. Click **OK**.

4 To keep your page neat, it's a good idea to use a table. Position the cursor on the page by pressing the **Return** key, go to the **Table** menu and select **Insert Table**. In the dialogue box select the number of columns and rows you'd like, then click **OK**.

Save as Web page
Web pages are created in a language called HTML (HyperText Markup Language). But you do not need to know the language because Microsoft Word will create the HTML for you.

When you open a blank document in Word, go to the File menu and select Save as Web page. If this option is not offered, select Save As and then choose Web page in the 'Save as type' box. Create a new folder to save it to, and name the document 'home'. When saving a file for use on the Web, always give it a one-word name, typed in lower case (some servers won't recognise file names with capital letters or spaces).

To edit your page, open Word, go to the File menu and select Open. Then use the dialogue box to locate the page. To view your page in your browser, and test links before publishing, double-click on the file icon.

Why use a table?
Without using a table as the framework for your Web page it is difficult to position your text and pictures precisely. For this project two columns were chosen, one for pictures and one for text. Four rows were chosen to accommodate the content of the page, but it is easy to add more rows. With your cursor in the table, go to the **Table** menu, select **Insert**, then **Rows Above** or **Rows Below**.

Watch out
*When you insert your table, you may not at first be able to see it. To make the table visible, go to the **Table** menu and select **Show Gridlines**. To hide the gridlines, select **Hide Gridlines** in the Table menu.*

Bright idea
Word offers a variety of design elements to use when creating your Web pages. More backgrounds, buttons and rules can be obtained from the Web and disks cover-mounted on PC magazines.

5 To adjust the width of a column, place the mouse pointer over the column edge. When it changes to a double-headed arrow, press the left mouse button and drag the line across to the required width.

6 To place text in the table, click in the relevant column and row and simply type it in. The row height will adjust automatically to accommodate your entry. Style the text as in Step 3.

7 To insert a picture in the table, click in the relevant column and row (here, in the first row of the first column). Go to the **Insert** menu and select **Picture**, then **From File**. This lets you import scanned pictures stored on the hard disk.

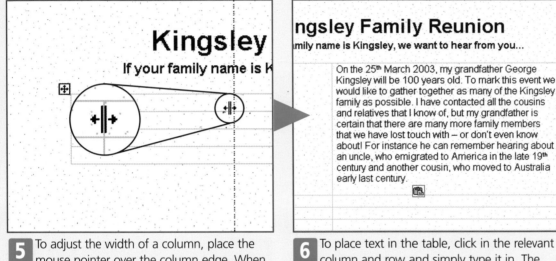

Preparing images

In order for your Web pages to carry the maximum amount of information and be downloaded quickly, pictures should use as little memory as possible. It's best, then, to use small images saved in a compressed format. To do this, you'll need an image-editing package such as Paint.

Open the image, go to the **Image** menu and select **Attributes**. Set the image to 200 pixels high and reduce the width by a similar degree (this reduces the memory required by the image file). Click **OK**.

Go to the **File** menu and select **Save As**. In the 'Save as type' box, select either **JPEG** (Joint Photographic Experts Group) or **GIF** (Graphic Image Format). JPEG is best for images like photographs that have graduated colours; GIF is a better way to save diagram-like images with solid colours. Pictures saved in these formats are compressed to use less memory.

If the images files you are using are not already held in your publishing folder, you must save them in it. This is important as they need to be here when you publish.

The Web is made up of millions of linked pages. You can also add links from your home page to other pages that you have created or to other sites on the Web.

LINKING PAGES

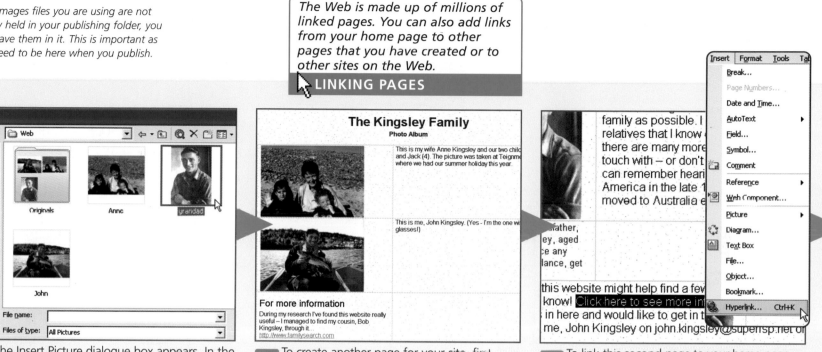

The Kingsley Family
Photo Album

This is my wife Anne Kingsley and our two child
and Jack (4). The picture was taken at Teignm
where we had our summer holiday this year.

This is me, John Kingsley. (Yes - I'm the one wi
glasses!)

For more information
During my research I've found this website really
useful — I managed to find my cousin, Bob
Kingsley, through it...
http://www.familysearch.com

family as possible. I
relatives that I know
there are many more
touch with – or don't
can remember heari
America in the late 1
moved to Australia e

...father,
ey, aged
ce any
lance, get

this website might help find a fev
know!
in here and would like to get in t
me, John Kingsley on john.kingsley@superisp.net or

Insert | Format | Tools | Tab

- Break...
- Page Numbers...
- Date and Time...
- AutoText ▶
- Field...
- Symbol...
- Comment
- Reference ▶
- Web Component...
- Picture ▶
- Diagram...
- Text Box
- File...
- Object...
- Bookmark...
- Hyperlink... Ctrl+K

8 The Insert Picture dialogue box appears. In the 'Look in' box find the folder that contains your images. Click on the image you wish to import, then click **Insert**. The image appears in the table. To resize the picture, click on it, then click and drag a corner handle.

9 To create another page for your site, first open another blank Web page as in Step 1. Save it in the same folder as your first page. Insert a table, type in your text then style it in a similar way to your previous page.

10 To link this second page to your home page, you need to set up a 'hypertext' link. Open the home page, highlight a word or words you want to act as the link, then go to the **Insert** menu and click on **Hyperlink**.

Key word
Link *A set of words or an image which, when clicked on, takes the user to another page on the World Wide Web. Text links usually appear underlined and in different coloured type.*

Close up
*To remove a link, highlight the words that activate the link, go to the **Insert** menu and select **Hyperlink**. In the Edit Hyperlink dialogue box click on the **Remove link** button.*

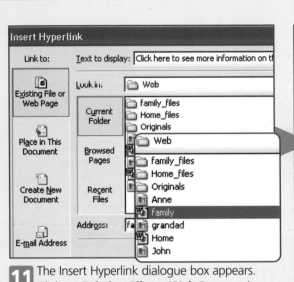

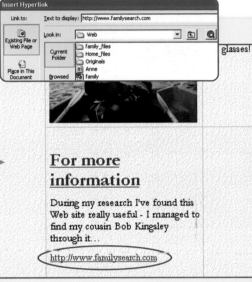

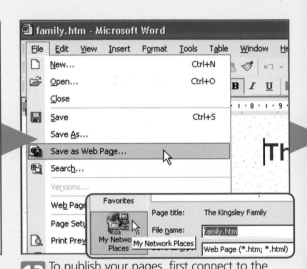

11 The Insert Hyperlink dialogue box appears. Click on **Existing File or Web Page** and **Current Folder** to find your linking page. When you find it, click on it then click **OK**. The text you selected appears as an underlined link. Hold down **Ctrl** and click on the text to see the linked page.

12 To create links to other Web sites, type a Web address into a page, highlight it, go to the **Insert** menu and select **Hyperlink**. In the dialogue box, the text you have typed will appear in the 'Address' window. Click **OK**. The underlined link appears on your page. Click on it to go to that site.

13 To publish your pages, first connect to the Internet. Go to the **Start** menu, click on **Connect To** and then on your dial-up connection. Once you are connected, return to Word. Go to the **File** menu and click on **Save as Web Page**. Click on **My Network Places** at the bottom of the left-hand column.

Using Windows XP Web Wizard

If you don't have any web space of your own, you can use Microsoft's services via its Web Publishing Wizard. Go to the **Start** menu and select **My Documents**. Locate the document you wish to put on the web, and click on **Publish this file to the Web** in the File and Folder tasks. The Web Publishing Wizard will open. Follow the steps – you will be asked to choose between Xdrive plus and MSN Groups. Choose one and complete any information you are asked for. You may be required to make a payment.

⚠ Watch out

*Make sure you are connected to the Internet before you complete the instructions in the Web Publishing Wizard and click on **Finish**. Otherwise the Wizard will not be able to publish your pages.*

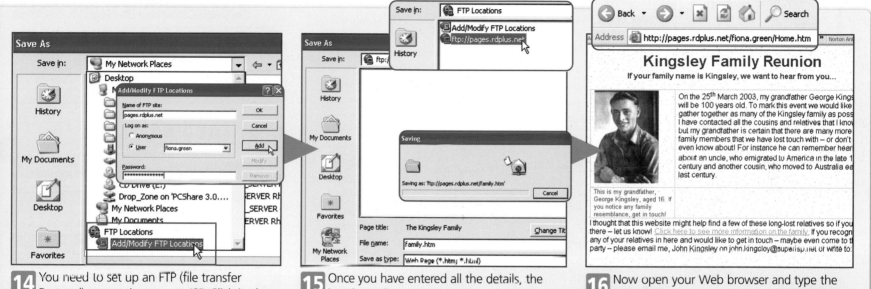

14 You need to set up an FTP (file transfer Protocol) connection to your ISP. Click in the 'Save in' box. Choose **Add/Modify FTP Locations** from the drop-down list. A dialogue box will open asking you to enter the details your ISP has given you about the location of your personal web space. Complete the boxes and click **OK**.

15 Once you have entered all the details, the location will appear in the 'Save in' box. Double click on the desired location and then on **Save**. All the files necessary to make up your page will be transferred over to your web space (this make take some time).

16 Now open your Web browser and type the Web address for your pages into the address box. Click on **Go** (or press **Enter** or **Return**). After you connect to the Web your home page will be located and displayed – just as Web users across the globe will see it.

🔑 Key word

Server *This refers to the computer that holds your Web pages. When you publish your Web pages you are transferring them to that computer. This means that you do not have to be on-line yourself for someone to see your pages.*

Do research on the Net

Use today's technology to learn about our yesterdays

The World Wide Web is a great tool for historical research. Whatever your field of interest, there are almost bound to be sites, discussion groups and library resources dedicated to that topic.

If, for example, you are interested in the First World War, you will find thousands of resources on the Web. Some will be pages produced by amateur historians, some will be educational sites aimed at children, some will be highly academic.

The first step is to do a search. Here we use a search engine called AllTheWeb, but you can use any one you like, and pick your own path through the wealth of information on the Great War.

Make a note of which direction you want your search to take. Be as specific as possible to limit the number of 'hits'. For example, search for 'Somme' rather than 'battles'.

BEFORE YOU START

1 Connect to the Internet as usual. In your Web browser's address box type in the address of a search engine then click **Go** or **Enter**. The engine's home page will appear. Type a key word or words into the search box then click the **Search** button.

Popular history sites

Sites with information on war history include:
- www.historychannel.com (general history site)
- www.encyclopedia.com (free on-line encyclopedia)
- www.worldwar1.com (reference works and discussions)
- www.bbc.co.uk/history/war (numerous war articles)

Key word

Home page *This is the opening page for any Web site. It will tell you what the site includes and provide links to the various parts of the site.*

2 A list of Web sites will appear. A search for 'World War I' yields more than one million items, including sites on women's roles in the war, picture archives and eye-witness accounts. Scroll down and click on **World War I - Trenches on the Web**.

3 When the site opens, use the slider bar on the right-hand side of your window to scroll down the home page some considerable way. You will find a list with the heading 'Good Starting Points'. Click on **Reference Library**. This is a good place to begin your research.

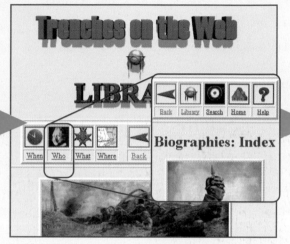

4 Through the Reference Library you can access huge amounts of data, including biographies, maps, artwork and even sound recordings of the period. Click on one of the buttons at the foot of the home page to access an area of your choice.

Results by category

AllTheWeb groups together related Web sites in its Fast Topics section. This is extremely useful as it means you don't have to trawl through thousands of sites to find ones you may be interested in.

After your initial search it organises the sites found into a number of fast topics, which appear on the right-hand side of the results page. Each fast topic offers the results of a more precise search based on your initial query.

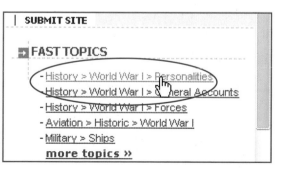

Remember to use your Web browser's Back and Forward buttons to revisit Web sites and pages you have opened since going on-line.

Bright idea
When you come across interesting sites,
bookmark them (see page 96). This way you can
revisit them quickly, without having to search for them
again or remember their address.

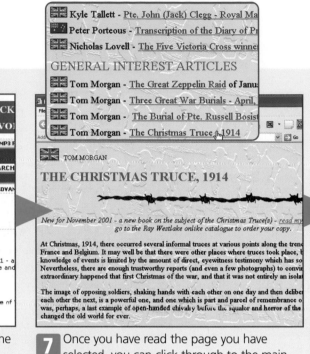

5 To find other sites of interest, click on your
Web browser's **Back** button to return to the
AllTheWeb site. Click on another site, such as
Photos of the Great War.

6 For a search on a more detailed aspect of the
Great War, return to the AllTheWeb site.
Enter your search term and select a page from the
results returned. Below the title of each page is
short 'description' – in fact a series of excerpts
from the page – to give an idea of its contents.

7 Once you have read the page you have
selected, you can click through to the main
contents page of the site you're visiting to see
other information. When you have finished, you
can use your browser's **Back** button to return to
your original search results.

Saving pictures

To save an image onto your
hard disk, right-click on the
image and select **Save
Picture As** from the
pop-up menu that appears.
Click on the arrow beside
the 'Save in' box, scroll through and
select a folder in which you want to save
the image. Give the image a name in the
'File name' box then click **Save**.

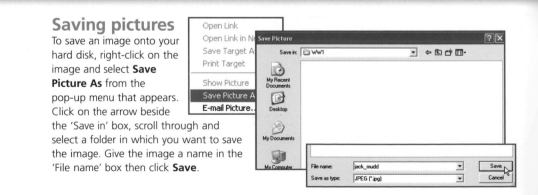

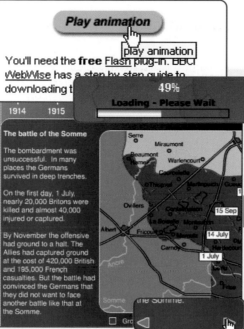

8 Some of the most impressive resources on First World War history can be found at www.bbc.co.uk/history/war. The BBC's web site contains a detailed timeline of the war's events and fascinating features. One is an animated map showing how the Western Front developed.

9 The map uses the Flash plug-in for Internet Explorer – you will be asked if you would like to install it if you have not already done so. Once the map has downloaded you can follow the evolution of the trenches, with animations showing the key battles.

10 The BBC site also covers the human side of the war, with stories about individuals from the major fighting powers. The options at the top of the page allow you to choose different ways to browse through the site's extensive contents: by topic; by time; or by people.

Printing a Web page

To print out a Web page for future reference, go to the **File** menu on your browser's menu bar at the top of the screen and click on **Print**. In the Options tab of the Print dialogue box you can choose how to print out web pages with frames (separate elements that may not all print out at the same time).

Primary school learning

Help your children expand their knowledge through the Net

The World Wide Web is, among many other things, a learning resource. It is full of material that can enhance children's understanding of their school subjects and of the world around them. There are thousands of educational sites, along with related sites that both parents and children will find useful. This project shows you a selection – some are bright and breezy interactive sites, others contain details of the National Curriculum.

Using the Internet for education is fun, and it equips primary-age children with learning skills they are likely to use throughout their school years, and beyond.

Make a daily study plan so that you can work out exactly which subjects are to be studied and when. This way, you can limit time spent on-line.

▶ BEFORE YOU START

Address 🔍 http://www.yahooligans.com

YAHOOLIGANS!
the Web Guide for Kids

Wednesday June 19, 2002

- Games
- Movies
- Jokes
- Science
- Reference
- Ask Earl
- News
- Sports
- Astrology
- Cool Sites

Yahooligans! News
Heads Up! - *Associated Press*
Snake handler Peter Morningstar has his brow bitten by a 7 kilogram (15.5 pound), 3 meter (10 feet) long carpet snake during a photo shoot for a newspaper in Brisbane, Australia. More...

The Solar System | Search

Yahooligans! Directory

Around the World
Countries, U.S. States, Holidays...

School Bell
Lang. Arts, Math, Social Studies...

Arts & Entertainment
TV, Movies, Jokes, Music...

Science & Nature
Space, Animals, Dinosaurs...

1 Connect to the Internet. In the browser's address box type in a search engine address – here, www.yahooligans.com, an engine specially for children. Press **Return**. When the home page loads type a key word into the search box and click on **Search**.

Searching by category

In addition to a search box, some search engines let you search by category. You narrow your search by clicking on subdivisions that have been made already. This is useful for children who might misspell key words.

Arts & Entertainment
TV, Movies, Jokes, Music...

Science & Nature
Space, Animals, Dinosaurs...

Close-up
Keep a record of a Web site's address by adding it to your Web browser's Favorites or Bookmarks file (see page 96). Once entered, all you need do to view the site is click on the entry instead of typing in the Web address every time.

Back

*Click on the **Back** button to revisit sites and pages already viewed since you have been on-line.*

(see page 96)

43. Arty **the** Part Time Astronaut
     information about **the** solar system
     http://www.artyastro.com
     More sites about: Astronomy and S

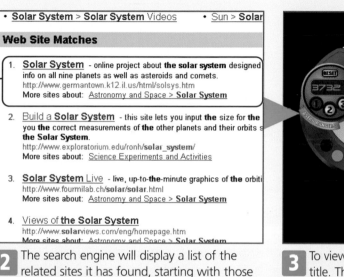

- Solar System > Solar System Videos   • Sun > Solar

Web Site Matches

1. **Solar System** - online project about **the solar system** designed
    info on all nine planets as well as asteroids and comets.
    http://www.germantown.k12.il.us/html/solsys.htm
    More sites about: Astronomy and Space > **Solar System**

2. Build a **Solar System** - this site lets you input **the** size for **the**
    you **the** correct measurements of **the** other planets and their orbits s
    the Solar System.
    http://www.exploratorium.edu/ronh/**solar_system**/
    More sites about: Science Experiments and Activities

3. **Solar System** Live - live, up-to-**the**-minute graphics of **the** orbiti
    http://www.fourmilab.ch/**solar/solar**.html
    More sites about: Astronomy and Space > **Solar System**

4. Views of **the Solar System**
    http://www.**solar**views.com/eng/homepage.htm
    More sites about: Astronomy and Space > **Solar System**

2 The search engine will display a list of the related sites it has found, starting with those that most closely match your requirements.
Use the scroll bars to the right of the page to browse the list.

Most search engines provide a brief description of the contents of a Web site. This helps you to decide whether the site is likely to be useful or not.

3 To view a Web site, click on its underlined title. The home page of that site will then appear. Click on any buttons or links (indicated by different coloured text and underlining) to explore the site. To return to the list of other sites click on the **Back** button.

4 Arty the Part time Astronaut is a site that uses exciting animations and graphics to explain how the Solar System works. To view some of the features you will need the Flash plug-in, an add-on to your browser. Most PCs will have the plug-in preinstalled; if not you will be asked if you want to download it.

Useful educational sites
You may find these Web sites and search engines particularly useful for children under 11:
- www.bbc.co.uk/education (contains a dedicated section to primary school learning)
- www.quia.com/web/ (fun and games for all ages)
- www.nationalgeographic.com/world/index.html (visit the Kids Network)

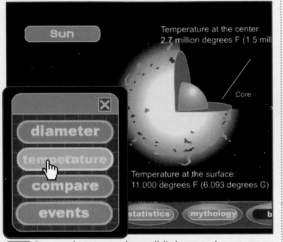

Bright idea
*Teach children how to read long Web pages off-line (using a Web site without staying on the phone line) to keep your phone bill down. If you're using Internet Explorer, go to the **File** menu and click on **Work Offline**.*

5 Remember to explore all links to other areas within the same site or to related sites. This can take a lot of time, so keep an eye on the clock or sign-up for a flat-fee ISP service that gives you unlimited time on-line.

1 Reading and storytelling are key parts of primary school learning. The Stories From The Web site (www.storiesfromtheweb.org) is an eye-catching site, containing stories, clubs and interactive elements. Click on the **Stories** for a good read.

2 As your mouse pointer passes over links, it will change its appearance to a hand sign. The site organises stories by Authors, Poetry, Titles and Types of Story – clicking on a section header opens the link.

*When you find a page that contains useful information, you may want to print it. Click on the text first, then go to the **File** menu and click on **Print**.*

The Stories From The Web site offers guidelines for both parents and children. It also has an e-mail address should you want to contact the site administrators.

As you read stories on The Stories From The Web site, a page counter in the top right-hand corner of the screen will help you keep track of how far you have got.

Well-organised Web sites such as the one below will give you a guarantee that their pages and the sites they contain links to are child-friendly and safe.

For Grown-Ups   PRIVACY POLICY   About MaMaMedia
Legal Terms and Conditions   Advertising Information   Tech Help

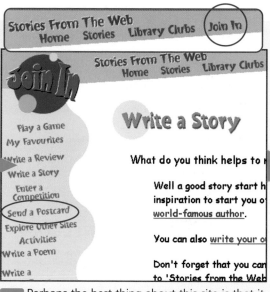

3 The stories appear on screen, page by page. You have to click on the **Read On** button to start and then the **Next Page** button to turn the pages – a page counter in the corner tells you how many pages the book has.

4 Perhaps the best thing about this site is that it encourages children to write their own stories, review new ones and send in suggestions of their favourites. Click on the **Join In** link, then on a section from the panel on the left of the page.

5 Learning is easier when it's fun. The MaMamedia site (www.mamamedia.com) contains lots of movement, colour and energy. This is definitely one to work through and enjoy, maybe as a break from homework.

The Send a Postcard section allows youngsters to select a special picture from the site's image library to send as an e-mail to a friend.

To send a postcard just follow these steps....

Step 1. Choose a picture and click the button to select it.

○ 3 Bears   ○ Greensmoke

Step 2. type in your name   Jack Grimshaw

Step 3. and your email address?   jack@grimshawshack.ou

Step 4. and the name of the person you are sending the card to?   Millie Peters

Step 5. and their email address?   Milliepede@petersfamily

Watch out
To prevent children accessing unsuitable material on the Internet, consider buying a Web-screening program, such as Net Nanny or Cyber Patrol (see page 99).

Close-up
Links to other Web pages and sites usually appear underlined and in a different colour from the body text of a page. A mouse pointer will always change to a pointing hand when it passes over a link. A single mouse click opens a link.

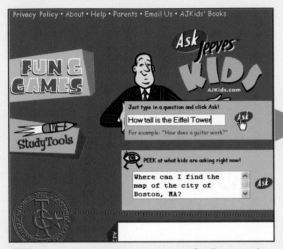

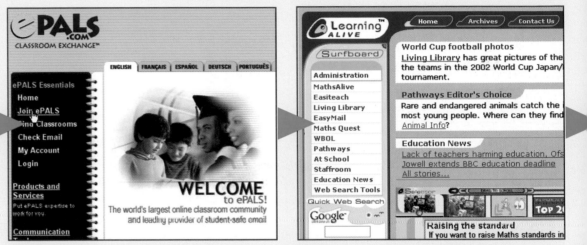

6 There are search engines specifically geared towards children. Ask Jeeves For Kids (www.ajkids.com) is one example. A child can type in a question and Jeeves will help him find the answer by listing Web sites that might contain relevant information.

7 E-mail can also be used for learning. Epals (www.epals.com) is a Net-based organisation that links schoolchildren from around the world via e-mail. Epals can bring together pupils of a similar age who are studying similar types of subject.

8 Parents of primary schoolchildren can also use the Internet to check the Web sites of prospective secondary schools. Learning Alive (www.learningalive.co.uk) is a good place to start.

Navigating between windows

Sometimes, when you click on a link to another site, a new window opens in front of the original window. If you want to return to the original site, you have to make the original window 'active'.

To make the original window active, minimise or close the new window then click on the original window (clicking the **Back** button in the new window will not work).

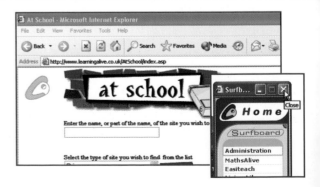

Key word

E-mail Electronic mail (e-mail) is a form of high-speed communication that is supported by the Internet. Messages can be sent down telephone lines to people on the other side of the world in seconds.

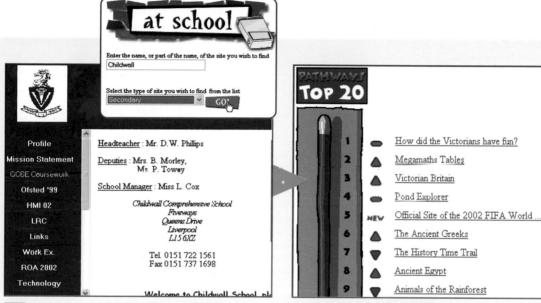

9 Click on the **At School** link and wait for the page to load. Next, click on the **at school Directory** link. Type in the name of the school in the search box (this can be narrowed down in the box below) and click on **Go**. If the school has a Web site, it will appear.

10 Using your Web browser's **Back** button, return to the Learning Alive home page and click on **Pathways**. This is a useful page full of links relevant to the National Curriculum selected by site visitors and the site editor, including a page with the top 20 sites.

11 Finally, combine learning with fun. Take a look at The Yuckiest Site on the Internet (http://yucky.kids.discovery.com), a child-friendly interactive science site that provides education and entertainment.

Secondary school learning

Gather material to help you study for your examinations

The Internet is a valuable aid to learning and study. In addition to helping with research for everyday school work, students can find lots of useful material that relates to GCSE and A-level syllabuses.

Certain sites offer the chance to browse past examination papers, take part in question-and-answer sessions, and chat with other students on-line. And when it comes to preparing for exams, students can get help setting up revision timetables.

But not all Web-based learning is geared towards specific exams. Language students can hone their skills by reading on-line foreign-language magazines, and everyone can find resources to help with all areas of study.

First make a list of the subject areas you wish to study, then make a note of appropriate key words and phrases to search by.

BEFORE YOU START

1 Connect to the Internet. In your Web browser's address box type the address of a search engine (here, www.google.co.uk), then press the **Return** key. After a few seconds the home page will load and appear on screen.

Close-up
Although the full address for Web sites includes 'http://' before the 'www…', you don't need to type this into the Address box. For most Web sites, you can simply start the address with 'www'.

The Google search engine highlights every occurrence of your key words to help you make your choice of Web sites.

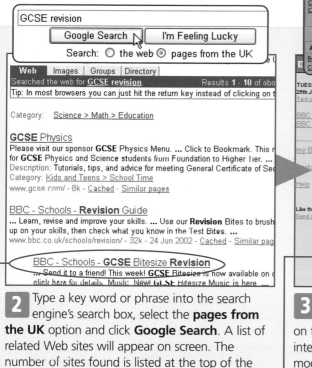

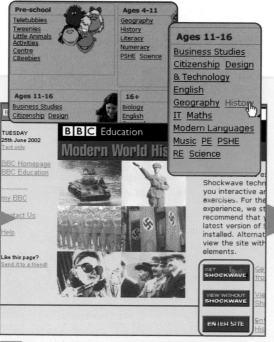

Watch out

When you do a word search, be as specific as you can. A search for, say, 'GCSE exams', might yield unsuitable results, such as personal CVs listing GCSE passes. See page 94 for advice on searches.

2 Type a key word or phrase into the search engine's search box, select the **pages from the UK** option and click **Google Search**. A list of related Web sites will appear on screen. The number of sites found is listed at the top of the page. To open a particular site, click on its address.

3 A good place to start for general study is the BBC Web site (www.bbc.co.uk/schools). Click on the link for **Ages 11-16** or **16+**. The site has interactive games, tests and creative learning modules to help with National Curriculum subjects.

4 Some sites, such as AngliaCampus (www.angliacampus.com) are subscription sites, whereby users have to pay a fee to access services and information beyond the 'guest' facilities. You are given sample content to help you decide whether it's worth subscribing.

Extra software

In order to interact with this particular site you need a Shockwave plug-in. If you don't already have this, you can download it by clicking on the button on the page. (See page 100 for more information on plug-ins.)

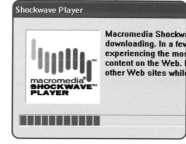

Subscribing tips

Well-managed Web services such as AngliaCampus will offer you the choice to sign up either on-line or by fax. Read their terms and conditions very carefully. If you are asked to pay on-line you should be informed that the server is secure, and that your credit-card details cannot be viewed by unauthorised parties.

You can subscribe by:
- Post
- Fax
- Credit Card online
- Purchase Order

Subscribe by post

1. Download and print out the Subscription Application form. Comp[...] your school order form or payment. Please make your cheque p[...] Ltd.
2. Read the terms and conditions information. Sign your form to in[...]
3. Send your form to:

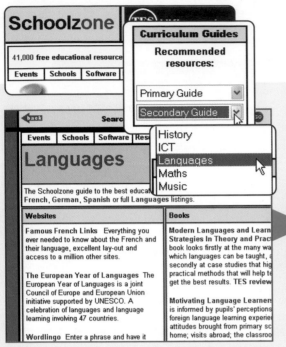

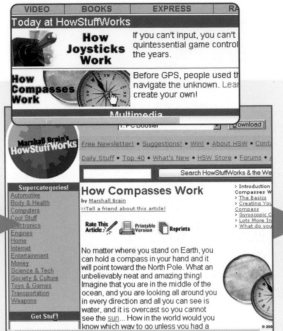

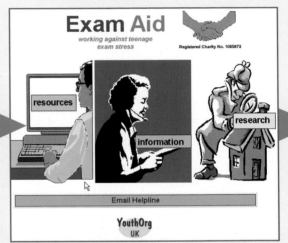

5 Another site packed with useful information is Schoolzone (www.schoolzone.co.uk). On the home page click on **Secondary Guide** in the Curriculum Guides box, then select a subject. This takes you to a list of recommended books, curriculum information and links to other sites.

6 A great site to find out the workings of just about anything is How Stuff Works (www.howstuffworks.com). It covers a range of subjects, from car engines to tornadoes, and offers an extensive question-and-answer section.

7 Search engines will help you find sites that can help with other exam-related issues. For example, www.examaid.co.uk is a Web site working against teenage exam stress. It provides information on organisations that can help with stress management, careers, bullying and health.

Keep yourself posted

It's not just links to other Web sites that are underlined on Web pages. Links to e-mail addresses are, too. Look out for free subscriptions to educational newsletters, which you can receive via e-mail.

Thankyou for registering with Schoolzone.co.uk. We will send you monthly updates during term time informing you about new items on Schoolzone. Please read our Privacy Policy at :-
http://www.schoolzone.co.uk/documents/privac
MyZone: To activate MyZone, go to :-
http://www.schoolzone.co.uk/documents/myzon
and enter this PIN: 148425 then your

Attention parents

Chatting on-line can be addictive. If you allow your children to chat to other students on the Web, it's sensible to limit the time they spend doing so, just as you would do when they are on the telephone.

There are several on-line timer programs that help you keep tabs on time spent chatting and the cost. You can even set an alarm to go off when your chosen budget has been reached. Try Internet Timer by Rat Software (www.ratsoft.freeserve.co.uk).

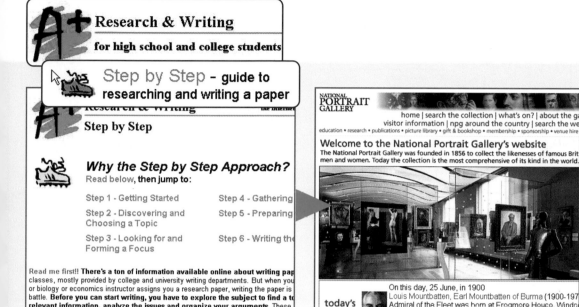

Research & Writing
for high school and college students

Step by Step - guide to researching and writing a paper

Research & Writing   the Internet

Step by Step

Why the Step by Step Approach?
Read below, then jump to:

Step 1 - Getting Started

Step 2 - Discovering and Choosing a Topic

Step 3 - Looking for and Forming a Focus

Step 4 - Gathering

Step 5 - Preparing

Step 6 - Writing the

Read me first!! There's a ton of information available online about writing pap classes, mostly provided by college and university writing departments. But when you or biology or economics instructor assigns you a research paper, writing the paper is battle. **Before you can start writing, you have to explore the subject to find a to relevant information, analyze the issues and organize your arguments.** These more time and require different skills than the final step--writing the paper. And many

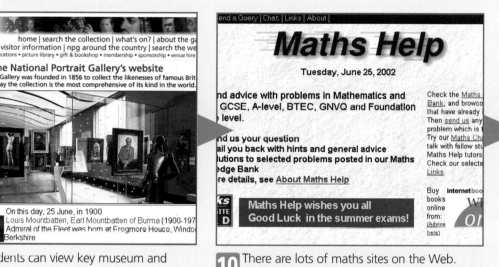

8 For help on researching and writing an essay, visit www.ipl.org/teen/aplus at the Internet Public Library. This useful site gives practical step-by-step information on planning, researching and writing an essay or project, even down to compiling a timetable.

9 Arts students can view key museum and gallery exhibits at first hand with virtual guided tours. Visit the Museum of Modern Art in New York (www.moma.org) or the National Portrait Gallery, London (www.npg.org.uk), for seminal works of art.

10 There are lots of maths sites on the Web. Maths Help (www.maths-help.co.uk) offers a chat facility where you can talk on-line to other students. You will find listings of different chat times and subjects students will be discussing.

Don't lose your focus
It's easy to become sidetracked when going through search results. Be disciplined about assessing each page quickly and deciding whether a site is likely to contain useful information about the subject you are researching. If it does, save the site as a bookmark or a favourite (see page 96). Then click the **Back** button to return to the results page.

Useful educational sites
You may find these Web sites and search engines particularly useful for children aged 11-16:
● www.dictionary.com (on-line spelling and grammar guide)
● www.learn.co.uk (on-line lessons)
● www.studyweb.com (general educational resource)
● www.dfee.gov.uk/iyc/ (further education advice)

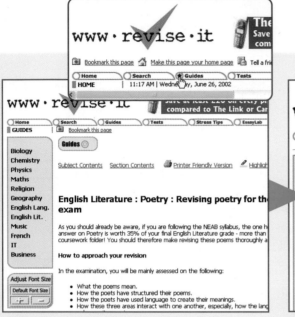

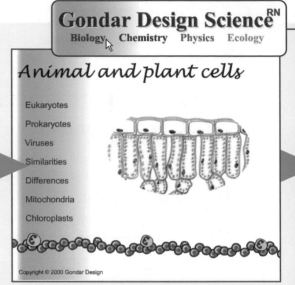

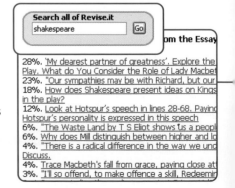

11 Revise it (www.revise.it) gives study tips and has revision guides written by teachers. Click on **Guides** then select a subject in the left-hand list. Next, choose a section within that subject. This takes you to topic sub-sections where you can focus your revision on specific areas.

12 Revise.it's EssayLab has hundreds of A grade essays covering GCSE and A-Level subjects. Use them to help structure your essays and as a guide to the key points of your question. When you take a break, there's a fun page with humorous real-life answers to previous GCSE questions!

13 Search engines will help you find sites that are written by academics or teachers but are not necessarily linked from larger sites. For example www.purchon.com is a site run by a teacher for pupils at his school, but is useful for anyone studying biology, chemistry, physics or ecology.

Losing a link

Web sites come and go on the Internet all the time. You might sometimes click on a link and get a message saying that the page either no longer exists or that 'A connection with the server cannot be established' (this often means the page no longer exists). So be prepared for the occasional disappointment.

Search a site

Many Web sites have their own search engines to help you locate a specific topic within the site. Type in a key word for the subject area you'd like more information on and wait for a list of results to be displayed

Watch out
Students using the Internet to study and revise should always check with their teachers to make sure that what they are looking at is relevant to their particular course.

If you find educational CD-ROMs expensive to buy, remember that you can borrow them from public libraries.

Bright idea
For further information and suggestions on how to write and design an eye-catching Curriculum Vitae, turn to page 154.

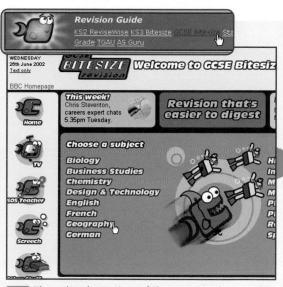

14 The schools section of the BBC site has an area devoted to GCSE revision. Go to the site's home page (see Step 3) and click on **GCSE Bitesize** in the Revision Guide box. You can test yourself, answer sample questions and read teachers' and examiners' notes.

15 You can also use the Internet to find and buy additional educational resources. For example, Ramesis (www.ramesis.com) sells educational CD-ROMs on-line. Use any search engine to locate other suppliers.

16 Prospective school-leavers can seek advice on writing their first Curriculum Vitae. Visit the Jobsite (www.jobsite.co.uk/career/write_cv.html) for detailed guidance.

Work off-line

If you find you're becoming engrossed in a single detailed Web page, remember that you can work off-line and so save the cost of your call. With Internet Explorer, for example, go to the **File** menu and click on **Work Offline**.

Games on the Internet

You'll never lack a playing partner when you're on-line

The Internet is an unrivalled source of entertainment as well as information. In fact, when it comes to computer games, the Internet is in a league of its own, as it not only provides the games but the players, too.

Many on-line games are adventure or action-based, but there are plenty of gaming sites catering to more diverse tastes. There are, for example, a large number of chess-related services, some of which allow you to play against opponents from around the world in 'real time', that is, live over the Internet. If, however, you do not want to spend money connected to the Internet while you play, you can opt to play games by e-mail. You can also download games to play at your leisure.

For security reasons, when playing against others on-line, it is advisable not to divulge any personal details such as telephone numbers.

PLAYING GAMES BY E-MAIL

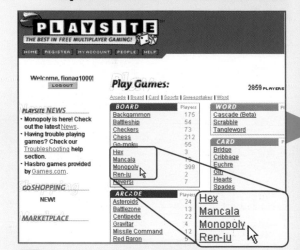

1 Connect to the Internet. To play a game of Monopoly on-line, go to www.playsite.com. Once you've registered (see below), click on **Monopoly** in the Board section. This takes you through to the main Monopoly window.

*Many game sites require regular users to register. To register on Playsite, click on **Register**, fill in your details, read the User Agreement then click **Register Me**.*

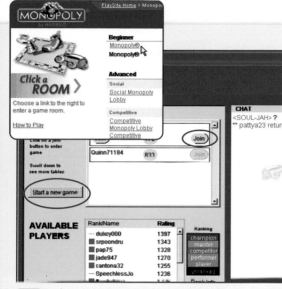

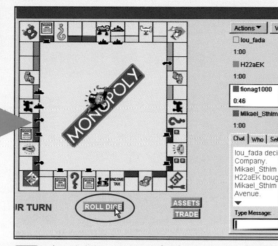

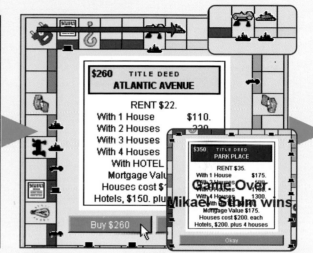

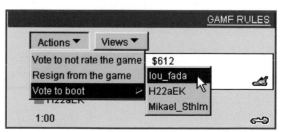

2 In the main Monopoly window, choose and click on a game room listed on the right. Once inside a game room you can join a game by clicking on the **Join** buttons on display in the Join tab, or you can start a new game by clicking the **Start a new game** button.

3 When joining a game, firstly choose a playing piece. The players are listed on the right with the current player highlighted. Follow your opponents' actions in the bottom-right chat box, where you can also type messages to them. When it's your turn to play, click on **Roll Dice**.

4 A red arrow indicates how your piece moves around the board. The centre of the board displays information about the property you are on, and icons of your playing piece indicate which properties you own. Play the game just like a regular version of Monopoly.

Game playing resources

A good way to prepare for a game is to browse through the options in the Resources tab in the main Monopoly window. Click on the links to read the rules, pick up useful tricks and tips and learn about the history of the game.

*You can resign from a game or vote to 'boot' another player who is holding up play by clicking on the **Actions** button.*

Watch out
Using a high-speed broadband connection can make on-line gaming faster and more fun. However, make sure you protect your system with a 'firewall' – software or hardware that stops other internet users accessing files on your PC.

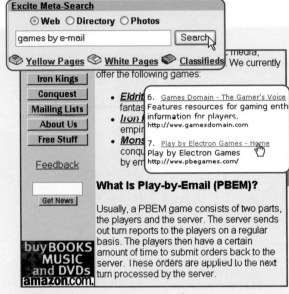

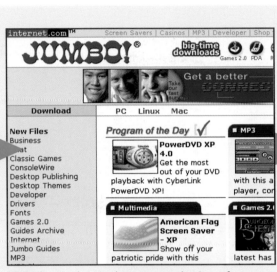

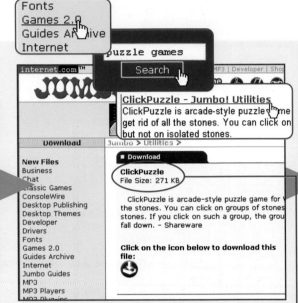

5 On the Internet you can also access strategy and fantasy games that work by sending your moves to your opponent(s) by e-mail. To find one of these, go to www.excite.com and type 'games by e-mail' in the Search box. Select a site from the search results listed.

6 The Jumbo site has a vast selection of programs, some of which are games, that users can download. In your Web browser's address box type in www.jumbo.com then press **Return**. Wait for the home page to load.

7 To see the games available click **Games 2.0** in the Download column. Type in a search term in the next window that appears, then click on the game that interests you in the results list. A screen appears with information about the game, with the option to download.

Software for free...
● **Shareware** is software that is distributed free for a limited period. When the license expires you should buy the program if you want to continue using it.
● **Freeware**, as the name suggests, is software that's distributed free of charge and can be used indefinitely. However, it often comes without any user support.
● **Demo/Sample software** is a reduced version of a commercial program. You use it to decide whether you want to buy the complete program.

File sizes
When you download a game file from the Internet you will usually be told the size of the file. A file of a couple of hundred kilobytes should take just seconds to download, but a file of several megabytes could take an hour or more. Games that contain lots of sophisticated graphics take the longest to download.

ClickPuzzle
File Size: 271 KB

Watch out

*Some games are free to download, but may still come with some restrictions. Read any licensing agreements before you play. Tick the 'I agree' box and then click on **Next** to continue with your install.*

Bright idea

Avoid deleting downloaded files after the programs have been installed. If possible, back them up onto a separate storage device, such as a floppy disk. The installation programs may be needed again at a later date.

8 Click on the download icon then click on **Save** to download the game. The Save As box appears. Select a place in which to save the file and click **Save**. It's a good idea to save it to your Desktop. Once the file has downloaded, click **Close** in the File Download window.

9 To install the file onto your hard disk, close your Internet connection and double click on the icon of the downloaded file on your Desktop. Read the Licence Agreement (see above left) and click **Start** in the Installing window. Click **OK** when the installation is 100% complete.

10 Untick 'View Readme File' and 'Run Installed Application' in the next Installing window, then click **OK**. To play your game, go to the start menu. Click on **All Programs** and select your game from the drop down menu.

Watch the clock

You may be given an estimate for how long the file will take to download. But estimates are not always accurate. You can get a better idea of downloading time by watching how quickly the clock counts down. Remember that time spent on-line costs money. Click on the **Cancel** button if you change your mind about downloading.

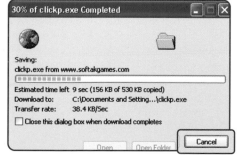

Remove a game

To delete a game from your computer, go to the Start menu and select **Control Panel**, then **Add or Remove Programs**. Click on the **Change or Remove Programs** option on the left. Highlight the program you wish to delete and click on the **Change/Remove** button.

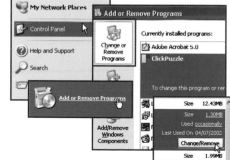

Chess is a popular game on the Web. You play against a computer or a person in real time. Because you play on-line, set a time limit on individual moves to keep costs down.

► PLAYING CHESS ON-LINE

Bright idea
Before you begin playing a game of chess, print out and study a copy of the game rules and any tips you are given for on-line chess etiquette.

Member Info

Required info

Please fill out the confidence by Ca

Browser Setup

There is that Cai in your Caissa

Java Test

The purpose of this test is to deter the Java programming language. T

Welcome A

Your account number is **#21233**. Please include this number i correspondence you submit. If you forget it, your account numbe available online in your Member Workspace.

Your free trial membership lasts for 30 days from today's that you use this time with no obligation other than to make sure service and that your Internet connection/Web browser is comp enough (we recommend using Netscape Navigator or Microsof Explorer with at least a 28.8kbps connection).

We will give you notice of the trial membership's impending co week before this date and request that you submit your yearly s you would like to subscribe at that time to pay. If you do not wish to subscribe, automatically. Also keep in mind that y

CONTINUE

Back

Address http://www.caissa.com/

CAISSA'S WEB ®

PLAY CHESS NOW! ™
Serving up over **3000 live games per day!**
ome to Caissa's Web, the World Wide Web's first full-service chess

LOG ON

NEW MEMBERS SIGNUP

SIGN ME UP!

Enter your handle:
(3-16 characters; upper/lower case letters and numbers; no spaces or special symbols)
fionag1000

Enter your password:
(3-16 characters; upper/lower case letters and numbers; your password should not be the same as your handle)
fifivert

Enter your rating:
(Elo-style rating, 1000-2500; leave blank if unknown)

Clear | Enter

11 A good site for playing chess on-line is www.caissa.com. Type this in your browser's address box and press **Return**. When the home page loads, click on **New Members Sign Up Here** – a new page appears, explaining how the site works. Click **Sign Me Up!** for a trial membership.

12 You will then need to complete a few questions. Type in a 'handle' (the name by which you want to be known when playing) and a password then click on **Enter**. Make sure you make your password easy to remember, as you will need it to log on to the site in future.

13 Fill in the Member Info window and click **Enter**. Adjust your browser setup following the instructions for Internet Explorer 5.x browsers and Click **Continue**. Then complete the Java test. Next you will be welcomed and given an account number. Click **Continue**.

Try before you buy
Some Web-based chess services are free, but others, including Caissa's site (above), are membership services for which you have to pay a fee. Free trials help you to decide whether it's worth paying for these services or not.

On-line etiquette
When playing games on-line remember that you are often playing against other people – not a computer – and so the usual rules of social etiquette apply.

For example, you should not leave your computer without a mutual agreement to stop playing. One of the Caissa site's particular rules is that you should never prolong a game that you are clearly going to lose.

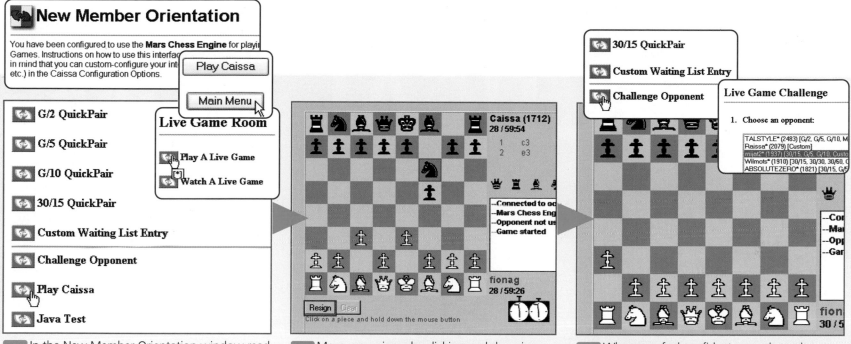

New Member Orientation

You have been configured to use the **Mars Chess Engine** for playing Games. Instructions on how to use this interface in mind that you can custom-configure your interface etc.) in the Caissa Configuration Options.

Play Caissa

Main Menu

Live Game Room

Play A Live Game

[*] Watch A Live Game

G/2 QuickPair

G/5 QuickPair

G/10 QuickPair

30/15 QuickPair

Custom Waiting List Entry

Challenge Opponent

Play Caissa

Java Test

Caissa (1712)
28 / 59:54

1   c3
2   e3

--Connected to oc
--Mars Chess Eng
--Opponent not us
--Game started

fionag
28 / 59:26

Resign Clear
Click on a piece and hold down the mouse button

30/15 QuickPair

Custom Waiting List Entry

Challenge Opponent

Live Game Challenge

1. Choose an opponent:

TALSTYLE* (2483) [G/2, G/5, G/10, M
Raissa* (2079) [Custom]
mijat2* (1937) [30/15, G/5, G/10, Custo
Wilmots* (1910) [30/15, 30/30, 30/60, C
ABSOLUTEZERO* (1821) [30/15, G/5

--Col
--Ma
--Op
--Gar

fion
30 / 5

14 In the New Member Orientation window read the Web site's rules, then click **Main Menu**. To play, click the **Live Game Room** button, then the **Play A Live Game** button. To play against the computer for practice, click on **Play Caissa**.

15 Move your pieces by clicking and dragging them. After every one of your moves you will see Caissa make a move. If you are clearly beaten, click on the **Resign** button at the bottom of the screen.

16 When you feel confident enough to play a person, go to the Live Game Room (click on your browser's **Back** button), and click on the **Challenge Opponent** button. Select a player and begin your game.

Added insight

If you prefer to learn how the system works before you play a game, watch one first. Click on the **Watch A Live Game** button, which you can find on the Web site's Live Game Room page (see above).

Live Game Room

Watch A Live Game

40 Active Games, **0** Tournament Games, **2** Games On Hold

White	Rating	Black	Rating	Speed
Slacker	1600/0	Caissa	1699	30/60
RandyH	1200/0	LawAndOrder	1740	30/15
FYA	1519	NH90	1600	G/2
Drozd2	1252	tengns1	1402	30/30

PRACTICAL HOME

This section will guide you, **step by step**, through **40 practical projects** over a range of subjects. Each task is self-contained – you require **no prior experience** of the program used. Suggestions are also made of ways you can bring the projects together to undertake more **ambitious events**, such as organising a reunion.

PROJECTS

Design a letterhead

Create your personal stationery with an individual look

A personalised letterhead will add a touch of flair and individuality to all your correspondence. Once you have mastered the skills involved in creating a letterhead, you can follow the same principles to design letterheads for different occasions – one for business stationery, perhaps.

When you have created your letterhead, save it as a template that you can use again and again, whenever you write a letter. And if your details change – for example, if you move house or acquire an e-mail address or mobile phone number – you can easily alter them on your template

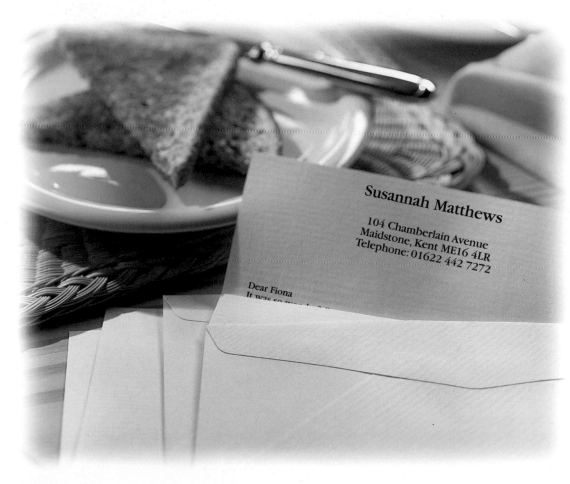

Susannah Matthews

104 Chamberlain Avenue
Maidstone, Kent ME16 4LR
Telephone: 01622 442 7272

Dear Fiona
It was so

Decide what you are going to use your letterhead for. If it is for letters to family and friends, you can be creative with your choice of fonts.

BEFORE YOU START

Document1 - Microsoft Word

| File | Edit | View | Insert | Format | Tools | Table | Window | Help |

New...   Ctrl+N
Open...   Ctrl+O
Close
Save   Ctrl+S
Save As...
Save as Web Page...
Search...
Versions...
Web Page Preview
Page Setup...
Print Preview
Print...   Ctrl+P

1 Go to the **Start** menu, click on **All Programs** and select **Microsoft Word**. A new document automatically opens. Go to the **File** menu and click on **Page Setup**.

*To create a letterhead in Microsoft Works, open Microsoft Works then click on the **Programs** tab. Choose **Works Word Processor** then **Start a blank Word Processor document**.*

OTHER PROGRAMS

 **Templates on CD-ROM**

Bright idea
If you have an e-mail address, remember to include it in your letterhead.

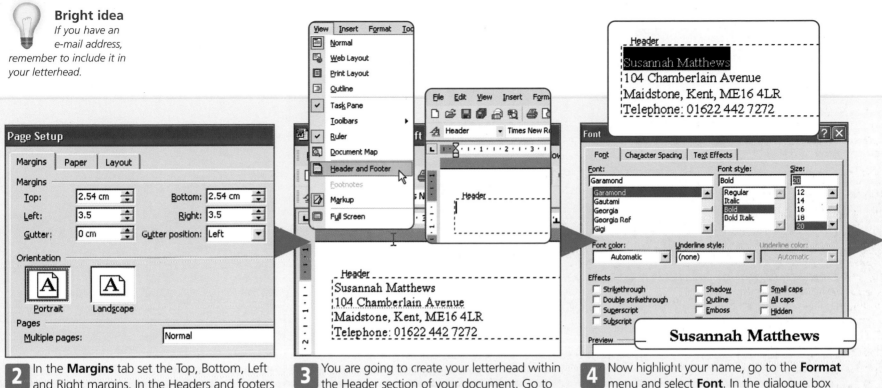

2 In the **Margins** tab set the Top, Bottom, Left and Right margins. In the Headers and footers section of the **Layout** tab, set the 'From edge' distances between the header and the top of the page, and the footer and the bottom of the page. Equal distances look neatest.

3 You are going to create your letterhead within the Header section of your document. Go to the **View** menu and click on **Header and Footer**. The cursor automatically appears in the Header section. Type in your name, address, postcode and telephone number.

4 Now highlight your name, go to the **Format** menu and select **Font**. In the dialogue box select a font, style and size, clicking on any to view them in the Preview window. Make your selection and click **OK**. Style your address in the same way.

Key word
Header and Footer These terms describe the information that appears at the top (header) and bottom (footer) of each page of a document – for example, running titles, reference details and page numbers.

Let the Wizard help

Microsoft Works has a useful device, called a Wizard, that can help you create personalised letterheads. Open Microsoft Works, and in the **Programs** tab click on **Works Word Processor**. Choose **Letters** and click on **Start this task** to launch the Letter Wizard. Click on **Create a Letterhead** then fill in the required details as you follow the on-screen steps.

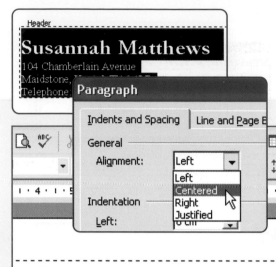

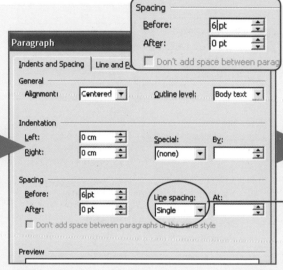

5 To position your letterhead in the centre of the page, highlight all the text in your Header section, go to the **Format** menu and click on **Paragraph**. Select the **Indents and Spacing** tab. Scroll through the Alignment options and click on **Centered**. Click on **OK**.

6 To adjust spacing above or below some text, highlight the relevant lines, go to the **Format** menu and click on **Paragraph**. Select the **Indents and Spacing** tab. Below Spacing click on the arrows beside Before or After to increase or decrease the spacing.

7 When you are happy with your design, save it as a template that you can use again and again. Go to the **File** menu and select **Save As**. Click in the 'Save as type' box at the bottom of the dialogue box and select the **Document Template** option from the drop-down list.

Use your toolbar

The toolbar buttons at the top of the screen help you style your text quickly. Highlight the text. Click on the relevant button to make it bold, to italicise it or to underline it. Change your text's position, too, by clicking on the left, centre or right alignment buttons.

*To adjust spacing between lines, highlight the relevant text, go to the **Format** menu and click on **Paragraph**. In the **Indents and Spacing** tab click on the arrow beside the 'Line spacing' box then click on a suitable measurement. Click **OK**.*

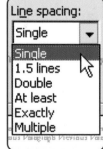

Works template

To save your letterhead as a template in Microsoft Works, go to the **File** menu and select **Save As**. In the dialogue box click on the **Template** button in the bottom right-hand corner. In the Save As Template dialogue box type in a name for your template then click **OK**.

Bright idea
*Save yourself time by using automatic dating for your letters. Click where you want the date to appear in your document, go to the **Insert** menu and click on **Date and Time**. In the dialogue box click on your preferred style then click on **OK**.*

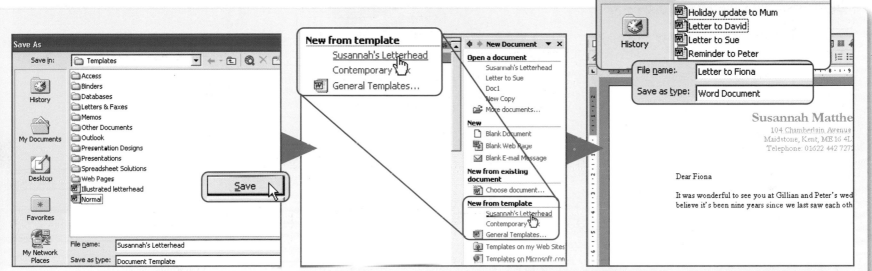

8 Word will automatically suggest saving your document in its Templates folder in the 'Save in' box. Save it here or choose your own location. Then type in a suitable name for your template in the 'File name' box. Now click on **Save**.

9 Whenever you want to use your template go to the **File** menu and click on **New**. A column appears on the right-hand side of the screen. Your new template will appear under the 'New from template' section. Click on the template title to open a new document.

10 When the template opens go to the **File** menu and click on **Save As**. Select a folder in which to save your letter, type in a name for it, then click on **Save**. The cursor will flash below your letterhead. Use the **Return** key to create a few blank lines before you start typing.

Changing your template
In Word, go to the **File** menu and select **Open**. From the 'Files of type' box select **Document Templates**. Double-click on your template in the Templates folder, make any changes to it then save it.

In Works, choose **Works Word Processor** in the Task Launcher. Click on your letterhead in the list of templates, select **Start this task**, make your changes, go to the **File** menu and select **Save As**. Double-click on the old file in the Templates folder to replace it with the new one. Click on **Yes** in the Dialogue box to confirm your choice.

Why not spruce up your letterhead with a graphic from the gallery that comes free with Word and Works? See page 186 to find out how.

▶ **OTHER IDEAS TO TRY**

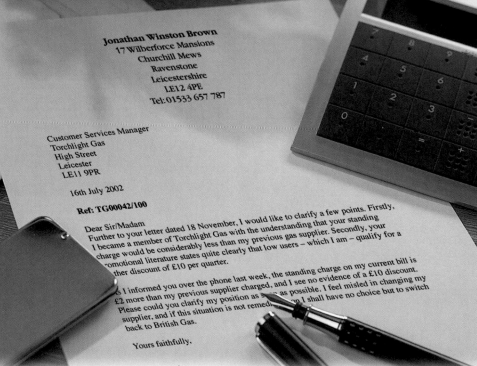

Assemble all relevant documents and make a quick note of the points you wish to make. Check that you are writing to the appropriate person to deal with your letter.

BEFORE YOU START

Save As

Save in:	Formal Letters

- Electricity Connection
- Mortgage Enquiry
- Planning Application

History

My Documents

Desktop

Favorites

My Network Places

Save

Cancel

File name: Torchlight Gas

Save as type: Word Document

1 Go to the **Start** menu, highlight **All Programs** and click on **Microsoft Word**. Save your new document by going to the **File** menu and selecting **Save As**. Select or create a suitable folder in the 'Save in' box, type in a file name then click on **Save**.

Send a formal letter

Give your business correspondence a professional look

Writing a formal letter can seem a daunting task, but with a personal computer it couldn't be more straightforward. On all your correspondence make sure you include your name, address and the date on which you are writing. For formal letters it is also usual to include the name, company position and address of the person you are writing to.

It's also a good idea to include an official reference. If you are writing to your bank, for example, this could be your account number. When replying to a letter, take a look at it to see if a reference is included, and repeat that.

You can also create a letterhead in Microsoft Works. Open Works then, in the Works Task Launcher, click on the **Programs** tab then on the **Works Word Processor** button.

OTHER PROGRAMS

*To see exactly how many line spaces you have used, click on the **Show/Hide** button on the toolbar.*

Watch out
You are in danger of losing your work if you do not save it frequently. Make a habit of saving your letter every few minutes.

Torchlight Gas - Microsoft Word

File   Edit   View   Insert   Format   Tools   Table   Window   Help

Normal + 11 pt   Times New Roman   11   B   I   U

Jonathan·Winston·Brown¶
17·Wilberforce·Mansions¶
Churchill·Mews¶
Ravenstone¶
Leicestershire¶
LE12·4PE¶
Tel:01533·657·787¶
¶
Customer·Services·Manager¶
Torchlight·Gas¶
High·Street¶
Leicester¶
LE11·9PR¶
¶
16·July·2002¶

2 Type in your name, address and, if you like, telephone number. Leaving a line space between each section (press the **Return** key), type in the title and address of the person you are writing to, the date and, if relevant, a reference or account number.

---

16 July 2002

Ref: TG0042/101

Dear Sir/Madam
Further to your letter dated 18 November I would like to cla... became a member of Torchlight Gas with the understanding be considerably less than my previous gas supplier. Secondl... tates quite clearly that low users – which I am – qualify for quarter.

As I informed you over the phone last week, the standing ch... than the previous supplier charged, and I see no evidence of... clarify my position as soon as possible. I feel misled in chan... is not remedied soon I shall have no choice but to switch ba...

Yours faithfully,

3 Leave one more line space then begin your letter. It is customary, if you do not know the name of the recipient, to address your letter to 'Sir/Madam' and sign it off at the end with 'Yours faithfully'. If you do know the name of the recipient, sign off with 'Yours sincerely'.

Jonathan Winston Brown
17 Wilberforce Mansions
Churchill Mews
Ravenstone
Leicestershire
LE12 4PE
Tel:01533 657 787

4 To position your own details in the centre of the page, highlight your name, address and telephone number then click on the **Center** button on the toolbar.

Smart Tags

Smart tags appear in Word documents as small icons around text. To find out what a smart tag can do, hover your cursor over it and click on the arrow that appears. This displays a number of options in a drop-down menu

Purple dotted lines beneath a name or address indicate a smart tag. Hover your cursor over it and a small 'i' icon appears. From the drop down menu you can

choose to send that person an e-mail or add their contact details to your Outlook address book. The appropriate window from the program that performs that function automatically opens for you.

In Word you may also see the AutoCorrect Options button and the Paste Options button (see right). These both have actions you can choose without clicking a button on the toolbar or opening a dialogue box.

Jonathan Winston

Person: Jonathan Winston Brown
Send Mail
Schedule a Meeting
Open Contact
Add to Contacts
Insert Address
Remove this Smart Tag

○ Keep Source Formatting
○ Match Destination Formatting
○ Keep Text Only
Apply Style or Formatting...

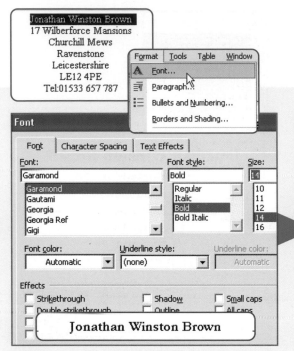

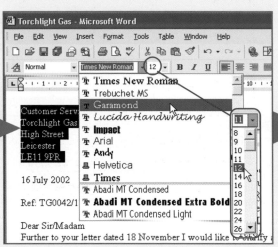

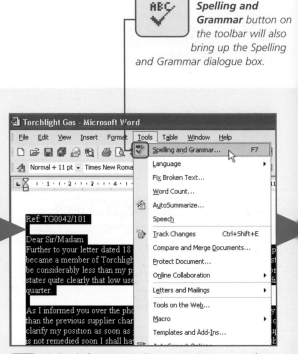

*Clicking on the **Spelling and Grammar** button on the toolbar will also bring up the Spelling and Grammar dialogue box.*

5 To style your letter first highlight your name at the top, go to the **Format** menu and select **Font**. In the dialogue box select a font, style and size, clicking on any that interest you to view them in the Preview window. Make your selection then click **OK**.

6 Continue to style the remainder of your text as you did in the previous step, highlighting individual sections as you go. For speed you can use the font and font size shortcuts on the toolbar as shown.

7 To check for any spelling mistakes, go to the **Tools** menu and select **Spelling and Grammar**. If you only want to check a section of the document, highlight the relevant text before going to the menu.

Select a font

If you know the name of the font you want to use, type its first letter in the Font box. All the fonts beginning with that letter will automatically appear at the top of the font window. This saves you scrolling through all your fonts.

Change the scale

If you want to magnify your document to see it in more detail, without adjusting the size of the type, you can change its scale by clicking on the arrow beside the Zoom toolbar function and selecting one of the options. If you can't see the Zoom function, you may need to maximise your window.

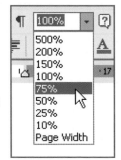

Bright idea
Before posting your letter read it through to check for errors then give it to a friend to proofread. Ask if it is clear and makes sense.

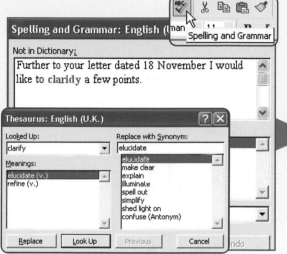

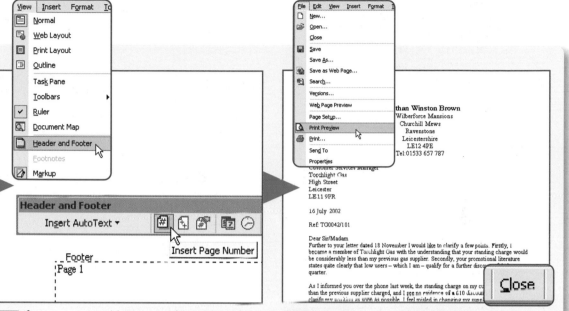

8 If Word questions a spelling, click **Ignore** or **Change** depending on whether the word is misspelled. If you can't think of the exact word you're looking for, use the Thesaurus. Go to the **Tools** menu, highlight **Language** and click on **Thesaurus** to find words with similar meanings.

9 If you want to add page numbers, go to the **View** menu and select **Header and Footer**. Click in the Footer section then click on the **Insert Page Number** button on the Header and Footer toolbar. If you wish, you can add 'Page' before the number and format the text.

10 To see how your letter will look, go to the **File** menu and select **Print Preview**. To revert back to your previous screen click on the **Close** toolbar button. When you are happy with how your letter looks, go to the **File** menu, select **Save** then **Print**. Click **OK**.

Make your point

If you are making a number of important points in your letter and wish to emphasise them, type each of them on a new line and go to **Format**, then **Paragraph** to put a line space between each one. Highlight the whole section then click on the **Bullets** toolbar button.

- I did not become a member of y therefore do not owe the full yea

- I was recommended to the club t reduced rate

- I joined with my wife, which me subscription

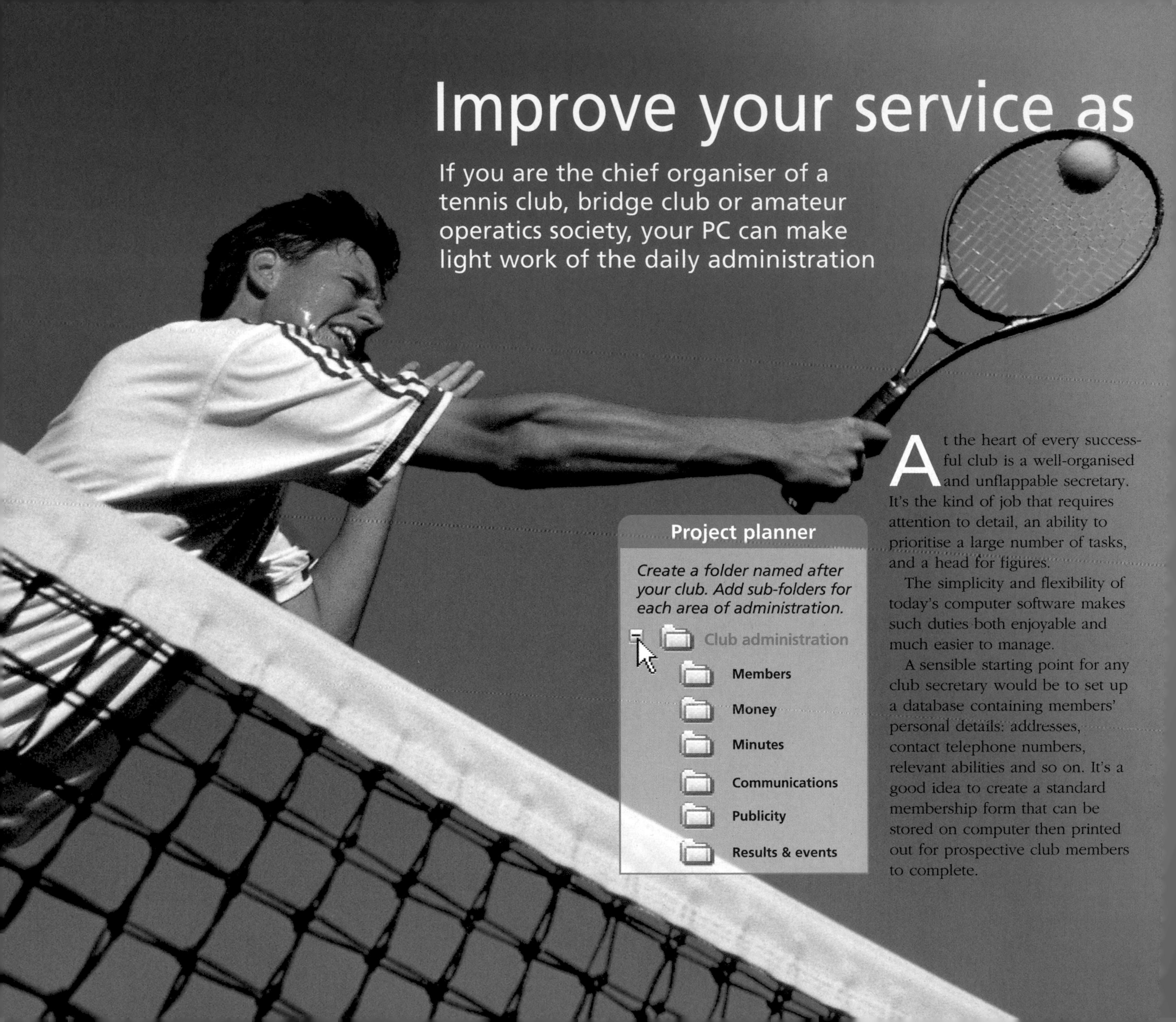

Improve your service as

If you are the chief organiser of a tennis club, bridge club or amateur operatics society, your PC can make light work of the daily administration

Project planner

Create a folder named after your club. Add sub-folders for each area of administration.

- Club administration
  - Members
  - Money
  - Minutes
  - Communications
  - Publicity
  - Results & events

At the heart of every success-ful club is a well-organised and unflappable secretary. It's the kind of job that requires attention to detail, an ability to prioritise a large number of tasks, and a head for figures.

The simplicity and flexibility of today's computer software makes such duties both enjoyable and much easier to manage.

A sensible starting point for any club secretary would be to set up a database containing members' personal details: addresses, contact telephone numbers, relevant abilities and so on. It's a good idea to create a standard membership form that can be stored on computer then printed out for prospective club members to complete.

a club secretary

Once you have a database set up, it's a simple task to produce address labels for club correspondence.

Using a second database, the secretary of a sports club can produce tables to show fixtures, results and club rankings.

Keeping club accounts and tracking membership fees are simple tasks once you set up a spreadsheet. You can use it for recruitment-based fiscal planning.

For communications with other organisations, create your own club stationery. You could design a club logo using Paint or another graphics program. The logo could then be used on club newsletters or, with the help of an outside supplier, on merchandise such as club ties and keyrings.

Consider compiling a pictorial club history on your computer. Somebody might like to write a short account that you could publish for members' interest.

And don't forget that many members will be on-line. If you compile an e-mail address book, you can send information on rankings, fixtures and social events to everyone at once. You could even post them on a club Web site which, of course, you could design and compile yourself.

With the introduction of on-line banking, monitoring your club accounts could not be simpler, And, provided there is the right software compatibility, you can download information straight from your bank to your spreadsheets and pay bills on-line.

Start the ball rolling

- Compile and collect all membership details and transfer them to your database
- Transfer a copy of the club's accounts to a spreadsheet on your computer
- Set up an on-line bank account
- Produce a club logo for all communications
- Arrange for all league or club information to be sent via e-mail to on-line members

Ideas and inspirations

Customise the following projects and ideas to suit the needs of your club. That way, you'll spend less time on administration, and far more time enjoying the club's benefits. Once you've set up the basic documents you need, maintaining them should be a quick and easy matter.

166 Membership database
Compile a handy reference document to keep a record of all your members' details.

272 Club accounts
Keep track of income and outgoings, and budget for projects, such as buying new equipment.

194 Illustrate your stationery
Liven up your correspondence with stationery that raises the profile of your club.

190 Design a greetings card
Send your members (or prospective members) cards for Christmas or to publicise a club event.

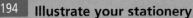

222 Painting on your PC
Design your own logo or artwork for stationery, club posters or Internet use.

Also worth considering...

With the paperwork now kept to a minimum, you might want to branch out onto the Internet.

114 Design a Web page
Refer existing and prospective members to your site and you'll save time fielding phone queries.

Write an eye-catching CV

Make the most of your experience and achievements

Your CV, or curriculum vitae, is intended to make a favourable impression on potential employers. As well as giving details of all the companies you have worked for and how long you were employed by them, explain what your responsibilities were and what skills you have developed.

Keep your CV brief and to the point. If possible, try to fit it on a single page. Select a clear, easy-to-read font and don't be tempted to make the font size too small in an effort to squeeze everything in. Also, keep your CV's design simple, with well-defined sections that make it easy to extract information.

To make sure all your dates of employment are correct, collect your old P45 forms and refer to them as you type in your details.

BEFORE YOU START

Personal Details
Simon Buckhurst
14 Carleton Street,
Tel: 020 8697 8766

Curriculum Vitae

Personal Details
Simon Buckhurst
14 Carleton Street, London N7 0ER
Tel: 020 8697 8766. Fax: 020 8697 8566

Employment
April 1994 - presen
Following promotio
administration resp
turnover and profit

1 Go to the **Start** menu, highlight **All Programs** and click on **Microsoft Word**. When your document opens type in your details, starting with 'Curriculum Vitae'. Press the **Return** key to put line spaces between the different sections.

*You can also create your CV in Microsoft Works. Open Works then, in the Works Task Launcher, click on the **Programs** tab then on the **Works Word Processor** button.*

OTHER PROGRAMS

Templates on CD-ROM

Watch out
*You may lose your work if you don't save it. Either go to the **File** menu and select **Save**, or press the **Ctrl** key and, keeping the Ctrl key pressed own, press the 'S' key, too.*

*Remember to use the function keys on your keyboard for frequently used commands. Press **F7** to bring up the Spelling and Grammar dialogue box.*

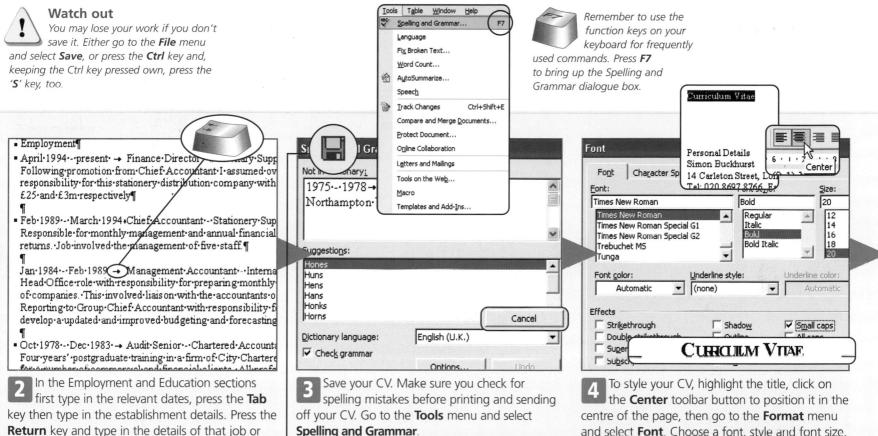

Tools **Table** **Window** **Help**

Spelling and Grammar... F7
Language
Fix Broken Text...
Word Count...
AutoSummarize...
Speech
Track Changes   Ctrl+Shift+E
Compare and Merge Documents...
Protect Document...
Online Collaboration
Letters and Mailings
Tools on the Web...
Macro
Templates and Add-Ins...

- Employment¶
- April·1994··present → Finance·Director ..ary·Supp
Following·promotion·from·Chief·Accountant·I·assumed·ov
responsibility·for·this·stationery·distribution·company·with
£25·and·£3m·respectively¶
¶
- Feb·1989··March·1994·Chief·Accountant··Stationery·Sup
Responsible·for·monthly·management·and·annual·financial
returns.·Job·involved·the·management·of·five·staff.¶
¶
Jan·1984··Feb·1989 → Management·Accountant··Interna
Head·Office·role·with·responsibility·for·preparing·monthly
of·companies.·This·involved·liaison·with·the·accountants·o
Reporting·to·Group·Chief·Accountant·with·responsibility·f
develop·a·updated·and·improved·budgeting·and·forecasting
- Oct·1978··Dec·1983 → Audit·Senior··Chartered·Accounta
Four·years'·postgraduate·training·in·a·firm·of·City·Chartere

Spelling and Grammar

Not in Dictionary:
1975··1978→
Northampton·

Suggestions:
Hones
Huns
Hens
Hans
Honks
Horns

Cancel

Dictionary language: English (U.K.)
☑ Check grammar

Options...   Undo

Font

Curriculum Vitae

Personal Details
Simon Buckhurst
14 Carleton Street, Loff
Tel: 020 8697 8766, F

Center

Font | Character Sp

Font:
Times New Roman
Times New Roman
Times New Roman Special G1
Times New Roman Special G2
Trebuchet MS
Tunga

Bold
Regular
Italic
Buld
Bold Italic

Size:
20
12
14
16
18
20

Font color: Automatic
Underline style: (none)
Underline color: Automatic

Effects
☐ Strikethrough   ☐ Shadow   ☑ Small caps
☐ Double strikethrough ☐ Outline   ☐ All caps
☐ Super
☐ Subscr

CURRICULM VITAE

2 In the Employment and Education sections first type in the relevant dates, press the **Tab** key then type in the establishment details. Press the **Return** key and type in the details of that job or course on a new line.

3 Save your CV. Make sure you check for spelling mistakes before printing and sending off your CV. Go to the **Tools** menu and select **Spelling and Grammar**.

4 To style your CV, highlight the title, click on the **Center** toolbar button to position it in the centre of the page, then go to the **Format** menu and select **Font**. Choose a font, style and font size, clicking on any to view them in the Preview window. Click **OK**.

Bright idea
Type in your details under the following headings: 'Personal Details', 'Employment', 'Education', 'Computer Skills' and 'Hobbies and Interests'. List jobs and qualifications in chronological order, beginning with the most recent.

*Clicking on the **Save** toolbar button will bring up the Save As dialogue box. When you have located a suitable place in which to save your CV, type in a file name then click on **Save**.*

Save As

Save in: ☐ Correspondence

☐ Administration
☐ Business Letters
☐ Household business
☐ Personal letters

History

My Documents

File name: Curriculum Vitae
Save as type: Word Document

Let the Wizard help
Microsoft Works has a Wizard that can help you create a CV. Open Microsoft Works. In the Task Launcher, click on **Programs** at the top, then **Works Word Processor** in the left-hand column and choose **Resume (CV)** from the list of tasks. Click on **Start this task** and follow the on-screen instructions.

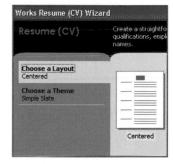

Works Resume (CV) Wizard

Resume (CV)   Create a straightfor
                  qualifications, emplo
                  names.

Choose a Layout
Centered

Choose a Theme
Simple Slate

Centered

Bright idea
*Be prepared! Update your CV on
a regular basis, remembering to
add details of any training courses, new
interests and areas of responsibility.*

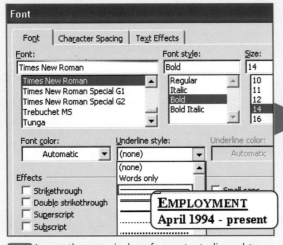

5 Leave the remainder of your text aligned to
the left of the page but choose fonts and font
sizes for it in the same way as before. Emphasise
section headings by selecting a bold font, putting
them in small capital letters and underlining them.

6 For each job and educational establishment,
make the font size of the first line slightly
larger than the subsequent lines, and choose a
bold font style or a bolder font.

7 Highlight these lines in turn, go to the
Format menu and select **Tabs**. In the Tabs
dialogue box type in 5 cm as the Tab stop position.
Click **OK**. The second half of these lines will now
appear neatly above each other. If necessary, adjust
the spacing to suit your text.

Use your toolbar
For speed, use the Underline
button on your toolbar to put
a line beneath text. Simply
highlight the relevant text
then click on the button.

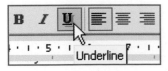

Bright idea
*When you write your accompanying letter of
application, use the same fonts as in your CV.
Not only will your letter and CV complement each other,
but they will also have a professional appearance. A
potential employer may well form the impression that
you pay attention to detail.*

Short cut
To close the Print Preview window and revert back to the previous screen, press the **Esc** key on your keyboard.

Print your CV for the first time on normal paper. If you are happy with how it looks, use better-quality paper for the finished result.

FINISHING TOUCH

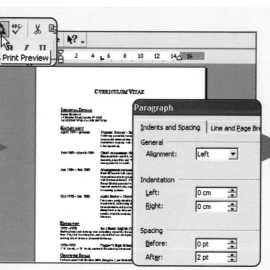

8 Now highlight the lines that describe what each job entailed, go to the **Format** menu and select **Paragraph**. In the Indents and Spacing tab, beside Left in the Indentation section, type in the same measurement you used to set the first tab stop in Step 7. Click **OK**.

9 To see how your CV looks, click on the **Print Preview** button. To increase space below headings, press **Esc** to go back into editing mode. Highlight a heading, go to the **Format** menu and select **Paragraph**. In the Spacing section click on the uppermost arrow to the right of After.

10 To adjust line spacing, highlight the lines in question, go to the **Format** menu and select **Paragraph**. In the Line spacing section scroll through the options available. When you are happy with your CV, go to the **File** menu and select **Save** then **Print**.

Add page numbers

To add page numbers, go to the **View** menu and select **Header and Footer**. Scroll to the bottom of the page and click in the Footer section. In Word, go to the Header and Footer toolbar, click on **Insert AutoText**, then on **PAGE**.

In Microsoft Works, go to the **Insert** menu and select **Page Numbers**. If you wish, you can add 'Page' before the number and format the text in either program.

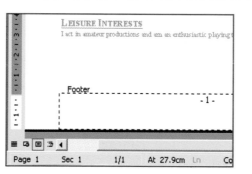

Page Setup

Margins	Paper	Layout

Margins

Top: 2.5   Bottom: 2.5
Left: 2.5   Right: 2.5
Gutter: 0 cm   Gutter position: Left

Orientation

Portrait   Landscape

Pages

Multiple pages: Normal

1 To make menus, go to the **Start** menu, select **All Programs** then **Microsoft Word**. Go to the **File** menu and click on **Page Setup**. Set the margins to 2.5 cm and change the orientation to landscape then click **OK**. Create two columns (see above right).

Design a dinner party menu and place cards

Impress your guests with specially designed table decorations

Great food and good company are the key ingredients of a dinner party, but to make the evening really special, you need to pay attention to detail. One way to set just the right tone for your party is by designing and printing your own menus and place cards. Whether the mood is formal, fun, festive or themed, you will be able to find fitting fonts, colours and Clip Art graphics on your computer.

Templates on CD-ROM

To set columns, go to the **Format** menu and select **Columns**. Select **Two** in the Presets section, then click **OK**.

If you can't see your 'Return' symbols click on the **Show/Hide** toolbar button. (In Microsoft Works go to the **View** menu and click on **All Characters**.)

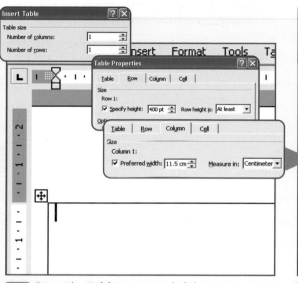

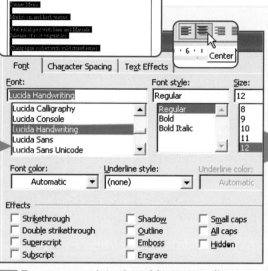

2 Go to the **Table** menu and click on **Insert**, then **Table**. Set the rows and columns to 1. Click **OK**. Return to the **Table** menu and select **Table Properties**. Click the **Row** tab and set the height to '400pt' 'At Least'. Click the **Column** tab and set the width to 11.5cm. Click **OK**.

3 Type your text into the table. Leave a line space between courses by pressing the **Return** key twice. Highlight the text and click on the **Center** toolbar button. Go to the **Format** menu and click on **Font**. Choose a font, style and size for your text then click **OK**.

4 To adjust the spacing between courses, highlight the first 'Return' symbol, go to the **Format** menu and click on **Paragraph**. In the 'Spacing section' click on the arrows to the right of the Before and After boxes until you are happy with the result. Repeat for all blank lines.

Checking your spelling

Any words that your computer doesn't recognise will appear on the screen with a wavy red line underneath. To check the spelling of these words go to the **Tools** menu and select **Spelling and Grammar**. But just because a computer doesn't recognise a word, it doesn't mean it doesn't exist. It's best to double-check in a dictionary.

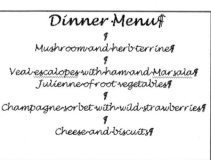

Let the Wizard help

Microsoft Works includes templates for several types of menu, with a variety of eye-catching styles to choose from.

To use a template, open the Works Task Launcher, click on **Programs** then on **Works Word Processor**. Choose **Menus** from the list of tasks and click on **Start this task** to launch the Menu task wizard. Choose your design and follow the on-screen instructions.

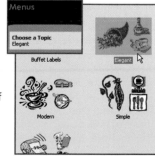

For uniformity, design your place cards using the same Clip Art and fonts that you used in the menu.

DESIGNING PLACE CARDS

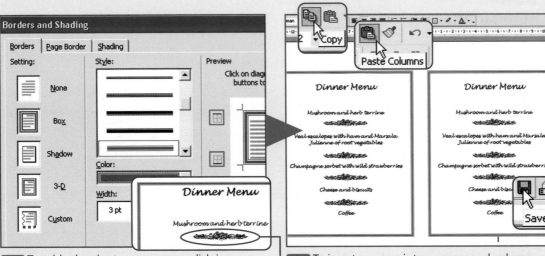

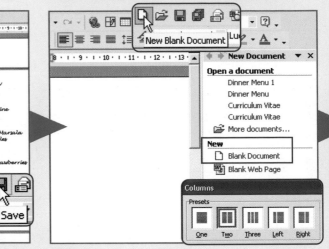

5 To add a border to your menu, click in your table, then go to the **Table** menu, choose **Select**, then **Table**. This highlights the table. Go to the **Format** menu and click on **Borders and Shading**. Under the Borders tab select a setting, style, colour and width. Click **OK**.

6 To insert a menu into your second column, press the **Ctrl** key and the letter '**A**' together to select the table. Click on the **Copy** toolbar button. Click below the table and press **Return**. Click on the **Paste** toolbar button. Click on the **Save** toolbar button, name and save your file.

7 Either go to the **File** menu and click on **New** in the scroll down menu, or click the **New Blank Document** toolbar button. Then go to the **Format** menu and select **Columns**. Select Two in the Presets section, then click **OK**. Save and name your new file.

Adding Clip Art

Use Clip Art to enliven your menu. Click in the document, go to the **Insert** menu and select **Picture**, then **Clip Art**. The 'Clip Organizer' column appears on the right of the screen. Find an image by typing in a search term then click **Search**. The results will be displayed in the column. Hover the cursor over your selected image and click the bar that then appears at the side. Select **Insert** from the pop-up menu. The image will then appear in your document. To learn how to size and position the Clip Art, see page 187.

Now copy and paste the Clip Art between each course using the **Copy** and **Paste** toolbar buttons.

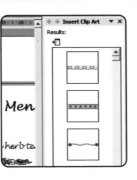

When you set the width of your columns, the spacing between the columns adjusts automatically.

Add a Clip Art image as before. See Step 5.

Close up
*Your place cards may not all fit on a single sheet of A4. To add another page to your document press the **Return** key at the end of the first page – a second page appears automatically.*

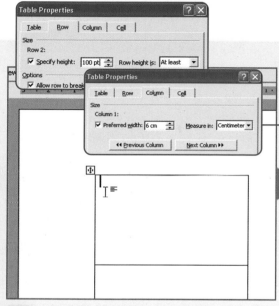

Nicholas Vincent¤

Melanie Swift¤

2 Copy

Paste by Appending Table

Rudr Wilson¤

Helen Maslin¤

Nicholas Vincent¤

8 In the **Table** menu click on **Insert**, then **Table**. Set columns to 1 and rows to 2. Click **OK**. Return to the **Table** menu and select **Table Properties**. Click the **Row** tab and set the height to '100 pt' 'At Least'. Click the **Next Row** button and repeat the value. Click the **Column** tab and set the width to 6 cm. Click **OK.**

9 Click in the lower of the two cells (the top will be the back once the card is folded). Press the **Return** key twice then type in a guest name. Highlight it, go to the **Format** menu and click on **Font**. Select a font, size and style. Click **OK**. Click on the **Center** toolbar button.

10 To duplicate your card, select the table and click on the **Copy** button. Click below the table and press **Return** twice. Click on the **Paste** toolbar button. Replace the first guest's name by highlighting it and typing in the next guest's. Repeat for other cards.

Bright idea
It's worth buying a small guillotine to cut your place cards after you have printed them out. Cutting with a guillotine rather than scissors will ensure the edges of your cards are neat and precise.

To help you organise the menu for your dinner party, why not set up a database of recipes? Turn to page 282 to find out more.

OTHER IDEAS TO TRY

Create a family newsletter

Keep in touch with distant friends and relatives

A regular newsletter is a great way to keep family members in touch with each other. The first step is to ask your relatives whether they would like to contribute any news, such as a new job or a recently passed exam. They may even like to send in favourite recipes or poems they have written.

Impose a deadline and suggest they send anything to you on a floppy disk or, even better, via e-mail to save you typing in their text.

Once the contributions have arrived write your own stories to incorporate them. Finally, decide what you are going to call the family newsletter. It's tempting to use your surname in the heading, but remember that not all family members share the same name.

Prioritise your contributions. If there isn't enough space for all your news in the current edition of the newsletter, save some for the next.

BEFORE YOU START

Page Setup

| Margins | Paper | Layout |

Margins

Top: 2 cm   Bottom: 2 cm

Left: 2 cm   Right: 2 cm

Gutter: 0 cm   Gutter position: Left

Orientation

Portrait   Landscape

Pages

Multiple pages: Normal

1 Go to the **Start** menu, select **All Programs** and click on **Word**. Go to the **File** menu and click on **Page Setup**. With the Margins tab selected, set the sizes for the Top, Bottom, Left and Right margins. Click **OK**.

*You can also create a newsletter using Microsoft Works. Open Works then, in the Works Task Launcher, click on the **Programs** tab then on the **Works Word Processor** button.*

OTHER PROGRAMS

Templates on CD-ROM

Family News

Top marks!

Congratulations to Anna Taylor, Jim and Jo's eldest daughter, for passing her degree in Spanish. She really deserved the 2.1 she got.

We went to her graduation in July at Birmingham Cathedral and I have to admit that I nearly burst with pride when she shook hands and received her degree from the Chancellor of her university.

Anna is planning to travel and work in Spain for a year, starting in Barcelona and travelling to the south coast in time for the summer's tourist season.

All the family will really miss Anna but I'm sure you'll join us in wishing her good luck and 'bon voyage!'

Making a splash

Our son, Paul Taylor, has been indulging in his favourite watery pastime - swimming.

This time it's in a good cause because his school is collecting money for the charity Children in Need, so Paul asked friends and neighbours to dig deep into their pockets and sponsor his watery antics.

His father, Jim, and I went along to watch his efforts along with plenty of other weary but devoted parents and were pleased that he swam so well.

Children in need will be pleased too when they receive the school's cheque for £297 to help their charity work, including Paul's contribution of £31.80. A valiant effort.

It's a girl

Sally Stafford gave birth to Sarah Jane on 4th July. Congratulations! Mother and baby are doing well and the family hopes to come to England early next year. Better put the kettle on...

Fun in the sun

After all their efforts, Jim and I felt that the kids deserved a holiday. So we had a fortnight in Majorca....

The neighbours kindly took Barney and he was quite happy to go as they feed him chocolate. We packed our bags (so much luggage!) and headed for the sun.

The children chose a hotel near the beach with a pool for Paul and his friend Sam and plenty of Spanish waiters for Anna and her friend Sue to practise their Spanish with.

Now that the kids are older, we didn't mind leaving them at the hotel while we went exploring the island in a jeep. It really is quite beautiful but the hair-raising mountain roads took some negotiating!

We all returned, bronzed, relaxed and ready to argue about next year's break.

Celebration!

Margaret Taylor will be celebrating her 100th birthday in December. To celebrate this wonderful event we are holding a surprise party at her home in Sussex. Hope to see you there on the 8th!

For even more precise picture wrapping options click on the **Advanced** *button in the Layout tab. You can set the distance between the picture and text.*

Family·News¶
Top·marks!¶
Congratulations·to·Anna·Taylor,·Jim·and·Jo's·eld
in·Spanish.·She·really·deserved·the·2.1·she·got.¶
We·went·to·her·graduation·in·July·at·Birmingham
nearly·burst·with·pride·when·she·shook·hands·and·receiver·her·degr
Chancellor·of·her·university.¶
Anna·is·planning·to·travel·and·work·in·Spain·for·a·year,·starting·in·I
travelling·to·the·south·coast·in·time·for·the·summer's·tourist·season.
will·really·miss·Anna·but·I'm·sure·you'll·join·us·in·wishing·her·goo
voyage!'¶
¶
Making·a·splash¶
Our·son,·Paul·Taylor,·has·been·indulging·in·his·favourite·watery·pas
This·time·it's·in·a·good·cause·because·his·school·is·collecting·mone
Children·in·Need,·so·Paul·asked·Friends·and·neighbours·to·dig·deep
and·sponsor·his·watery·antics¶
His·father,·Jim,·and·I·went·along·to·watch·his·efforts·along·with·ple
but·devoted·parents·and·were·pleased·that·he·swam·so·well.¶
Children·in·need·will·be·pleased·too·when·they·receive·the·school's

2 Type in your heading then press the **Return** key. Type in your articles, giving each its own title and leaving a line space between them (press the **Return** key).

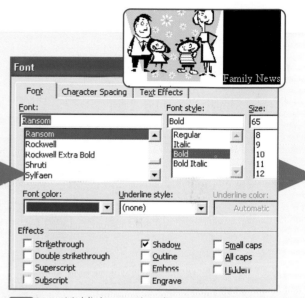

Top marks!
Congratulations to Anna Taylor, Jim and Jo's eldest daughter, for passing h
in Spanish. She really deserved the 2.1 she got.
We went to her graduation in July at Birmingham Cathedral and I have to a
nearly burst with pride when she shook hands and receiver her degree from
Chancellor of her university.
Anna is planning to travel and work in Spain for a year, starting in Barcelo
travelling to the south coast in time for the summer's tourist season. All the
will really miss Anna but I'm sure you'll join us in wishing her good luck a
voyage!'

Making a splash
Our son, Paul Taylor, has been indulging in his favourite watery pastime

3 Add a Clip Art image for fun (see below). When inserted and resized, go to the **Format** menu and click on **Picture**. To control how your text wraps around your Clip Art image, click on the **Layout** tab. Click the **Tight** icon in the Wrapping style section. Click **OK**.

4 Now highlight your heading, go to the **Format** menu and click on **Font**. Choose a font, style, size and colour. As this is an informal document, choose a fun font. For a distinctive effect, click in the Shadow box and select a dotted rule in the Underline style box.

Add page numbers

To add page numbers, scroll to the bottom of the page then go to the **View** menu and click on **Header and Footer**. Click in the Footer section. In Word, go to the Header and Footer dialogue box, click on **Insert AutoText,** then on **PAGE**.

In Microsoft Works, go to the **Insert** menu and click on **Page Numbers**. The correct page number will appear at the bottom of each page. In either program you can resize and format the text as you wish.

Using images

To import Clip Art, place your cursor at the top of the document, go to the **Insert** menu, select **Picture** then click on **Clip Art**. A search bar appears on the right-hand side of the window. Enter a description, click on **Search** and choose from the images that appear.

To import photos, scan them in, or download them from a digital camera and save them on your PC (for details on scanning, see page 204). Go to the **Insert** menu, select **Picture** then click on **From File**. Find your photograph then click on **Insert**.

For more details on inserting and using Clip Art images and photos, see pages 186 and 209.

Close-up
*To see your text laid out in columns, go to the **View** menu and click **Print Layout**.*

Bright idea
For a professional look, style all your headings using the same font, font style and font size. Use colour only in the headings as coloured text can be difficult to read.

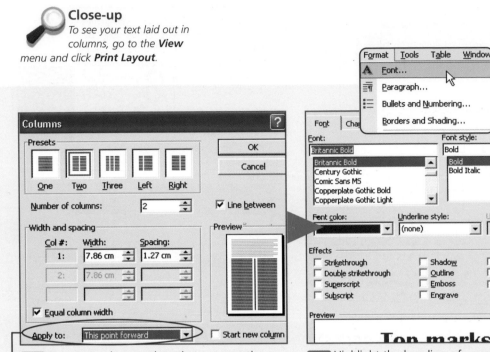

5 To create columns, place the cursor at the start of your first article, go to the **Format** menu and click on **Columns**. Select **Two** in the Presets section. Set the column width and the spacing between the columns. Ensure the 'Line between' box is ticked then click **OK**.

6 Highlight the heading of your first article, go to the **Format** menu and click on **Font**. Select a font, font style and size. If you are printing in colour, click on the arrow next to the Font color box, scroll through and select a colour. Click **OK**.

7 Highlight and style the first paragraph of your first article in the same way. Choose a bold font style to make it stand out. Highlight and style the remainder of the first article, selecting a regular font style.

Applying settings

To apply your column settings to the area of the document below the heading, click on the arrow to the right of the 'Apply to' box, scroll through and click on **This point forward**.

Columns in Works

To set columns in Microsoft Works, go to the **Format** menu and click on **Columns**. Set the 'Number of columns' and the 'Space between' them. Click in the 'Line between columns' box, then click **OK**. Note that all the text in your newsletter reflows into columns.

*In the Drop Cap dialogue box, click on the **Dropped** icon in the Position section. Select the number of lines you want it to drop by in the 'Lines to drop' box. Click **OK**.*

Drop Cap

Position

Lines to drop: 3
Distance from text: 0 cm

If you want to produce a regular newsletter, save your first one as a template that can be opened and altered for each edition.

CREATE A TEMPLATE

Indents and Spacing | Line and Page Breaks

General
Alignment: Left   Outline level: Body text

Indentation
Left: 0 cm   Special: (none)   By:
Right: 0 cm

Spacing
Before: 0 pt   Line spacing: Single   At:
After: 0 pt
☐ Don't add space between paragraphs of the same style

Preview

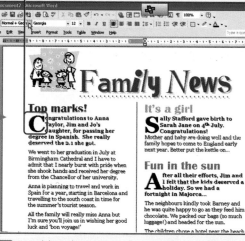

Save As

Save in: Templates
🖹 grapes
🖹 Normal

History
My Documents
Desktop
Favorites
My Network Places

File name: Family News
Save as type: Document Template

8 To adjust line spacing, highlight your first article (not the heading), go to the **Format** menu and click on **Paragraph**. Apply settings in the dialogue box (see below). Style the rest of your articles in the same way.

9 To add a 'drop cap', place your cursor in the first paragraph, go to the **Format** menu and click on **Drop Cap**. Apply settings in the dialogue box (see above). Click **OK**. To check how your document looks, go to the **File** menu and select **Print Preview**.

10 Go to the **File** menu and select **Save As**. In the Save As dialogue box type in a name in the 'File name' box. Click on the 'Save as type' box and choose **Document Template**. Word will save your newsletter in its Templates folder. Click **Save**.

Adjusting line spacing

To adjust spacing between lines, click on the arrow to the right of the 'Line spacing' box and scroll through. If you know which point size you want, click on **Exactly** then select the size in the At box.

To increase the space between paragraphs, click on the uppermost arrow to the right of After in the Spacing section. Finally, click **OK**.

Spacing
Before: 0 pt   Line spacing: Single   At:
After: 0 pt
☐ Don't add space between paragraph

Single
1.5 lines
Double
At least
Exactly
Multiple

Preview

Tabs...   OK   Cancel

Finishing touch

Don't forget to add your name and contact details at the end of the newsletter, and explain how to submit articles for future editions.

Family News

Top marks!

Congratulations to Anna Taylor, Jim and Jo's daughter, for passing her degree in Spanish. She really deserved the 2.1 she got.

We went to her graduation in July at Birmingham Cathedral and I have to admit that I nearly burst with pride when she shook hands and received her degree from the Chancellor of her university.

Anna is planning to travel and work in Spain for a year, starting in Barcelona and travelling to the south coast in time for the summer's tourist season.

All the family will really miss Anna but I'm sure you'll join us in wishing her good luck and 'bon voyage!'

It's a girl

Sally Stafford gave birth to Sarah Jane on 4th July. Congratulations!
Mother and baby are doing well and the family hopes to come to England early next year. Better put the kettle on...

Fun in the sun

After all their efforts, Jim and I felt that the kids deserved a holiday. So we had a fortnight in Majorca...

The neighbours kindly took Barney and he was quite happy to go as they feed him chocolate. We packed our bags (so much luggage!) and headed for the sun.

The children chose a hotel near the beach

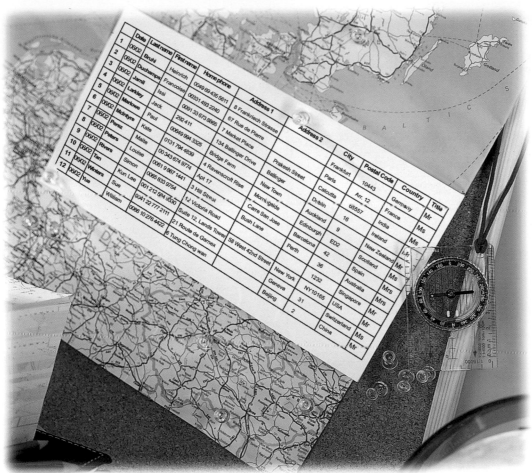

Make an address list

It can be easy to keep in touch with friends and contacts

One of the most useful things you can do with a database is make an address list. There are many advantages to doing this on your PC. You can easily update it when people move house or change their name; you can sort addresses; you can even create group e-mail lists to send all your friends the same e-mails at once. You can also search your database for individual words (if, say, you can remember that someone was called Jim but you have forgotten his surname). And you can always print it out if you need to.

| Home | Tasks | Programs | History | Customize |

PROGRAMS
Type your question and click Search, or click a program.

Keep track of all your friend numbers, mailin

[Search]

📖 **Start Address Book**

Address book
Address book converter

Works Word Processor
Works Spreadsheet
Works Database
Works Calendar
Address Book

1 Go to the **Start** menu, select **All Programs** and click on **Microsoft Works**. In the Programs tab select **Address Book** in the list on the left. To launch the application, click on **Start Address Book** when it appears on the right.

Templates on CD-ROM

Key word

Field *This is a category of information in a database that appears in all entries – for example, 'Name', 'Street Address' and 'Phone'.*

2 If you have not created an identity for yourself (see below) the Address Book opens in the default identity. To create a new folder for your addresses go to **New** then select **New Folder**. Name the folder and click **OK**. The folder is now listed on the left. Click on it to highlight it.

3 With your folder highlighted, create new contacts to save in it. Go to **New** and select **New Contact**. In the Name tab, type in your contact's first and last names – these automatically appear in the display name field. You can change the display name by typing in a different name.

4 There are several other tabs where a variety of other information can be added. Click on each tab and fill in the details. Only click **OK** when you have filled in all the information you want to record. With your folder highlighted on the left, your new entry now appears listed on the right.

Switching identities

Creating identities is a way for several people to use Outlook Express and the Address Book on the same computer. Creating a different identity for each user allows them to see their own mail and contacts when they log on under their identity.

To switch between identities in the Address Book, go to the **File** menu and select **Switch Identity**. Highlight your identity in the dialogue box, then **Click OK.**

Adding e-mail addresses

Be sure to include e-mail addresses for your contacts as they can be used in Outlook Express. You can set up Outlook to automatically add addresses to your Address Book whenever you reply to an e-mail. To do this, launch Outlook Express. In the **Tools** menu, click **Options**. On the **Send** tab, click **Automatically put people I reply to in my Address Book**.

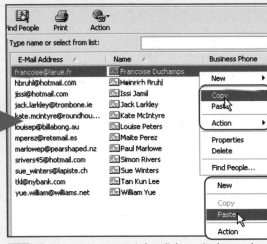

File	Edit	View	Tools	Help
New	Properties	Delete	Find People	

*To delete a folder or contact, click on it in the list to highlight it. Click on the **Delete** button on the top toolbar. Then click **Yes** in the dialogue box to permanently erase all its contents.*

5 You can organise your Address Book in several ways. To sort contacts by name, click on the **Name** column header. Click several times to display the list in alphabetically ascending or descending order of either first or last name. You can also sort by e-mail and telephone numbers.

6 To copy a contact, right-click on it then select **Copy** in the drop-down menu. To paste the contact into another folder, click on the folder to open it, then right-click your mouse, select **Paste**, and click **OK** in the next dialogue box. Your contact will now appear listed in the new folder.

7 To create a 'group' of contacts, go to **New** and select **New Group.** Give the group a name. The next time you use Outlook Express simply type that name in the 'To' box to e-mail all the people in your group at once. To add contacts to your group, click **Select Members**.

To change the order of the columns in your Address Book, point to a column and then drag the column to the left or right until it is located where you want it.

E-Mail Address	Name	Business Phone	Home Phone
francoise@larue.fr	Francoise Duchamps		00 331 493 2240
hbruhl@hotmail.com	Heinrich Bruhl		00 49 69 435 5...
jissi@hotmail.com	Issi Jamil		00 91 33 673 8...
jack.larkley@trombone.ie	Jack Larkley		292411
kate.mcintyre@roundhou...	Kate McIntyre		0131 794 4839
louisep@billabong.au	Louise Peters		00 61 9867 1441
mperez@retemail.es	Maite Perez		00 343 674 9774
marlowep@pearshaped.nz	Paul Marlowe		00 649 994 3325
srivers45@hotmail.com	Simon Rivers		00 65 833 9754

Searching for contacts

To find a contact in your Address Book, go to the Edit menu then select **Find People**. In the Find People dialogue box set the 'Look in' box to Address Book. Type in a key word, or words in one or more of the fields displayed, then click on **Find Now**. The search results will be listed below.

Now that you have completed your address list, why not use it to print out address labels? See page 170 to find out how.

OTHER IDEAS TO TRY

See page 170

Short cut
To print, hold down the **Ctrl** key and press '**P**' to bring up the Print dialogue box.

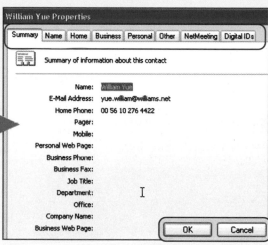

8 In the Select Group Members dialogue box, scroll down the folder list to select the folder from which you want to take your contacts. To select a group member, highlight the contact and click on **Select**. Click **OK** when all group members have been chosen.

9 To change a contact's details, double click on the entry in the folder list. The contact opens with a summary tab highlighting some of the details you have entered. Details cannot be edited in this tab. Click on the appropriate tab, make your changes and click **OK**.

10 To print your Address Book information, select the contacts whose details you'd like to print by highlighting them in their folder. Then go to the **File** menu and select **Print**. In the Print dialogue box, chose your Print Style and number of copies then click on **Print**.

Hold a net meeting

If you use Microsoft NetMeeting or other conferencing software you can make a conferencing call directly from the Address Book.

Double click on a contact name and in the NetMeeting tab, fill in the Conferencing Server address and Conferencing Address for the contact. Click **Add**. Click **Call Now** in this tab to initiate a net meeting.

Make address labels

Save time and effort by printing your own labels

Computers come into their own when there are repetitive or time-consuming tasks to be done. Writing addresses on envelopes – at Christmas or for a charity mailshot – is one such task. Why not use your PC to create and print out address labels? It will spare you the tedium of writing them out by hand, and you give your envelopes a professional look.

You can create labels with a wide variety of designs, text styles and sizes, and you can save them to use over and over again.

You must have the addresses you want to print compiled on a database. To do this, see Make An Address List *on page 166. You also need to buy sheets of sticky labels.*

BEFORE YOU START

1 Go to the **Start** menu, select **All Programs** then click on **Microsoft Works**. Once the application has launched, click on **Works Word Processor** in the Programs tab. Then select **Start a blank Word Processor document**.

*You can also create address labels in Microsoft Word. Go to the **Tools** menu and click on **Letters and Mailings**, then **Mail Merge Wizard** and follow the prompts.*

OTHER PROGRAMS

Templates on CD-ROM

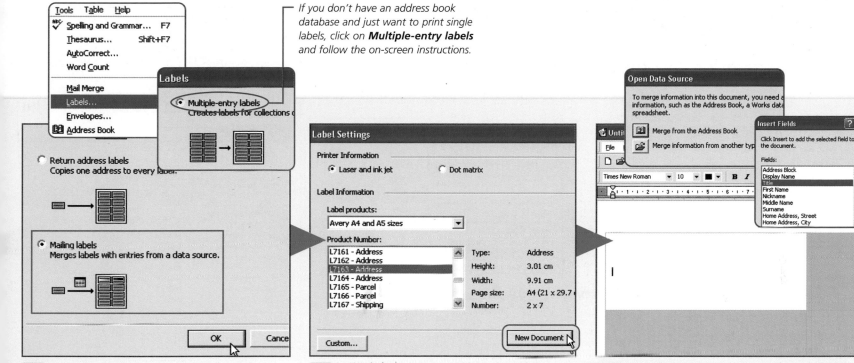

*If you don't have an address book database and just want to print single labels, click on **Multiple-entry labels** and follow the on-screen instructions.*

2 Go to the **Tools** menu and click on **Labels**. The Labels dialogue box appears. Select **Mailing Labels**. This enables you to merge the addresses you have stored in your Address Book into your labels document. Click **OK**.

3 In the Label Settings dialogue box click on the arrow at the side of the 'Label products' window and scroll down to select the correct label brand and type. Then scroll through the Product Number menu and click and highlight your label number. Click on **New Document**.

4 In the Open Data Source dialogue box, click on **Merge from the Address Book**. The Insert Fields dialogue box appears. Click on the first field you would like to use then click **Insert**.

Close-up

Address labels come in a variety of sizes, each with their own reference number. You can buy labels that fill the whole of an A4 page. Specialist labels to put on floppy disks, videos, cassettes and other items are also available. One of the most common address labels is the L7163, with 14 labels to an A4 page.

Searching for a database

The Open Data Source dialogue box also gives you the option of merging information from other databases you have created.

Click on **Merge information from another type of file** to locate a different data source. Scroll down the 'Look in' window to locate your file. Scroll down the 'Files of type' window to ensure the kind of file you created is displayed.

Watch out
If you skip the Select Names step all the addresses from all the folders in your Address Book will merge into your labels document.

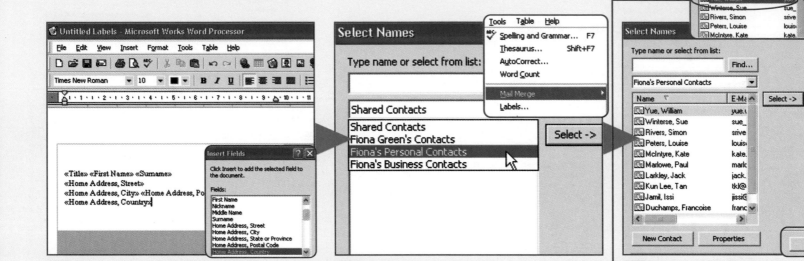

5 Add all the required fields in order. To ensure correct spacing on your labels, press the **Space bar** between fields that appear on the same line. Press **Return** to place fields on different lines. The fields are displayed in the top left-hand label of your document.

6 To choose your addresses, go to the **Tools** menu and select **Mail Merge**, then click on **Select Names**. In the Select Names dialogue box, scroll down the folders menu to select an Address Book folder. Once you have chosen a folder, all the contacts from that folder appear on the left.

7 To select an address, click on it to highlight it then click on **Select**. The recipient's name then appears in the 'Merge Recipients' window. Once you have selected all the recipients, click **OK**.

Your Address Book identity

If you share the Address Book program with another family member and have created more than one identity (see page 167) you can set your identity as the default for mail merging.

Open the Address Book in Works. Go to the **File** menu and select **Switch Identity**, then click on **Manage Identities**. Set 'Use this identity when starting a program' to your identity, then click **Close**.

*To select more than one recipient at a time click on your first contact and hold down the **shift key** whilst clicking on the rest in turn. Click **Select** and all the names you have highlighted will then appear in the 'Merge Recipients' window.*

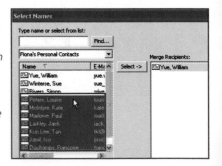

Bright idea
If you design a label that you think you might use again, remember to save it. You will be prompted to do so before you close the document.

Watch out
Don't waste your sticky labels. Before printing do a test on a sheet of paper, then overlay the paper on your sheet of labels to check the fit. If necessary, add or remove line spaces to improve the layout.

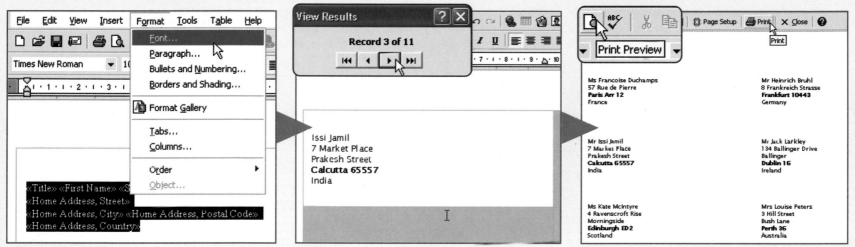

8 The first entry in your database appears in the top left hand side of your document. To style your addresses, highlight this entry and go to the **Format** menu. Select **Font**, then chose a font style and size. The style you select for this entry will apply to all the addresses in your document.

9 Using the View Results dialogue box that appears, scroll through all your entries. As you hit the right single arrow button, they will appear one by one in the top left-hand side of the document. You can check each in turn to ensure the details are correct.

10 To view the whole page of labels, click on the Print Preview icon in the toolbar. To print your labels, click on **Print** in the Print Preview window.

Selecting fonts

With your text selected in your document, you can also change the font style by using the drop down menu in the Font window of the formatting toolbar. Click on the arrow at the side of the window and scroll down.

Make a home

Let your computer take care of the

Project planner

*Create a folder named
after your business. Add
sub-folders for each of its
various aspects.*

📁 **Business**

📁 **Clients**

📁 **Suppliers**

📁 **Finance**

📁 **Product
development**

📁 **Publicity**

Millions of people around the world have seized the opportunity to start their own business. There is a real thrill to be had from making a go of your own idea, from being your own boss and taking your financial destiny into your own hands.

But with this opportunity come new responsibilities: for accounting, correspondence, and publicity; for dealing with suppliers, your bank manager and the tax man, and – perhaps most importantly – for finding your next client.

In fact, most of your time could easily be taken up with anything

business work

details while you take care of the profits

other than realising your original business idea.

Your PC can reduce the time spent on many of these tasks. It can even help you to research your business idea before you invest heavily in it.

For correspondence and publicity you could design a logo using Paint or another drawing program. It's often easiest to design your stationery and produce correspondence from a template, and keep a record of all your communications either on your computer's hard disk or backed-up on portable disks.

You can use your PC's database program to create a client database and, from that, customer name and address labels.

Ensure you never miss an appointment by running your

business diary from your Desktop. If you use a car for work, you can work out your running costs to claim them as business expenses. And your spreadsheet program will make dealing with your accounts less of a headache.

With your PC you can design your own business cards, or you can advertise much farther afield with your own Web site.

You can also use the Internet to correspond by e-mail, compare competitors' prices and services, and surf the Web for trade leads – some companies even post supply requirements on Government sites set up to encourage trade.

Before long, your computer will establish itself as your most productive and versatile employee, leaving you more time to enjoy your work.

Minding your own business

- Research the market for your business
- Research prices and costings for your product and those of competitors
- Prepare a business plan
- Arrange and prepare start-up finances
- Seek an accountant's advice on running a business
- Officially register as a business

Ideas and inspirations

Below are some suggestions for limiting the time you spend taking care of your business and maximising its efficiency. The projects can be adapted depending on your own circumstances. If you have business partners, you may agree to divide the tasks between yourselves.

252 Do your own accounts
Organise your income, outgoings and overheads; project future expenditure and profit.

194 Illustrated business stationery
Increase the profile of your business and make communications more effective.

166 Compile a client database
Make sure you don't lose track of anyone by storing their details in an updatable record.

180 Set up a business diary
Keep track of your appointments and timetable a variety of tasks in an on-screen diary.

114 Design your own Web page
Advertise your products or services on the Internet and invite potential clients to e-mail you.

Also worth considering...

Use pictures as well as words to sell your product – to get the message home to potential clients.

286 Create a press pack
With the same techniques used to produce a baby book you can design a mailshot or brochure.

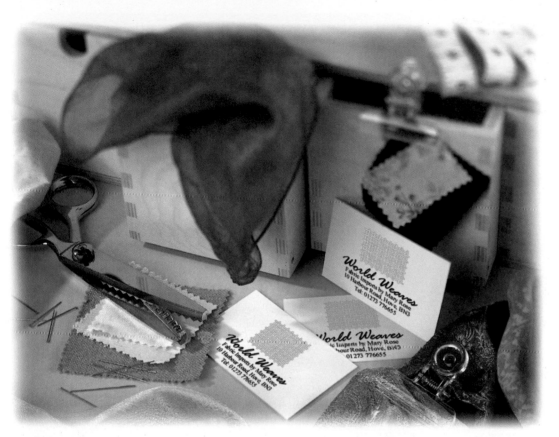

Design a business card

Make a good impression on colleagues, associates and friends

A well-designed business card can make a huge impact on potential clients and on your business. It reflects on your professionalism and its design can impart key aspects of your business. For example, a cake decorator who uses a picture of a traditional wedding cake and traditional fonts on their business card is likely to attract a different clientele than one who uses a picture of a more unusual cake and modern fonts.

A business card, or visiting card for social occasions, can easily be created using Word, and you can personalise it with your choice of text style and graphics. Alternatively you may wish to design a card for a society or association with which you are involved.

Make sure you have the formatting toolbar active before starting this project.

BEFORE YOU START

Page Setup

| Margins | Paper | Layout |

Margins

Top: 2.54 cm   Bottom: 2.54 cm
Left: 1   Right: 1
Gutter: 0 cm   Gutter position: Left

Orientation

Portrait   Landscape

Pages

Multiple pages: Normal

OK

1 Go to the **Start** menu, select **All Programs** and click on **Microsoft Word**. Go to the **File** menu and click on **Page Setup**. With the Margins tab selected, type in 1 cm for the Left and Right margins, so that two standard-sized cards will fit side by side on an A4 sheet. Click **OK**.

It is possible to style text and import Clip Art in Works' word processing program. You can also size your card accurately in Works, making it a suitable alternative to Word for this task.

OTHER PROGRAMS

Templates on CD-ROM

When you adjust the width of your columns, the spacing between them adjusts automatically.

Close up
*When inserting your table, rulers should appear at the top and to the left of your document. If they do not, go to the **View** menu and click on **Ruler**.*

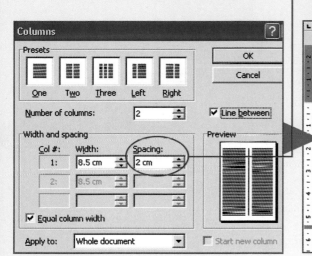

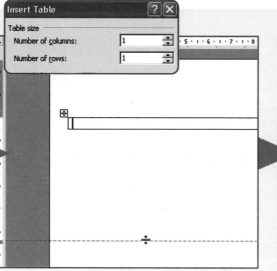

2 Go to the **Format** menu and select **Columns**. In the Presets panel, click on **Two**. In the Width and spacing panel make the Width 8.5 cm (Spacing adjusts automatically). Ensure the 'Equal column width' and the 'Line between' boxes are ticked (to tick, click in them). Click **OK**.

3 Go to the **Table** menu and click on **Insert Table**. Set the columns and rows to one. Click **OK**. A box appears. Move the mouse pointer over the bottom line. When it becomes a double-headed arrow, drag the line to the 5.5 cm mark on the left ruler.

4 Click inside the table and type in your text. To align it in the centre, highlight it then click on the **Center** toolbar button. Now highlight sections of text and style them by going to the **Format** menu and clicking on **Font**. Select a font, size and style. Click **OK**.

Save your document

Soon after opening your new Word document, remember to save it. Go to the **File** menu and select **Save As**, or click on the **Save** toolbar button. Save your business cards into a suitable folder.

Watch out

It may be tempting to use an unusual font for fun, but make sure your text is legible. If your card can't be read easily, there's little purpose in having one in the first place.

Watch out
Position your Clip Art image so that there is an equal amount of space around it. This will look balanced and more professional.

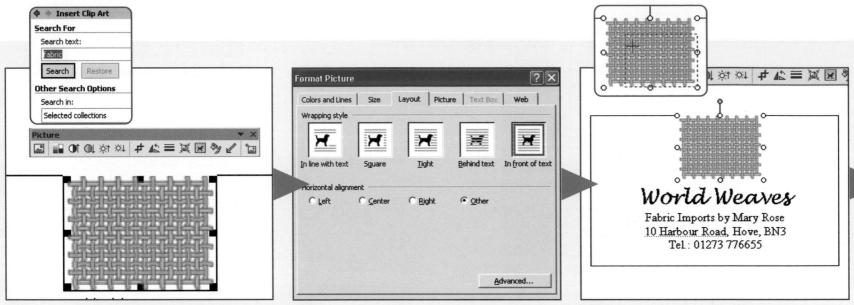

5 Add a Clip Art graphic. Go to the **Insert** menu, select **Picture** and click on **Clip Art**. Type a search term in the column that appears on the right and click **Search**. Scroll through to find a suitable graphic, then click on the image and select **Insert**. The graphic appears above the table.

6 Go to the **Format** menu and select **Picture** and click the **Layout** tab. The default Wrapping style setting is 'In line with text'. This allows you to move the image by hitting the return key on the keyboard. Other options allow you to move the image by clicking and dragging it.

7 To alter the size of your Clip Art image, click on one of its corners and drag it across your screen to the desired size. To position the image in the centre of your card, (when the Wrapping style in Step 6 is set to 'In line with text'), click on it then click on the **Center** toolbar button.

Add space around your Clip Art
To add more space around your picture (when the Wrapping style in Step 6 is set to 'In line with text') click on it and go to the **Format** menu. Click on **Paragraph**. In the Spacing section click on the uppermost arrows beside Before and After to increase the spacing.

Undoing changes
If you have experimented with spacing and formatting, but find you don't like the results, the quickest way to remove the changes is to click on the **Undo** button on the Word toolbar. Each click you make takes you back a stage in the development of your document.

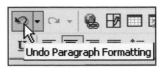

Bright idea
To get the best results print your cards on card that is 250gsm or thicker. Most home printers only handle card up to 160gsm thick – check the manual – so consider having the file printed at a print shop.

Close up
To remove a card, click on it, go to the **Table** menu and click on **Select Table**. Go back to the **Table** menu and select **Delete Rows**.

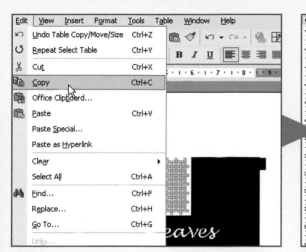

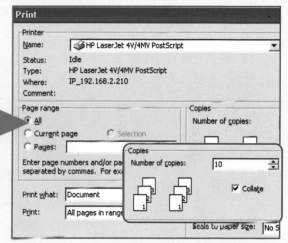

8 To create several cards, simply copy and paste the original. Click anywhere inside the table, go to the **Table** menu and click on **Select**, then **Table**. Go to the **Edit** menu and select **Copy**. A copy of your business card is now stored in the computer's memory, ready for pasting.

9 Click below the original table and press **Return**. Go to the **Edit** menu and select **Paste**. The image and text appear. Click on the **Paste Options** button just below and select **Display as table**. Repeat to fill the page with cards. When you reach the end of the first column, Word automatically moves onto the second one.

10 Once you're happy with the design of your cards, go to the **File** menu and select **Print**. Choose the page range and number of copies you want then click **OK**.

Professional results
If you want to print the card at a print shop, save it onto your hard disk and also onto a floppy disk.

Place your disk in the floppy disk drive and with your document open go to **File**, then **Save As**. In the 'Save in' box select **My Computer**. Click on **3½ Floppy [A:]** as the destination for saving your document then click **Save.**

Create your own diary

Organise your life – use a computer to help you plan

Many people have such pressurised schedules that it is easy to lose track of everything that needs to be done. By creating a diary using the Microsoft Office program Outlook, you need never miss an appointment again.

Outlook allows you to enter appointments, events, meetings and tasks into your diary and view them by the day, week or month. It allows you to print out a schedule for your day, attach important documents to relevant entries in your diary, and it even reminds you of your appointments well before they catch up with you.

Ask your family or work colleagues if there are any events, tasks or appointments that you should add to your diary immediately.

BEFORE YOU START

1 Go to the **Start** menu, select **All Programs** then click on **Microsoft Outlook**. Click on the **Calendar** icon. A blank schedule for the day appears. It includes sections for each hour of the day, a view of the next two months and a blank list of tasks in the TaskPad.

*You can make a calendar in Microsoft Works. Open Works then, in the Programs tab, click on **Works Calendar**. Click on **Start the Calendar** to launch the program.*

OTHER PROGRAMS

Bright idea
The small arrows beside the name of each month in the daily or weekly view enable you to quickly move to the previous or following month.

Short cut
To add a new appointment when you are displaying your daily calendar, double-click at the new appointment time and enter the details.

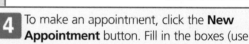

2 Customise the way you view your diary. If you want to view it week by week, click on the number **7** toolbar button. To view a whole month at a time, click on the number **31** toolbar button. To return to the day-by-day view, click on the number **1**.

3 Alter the calendar settings to suit your needs. Go to the **Tools** menu and click on **Options**. In the Preferences tab, click on the **Calendar Options** button. Amend settings by clicking on the arrows beside each box and scrolling through the options. When you have finished, click **OK**.

4 To make an appointment, click the **New Appointment** button. Fill in the boxes (use the bottom panel for extra data). To set an alert before the meeting, click in the Reminder box to tick it, and set how far in advance you want the warning to happen. Click **Save and Close**.

Terms used in Outlook
Outlook allows you to make four types of entry through the File and Calendar menus:
● An appointment is an activity that you reserve time for, but which does not involve other people.
● A meeting is an appointment to which you are inviting other people.
● An event is an activity that lasts at least 24 hours. It appears as a banner at the start of each relevant day.
● A task is a duty that you can check off on completion.

Working hours
When you set your 'Calendar working hours', Outlook displays them as yellow, and your leisure hours are displayed in an olive colour (using the default colour scheme). Clicking on an hour highlights it in blue.

05⁰⁰	
06⁰⁰	
07⁰⁰	
08⁰⁰	
09⁰⁰	
10⁰⁰	

For your alarm to work, Outlook must be running. As part of your daily routine, open the program and minimise it, so that it appears as a button on the Taskbar.

Short cut
*If you want to delete an appointment in your diary or a task in your TaskPad, click on the item then click the right mouse button. Click on **Delete** in the pop-up menu.*

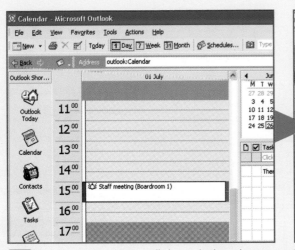

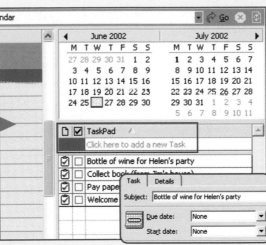

5 To view your entry, scroll through the relevant day's calendar. To move an entry to a new time, click on the coloured bar to its left and drag it to the new time, releasing the mouse button to put it in place.

6 To add a task in the TaskPad, double-click on **Click here to add a new Task**. Type in the details. Click **Save and Close**. When you complete the task, click on the box beside it.

7 To add an event, go to the **Actions** menu and click on **New All Day Event**. Enter the details in the window that appears. Click **Save and Close**. The event appears as a banner at the top of the relevant day or days.

Altering entries

To change an entry's duration, first click on it. Place your cursor over the top or bottom edge of the appointment box. When the cursor becomes a double-headed arrow, click and drag the edge of the box up or down.

Different views

You can view your diary in a number of ways. Go to the **View** menu, select **Current View** then click on one of the options available.

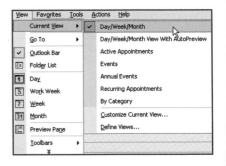

Close-up
You don't need to save your diary as you would any other document – it will save itself when you close it. When you open Outlook again it will appear automatically.

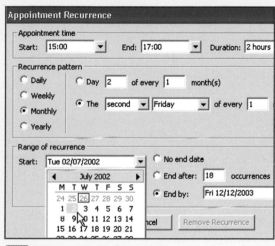

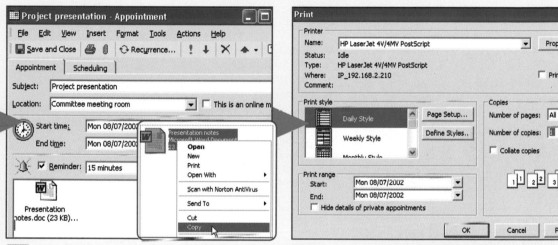

8 To set up a regular appointment, go to the **Actions** menu and click on **New Recurring Appointment**. Fill in your information, then click **OK**. To set up a regular event, select **New All Day Event** from the Actions menu, fill in the details and click the **Recurrence** button to set it up.

9 If you have a document relevant to an appointment, you can attach a copy to your diary entry. Go to the **Start** menu, select **My Documents** and locate your file. Right-click on it and select **Copy**, then right-click in your appointment window and select **Paste**.

10 To print out a daily schedule, go to the **File** menu, select **Page Setup** then click on **Daily Style**. Select your Layout options (see below left) then click on **Print**. In the Print dialogue box click on **OK**.

Setting print options

In the Page Setup dialogue box you can set options for how you want your diary to print. These include printing the day over one or two pages, adding your list of tasks, choosing which hours of the day to cover, and which fonts to use.

Finishing touch

Add a title and date to your diary. In the Page Setup dialogue box click on the **Header/Footer** tab. Type your title in the Header section, and the date on which you printed the diary in the Footer section (you can also add a page number and your name). Click on the **Font** button and choose a font and size in the dialogue box.

Form a pressure group to

Whether you're campaigning to save the rain forest or your local

Project planner

Create a folder named after your group. Add sub-folders to it for each mini-project.

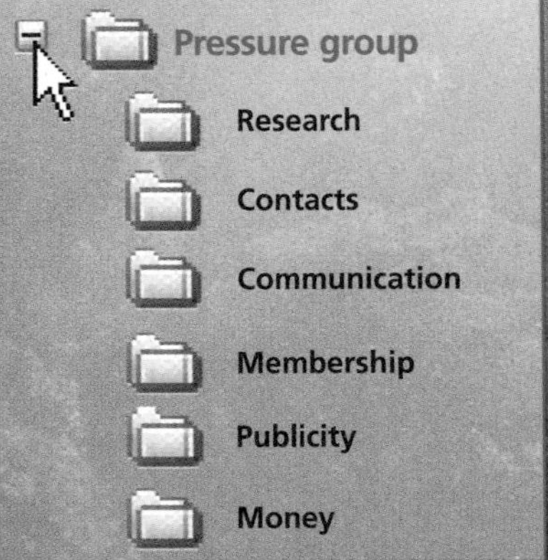

- Pressure group
  - Research
  - Contacts
  - Communication
  - Membership
  - Publicity
  - Money

Across an enormous range of concerns – from the global movement to preserve the rain forest, to local campaigns petitioning for traffic-calming measures – the number of people involved with lobbying official bodies has never been greater.

Whether you are starting a new group or opening a local branch of an existing one, it is important to recruit and organise committed members, accrue campaign donations and maintain momentum. Many pressure groups are run by volunteers on slender resources. Your computer can help to make the best use of both.

Increasingly, pressure groups are turning to the Internet to formulate and publicise their campaigns. Researching topics on-line is an obvious starting point. Many educational facilities and research centres release reports via the Net, and the introduction of more 'open

make a difference

park, your PC can get the message across

government' in some countries has led to the publication on the Web of a vast quantity of official statistics and information which can aid a campaign.

Newsgroups also offer fertile ground for pressure groups. There are issue-specific noticeboards and forums, where information is traded and debates instigated by interested parties, such as members of other groups and contributors with expert knowledge. Any pressure group would do well to post its details and aims on suitable sites, both to attract members and donations and to collect new information.

A Web site is the cheapest way to publicise a cause, and is the only medium with a truly global reach. The cost of maintaining a site is minimal once it has been set up.

Beyond research and publicity, your computer can be used to manage your organisation or branch. You can set up a membership database in Microsoft Works, use a spreadsheet package to manage the group accounts, and produce newsletters and press releases using a word-processing program. You can also create a mailing list, an e-mail list and print address labels. Consider producing questionnaires or petitions using your database's Form Design feature, and lobby local politicians via e-mail.

Form your plan of action

- Arrange venue/date/agenda for launching group
- Publicise launch meeting
- Arrange a visiting speaker
- Appoint officers and detail responsibilities
- Organise street publicity, collect shoppers' signatures and recruit new members
- Plan local demonstrations/publicity campaign
- Design and produce publicity material and flyers

Ideas and inspirations

Adapt the following projects and ideas to enhance your pressure group's profile, attract new members and make the most of your existing members' time and your group's resources. You may even think of other ways to apply your new skills and your computer's capabilities.

94   Internet research
Find the facts to formulate your argument, or simply keep up to date with affiliated groups.

166   Make an address list
Create a handy, easy-to-manage reference file for all your membership and contact details.

162   Create a newsletter
Keep your members updated about ongoing developments with a short publication.

32   Design a questionnaire
Use database software to gather information on members' opinions and concerns.

272   Accounts
Set up a spreadsheet to keep a close track of membership fees, donations and outgoings.

Also worth considering...

Once your pressure group is up and running, make regular mailshots easier on yourself.

170   Make address labels
Use your membership database as the basis for time-saving printed stationery.

Using Clip Art images

Give a touch of creativity to your work by adding illustrations

Clip Art illustrations are predesigned graphic images or pictures that you can incorporate into any document to give it a professional look. A gallery of such images is included free with Word and Works.

The images are generally arranged in such categories as 'Christmas', 'Children' or 'Travel'. They can be used as logos, borders, dividers or just as decorative devices. You can also alter the look of an image, cropping it, framing it and colouring it as you wish.

It is not always easy to get the best, most polished results at the first attempt, so be sure to experiment with Clip Art. Soon you will be making your own greetings cards, wrapping paper, invitations and address labels.

1 To insert Clip Art into a Word document, place the cursor where you want the image to go. Go to the **Insert** menu, select **Picture** and click on **Clip Art**. A column appears down the right-hand side of the screen with a Clip Art search facility at the top.

A Clip Art gallery comes as standard with Word and Works. You can also buy Clip Art on CD-ROM, download it from the Internet or scan in your own designs to use as Clip Art.

OTHER SOURCES

Clip Art on CD-ROM

*To see Word's Picture toolbar, go to the **View** menu,*  *select **Toolbars** then click on **Picture**. To find out what an icon on the Picture toolbar does, place the mouse pointer over it and an explanatory note will pop up.*

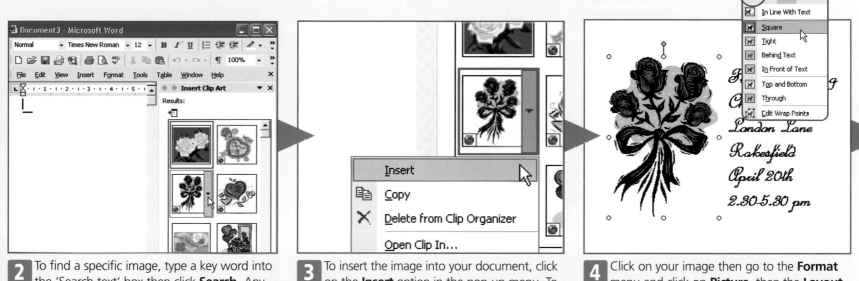

2 To find a specific image, type a key word into the 'Search text' box then click **Search**. Any images matching your criteria will then be displayed. When you hover the cursor over on an image that interests you, a toolbar appears. Click on the toolbar and a pop-up menu is displayed.

3 To insert the image into your document, click on the **Insert** option in the pop-up menu. To resize it, while keeping it in proportion, click on one of the corner handles and drag it to the required size.

4 Click on your image then go to the **Format** menu and click on **Picture,** then the **Layout** tab; or click on the **Text Wrapping** button in the Picture toolbar. Select 'Square'. Any text you type into your document will now appear to the right of the image. To move the image, click on it and drag it to the correct position.

Clip Art on-line

To insert Clip Art from the Internet, go to the **Insert** menu, select **Picture** then click on **Clip Art**. Click on **Clips Online** at the bottom of the column that appears on the right-hand side of the screen. This launches an Internet browser window. Type in a search term and browse the images. When you find an image, right click on it and go to **Save Picture As** in the pop-up menu.

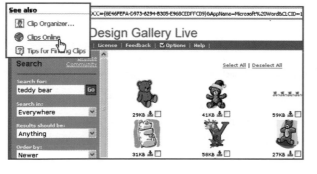

Using text in Works

In Microsoft Works you have three options when positioning text around an image. With the image selected, go the **Format** menu, choose **Object** and select the **Wrapping** tab. **In line with text** places the bottom of the image in line with the text it precedes. The **Square** option makes text wrap in a straight-sided box around the image. **Tight** makes the lines of text follow the shape of the image.

5 To put a frame around the image, click on the **Line Style** button on the Picture toolbar and select a line width from the menu. You can also give your line a dashed effect by clicking on **More Lines** and choosing an effect in the Dashed box of the Format Picture dialogue box

6 To give your image a background colour, click on the **Line Style** button and select **More Lines** or go to the **Format** menu, click on **Picture** and the **Colors and lines** tab. Select a fill colour. To get rid of your frame and background colour, select **No Fill** and **No Line** in the two Color boxes.

7 If you want to shape text closely around the image, click on the **Text Wrapping** toolbar button and select **Tight**. To adjust the wrap, click on **Edit Wrap Points** from the Text Wrapping menu. Click on the points that appear and drag them accordingly.

Using images with text

If you want to use text with Clip Art on a page of typescript, you need to decide how to position the text and images together in your document. Click on the image, go to the **Format** menu and click on **Picture**. Click the **Layout** tab. In the Wrapping style section there are a number of options and an advanced button for even more choices. Experiment with your layout by clicking on each in turn and seeing how this affects the position of your text and picture on the screen. You will need to click **OK** for each selection and then go back to the Layout tab to experiment with the next option.

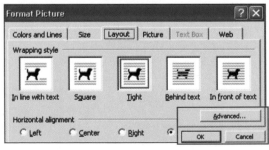

*If you're unhappy with your image adjustments, click on the **Reset Picture** button on the Picture toolbar. The image will then look exactly the same as when you first inserted it.*

Bright idea

In Word you can customise Clip Art. Click on the image, go to the **View** *menu, select* **Toolbars** *then click on* **Drawing**. *On the Drawing toolbar, click on* **Draw** *and select* **Ungroup**. *Click off the image. You can now select an area of the image and change the colours as you prefer, and add 3D or shadow effects to your image.*

8 You can crop your image, that is, remove part of it. Click on the **Crop** toolbar button then on the image. Drag a handle into the image to crop out the areas you don't want, then click the **Crop** button again. To restore the image, click the **Crop** button and pull the handle back out.

9 If you select **Behind Text** from the Text Wrapping menu, the text will appear on top of the image. This can look messy but you can make the text stand out by reducing the vibrancy of the image. Click on the image, then the **Image Control** button and select **Washout**.

10 To centre your text on top of the image, highlight the text and click on the **Center** button on the main toolbar. Then drag the image to sit below the text.

Changing the image

You can alter the way your Clip Art looks by clicking on the **Image Control** button on the Picture toolbar. You can choose more than one option at a time.

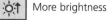

● **Automatic** gives a normal image and is the default setting.
● **Grayscale** produces a faint shaded monochrome image.
● **Black and white** gives a monochrome image.
● **Washout** gives a faint colour image.

You can also adjust the brightness and contrast of the image using four buttons on the toolbar:

 More contrast

Less contrast

More brightness

Less brightness

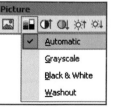

Design a greetings card

Send a personal message with your own special occasion cards

Making your own greetings cards allows you to combine a personal message with an appropriate – even unique – choice of image, and ensures that you always have the right card for any occasion.

On a Christmas card, for example, you could insert a series of photographs showing things that you and your family have done over the past year. And for birthday cards you could scan in and use pictures your children have painted (see page 204).

Anyone who receives personalised cards such as these will greatly appreciate all the thought and effort that has gone into producing them.

Look at your printer manual to find out the maximum thickness, or weight, of paper your printer can take. Consider mounting thinner paper onto card to give it strength.

▶ BEFORE YOU START

1 Go to the **Start** menu, select **All Programs** and click on **Microsoft Word**. To name and save your document go to the **File** menu and click on **Save As**. Select a suitable location in the 'Save in' box, type in a file name, then click on **Save**.

*You can create greetings cards in Microsoft Works. Open Works then, in the Works Task Launcher, click on the **Programs** tab then on the **Works Word Processor** button.*

▶ OTHER PROGRAMS

 **Templates on CD-ROM**

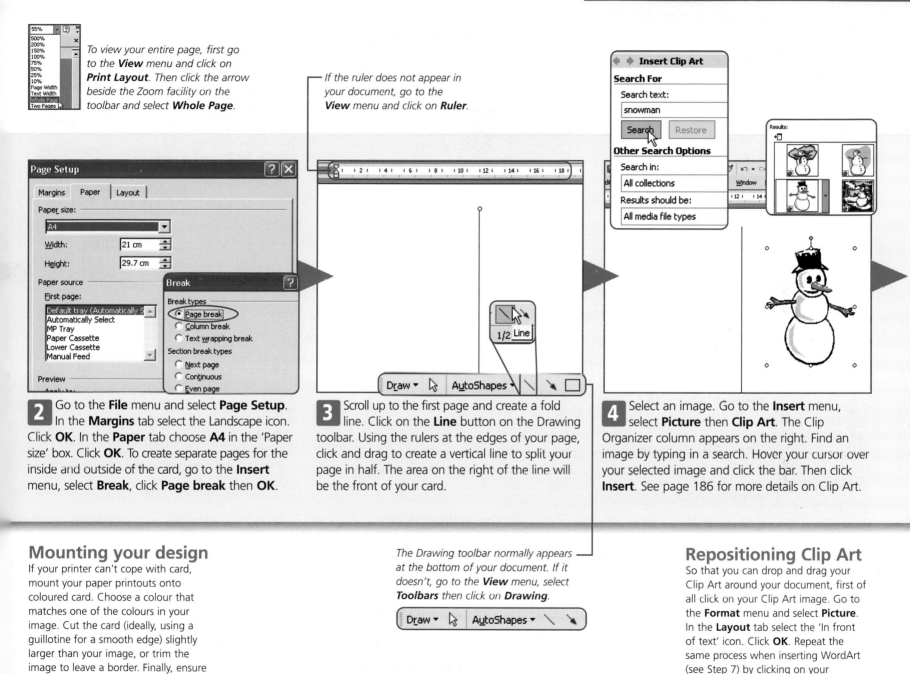

*To view your entire page, first go to the **View** menu and click on **Print Layout**. Then click the arrow beside the Zoom facility on the toolbar and select **Whole Page**.*

*If the ruler does not appear in your document, go to the **View** menu and click on **Ruler**.*

2 Go to the **File** menu and select **Page Setup**. In the **Margins** tab select the Landscape icon. Click **OK**. In the **Paper** tab choose **A4** in the 'Paper size' box. Click **OK**. To create separate pages for the inside and outside of the card, go to the **Insert** menu, select **Break**, click **Page break** then **OK**.

3 Scroll up to the first page and create a fold line. Click on the **Line** button on the Drawing toolbar. Using the rulers at the edges of your page, click and drag to create a vertical line to split your page in half. The area on the right of the line will be the front of your card.

4 Select an image. Go to the **Insert** menu, select **Picture** then **Clip Art**. The Clip Organizer column appears on the right. Find an image by typing in a search. Hover your cursor over your selected image and click the bar. Then click **Insert**. See page 186 for more details on Clip Art.

Mounting your design

If your printer can't cope with card, mount your paper printouts onto coloured card. Choose a colour that matches one of the colours in your image. Cut the card (ideally, using a guillotine for a smooth edge) slightly larger than your image, or trim the image to leave a border. Finally, ensure that you have envelopes large enough to hold your cards.

*The Drawing toolbar normally appears at the bottom of your document. If it doesn't, go to the **View** menu, select **Toolbars** then click on **Drawing**.*

Repositioning Clip Art

So that you can drop and drag your Clip Art around your document, first of all click on your Clip Art image. Go to the **Format** menu and select **Picture**. In the **Layout** tab select the 'In front of text' icon. Click **OK**. Repeat the same process when inserting WordArt (see Step 7) by clicking on your WordArt and selecting **WordArt** in the **Format** menu.

Key word

WordArt This describes the Microsoft library of text formats that you can customise. All you need do is select a form of WordArt then type in your text. You can colour the text and style it however you wish.

Click and drag your WordArt into position. To resize it, click and drag on one of its corner handles.

5 If you want to add snowflakes, click on the **AutoShapes** button on the Drawing toolbar and select **Stars and Banners**. Click the shape you want, then click and drag to draw it on the page. Use the white handles to resize the item, and the yellow one, if there is one, to alter its shape. The green handle allows you to rotate an image.

6 To add colour to your snowflakes, right-click on one of the flakes and select **Format AutoShape** from the pop-up menu. In the dialogue box the Colors and Lines tab is selected. Click the arrow beside the Color box in the Fill section and select a colour. Click **OK**.

7 Add a message to the front of the card. Go to the **Insert** menu, select **Picture** then **WordArt**. In the WordArt Gallery click on a style, then **OK**. A box appears asking you to type in your text. Do so, selecting a font, size and style at the same time. Click **OK**.

Create a frame

You can easily place a border around the front of your card. Click on the **AutoShapes** button on the Drawing toolbar, select **Basic Shapes** and then the Rectangle option. Click and drag on the document to create a frame of the appropriate size.

Click on the **Line Color** toolbar button then click on **Patterned Lines** from the colour palette. Select a pattern, foreground and background colour, then click **OK**. Click the **Fill Color** toolbar button and then click **No Fill** to ensure your ClipArt is visible.

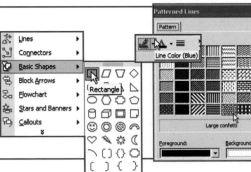

Colouring WordArt

You can change the colour of some types of WordArt. Select your WordArt, then click on the **Format WordArt** button on the toolbar. In the Fill section of the **Colors and Lines** tab select a colour for the text, and in the Line section select a colour and style for the outline of your text. Click **OK**.

*To change a WordArt message, double-click on it and type in your new text. To change its format, click on the **WordArt Gallery** button on the WordArt toolbar, then double-click on the style you want. Your text will remain the same.*

Use the alignment toolbar buttons to position text within your text box.

*Before you print, remove the fold lines you have used as guides. Click on each of them and press the **Delete** key.*

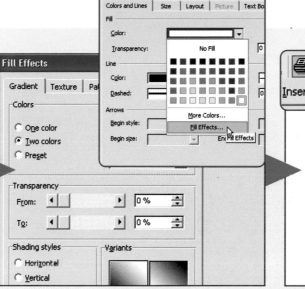

8 Scroll down to the second page and draw a fold line as in Step 3. Go to the **Insert** menu, select **Text Box** and click and drag to draw a box on the right hand side of the page. Type in your text, highlight it, go to the **Format** menu and select **Font**. Choose your font options. Click **OK**.

9 To give the text box a background colour, double-click on the edge of the box. In the Fill section of the dialogue box click on the arrow beside the Color box and select **Fill Effects**. Under the Gradient tab, select your colours, shading style and variant. Click **OK**.

10 Now go to the **File** menu and click on **Print Preview**. If you are happy with your card, choose **File** then **Print**. Print page 1 only, then place the paper or card back in the printer (you will need to experiment with orientation) and print page 2 on the reverse.

*If you give your text box a background colour (see Step 9), remove the border around it before you print. Double-click on the edge of the box then, in the Line section of the dialogue box, click on the arrow beside the Color box and select **No Line**. Click **OK**.*

193

Illustrate your stationery

Be creative **with your** personal **and** business correspondence

Using an image on your business stationery illustrates the nature of the business and adds a professional touch. On letters, compliments slips and business cards, a distinctive logo sends out an impressive message. On personal stationery, imagery can also reflect your personality and set a tone.

Your computer makes it simple to design and produce high-quality stationery. These pages cover business stationery, but the same principles apply for personal stationery. The word processing programs in Microsoft Office and Works offer a wide range of fonts, styles and colours, as well as Clip Art images. For personal stationery you could use an image of your house or a family coat of arms.

Make sure you have all the correct details at hand, especially postcodes and e-mail addresses.

BEFORE YOU START

1 Go to the **Start** menu, select **All Programs** then click on **Microsoft Word**. After your document opens, save it. Go to the **File** menu and click on **Save As**. Select a folder in which to save it in the 'Save in' box. Give it a file name, such as 'Letterhead'. Click on **Save**.

*You can also create stationery in Microsoft Works. Open Microsoft Works then, in the Works Task Launcher, click on **Programs** then on **Works Word Processor**.*

OTHER PROGRAMS

 Templates on CD-ROM

*For different ways of positioning your image, click on it then go to the **Format** menu. Select **Picture** then the **Layout** tab. Choose how to position your image with your text For details on using Clip Art, see page 186.*

For details on using Clip Art, see page 186.

Key word
Template *This is a predesigned file. It is useful for any kind of standard document – invoices or letterheads, for example – where the basic look of the document is always going to be the same.*

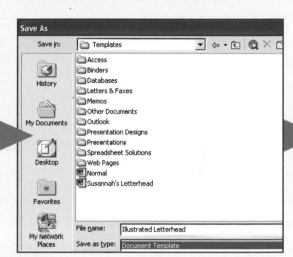

Font

Font | Character Spacing | Text Effects

Font:
Tempus Sans ITC

Symbol
Tahoma
Tempus Sans ITC
Times
Times New Roman

Font style:
Bold

Regular
Italic
Bold
Bold Italic

Size:
36

24
26
28
36
48

Font color: ▼
Underline style: (none) ▼
Underline color: Automatic

Effects
☐ Strikethrough
☐ Double strikethrough
☐ Superscript
☐ Subscript

Great Grapes
Wine Merchants
15 Vine Street, London NW6 4PE
Tel/Fax 020 7100 2000

Insert Clip Art
Results:

Insert
Copy
Delete from Clip Organizer
Open Clip In...
Tools on the Web...

Great Grapes
Wine Merchants
15 Vine Street, London NW6 4PE
Tel/Fax 020 7100 2000
Email:james@greatgrapes.co.uk

Save As

Save in: Templates

History
☐ Access
☐ Binders
☐ Databases
☐ Letters & Faxes
☐ Memos
☐ Other Documents
☐ Outlook
☐ Presentation Designs
☐ Presentations
☐ Spreadsheet Solutions
☐ Web Pages
☐ Normal
☐ Susannah's Letterhead

My Documents

Desktop

Favorites

My Network Places

File name: Illustrated Letterhead
Save as type: Document Template

2 Type in your company name and contact details. To style your text, highlight the company name, go to the **Format** menu and click on **Font**. Select a font, style, size, colour and effect from the lists, then click on **OK**. Style the remainder of your text in the same way.

3 To insert a Clip Art image, go to the **Insert** menu, select **Picture** then click on **Clip Art**. Type a search term into the box at the top of the right-hand column that appears, then click **Search**. Click on your selected image then click on **Insert** in the toolbar that appears.

4 Go to the **File** menu and click on **Save As**. Scroll through the 'Save as type' box and click on **Document Template**. Word will suggest saving your document in its Templates folder in the 'Save in' box. Type in a name in the 'File name' box, then click on **Save**.

Inserting e-mail addresses
When you type in an e-mail address in Word, it will try to create a link to your e-mail software. To style the text as you wish, turn off this function. Go to the **Tools** menu and select **AutoCorrect**. Click on the **AutoFormat As You Type** tab. Click in the box beside 'Internet and network paths with hyperlinks' (this removes the tick), then click **OK**.

james@greatgrapes.co.uk

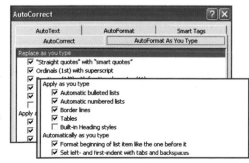

AutoCorrect

AutoText | AutoFormat | Smart Tags
AutoCorrect | AutoFormat As You Type

Replace as you type
☑ "Straight quotes" with "smart quotes"
☑ Ordinals (1st) with superscript
☑
☑
☑
☐

Apply as you type
☑ Automatic bulleted lists
☑ Automatic numbered lists
☑ Border lines
☑ Tables
☐ Built-in Heading styles

Automatically as you type
☑ Format beginning of list item like the one before it
☑ Set left- and first-indent with tabs and backspaces

Let the Wizard Help
Microsoft Works has a useful device, called a Wizard, to help you create a letterhead. When you open Works, the Works Task Launcher appears. Select **Tasks**, then **Letters and Labels** from the list on the left. Further options appear to the right. Select **Letters** then **Start this task** to start up your Wizard.

Microsoft Works Task Launcher

Home | Tasks | Programs | History | Customs

TASKS

Search

E-mail & Internet
Letters & Labels
Newsletters & Flyers
Research & Education
Household Management

Cover letters
CV (resumé)
Envelopes
Faxes
Letters
Mailing labels

Close-up
You cannot paste Clip Art into text boxes so, in order to copy and paste text from your letterhead template, you must delete the Clip Art first. When you close your letterhead template, do not save any changes.

The Copy and Paste toolbar buttons allow you to duplicate text. Click and drag your mouse over the text in question to highlight it, then click on the **Copy** button. Click on the **Paste** button to place the text.

Once your letterhead is designed, create further items of stationery by copying and pasting the details.

COMPLIMENTS SLIPS

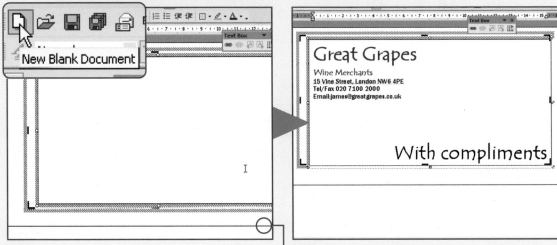

New Blank Document

Great Grapes
Wine Merchants
15 Vine Street, London NW6 4PE
Tel/Fax 020 7100 2000
Email:james@greatgrapes.co.uk

With compliments

Great Grapes
Wine Merchants
15 Vine Street, London NW6 4PE
Tel/Fax 020 7100 2000
Email:james@greatgrapes.co.uk

With

5 Click on the **New** toolbar button to open a new file. Set up your page (see below) then save it. To create a box in which to place data, go to the **Insert** menu and click on **Text Box**. Click at the top of the page and drag the mouse diagonally to create a box.

6 Open your letterhead template, delete the Clip Art and copy the text (see above, right). Click in your new text box and paste the copied text. Press **Enter** and type in the words 'With compliments'. Style the text (see Step 2) then drag the box into place.

7 Click outside your text box and insert the same Clip Art image that you used in your letterhead (see Step 3). Resize and reposition the image in the same way.

Setting up
You can fit three compliments slips on one A4 sheet. To get the maximum print area, go to the **File** menu and click on **Page Setup**. Set the Top and Bottom margins to 0cm. Click **OK**. A warning box appears, alerting you about small margins. Click **Fix**, then **OK**.

Page Setup

| Margins | Paper | Layout |

Margins
Top: 0
Left: 3.17 cm

Microsoft Word
One or more margins are s button to increase the app

Adding guidelines
Divide your page into thirds with guidelines. To access the Drawing toolbar, go to the **View** menu, select **Toolbars** then click on **Drawing**.
Click on the **Line** toolbar button. Move the cursor to just short of the 10cm mark on the vertical ruler, then click and drag the cursor across the page. Draw the second line, starting just short of the 20cm mark.

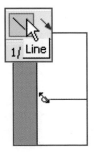

1/ Line

Short cut
If you ever need to change the details within your stationery, amend the text in your letterhead first, then copy and paste that text into your compliments slips.

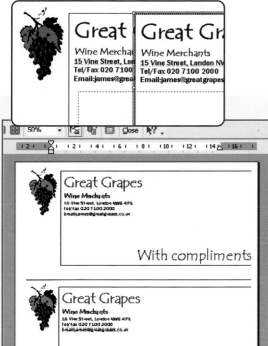

You do not want your guidelines to print out. To delete them, click on each of them in turn and press the **Delete** key.

Your business card will carry the same information and graphics as your letterhead and compliments slip.

BUSINESS CARD

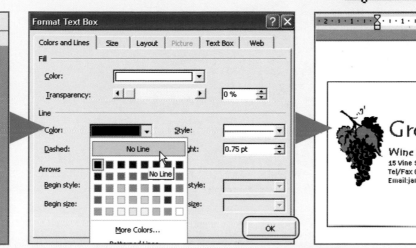

8 Click on an edge of the text box, right-click and select **Copy** from the menu. Click outside the box, right-click and select **Paste**.
Another text box appears in front of the first. Click on it and drag it down to the second slip. Repeat for the third slip and then your image.

9 To ensure the text box border does not print, click on the box, go to the **Format** menu and click on **Text Box**. With the Colors and Line tab selected, go to the Line section, click on the Color box then on **No Line** and OK. Go to the **File** menu and click **Print**.

10 Now that you have designed your letterhead and a compliments slip, use a similar process to create a business card.
Creating a business card is explained in full on page 176.

Using Works

With Works, you enter text into a box which you can then move around the page. In the **Insert** menu choose **Picture**, then **New Drawing**. In the window that opens, click on the **Rectangle** icon. Now click on the page and drag the cursor diagonally to draw a box (click on and drag a corner to resize).

Click on the **Text** button, click inside the box and type your text. To style it, click on the sections, go to the **Text** menu and select the font and style you want.
Close the window to insert the drawing onto the Works page. Click on the handles around the drawing to resize it. Add Clip Art as described in Step 3.

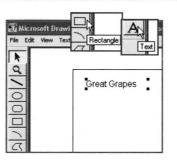

It's a surprise party!
Shhh...
Andy's 30th Birthday

At: 24 Chapel Road, Bath
On: Saturday 9th December
Time: Please be there by 7.30pm
RSVP: Lynn 01234 654 321

Create an invitation

Make a special occasion even better with your own design

Making your own invitation allows you to create a design that reflects the type of event you are organising – and the type of person you are arranging it for. If it is going to be a lively party, use bright colours and fun fonts. If it is for a more sober dinner party, choose more subtle colours and traditional fonts.

Before designing your invitation, make a note of the relevant information guests will need, including the date, time, location of the event – and any dress requirements.

Decide what size you want your invitation to be. For convenience, it's a good idea to print two or four per sheet of A4 paper.

BEFORE YOU START

1 Go to the **Start** menu, select **All Programs** and click on **Microsoft Word**. A new document appears. Save it by going to the **File** menu and clicking on **Save As**. Select a location in the 'Save in' box, type in a file name, then click on **Save**.

*You can create an invitation in Microsoft Works. Open Microsoft Works then click on **Programs** then on **Works Word Processor** and finally on **Invitations** (see opposite).*

OTHER PROGRAMS

Templates on CD-ROM

2 Go to the **File** menu and click on **Page Setup**. Click the **Paper** tab and make sure that A4 is selected in the 'Paper size' box. Click the **Margins** tab and set the Top and Bottom margins to 0 cm. Click **OK**. A warning box comes up, click **Fix** then **OK**.

3 Type in your text. To style it, highlight the first part, go to the **Format** menu and click on **Font**. Select a font, style, size, colour and effect, then click **OK**. Now style the rest of your text, or use the special graphics effect facility, WordArt.

4 The WordArt Gallery contains a selection of text designs that you can edit and customise for your own use. Highlight the relevant text then click on the **Cut** toolbar button. This removes the text from the page and places it on the Clipboard – keeping it temporarily in your PC's memory.

Close-up

If you want to design a classic, traditional invitation, choose from the following fonts: Book Antiqua, Copperplate Gothic Light, Garamond, Monotype Corsiva or Palatino Linotype . For a more fun look, try Comic Sans MS, Curlz MT, Kristen ITC or Bradley Hand ITC.

Let the Wizard help

Microsoft Works has a Wizard that makes it even easier to design an invitation. Go to the **Start** menu, select **All Programs** and click on **Microsoft Works**. In the Works Word Processor, scroll down the list on the right and click on **Invitations**. Then click **Start this task**, select a Works Invitations Wizard style and customise your template.

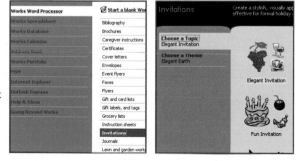

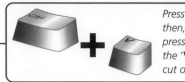

*Press the **Ctrl** key then, keeping it pressed down, press the '**V**' key to paste cut or copied text.*

You can exaggerate the effect of the WordArt shape by clicking on the yellow square and dragging it across the screen.

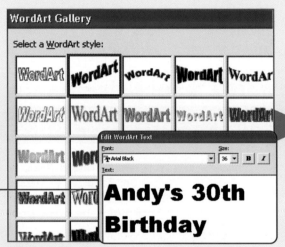

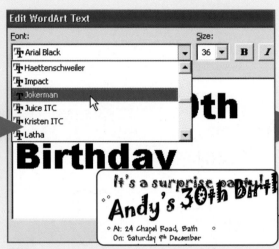

5 Go to the **Insert** menu, select **Picture** and click on **WordArt**. In the WordArt Gallery click on a style then click **OK**. A dialogue box asks you to type in your text. Hold down the **Ctrl** key then press the '**V**' key to paste in your text.

6 In the same dialogue box select a font, size, colour and style for your WordArt text then click **OK**. Your text will now appear in the document in your chosen WordArt form. If you wish, select a different colour for it.

7 Go to the **Format** menu, select **WordArt** then the **Layout** tab. Select the 'In front of text' wrapping style. Click **OK**. To move WordArt, click on it and drag it. To resize it, click on one of its corner handles and, keeping the mouse button pressed down, drag it across the screen.

Letter spacing in WordArt

You can adjust the spacing between WordArt letters, or characters. Click on the **Character Spacing** button on the WordArt toolbar, then click on your choice from the pop-up menu.

Colour in WordArt

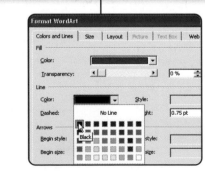

You can change the colour of some WordArt. Click on the **Format WordArt** button on the WordArt toolbar. In the Colors and Lines tab, choose a colour in the Fill section for the body of your text; and in the Line section choose a colour to outline the words.

Bright idea
For a professional look, print your invitations on card. Not all printers can handle card, however, so you may need to store the document on a floppy disk and take it to a print shop.

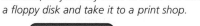

8 To adjust the shape of your WordArt, click on it, then click on the **WordArt Shape** button on the WordArt toolbar. A palette pops up offering you a selection of effects. Click on your choice.

9 To position the remainder of your text, highlight sections in turn then click on the **Left**, **Center** and **Right** alignment toolbar buttons. Add a ClipArt image if you wish. You can now copy your invitation into the second half of the page.

10 Hold down the **Ctrl** key and press '**A**' to highlight the text and ClipArt. Click on the **Copy** toolbar button. Place the cursor at the end of the text, press the **Return** key several times and click on the **Paste** button. Adjust the spacing if necessary and print the invitations.

Adding Clip Art

Place the cursor where you want the Clip Art to appear, go to the **Insert** menu, select **Picture** then **Clip Art**. A column appears down the right hand side of the screen. Type in a search term then scroll down the images and click on your choice, then click **Insert** on the pop-up toolbar.

For further details on how to manipulate your image, see page 186.

Plan the perfect party for

Use your computer to help organise your celebration

An informal get-together at home is one thing, but it is quite a different matter to arrange the kind of special party your friends and relations talk about for years after.

Silver weddings, landmark birthdays, marriages and christenings – these occasions do not come around very often, but when they do you want to be sure it all goes right. The preparations can take months and the planning will have to be meticulous. Venue, catering, entertainment, guests and accommodation – if people are coming a long way – must be booked and confirmed well in advance. You also need to plan the cost of it all.

One of the main areas in which your computer can help is in compiling a guest list. The

Project planner

Create a folder called 'Party'. Add sub-folders to it for each mini-project.

- Party
  - Guest list
  - Invitations
  - Letters to suppliers
  - Budget
  - Menus
  - Reminders

a special occasion

and ensure you have a day to remember

Microsoft Works database will store the contact details of guests and of key suppliers, such as caterers. Use your PC's design capabilities to produce invitations, then address them instantly by making labels from your guest database. As people reply, input the information into the database for a record of confirmed numbers.

Using a database means you'll only have to compile the list once, and you can then use it to note additional details: the number of people in each group; who has small children; who is a vegetarian and so on. Now you can estimate the number of people attending,

and use a spreadsheet to prepare a budget. Allocate a sum for the cost of the venue and entertainment, and an amount per head for food. If you need to contact and select caterers, DJs and so on, send out letters written in your word-processing program giving your requirements and requesting quotes. Use the word-processing program to create menus and place cards, too.

Now set up a planning spreadsheet in the form of a 'Celebration Countdown'. Use it to schedule remaining tasks.

Once everything is in place, you can relax and start looking forward to the big day.

Pay attention to detail

- Compile guest list
- Book venue
- Organise caterer
- Design and send out invitations
- Book disc jockey and Master of Ceremonies
- Compile 'Celebration Countdown'
- Write and send reminders/directions

Ideas and inspirations

These suggestions will get you started on organising your event. All the projects can be adapted depending on the nature of your occasion. For example, on your invitation you could include your e-mail address so guests can respond by computer.

166 Guest list and address labels
Set up a guest list to keep track of who you invite and use labels to mail your invitations.

198 Create an invitation
A little imagination – and the versatility of Word and Works – will ensure a good response.

148 Send a formal letter
Use Word to produce businesslike letters to suppliers, to check availability and prices.

272 Project-based budgeting
Compile a spreadsheet to help keep track of all your party's expenses.

308 Celebration countdown
In the same way you plan a holiday, create a spreadsheet to organise last-minute tasks.

Also worth considering...

Whether you have a caterer or are doing the food yourself, guests might like to see the menu.

158 Dinner party menu
If your party involves catering, you could save money by asking guests to select their choice in advance.

Add your own images

Scan in your favourite photographs to liven up your documents

There is no limit to the variety of images you can use in your documents. If you have a scanner, you can transfer photographs, or pictures from newspapers or books, to your own computer.

A scanner takes a digital copy of an image that you can manipulate in any way you wish before placing it in a newsletter, invitation or card (but be aware that the use of printed material is covered by copyright laws).

There are several different ways to scan images using Windows XP. They range from simple Wizards that do almost everything automatically to utilities that allow you to fine-tune the scanning process to get the best results possible.

The following steps apply to one type of scanner. As products vary, be aware that on other hardware some of the screens may look different.

BEFORE YOU START

1 If it is the first time you have used your scanner, Windows XP will recognise the new hardware when you connect its USB lead. Install the scanner's drivers either from the CD that came with it or by downloading them from the manufacturer's Web site.

⚠️ **Watch out**
Most printed material is covered by copyright laws. Unless you are copying it purely for your own use and not for distribution, it is not available for you to use freely. As a general rule, if you are designing a newsletter or poster, you will be breaching copyright laws if you use images from published sources without the copyright owner's permission.

The Scanner and Camera Wizard in Windows XP is simple and easy to use. To have greater control over the scanning process, see overleaf.

USING THE WIZARD

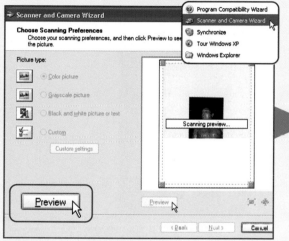

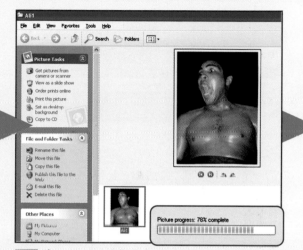

2 Go to the **Start** menu and click on **All Programs**, then **Accessories** then **Scanner and Camera Wizard**. The Wizard will launch. Click **Next**, then **Preview**. This makes the scanner do a quick, low-resolution pass over your picture so that you can decide how to crop it.

3 Choose the type of picture that you are scanning. For greater control, click on **Custom Settings** and adjust the brightness and contrast and resolution of your scan, then click **OK**. When you are happy with the chosen settings, click **Next**. Choose a name, file format and location for your scanned picture then click on **Next**.

4 The scanner will make the scan. When it has finished you will be asked if you want to publish your picture to the Internet, order prints of it on-line or do nothing. Make your choice, then click **Next**. In the last screen click **Finish**. The folder with your new scan in it will open.

Push-button scanning

Many modern scanners have buttons that you can press to launch an automatic scan of a picture. This Epson scanner has a set of buttons that includes one that will scan a document at a resolution suitable for sending in an e-mail message. Other buttons launch processes such as scanning an image for a Web site or sending a scanned image direct to a printer. The exact way that these buttons work depends on your hardware and software.

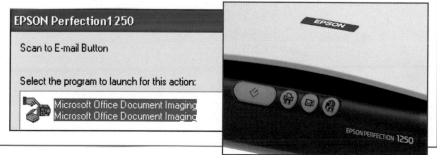

To make adjustments to the area to be scanned, place the cursor over one of the dotted lines and, when it becomes a double-headed arrow, click and drag the line to the required position.

For more control over your scanned image, some models come with software, called a TWAIN driver, that works within an image editing program such as Jasc® Paint Shop Pro™.

ADVANCED SCANNING

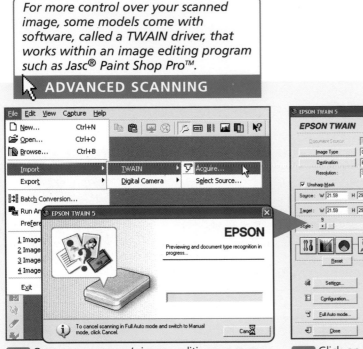

To switch to Manual mode, click Manual Mode.

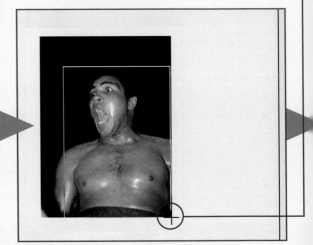

5 Open your scanner's image editing program. In the **File** menu click on **Import** then **TWAIN** and **Acquire**. The Espon TWAIN utility will launch. If it is in Full Auto mode, it will start scanning straight away, without allowing you to adjust the scanning settings. Click **Cancel** to stop the automatic scan.

6 Click on **Manual mode**. The TWAIN utility will launch. First of all you need to do a quick scan to let you experiment with the settings. Place the photo in the scanner and click on **Preview**. The image appears in the preview window.

7 A dotted frame over the image defines the area that will be scanned properly. Draw a new frame by clicking at an appropriate point in the top left-hand corner and dragging the cursor down and to the right, or resize and reposition it as shown above.

What is TWAIN?

Although it looks like yet another computer acronym, TWAIN does not in fact stand for anything. The name was coined at a time when it was very difficult to get scanners and computers to communicate with each other and is taken from the line "...and never the twain shall meet..." in 'The Ballad of East and West' by Kipling.

Scanning a printed image

If you are scanning an image from a newspaper, you may find the scan appears slightly distorted. This arises from the hexagonal pattern of ink dots that printing produces.

You may find a 'de-screen' setting within your scanning controls that contains different settings in 'lpi' (lines per inch). For glossy, printed material select 133-200 lpi; for newspapers select 65-120 lpi. If you don't have these settings try to improve the scan by reducing the sharpness setting to lessen the distortion (see Step 8).

Bright idea
Experiment with different settings until you get the look you want. Your image doesn't have to appear exactly as it did in its original context, and you can double the image's impact by editing it to suit your own material.

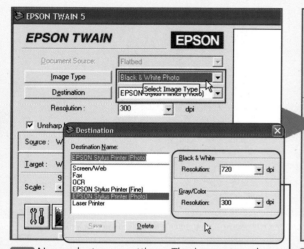

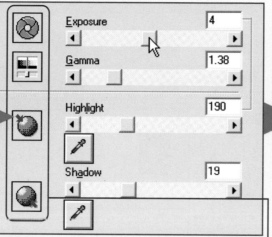

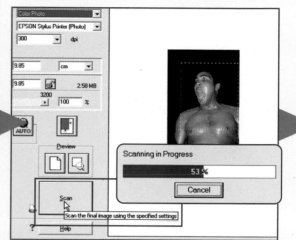

8 Now select your settings. The image type box lets you choose to scan in Black and White, while the resolution box lets you set the amount of detail that is picked up (see below). The Destination box allows you to scan at suitable settings for printing, faxing or viewing on screen.

9 There should be a set of tools that lets you make detailed adjustments to your scan. Image Controls, for example, lets you adjust the brightness and contrast of your image to a fine degree. Similar tools let you change colour settings and tones.

10 Once you have chosen your settings, click on the **Scan** button. You will hear the scanning head passing across your image, more slowly than it did when you previewed the image. You will also see a progress bar showing how much of the scan has been completed.

Conserving space
The amount of space your file uses relates both to the resolution at which the image has been scanned in and to its dimensions (height and width). By increasing just the resolution of this scan from 72 dpi to 200 dpi, the amount of memory it uses increases by more than ten times.

 Exposure *either lightens or darkens the image*

 Shadow *lets you apply dark areas to the scan*

 Gamma *sets the contrast between dark and light tones*

 Threshold *scans grey shades as black or white*

 Highlight *lets you apply light areas to the scan*

Ensure the Bitmap (.BMP) file format is selected in the File Format box. This means the scanned file can be imported into Word, Works and Paint, the Windows accessory program.

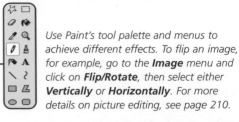

Use Paint's tool palette and menus to achieve different effects. To flip an image, for example, go to the **Image** menu and click on **Flip/Rotate**, then select either **Vertically** or **Horizontally**. For more details on picture editing, see page 210.

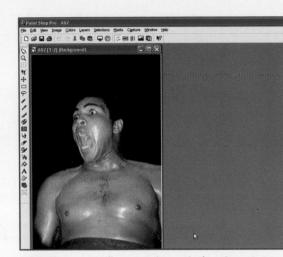

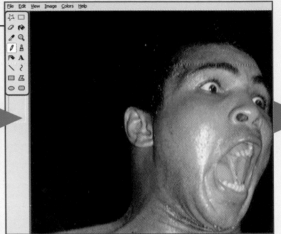

11 The scan will appear in a window in your image editing program. You may need to minimise the TWAIN Utility to see it properly. If you are not happy with the image you may be able to edit it and fine-tune its colours, or you might need to rescan it using different settings.

12 Now save your scan. Click on **Save As**, and choose a name and location for your scanned image. If you want to use or edit it in other programs it's best to save it as a Windows bitmap (shown by a .bmp at the end of the file name).

13 You can edit your image in the software that was supplied with your scanner (such as Paint Shop Pro) or in Paint. Go to the **Start** menu, select **Programs**, then **Accessories**, then **Paint**. When it opens, go to the **File** menu and select **Open**. Locate your scan then edit it.

Create a background

You can use a scanned photo as the background picture on your desktop if you saved it as a .bmp, .gif or .jpg file. Open the folder containing the image and right-click on it. Click on **Set as Desktop Background**. To adjust the desktop appearance right-click on it and choose Properties. Change the settings in the Desktop tab.

Now try placing your scan into a document to make, say, a card, a mini-magazine or a newsletter.

▶ NEW PROGRAM

To crop the image, click on the **Crop** *tool in the Picture toolbar then click on one of the side handles and drag it inwards. To resize the image, click on one of the corner handles and drag it diagonally.*

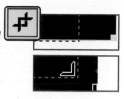

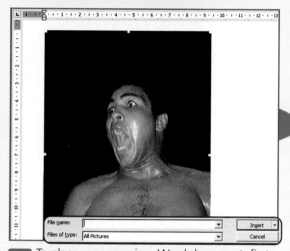

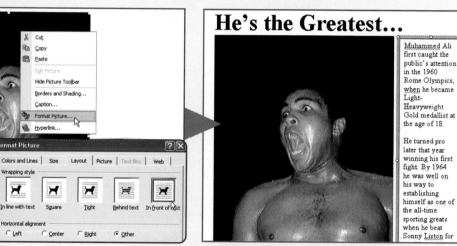

He's the Greatest...

Muhammed Ali first caught the public's attention in the 1960 Rome Olympics, when he became Light-Heavyweight Gold medallist at the age of 18.

He turned pro later that year winning his first fight. By 1964 he was well on his way to establishing himself as one of the all-time sporting greats when he beat Sonny Liston for

14 To place your scan in a Word document, first open the document. Place the cursor where you want the image to appear, go to the **Insert** menu, select **Picture**, then click on **From File**. Locate the scan through the 'Look in' box, then click **Insert**.

15 To move your image, right-click on it and click on **Format Picture**. Click on the **Layout** tab and then on **In front of text**. You should now be able to move the image around the page by clicking and dragging it. To resize and crop the image, see above.

16 To add text, go to the **Insert** menu and select **Text Box**. The cursor will change to a large cross. Draw two boxes – one for the heading and one for a caption. Size them in the same way you did for the picture. Click on the boxes and type in your text.

Using photos in Works

Inserting a photograph in Works is very similar to the procedure in Word. Go to the **Insert** menu, click on **Picture**, then **From File**. Navigate to the folder containing your photograph, click on it and then on **Insert**. The picture will appear in the document. You can resize the picture by clicking and dragging on one of the handles at the corners and the sides of the image. To keep the photograph in proportion, hold down the shift key as you drag a corner handle. Unlike Word, however, you cannot crop or adjust the colours of pictures in Works.

You will need to scan your picture in (see page 204) or get it scanned in at your local copy shop. Make sure it is saved in Bitmap (.bmp) format so that Paint can read it.

▶ BEFORE YOU START

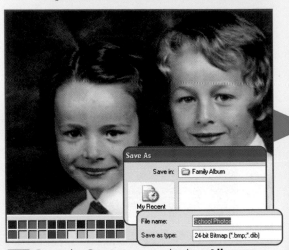

1 Go to the **Start** menu and select **All Programs**, then **Accessories**, then **Paint**. Go to the **File** menu and click on **Open**. Locate and click on your image, then click **Open**. Go to the **File** menu and click on **Save As**. Save as a 24-bit Bitmap file.

Use Paint to edit images

The camera never lies, but your PC can embellish the truth

Looking over old photographs can evoke many treasured memories, so it can be quite upsetting when they become faded, torn or scratched. Fortunately, you can use Paint, one of Windows accessory programs, to help create a 'blemish-free' version of the photograph. You can even use it to improve on the original image, removing 'red eye' and unwanted objects. And once you know the program, you can try creating special effects, such as adding elements of one photograph to another.

Paint comes with Windows and is a good place to start image editing. Advanced programs are available, including Adobe® Photoshop®, Corel Photo-Paint® and JASC® Paint Shop Pro®.

▶ OTHER PROGRAMS

⚠ Watch out
A scratch cannot be disguised using just one colour. As you work along the scratch, pick up colour from the surrounding area (see Step 3 for details).

🔑 Key word
__Pixel__ A computer image is made up of row upon row of tiny, coloured squares called pixels. Barely visible to the naked eye, they appear clearly when you enlarge your image using the View menu.

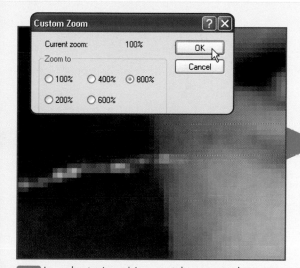

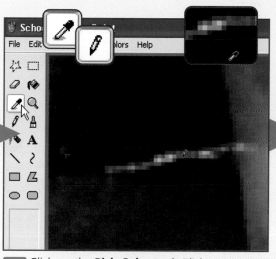

2 In order to 'repair' a scratch you need to magnify the image. Go to the **View** menu and select **Zoom** then **Custom**. In the Custom Zoom dialogue box, click the 800% option, then **OK**. Now use the scroll bars to find an area of the image to work on.

3 Click on the **Pick Color** tool. Click on an area of colour close to the blemish to 'pick up' that colour. Now click on the **Pencil** tool and click and drag over the blemish. If the colour is not quite right, use the **Pick Color** tool to select another one. Repeat for other areas.

4 Once you have finished a section, go to the **View** menu and select **Zoom** then **Normal Size**. Now assess how your changes look. To make further adjustments, repeat Steps 2 and 3. When satisfied, go to the **File** menu and click on **Save**.

Losing red eye

One of the most common photographic problems is red eye, the result of using a flash. It is possible to correct this in Paint, but you will almost certainly have to use several colours in order to ensure the eye looks real. To broaden Paint's colour palette, see right.

Create new colours

To add a new colour to the standard palette available in Paint, customise an existing one.

Double-click on the colour you want to customise in the Color box. In the Edit Colors dialogue box click on the **Define Custom Colors** button. Click and drag the slider next to the graduated colour palette until you get the right tone in the Color/Solid pane.

To save your colour, click on the **Add to Custom Colors** button. When you want to use it again, click on the Color box colour you customised. In the Edit Colors dialogue box the new colour will appear in the 'Custom colors' section. Click on it to select it.

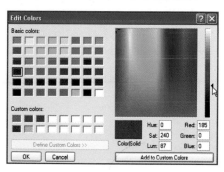

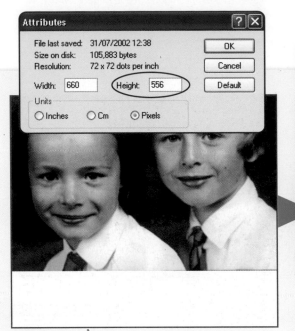

5 To add a caption to your picture, go to the **Image** menu and click on **Attributes**. In the Height box, increase the value by about 100 pixels then click **OK**. Scroll down the window and you will see a section of white has been added at the base of the image.

6 Click on the **Text** tool, then click and drag across the white space to create a text box. Type in your caption. Use the text toolbar to select a font, font size and style for your text. If the toolbar doesn't appear, go to the **View** menu and click on **Text Toolbar**.

7 Once you are happy with your image, go to the **File** menu and select **Save**. Return to the **File** menu and select **Print Preview** to see how the file looks before printing. Either print it yourself or take it to a print shop for a higher quality result.

Family treasures

You'll get particularly good results when restoring old black-and-white photos in Paint. Use the same technique as for colour, and remember that the depth of grey will vary across the photo. You'll see the huge range of shades when you magnify the image.

Mistakes with text

Once you click outside the text box you can't select your text and alter it. If you realise in time, you can correct your last three actions or commands by going to the **Edit** menu and selecting **Undo**. This will reopen the text box for you to correct the mistake.

If you notice your error after you have completed three more actions, click on the **Select** tool and click and drag to draw a rectangle around the text. Go to the **Edit** menu and select **Clear Selection**. Then create a new text box and type.

You can use Paint to add elements of one photograph to another. Simply select and copy part of one picture then paste it into another.

WORK WITH TWO IMAGES

Bright idea
Where possible, paste an image on to a plain, rather than a multi-coloured, background. This makes disguising the manipulation much easier.

8 Scan in your two pictures. Open the file from which you want to copy an element. Click on the **Free-Form Select** tool, then click and carefully drag the cursor around the section you want to copy. Go to the **Edit** menu and click on **Copy**.

9 Open the second file. Go to the **Edit** menu and click on **Paste**. The copied element then appears in a white box. To lose the background, click on the **Paste Transparent** tool. Click on the pasted image and drag it into position. Click off it only when it is in position.

10 Use the colour-filling method in Steps 2-4 to remove the unwanted outline around the pasted image and to blend the images into each other. When you are happy with the result, save the finished image.

Close-up
*When you are selecting the section of image you wish to copy and paste, magnify the image to fill the window (see Step 2). If you make a mistake, go to the **Edit** menu, click on **Undo**, then start again.*

Tidying up
If you simply want to remove a detail from a photo, select the image, go to the **Edit** menu and click on **Cut**. To fill the gap left, click on the **Pick Color** tool then 'pick up' a colour from the surrounding area. Click the **Fill With Color** tool then click in the white space.

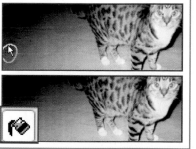

Design your own poster

Use graphics and text imaginatively to get your event noticed

When it comes to advertising an event, a colourful, eye-catching poster can really pull the crowds in. You can make a poster for almost any event, from a company dinner to a jumble sale. With a computer you don't need to be artistic to design an effective poster.

Posters should catch the attention of any passers-by and impart all the essential details of the event – the date, time, place, entry cost and purpose. If you use ClipArt, unusual fonts and WordArt (graphically enhanced text) be careful that you do not confuse readers with too many elements.

Check that all the information you want on your poster is correct, and think about which type of image will make the greatest impact.

▶ BEFORE YOU START

1 Go to the **Start** menu, select **All Programs** and click on **Microsoft Word**. Go to the **File** menu and select **Page Setup**. In the Page Setup dialogue box type in measurements for the Top, Bottom, Left and Right margins (at least 1 cm). Click **OK**.

*You can also design a poster in Microsoft Works. In the Works Task Launcher, click on **Works Word Processor** in the left-hand column. Select **Event flyers** on the right.*

▶ OTHER PROGRAMS

Templates on CD-ROM

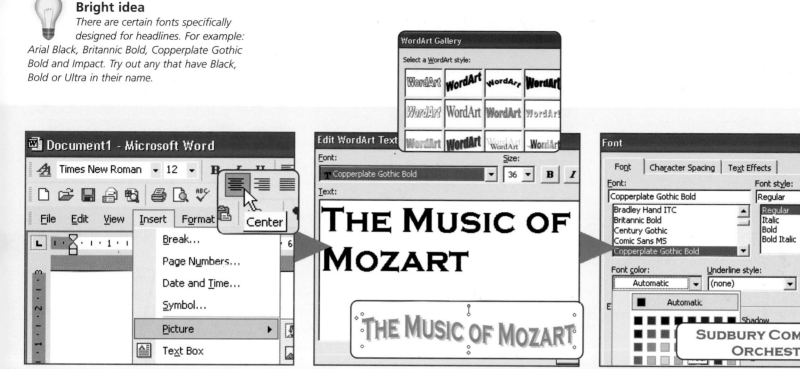

Bright idea
There are certain fonts specifically designed for headlines. For example: Arial Black, Britannic Bold, Copperplate Gothic Bold and Impact. Try out any that have Black, Bold or Ultra in their name.

2 Type in your text. To position it in the centre of your document, highlight it then click on the **Center** toolbar button. To insert WordArt, place your cursor where you want it to appear, then go to the **Insert** menu, select **Picture** and click on **WordArt**.

3 You will be presented with the WordArt Gallery. Click on a style you like, then **OK**. Type your heading into the dialogue box provided and select a font and font size. Click **OK**. Your heading will appear as WordArt (a type of image) in your document.

4 Now style the remainder of your text. Highlight each section in turn, go to the **Format** menu and click on **Font**. Select your choice of fonts, styles and font sizes. You can also choose from a selection of different text effects, including embossing.

Choosing the page size

When you open a new document, the paper size is automatically selected as Letter, and the orientation as Portrait (upright). To change the size, click on the **Paper** tab in the Page Setup dialogue box. Click on the arrow to the right of the 'Paper size' box, scroll through and select your preferred size. To change the orientation, select the Landscape option in the **Margins** tab.

Using WordArt

With your WordArt image selected click on the **Format** menu, select **WordArt**, then the **Layout** tab. The default setting is 'In line with text'. When WordArt is set to this option you can move it around the screen by hitting the return key on the keyboard. To be able to click and drag the object around the screen, select one of the other options. To adjust the size of your WordArt, click on one of the handles and drag it across the screen, and to distort the WordArt click and drag on the yellow square.

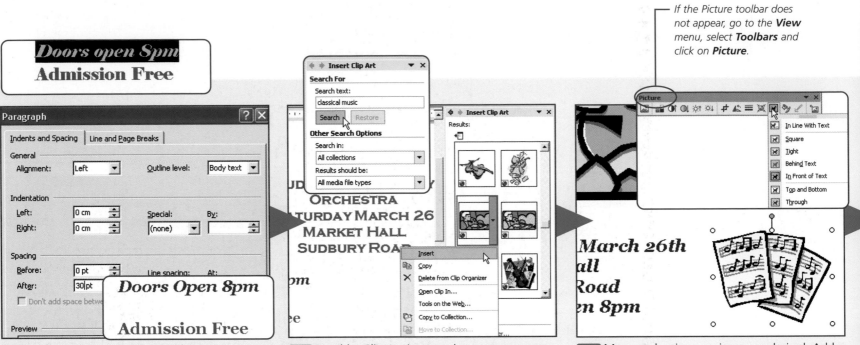

*If the Picture toolbar does not appear, go to the **View** menu, select **Toolbars** and click on **Picture**.*

5 To add space between text, place your cursor at the end of each section and press the **Return** key. For finer adjustments, highlight a section, go to the **Format** menu and click on **Paragraph**. In the Spacing section click on the uppermost arrow beside After.

6 To add a Clip Art image, place your cursor where you want it to appear, go to the **Insert** menu, select **Picture** and click on **Clip Art**. Type in the subject of your poster in the 'Search text' box in the right hand column and press **Search**. Click on an image then on **Insert** in the pop-up menu.

7 Move and resize your image as desired. Add as many images as you like. To ensure text flows around an image, click on it. The Picture toolbar will appear. Click on the **Text Wrapping** button then click on one of the options.

Importing images

If you want to use your own image from a CD-ROM or your scanned picture folder, go to the **Insert** menu, select **Picture** and click on **From File**. In the dialogue box scroll through and click on the location of your image. When you have located your image, click on it, then on **Insert**.

Cropping images

If you do not want to use all of the Clip Art image in your poster, crop out the unwanted parts. Click on the **Crop** tool in the Picture toolbar then click on and drag one of the picture handles. Drag the handles in or out to cut or restore the sides of your image.

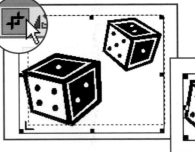

Watch out
A Clip Art image may be too large to fit where you want it to, in which case it will drop onto the next page. Reduce its size by clicking and dragging its picture handles then move it to your desired location.

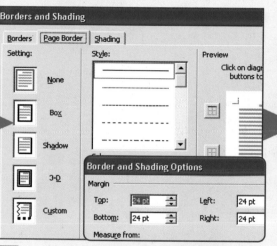

8 The Square option allows you to position text neatly above, below and at either side of your image. Tight keeps the text close to the image. With Edit Wrap Points you define the exact path the text takes around the picture by moving the wrap points.

9 To add a border, go to the **Format** menu and click on **Borders and Shading**. Click on the **Page Border** tab. Choose a style, colour, width and setting. (If necessary, click on **Options** and set the gap between the border and the edge of the page.) Click **OK**.

10 To view your poster, go to the **File** menu and click on **Print Preview**. If you need to make any alterations, press the **Esc** key and edit as necessary. To print your poster, click on the **Print** toolbar button.

Inserting an indent

When you type in text to a new document it automatically aligns to the left of the page. However, you may prefer to have more space between the text and the left-hand side of the page. Do this by adjusting the left indent.

Highlight your text and click on the **Increase Indent** toolbar button until you get the look you want. Click on the **Decrease Indent** button (to its left) to reduce the indent.

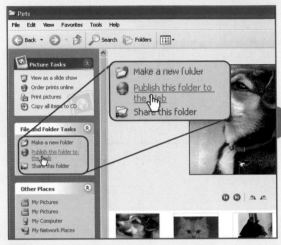

1 Gather all the photographs you intend to publish to the Web into one folder. To avoid very long downloads, make sure they are all under 1MB in size. Click on **Publish this folder to the Web** in the left hand column.

Build an on-line album

It's easy to create a photo album on the Web using Windows

Most people take more photographs than they ever put into an album. As a result, everyone has memory-filled shoe boxes that rarely see the light of day.

If you scan your pictures into your PC or upload them from a digital camera, you can create a kind of virtual photo album on-line. Windows XP has a built-in Web Publishing Wizard that takes your photos and publishes them on the World Wide Web, for all your friends and relatives around the world to see.

The process is very straightforward (as long as you have an Internet connection – see page 88). The web page you create is free apart from a few pence incurred in call charges while you're uploading the files.

Key word

.NET passport This gives you access to a raft of different services from Microsoft and other companies. Most people will come across it if they use Hotmail – Microsoft's very popular e-mail service. You also need a .NET passport to use Windows Messenger (see page 102) and a growing range of other services.

2 The **Web Publishing Wizard** will open. Click on **Next** and then choose each picture you want to upload to the Internet by making sure there is a tick in the box next to it. Buttons let you select all the pictures in the folder or clear your choices and start again. When you have completed your selection, click **Next**.

3 You will now need to connect to the web. If you have a dial-up connection, make sure your modem is plugged in and click on **Connect**. Once you are connected, a window opens showing a choice of places to store your files. Choose MSN Groups, then click on **Next**.

4 MSN Groups is a Microsoft service that lets you create 'meeting places' on the Internet where you can share family pictures for example. You'll need a .NET Passport to use the service – if you have not already got one, you will be asked to sign up for free.

Connecting a digital camera

Windows XP makes it easy to get pictures from a digital camera. Most cameras sold recently include a USB cable. Connect this to a vacant USB socket on your computer, switch the camera on and it should be recognised and configured automatically. You will see a dialogue box asking what you want to do each time you connect. You can choose whether to print all of the pictures in the camera's memory, view them as an on-screen slide show or copy them across to a folder on your computer.

Bright idea
Cropping your pictures so that the main subject of the photo is at the centre of the image makes for a more eye-catching display.

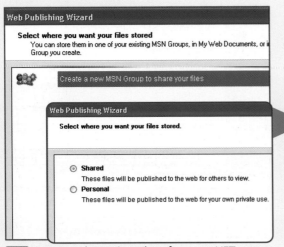

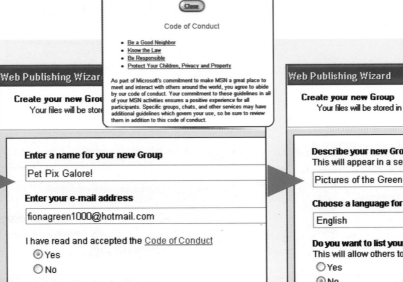

5 Once you have signed up for your .NET Passport, you can set up a new MSN Group. Click on **Create a new MSN Group to share your files**, then **Next**. Decide whether others will be able to view the files ('Shared') or not ('Personal'), then click **Next** again.

6 Enter a name for your group, along with the e-mail address you will have been given as part of the .NET Passport signup process. Click on **Code of Conduct** and read it carefully, then click next to 'Yes' and then on **Next**.

7 Add a description of your group for search engines to use. Set other options, then click on **Next**. Note the web address of your new group, and choose whether to have it added to the Favourites list in your web browser program, then click on **Next**.

Images on the Internet

The Web Publishing Wizard saves your photos in a format that is suitable for the Internet, but you may also want to send images as attachments to e-mails. To do this, you should compress pictures as either JPEG or GIF files (go to the **File** menu and click on **Save As** in a program like Paint). The JPEG is usually best for photographs, and allows you to choose how much compression to apply – too much means a loss of quality.

Bright idea

For those with a slow Internet connection, it can be annoying to be sent a large picture by e-mail and wait for it to download. So, rather than e-mailing a large picture file to your friends, publish it to a Website, and send them the Internet address of the Website in an e-mail, allowing them to choose whether to view it.

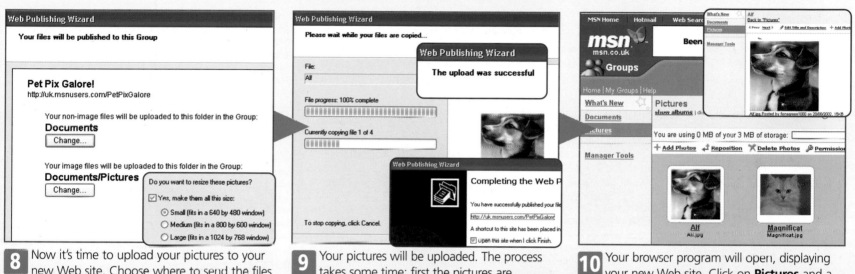

8 Now it's time to upload your pictures to your new Web site. Choose where to send the files (the suggested choices are usually fine) and click on **Next**. In the following window you can choose to have your pictures resized for the Internet. Make your choice then click on **Next**.

9 Your pictures will be uploaded. The process takes some time: first the pictures are processed and resized ready for the web, then they are transferred over to MSN's server. When all the files have been sent, click on **Next**. A confirmation will appear – click **Next** then choose to open the site in your browser before clicking **Finish**.

10 Your browser program will open, displaying your new Web site. Click on **Pictures** and a page will open showing your pictures as a series of thumbnails. Click on each image or the label below to see a full-sized version.

Order prints on-line

Windows XP lets you order high-quality prints of your pictures on-line. First connect to the Internet, then open the folder containing the pictures you want printed. Click on **Order prints online**. Follow the steps on screen. You will be asked to choose which pictures to print, and which printing service you want to use. This service is only worthwhile for high-quality images, which will take a long time to transfer if you have a slow Internet connection.

Painting on your PC

Create impressive works of art at the touch of a button

Fun, flexible and user-friendly, Paint is one of the most exciting Windows XP accessory programs. Even if you have never picked up a real paintbrush, you can create a piece of art to be proud of. Use it to paint abstract designs or familiar scenes, then transform your pictures into such things as greetings cards or party invitations.

The program has a variety of paintbrushes, pencils and airbrushes. And you can mix any colour you want using the Color box. Another advantage that Paint has over conventional oils or watercolours is that you can easily make 'authentic' copies of your work.

You might want to make a quick pencil sketch of your picture to give you a rough guideline to follow as you work on your PC.

▶ BEFORE YOU START

Attributes

File last saved:	Not Available
Size on disk:	Not Available
Resolution:	81 x 81 dots per inch

Width: 400   Height: 300

Units
○ Inches   ○ Cm   ◉ Pixels

OK

Colors
○ Black and white   ◉ Colors

1 Go to the **Start** menu, select **All Programs**, then **Accessories**, then **Paint**. Go to the **Image** menu and click on **Attributes**. Click on a measurement option in the Units section, then set the width and height of your canvas. Click **OK**.

Paint is the only graphics program available in Windows. But you can buy other, more sophisticated graphic packages – CorelDraw, for example – from computer shops.

▶ OTHER PROGRAMS

Close-up

The Attributes default setting for your picture size is 400 x 300 pixels, which is approximately 10.5 cm x 8 cm (4 in x 3 in). A pixel is the smallest area of the canvas which you can colour in order to create a picture.

Watch out

*When you use the **Fill With Color** tool in an enclosed space, the colour will appear only in that area. If the area isn't entirely enclosed, the colour will leak onto the rest of the picture.*

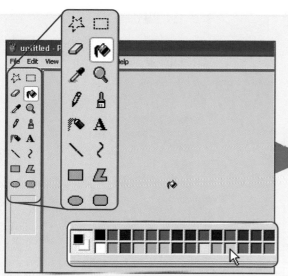

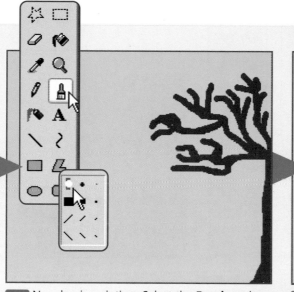

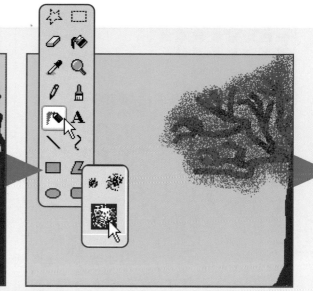

2 Start your picture by adding a background colour – you can then add other colours over this. Click on the **Fill With Color** tool then click on your choice of colour from the Color box at the bottom of the screen. Click on the canvas to add the colour.

3 Now begin painting. Select the **Brush** tool and click on a type of brush from the options below the Tool Box. Click on your choice of colour from the Color box. To make a brush stroke, click on the canvas and drag.

4 You can also use a spray-paint effect. Click on the **Airbrush** tool and click on a size of spray from the options below the Tool Box. Click on a colour from the Color box. Apply the colour as you did in Step 3.

Using the Tool box

Some tools, such as the brush tools, have a variety of styles which appear below the tool panel. Click on a style before using the tool. The functions of the tools are described below (the 'shape' tools are described on page 224):

Free-Form Select Selects an irregular-shaped area. Click and drag the pointer to select.

Select Selects a rectangular area. Click on the canvas and drag diagonally.

Eraser/Color Eraser Acts just like a rubber. Click and drag the pointer over the area to clear it.

Fill With Color Places a solid colour in an area. Choose a colour and click on the relevant area.

Pick Color Picks up a colour from the canvas. Apply the colour elsewhere by selecting another tool.

Magnifier Shows an area in close-up. Just click on the area. Also demagnifies magnified areas.

Pencil Draws a thin, freehand line. Click and drag the pointer to draw.

Brush Used for a brushstroke-style line. Select a style of brush then click and drag the pointer.

Airbrush Gives a spray-paint effect. Choose a spray radius then click and drag the pointer.

Text Inserts text into the picture. Click on the tool to draw a text box first, then add the text.

Line Draws a straight line. Select a thickness then click and drag the pointer.

Curve Used to draw a curve. You draw a line first then click on it and drag it to make a curve.

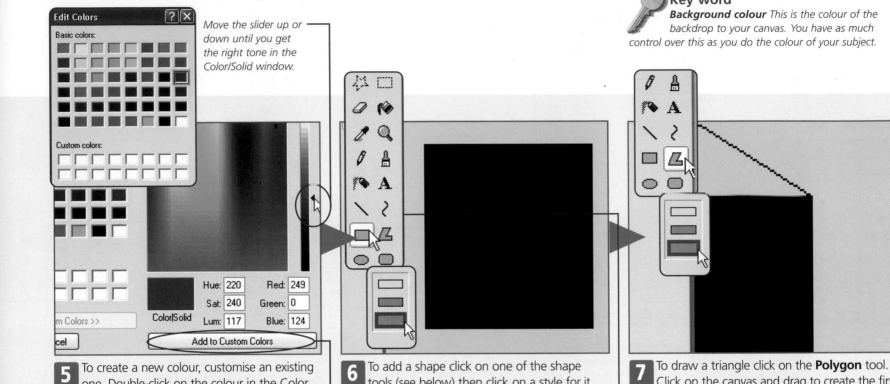

Move the slider up or down until you get the right tone in the Color/Solid window.

Edit Colors

Basic colors:

Custom colors:

Hue: 220   Red: 249
Sat: 240   Green: 0
Color|Solid   Lum: 117   Blue: 124

m Colors >>

cel   Add to Custom Colors

5 To create a new colour, customise an existing one. Double-click on the colour in the Color box. In the Edit Colors dialogue box click on the **Define Custom Colors** button. Create your colour (see above) then click **OK**.

6 To add a shape click on one of the shape tools (see below) then click on a style for it from the options below the Tool Box. Click on a colour from the Color box, then click on the canvas and drag to draw the shape.

7 To draw a triangle click on the **Polygon** tool. Click on the canvas and drag to create the first line. Release the button then click where the second side will end. A line will appear between this point and the first side. Repeat to complete the triangle.

To save your new colour, click on the **Add to Custom Colors** button. When you want to use it again, click on the Color box colour you customised. In the Edit Colors dialogue box your new colour appears in the 'Custom colors' section. Click on the colour to select it.

Shape tools

There are four shape tools to choose from – a rectangle, polygon (used to create irregular shapes), rounded rectangle and ellipse.

When you select a shape you are given three style options for it below the Tool box. The top one draws an outline in the colour of your choice; the middle one draws a coloured outline and fills the shape centre with the background colour; and the bottom one draws the shape and fills it with the colour of your choice.

Watch out
When you select a section of your canvas and move it, only click off it when you are happy with its new position. Once you click off it, you will have to reselect it before you can move it again.

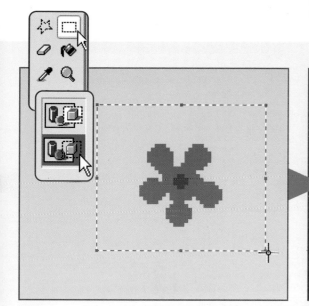

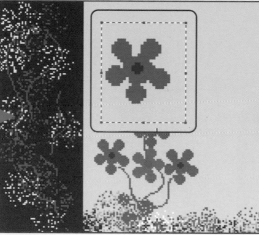

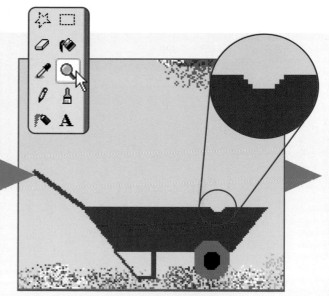

8 If you draw an item that you would like to repeat elsewhere on the canvas, click on the **Select** tool then click on the lower of the two options you are given below the Tool box. Click and drag over the item, go to the **Edit** menu and select **Copy**.

9 Return to the **Edit** menu and select **Paste**. The copied image appears at the top of the screen. Click on it and drag it to its new position. To change the colour of the item, click on the **Fill With Color** tool, select a different colour and click on the item.

10 Use the Magnifier to check for errors. For instance, you may have accidentally painted over part of another object. To undo this, click on the **Pick Color** tool and click on the correct colour on the canvas. Click on the **Brush** tool, select an option, then re-paint the area.

Stretch and skew

To stretch or skew part of your picture, go to the **Image** menu and click on **Stretch and Skew**. Experiment with measurements in either the Stretch or Skew sections.

Stretch and Skew		? X
Stretch		OK
↔	Horizontal: 60 %	Cancel
↕	Vertical: 60 %	
Skew		
↔	Horizontal: 0 Degrees	
↕	Vertical: 0 Degrees	

Flip and rotate

To flip or rotate part of your picture, click on the **Select** tool and select the area in question. Go to the **Image** menu and click on **Flip/Rotate**. To change the way it faces select the 'Flip horizontal' option; to turn it upside-down select the 'Flip vertical' option; to move it around by increments of 90° select the 'Rotate by angle' option, then the relevant degree option.

Flip and Rotate

Flip or rotate
- ● Flip horizontal
- ○ Flip vertical
- ○ Rotate by angle
  - ● 90°
  - ○ 180°
  - ○ 270°

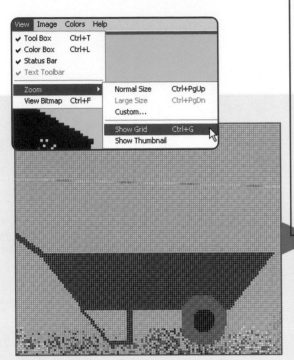

 There are two types of text box:
With this box you can add a background colour. Click on **Fill With Color**, select a colour then click in the box.
This option gives a transparent text box, through which you can see the background of the picture.

Once you have created your picture, Paint allows you to save it and use it in a number of ways, including as Desktop background.

USING YOUR IMAGE

 11 For precision corrections and drawing, magnify an area, go to the **View** menu, select **Zoom** then click on **Show Grid**. Now edit or draw, one pixel at a time.

12 To add text, click on the **Text** tool and select a box style (see above). Click and drag on the canvas to draw a box. Click on a colour from the Color box for your text, then start typing. To style text, highlight it, go to the **View** menu and select **Text Toolbar**.

13 Go to the **File** menu and click on **Save As**. Select a location and type a file name. To insert a Paint file into other documents, select **24-bit Bitmap** in the 'Save as type' box. To e-mail or add it to a Web page, choose either **GIF** or **JPEG**. Click **Save**.

Correcting mistakes

There are various ways to correct errors:

 Undo You can undo up to three changes at a time by going to the **Edit** menu and clicking on **Undo** for each correction. As a shortcut, press the **Ctrl** and 'Z' keys simultaneously.

 Erase Click on the **Eraser** tool and select a style option, then rub out the mistake on the canvas. Be aware that this rubs out all colour.

Paint over You can hide the error by painting over it. Click on the **Pick Color** tool, then click on the correct colour on the canvas. Select a brush and start painting over the error.

 Edit by pixel Click on the **Magnifier** tool then click on the appropriate part of the canvas. Go to the **View** menu, select **Zoom** then **Show Grid**. Now edit individual pixels.

Close-up
You can set your Desktop background as either Centered or Tiled. The first option places the image in the centre of your screen with a plain surround. The second covers your screen by repeating the image.

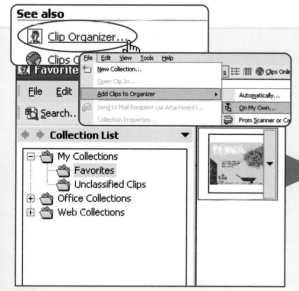

14 To use your image as Clip Art open a Word document. Go to the **Insert** menu, select **Picture**, then **Clip Art**. Click on **Clip Organizer** in the column that appears. In the Organizer select **File**, then **Add Clips to Organizer**, then **On My Own**. Find and click on your file then click **Add**.

15 You can use your picture as your Desktop background image (see above). Go to Paint's **File** menu and select either **Set As Background (Tiled)** or **Set As Background (Centered)**. See page 68 for more on personalising your Desktop.

16 Printing from Paint follows the same rules as in other programs. Go to the **File** menu and click on **Page Setup** to set your margins and orientation. From the **File** menu select **Print Preview** to check the look of your document, and **Print** if you are happy.

Now you have mastered Paint's tools, you can go on to edit photographs and other images. Turn to page 210 for more details.

▶ **OTHER IDEAS TO TRY**

227

Make your fête a day

There's no aspect of a fête (except the weather) that

Project planner

*Create a folder called 'Fête'.
Add sub-folders within it for
smaller projects.*

- 📁 Fête
  - 📁 Correspondence
  - 📁 Publicity
  - 📁 Finance
  - 📁 Ideas
  - 📁 Timetable
  - 📁 Floor plan

A successful fête is a matter of pre-planning and organisation. The main thing is to be sure that everything comes together at the right moment. It is a serious job making certain that everyone has fun on the day.

There are so many things to think about that the first job is to delegate some of the work. Form a committee and assign roles: someone to deal with drumming up publicity in the press and on the radio; someone to approach businesses for sponsorship or material help; and someone to be fête treasurer (this is particularly important if yours is a fundraising or charitable event).

Now you have to decide on a venue, and on a beneficiary if you plan to donate the proceeds of the fête to charity. Someone on the committee should keep careful notes of the discussions, and these should be typed up and circulated soon after each committee meeting. You may want to invite

in a million

you can't plan on your computer

your community police officer, or someone from the local council to take part in one of the meetings.

By now, you will have set up a timetable database on which you record the tasks that need to be carried out and when. Tick tasks off as they are completed – that way you can use the sort facility to separate completed tasks from those yet to be done, and so plan a weekly schedule.

If you are seeking sponsorship or prize donations, you might like to create an event letterhead for your correspondence. If you have e-mail or a fax modem, then use

them to keep in touch with all the clubs and organisations taking part in the fête. Meanwhile, use your PC to plan the location of all the stalls on the site.

As the day approaches, you can use your PC to create posters and flyers. By now you will know what the big attractions are and you can feature these on your publicity material (if you have asked a celebrity to open the fête, be sure that their photograph is on the poster).

When the big day eventually arrives, just relax and enjoy it – by now you'll have earned it.

Event organiser

- Form an organising committee. Arrange either monthly or weekly meetings
- Agree a date and beneficiaries of the profits
- Provisionally book the venue
- Approach local businesses for sponsorship
- Contact the police or local council to ensure date and venue are suitable
- Inform local press for advance and on-the-day coverage. Agree and implement publicity ideas

Ideas and inspirations

Listed here are a selection of projects you might want to use – or customise – to help you in the organisation of a successful community event. Allocate as much work as possible to other people, but keep a record of all developments on your computer.

180 Timetable database
Leave nothing to chance – produce a helpful diary of 'to do' tasks with your database.

144 Event letterhead
Correspond with stallholders and potential sponsors in a distinctive and memorable way.

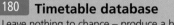

214 Design your own poster
Publicise the date, time and venue of your event locally, together with details of its attractions.

272 Accounts spreadsheet
Use a spreadsheet to keep track of all expenditure and income arising from your event.

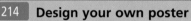

294 Stall planner
Create a simple, overhead 2D plan of the venue and organise your space effectively.

Also worth considering...

If your timescale and responsibilities justify it, you may find the following project makes things easier.

162 Create a newsletter
Keep the key people involved in the event informed of developments and progress.

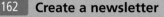

Create a Party CD

Compile and record **your own** music compilation

One of the best things about Windows XP is Windows Media Player. This program controls all forms of entertainment you're likely to use on your PC, from playing music CDs to viewing DVDs. The Media Player comes into its own, however, if you have a CD recorder or 'burner'. With it you can back up your files cheaply and reliably. More excitingly, it allows you to create CDs with the mix of music that suits you.

The right music can make a party go with a swing. Your guests will most likely become bored of hearing tracks by one artist. To avoid the chore of continually changing CDs, your computer allows you to create a compilation CD for special occasions.

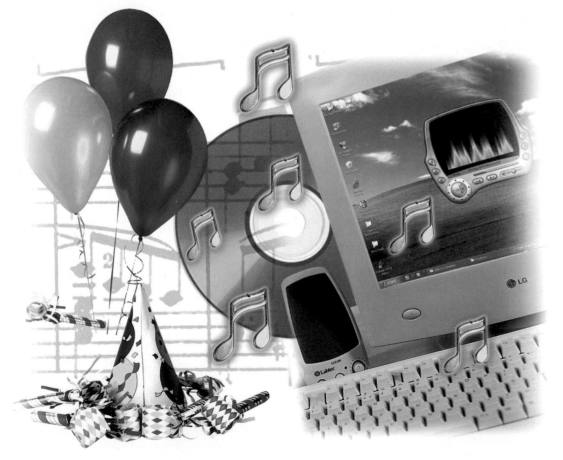

Go through your CD collection and choose music for your compilation. You don't need to have a chosen the order that they will play in.

► BEFORE YOU START

1 In the **Start** menu, click on **All Programs**, then **Windows Media Player**. The program will open and, if it's the first time you've used it, start playing a sample of music. Open your CD drive and insert an audio CD. The CD should start playing automatically – to see track names and details see below. Click on **Copy from CD**.

Naming Tracks

Windows Media Player can look up your CD against a database on the Internet and fill in the track title, artist and even the songwriters for you. Click on **Get names**. You will be asked to connect to the Internet. Once you've logged on to your Internet provider the search begins. The program will come back with what it thinks is a matching album – if it's correct (not always the case) click **Finish** to have your CD's details automatically completed.

Watch out

Respect copyright: it is illegal to copy and distribute the music on most CDs. You can make a single copy for your own use, but do not share files you copy with others.

2 Go to the **Tools** menu and click **Options**. In the Copy Music tab, set the slider to **Best Quality** (suitable for a CD) and click **OK**. Select the tracks to copy by clicking in the boxes to their left, then click on **Copy Music**. The track will be copied to your hard drive. Eject the CD and repeat the procedure for all the other tracks you want to copy.

3 Click on **Media Library**, then **New Playlist**. Name your Playlist then click **OK**. Click on **All Audio** in the left-hand column and drag tracks from the right-hand column to your new playlist. When you've finished, double-click on your new playlist to view it. Change the order of tracks by clicking and dragging them up or down.

4 Insert a blank CD-R in your CD burner and click on **Copy to CD or Device**, then on **Copy Music**. Your copied tracks will first be converted into a format suitable for CD, and then burnt to your CD-R. When it's finished, your CD will be ejected, ready to play.

Music Formats

The CD that you create using Windows Media Player does not contain exact copies of the tracks on your original CDs. When it copies songs to your hard drive, the program encodes in a special space-saving format (called a wmp file), with a slight loss of quality. When you burn your CD, the files are reconverted, but the lost quality cannot be restored.

Shedding Skins

Windows Media Player lets you radically alter its appearance. Click on **Skin Chooser**. A list of different skins will appear, each replacing the standard buttons and sliders with a themed look. When you find a skin that you like, click on **Apply skin** and the program will reclothe itself – maybe in rather a surreal way!

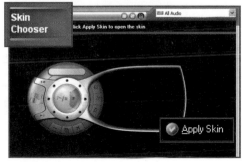

Introducing sound files

Have fun with the sounds that your computer makes

If your computer has a pair of speakers and a sound card (located inside your system unit), you can alter its 'tone of voice', or perform other tasks to do with sounds and music. For example, if your CD-ROM drive is not in use while you are working, you can use it to play music.

The addition of sound also maximises your enjoyment of computer games, and you can even use your PC's audio capabilities in conjunction with other software to make your own music.

It's also possible to add new sounds and assign them to tasks your computer performs, such as switching on or starting a piece of software. Windows even comes with a set of sound 'themes' which means you can change the entire acoustics of your system.

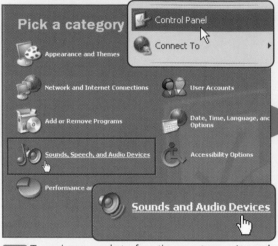

Ensure your speakers are plugged into the correct socket on the sound card (at the rear of your system unit) and that they are switched on.

BEFORE YOU START

1 To assign sounds to functions, set up a 'sound scheme' (a pre-set menu of sounds your PC plays when it carries out certain actions). Go to the **Start** menu, click on **Control Panel**, then **Sounds, Speech, and Audio Devices** then **Sounds and Audio Devices**.

Watch out

*When you select a different sound scheme you may be asked whether you want to save the previous scheme if you haven't already done so. Click **Yes**, type in a suitable name, then click **OK**.*

*To remove a sound from an event, click on the event and select **(None)** from the Name box in the Sound section.*

2 The Sounds and Audio Devices Properties box opens. Click on the **Sounds** tab, then the arrow beside the Sound scheme box. Click on **Windows Default**. You will be adding new sounds to this to make your own scheme.

3 The Program events pane at the bottom of the window shows every action to which a sound can be assigned. Those with a speaker icon already have a sound assigned. To find out the name of the sound that has been assigned, click on the event then look in the Sounds box.

4 To assign a different sound, click on the relevant event, scroll through the options in the Sounds box and click on your choice. Click on **Save As**. A box will appear asking you to name your new scheme. Type the name you want to use and click **OK**. Next, click on **Apply**, then **OK**.

Events on your PC

Assign sounds to the key events, or actions, that your PC performs:
- Start Windows
- Open program
- Program error
- Close program
- Maximise windows
- Minimise windows

To hear the sound assigned to an event, first click on the event then click on the arrow button to the right of the Sounds box.

Close-up

The most recent sound scheme you have saved will be loaded automatically when you switch on your PC. You won't have to reload it from the Control Panel.

You can have fun by recording your own set of sounds to assign to certain events. For this you will need a microphone.

► RECORDING SOUNDS

Bright idea
Before opening Sound Recorder, make sure your microphone is switched on. If you don't want to record your own voice, use music or dialogue from another source, such as a videotape.

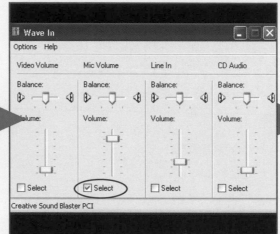

5 To record your own sounds, go to the **Start** button and select **All Programs**, then **Accessories**, then **Entertainment** and **Volume Control**. In the Volume Control dialogue box go to the **Options** menu and select **Properties**. Click the Recording option then click **OK**.

6 The 'Wave In' Recording Control dialogue box then appears. Make sure the box at the base of the 'Mic (Microphone) Volume Balance' section is ticked. This tells Windows that you are going to use a microphone as your source. Then close the dialogue box.

7 To open the Microsoft Sound Recorder, go to the **Start** menu and select **All Programs**, then **Accessories**, then **Entertainment** and finally **Sound Recorder**. Your PC is now ready to record any sound you enter via the microphone.

Setting up for recording

Plug your microphone into the sound card at the rear of the system unit beside the speakers socket (your speakers should already be connected). The microphone socket will probably be marked 'mic', or have a picture of a microphone by it. If the microphone itself has an on-off switch, make sure it is turned on. If your microphone needs a battery (few do), make sure it has one.

Other sound sources

As well as recording your own sounds, you can download some from the Internet. In order for Windows to read them they need to be in .wav format – they will have .wav after their names.

Watch out
If you switch off your speakers when you finish using your PC, remember to turn them on again when you want to hear sounds.

8 Click the **Record** button (the red dot) and speak (or play a pre-recorded sound) into the microphone. The green line in the sound recorder window becomes a waveform, giving a visual representation of the sound. When you have finished recording, click the **Stop** button.

9 To speed up, slow down, reverse, add an echo or alter the volume of your sound, go to the **Effects** menu and click on a relevant option. Click the **Play** button (with a single arrow) to listen to your changes. To save your sound, go to the **File** menu and click on **Save As** (see below).

10 To assign your recorded sounds to events, open the Sounds and Audio Devices Properties window (see Steps 1-4), and click on a program event. Click the **Browse** button and search through your hard drive to open your sounds folder. Select your sound and click **OK**.

Organising your sound files

Save all your sounds in the same folder so that it will be easy to find them. Create a new folder in My Documents, or put them in the Windows Media folder (go to the **Start** menu, click on **My Computer**, then double-click **[C:]**, then **Windows**, then **Media**). This is the folder where Windows automatically looks for sound files.

Link a music keyboard

Turn your PC into a musical instrument or recording studio

There are many ways to make music on your PC. With the correct software and an average sound card, you can generate sound without the need for separate instruments. You can record your voice and sample it, or use sound files from other sources such as the Internet or CDs.

You can link a keyboard to your PC using a MIDI (Musical Instrument Digital Interface) connector (some keyboards can also use a USB socket). This allows you to record your own tunes as you play them. You can then play back your music, edit and rewrite it, arrange and orchestrate it.

You can also buy software that allows you to write musical notation – a real advance over the long-winded business of writing compositions by hand on score paper.

Cubase • SX

Install Cubase SX
Install Acrobat Reader

1 Insert the music software CD in your CD drive. Your computer will automatically recognise it and begin to install it. You will also be asked if you wish to install Acrobat Reader (software that lets you read and print out help documentation for the program).

Watch out

Music-making can ask a lot of your computer, especially if you are recording and playing back lots of sounds at once. Music production programs run best if you have a lot of RAM available – at least 256MB is the usual recommended minimum.

Close-up

In order for your keyboard to be able to communicate with your PC, you must set it up correctly. Follow the instructions in the music keyboard's manual to help you do this.

Read Me File

Welcome to Steinberg's Cubase SL. This "read me" contains the latest information about Cubase SL 1.01 Please read the following information carefully.

IMPORTANT:

Read the Softwar
supplied with the
sending back the
yourself to be in a
contract.

If you want to rea
independently fro
to print the contr
CD-ROM in the 'L
several text files,
contains your ch

Cubase SL

Please enter the Name and S into the fields below.

Name
Dave Green

Serial Number
083160

Setup will install Cubase SL in the following folder.

To install into a different folder, click Browse, and select another folder.

You can choose not to install Cubase SL by clicking Cancel to exit Setup.

Destination Folder

C:\Program Files\Steinberg\Cubase SL   Browse...

Current Free Disk Space: 3532240 k
Free Disk Spa

< Back   Next >   Cancel

Current File

Copying file:
C:\...\Steinberg\Cubase SL\Default.cpr

All Files

Installation Complete

Cubase SL has been successfully installed.

Press the Finish button to exit this installation.

2 The program will ask you to read and agree to the software licence. You will need to fill in your name and owner serial number (this will be with your product documents). You may be prompted to confirm that the information is correct.

3 When asked to install the software, click on **Next** or **OK**. Your PC will suggest a folder in which to store it. Click **Next** to agree, or **Browse** to choose a different location. You may be asked if you wish to keep specialised files from a previous version of the program.

4 As the software installs you will see progress bars in screen showing how long there is to go. When the installation is complete you will be notified and asked if you would like to restart the computer to complete the process.

Setting up

Plug the MIDI lead into the sound card at the back of the system unit (this will probably be the joystick port). The other end of the lead splits into two. The two jacks plug into the keyboard's 'MIDI Out' and 'MIDI In' sockets. Alternativey you may be able to plug the keyboard directly into a USB socket. Now plug the keyboard into the mains socket and turn it on.

To combat software piracy, some software companies supply a special adaptor (a 'dongle') that must be plugged into a USB port. When you restart after installing, plug the dongle in and follow the steps to have it recognised.

Bright idea

A program is often updated after its CD-ROM has been pressed. Cubase will automatically look on-line for the latest updates to the program when your machine restarts – make sure your modem is plugged in and switched on, if necessary.

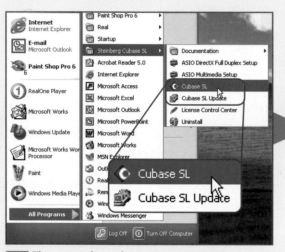

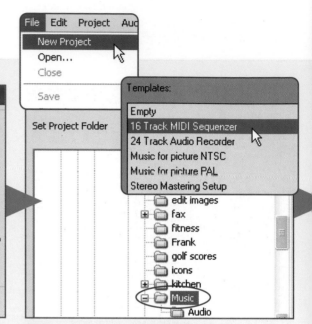

5 There may be a shortcut to your new software on your Desktop (double-click to open it). If not, go to the **Start** menu, select **Programs** then click on the program's name.

6 All MIDI software requires a 'device driver' to help it run. Because this is the first time you have opened your MIDI software, it will check your driver configuration. So, click **OK** to confirm that you want the driver tested.

7 To start a new project, go to the **File** menu, click on **New Project** and choose the **16 Track MIDI Sequencer** option from the list that appears. You will be promted to choose or create a folder to store the files that you create when you start recording music.

What is MIDI?

MIDI stands for Musical Instrument Digital Interface. This is a technical standard that allows musical data to be sent between different computers and specially equipped musical instruments.

It does not record specific sounds but instead records information about which notes you want in your compositions in a universal language which any computer can translate and – if connected to a MIDI sound source – replay.

The transport bar

Cubase's transport bar works just like the controls on an ordinary Hi-Fi system. As well as the usual Stop, Play and Record buttons, plus Rewind and Forward, you can set the tempo and time signature (4/4 etc) and check MIDI input and output.

Close-up

Keyboards are effective at emulating the sounds made by other instruments and are the most common MIDI instruments. But there are other MIDI instruments you can record and play with – guitars and drums are also popular choices.

*To return to the beginning of a tune, whether you are playing it or have just recorded it, double-click on the **Stop** button. If you just want to play a part of the song, click **Stop** then drag the 'Song position line' to where you want the playback to begin.*

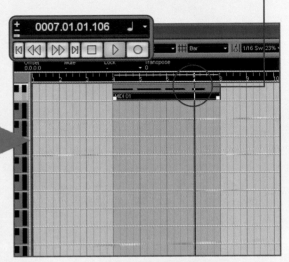

8 Check that Cubase can detect playing on your MIDI keyboard: play a note and look for lights in the In section of the transport bar. In the inspector (the panel on the left) click on out: and choose a MIDI instrument from the list. Now you should hear notes when you play.

9 To start recording click on the record button (marked with a circle) on the transport bar. You should hear 2 bars of metronome clicks to gauge the tempo, then your playing will be recorded. When you have finished click on the stop button (marked with a square).

10 Your tune appears as 'MIDI 01' in the arrangement window. Click the **Play** button (marked with an arrow) to hear it. Your PC and keyboard are now in harmony.

Get to know your keyboard

Keyboards have a range of different facilities. Like electronic synthesisers, some are more sophisticated than others. Some have two built-in libraries, one for instrument voices and another for rhythm styles. Some have facilities to construct and save their own rhythms. In addition to sound banks, your keyboard may have other useful features – for example, the ability to split the keyboard into two different voices, a built-in metronome to count off beats and keep time, automatic harmonisation and the facility to automatically alter the beat.

Music software – an overview

Composition software, such as Cubase, allows you to record any number of musical strands – called parts – separately, then play them back together at once as a single composition or arrangement. After you record your Parts you can then edit them, moving and lengthening notes, adding echoes and so on, to achieve the effect you want. (Edit mode also allows you to write musical notes on your screen and play them back through your sound card and/or MIDI instrument.)

Parts are recorded onto tracks. Cubase has two main types of tracks – MIDI tracks which store the notes you play on a MIDI instrument connected to a computer, and audio tracks which store actual sounds fed into your computer via the sound card.

Cubase and programs similar to it act like software versions of professional music studios, and have a wealth of complex features beyond the scope of this book. The two most basic techniques you will need to master are recording MIDI and audio tracks, which we demonstrate over the next few pages.

Working with music files

To make the best use of a program like Cubase you will need to have a MIDI keyboard attached to your computer (see page 236). Ideally the keyboard should be able to produce its own sounds, however you can also use it to trigger sounds generated by the computer itself. Windows XP incudes a standard set of MIDI sounds and Cubase adds to these with programs that emulate synthesisers and drum machines. To make the best use of this sort of feature – and of Cubase in general – you will need a fast PC with plenty of RAM (see page 237), lots of hard disk space and a professional quality sound card.

Compose your own music

Use specialist software to make music on your computer

Your PC can be a key compositional tool, helping you to create anything from a simple tune to a complex arrangement. In fact, with a sound card and/or MIDI instrument, you have access to a 'virtual' orchestra.

You don't need to be an experienced musician to enjoy composing music although, naturally, the more musical training you have, the more you can make of your PC's capabilities. Specialist software makes it possible for the novice to experiment with special effects, from simple fading in and fading out, to 'bending' and 'stretching' the sounds in ways that can't be achieved with a single instrument.

This project uses a MIDI keyboard and follows the creation of a simple arrangement composed of two piano parts which form a 'round', a rhythm track and a drum track.

The arrangement in this project was composed using Cubase SL music software. Whichever software you use, the basic principles of composition are the same. Consult your manual for specific guidance.

OTHER PROGRAMS

*If you'd like a metronome to keep time as you play your parts, click on the **Click** button on the transport bar.*

To set up your music keyboard and software, and to familiarise yourself with the key elements of Cubase, see pages 236-239.

BEFORE YOU START

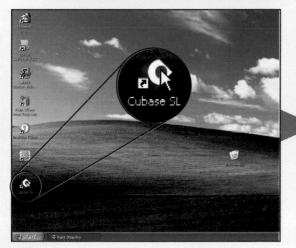

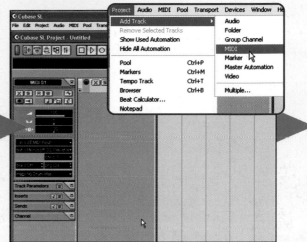

1 Launch your recording and sequencing software (in this case Cubase SL). Either double-click on the desktop icon, or go to the **Start** menu, click on **All Programs** then **Cubase**. The program will open in a new window.

2 To start a new project go to the **Start** menu and click on **New Project**. Choose the **Empty** option from the list that appears. Next choose a folder, or create a new one, to store your project in. This folder will be where Cubase places any sound files created as you record.

3 Add the first track to the project. Go to the **Project** menu, click on **Add track** then **MIDI**. The new track, called MIDI 01, will appear in the Project window.

Understanding the Project window

The Project window is the heart of a Cubase recording. From it you can control and manipulate most elements in your work. It is made of three main sections. In the middle is the track list, showing all the tracks, both MIDI and audio, that you have recorded. To the right is the arrangement area, where the individual parts are shown in position against a timeline at the top. You can zoom in and out of this view to look at recorded waveforms or MIDI notes, or to see the whole song in one window. To the left is the Inspector, which shows extra information about the currently selected track. Use the Inspector to choose instruments for a MIDI track, or to monitor levels on an audio track.

Close-up
*If you make mistakes with your recordings don't worry. Just stop playing and click the yellow **Stop** button on the transport bar. Then click on the part you have recorded and press the **Delete** key.*

Key word
Round *This describes a tune or song that is made up of the same parts that follow each other at equal intervals and at the same pitch.*

4 The Inspector allows you to choose the sound for the track. First choose the correct MIDI output for the track. Then click on **prg:**. You can change sounds by either clicking the up and down arrows on the keyboard or by directly typing in a number (up to 128).

5 Now record the first track. To hear a metronome click while you are playing make sure **Click** on the transport panel is lit. Click on the record button, listen to the 2-bar count-in and start playing. Click on the stop button to end your recording session.

6 Your new track will appear in the Project window. To hear it, click on the rewind button in the transport panel, then on the play button. If you're not happy with your recording simply hit delete to erase it.

Program controls

Whatever program you use, you will almost certainly have a set of controls to help you in your compositions. In Cubase, this set of controls is called the transport bar. You can make it appear, and disappear, by pressing the **F12** key at the top of your keyboard.

The transport bar is the control panel for playing and recording single tracks, and for setting their tempo and other features.

Parts do not always need to be recorded. You can draw drum parts, for example, in the pane on the right of the arrangement window, then fill in the notes, tempo, etc, afterwards.

▶ DRAWING PARTS

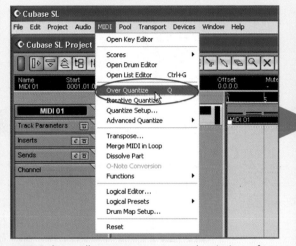

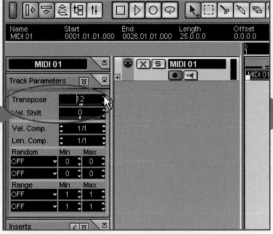

7 Cubase allows you to correct the timing of your playing by 'Quantizing' it. Click on a track then go to the MIDI menu and choose **Over Quantize**. Basic quantization simply forces notes to play right on the beat.

8 In the Inspector to the left of the Project window, click on **Track parameters**. Here you can alter parameters such as the relative loudness of the notes you recorded. You can also transpose your recording up and down by a chosen number of semitones – up 12 shifts the pitch up by an octave.

9 To correct individual notes, select a track, go to the **MIDI** menu and click on **Open Key Editor**. All the notes you recorded show on a piano-roll-like display. You can move notes up and down in pitch and forward or back in time. Click on the tools at the top to delete notes, split them or write new ones in.

Editing drum parts

Cubase, like many other music sequencers, has a dedicated Drum Editor for creating and correcting drum parts. It allows you to see the notes played on each percussion instrument arranged on a grid, and, if set up correctly, shows the name of each instrument in a particular drum set. The drum sets that you will have available depend on the MIDI instruments

attached to your computer or the sound card that you have installed. To make a MIDI part play drum sounds, you need to assign it to a drum map. In the Inspector on the left of the Project window click on **Map**. The GM Map should be an option – this allows you to play the drum sounds built into the General MIDI (GM) soundset that is part of Windows XP. To use other drum sets click on **Drum Map Setup**.

Pitch	Instrument
C1	Bass Drum
C#1	Side Stick
D1	Acoustic Snare
D#1	Hand Clap
E1	Electric Snare
F1	Low Floor Tom
F#1	Closed Hi-Hat
G1	High Floor Tom
G#1	Pedal Hi-Hat
A1	Low Tom

*To listen to any single track among the many that you have recorded, first click on the track then click the **S** (for Solo) button to the left. Finally, click the **Play** button on the transport bar.*

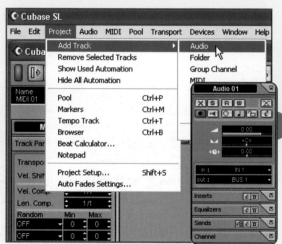

10 Now record an audio track. Close the Key Editor window and go to the **Project** menu. Click on **Add track** then **Audio**. A track marked Audio 01 will appear in the Project window.

11 Connect a microphone to the microphone input of your sound card. To check that sound is getting through, click on **Channel** in the Inspector. A channel meter will appear. Sing or play into the microphone and watch the the meter light up to show that a signal is getting through.

12 Click on the record button to start recording. You should hear your MIDI track in the background, allowing you to sing along. When you have finished, click on the stop button.

Special effects

Cubase has many built-in effects that can add depth and excitement to your recorded material. These include reverberations and echo units that help a dry recording sound more lifelike, as well as effects that exploit the digital nature of recording on a PC to make sounds that are anything but lifelike.

In theory you could add as many effects as you like to your recordings, but each new effect places further demands on your computer's processor – avoid this by using a fast PC with plenty of RAM.

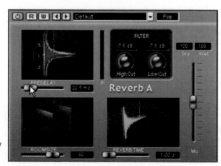

Bright idea
If you play a tape back faster than it was recorded, it will sound higher in pitch but will be shorter. Cubase, like most recording programs, can change the pitch of an audio file without changing its duration: something that was impossible before computer-based recording.

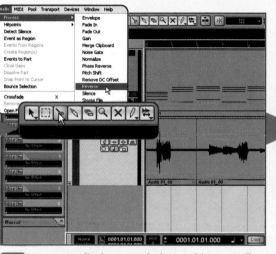

13 To listen to your recording, click on the rewind button on the transport panel, then on the play button. To view the recorded waves in more detail, use the sliders in the bottom right-hand corner of the Project window.

14 You can split the recorded sound into smaller sections that you can copy or repeat using the tools at the top of the Project window. You can also manipulate the sound in many different ways including reversing it, changing its pitch or lengthening it.

15 You can carry on adding audio and MIDI tracks to your recording up to a limit set either by your software or the capabilities of the computer system. Use the Track Mixer to adjust their balance (go to the **Devices** menu, then click on **Track Mixer**).

Repeating parts

If you're writing a piece of music that has repetitive elements – a drum pattern for instance – most recording programs will let you record the part once, then set how many times it is repeated. Cubase allows you to do this for both audio and MIDI tracks. Select the part that you want to repeat then go to the **Edit** menu and click on **Repeat**. The Repeat Events dialogue box will open. Type the number of times you want to repeat the part in the 'Count' box. If you click next to 'Shared Copies', the copies you make will change when you change the original part.

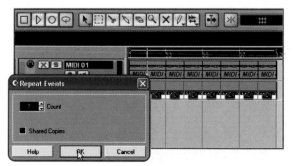

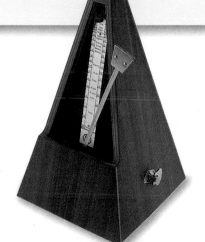

Learning to read music

Let your computer teach you the principles of musical notation

You don't have to be able to read music to compose it on your computer, and it is not necessary to know the names of individual notes to be able to play them or compose a tune. But as you become more confident and proficient at composition you may want to learn to read music. If so, a range of specialist software is available to help.

This project uses a program called Music Ace. Aimed at the complete novice, it teaches you notation through easy-to-follow lessons and related games. You will also be given the opportunity to test your knowledge by composing simple tunes. Much of the other educational music software available will follow these basic principles.

1 Go to the **Start** menu, select **Programs** then click on your music software. The opening screen of Music Ace contains musical notes playing a tune. Adjust the volume using the slide bar on the left of the screen. To begin, click on the **Start** button.

A range of music education programs, including Music Ace, can be sampled and downloaded from the Internet. A good starting point is the Shareware Music Machine Web site (http://www.hitsquad.com/smm).

▶ **OTHER PROGRAMS**

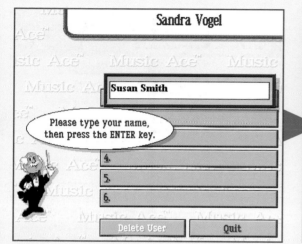

2 A music maestro will guide you through each stage of the program. Click in the first box, type your name then press the **Enter** key. Music Ace can accommodate several users, and it uses the names to keep track of each user's progress.

3 You are now presented with the Main Screen through which you choose whether to use the Doodle Pad (a music creation tool), follow a lesson or play a music game related to the lesson. To start a lesson click on the **Lesson** button.

4 Lesson 1 deals with basic music notation. An animated tutorial teaches you about the positioning of notes. After the tutorial you will be asked questions – click on the appropriate button to respond. Continue the exercises to the end of the lesson.

Set your preferences

The screen in which you elect to start a lesson or play a game also contains a Preferences button. Click on this to customise the way Music Ace works.

One set of choices, the Maestro Options, allows you to set the way in which on-screen help is delivered by the cartoon character, Maestro Max. If you wish, turn his voice or speech balloons off.

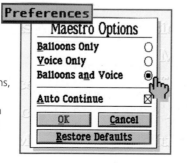

Use the Control Bar

Every lesson has a Control Bar running across the top of the screen. This provides access to basic options and settings.

To terminate the current lesson and return to the Main Screen click on the **Menu** button. The button to its right shows the name of the current lesson. To change the volume click on the **Vol** button. To move forwards or backwards in each lesson click on the relevant **Skip** buttons. Click on the **Pause** button to stop the lesson at the current point (the button changes to **Resume** – click on it to continue). To go straight to the game that relates to the lesson, click on the **Game** button.

Menu	1. Introduction to the Staff	Vol	◄◄ Skip	Pause ❚❚	Skip ►►	Game

Watch out
*Be aware that if you click on the **Skip** buttons to move forwards or backwards within a game your score will be set to zero.*

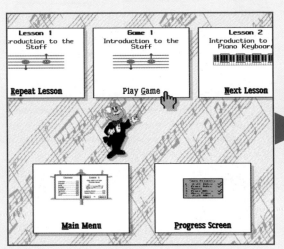

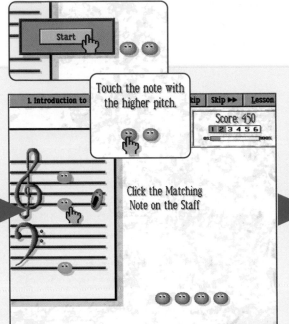

5 When a lesson ends you will be offered several options: to repeat the lesson, go to the main menu, check your progress, try the next lesson, or play the related game. To play the game click the **Play Game** button.

6 The game will encourage you to practise what you have learned in the lesson. To begin, click the **Start** button and follow the on-screen instructions. As you complete sections of the game your score will be displayed in the top right-hand corner of the screen.

7 When the game is finished choose the next lesson, another game, repeat the previous lesson or game, or view your progress. Alternatively, go to the Doodle Pad to try out what you have learned so far. Click on the **Main Menu**, then on the **Doodle Pad** button.

Assessing your progress

The lessons in Music Ace are broken down into sections. An indicator in the top right-hand corner of the screen shows you how far you have progressed through your current lesson. Completed sections are shown in green; the one you are working on in red.

Choosing lessons

You may not want to complete lessons or games in sequence – you may want to select specific ones to work on particular areas. You can do this from the Main Menu. Click on the **Next** arrow on the lesson page to leaf through the range of lessons available. When you find the one you want, click the **Lesson** or **Game** button to access it.

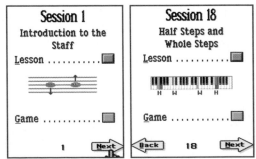

Key Word

Staff This describes the group of five lines on which notes are placed. Depending on where they are placed, the pitch of the note will change.

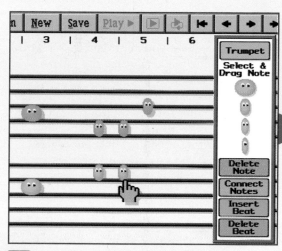

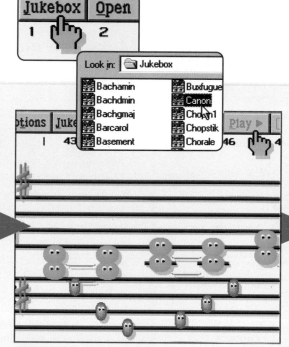

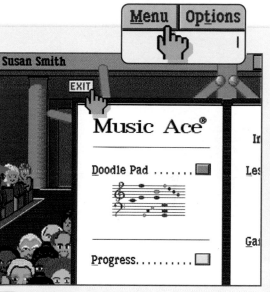

8 To move a note onto the 'staff' ready for playing, select and drag it from the box on the right of the screen. Move notes on the staff by dragging them. Each note plays as you move it. To hear your tune, click the **Play** button on the Control Bar.

9 Music Ace has a library of songs for you to listen to and edit. To open one in the Doodle Pad click on the Control Bar's **Jukebox** button, then double-click on a song. Click **Play** to hear it. Edit it by moving its notes on the staff and adding new notes.

10 To end your session, click on the **Menu** button on the Control Bar, then on one of the **Exit** buttons in the Main Menu. The next time you run Music Ace, click on your name from the user list – Music Ace will remind you of your progress.

Using the Doodle Pad

To change the instrument you are composing with, click on the instrument name at the top of the box on the right of the screen. Each time you click, a different instrument name will appear – Oboe, Marimba, Trumpet, Jazz Guitar, Clarinet and Grand Piano. When the instrument you want appears, all notes you create thereafter will sound like that instrument, and will appear in a different colour.

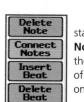

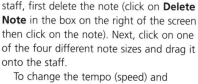

To adjust the length of a note on the staff, first delete the note (click on **Delete Note** in the box on the right of the screen then click on the note). Next, click on one of the four different note sizes and drag it onto the staff.

To change the tempo (speed) and loudness of your composition, drag the markers along the slide bar in the bottom left-hand corner of the screen.

Profit from your

Make the most of your money by using your

Investment circle

Create a folder called 'Investment circle'. Add sub-folders for each mini-project.

- Investment circle
  - Investors
  - Research
  - Accounts
  - Communications
  - Investments
  - Contacts

Investment circles have taken off around the globe, and the most successful have been known to outperform those of professional fund managers. These circles contain up to 15 people who enjoy making the most of their finances by selecting, purchasing and monitoring their own stocks and shares. They also save money by avoiding management charges.

All this has become possible in recent years because of the computerisation of the world's stock exchanges. People outside the world's financial citadels can act as their own fund managers, using their computers to access and act upon a wealth of up-to-date financial information: stock prices are updated on the Internet as soon as they change.

So if you are thinking of playing the markets, make the Internet your first stop. There are many sites where you can gather data on companies your group is thinking of investing in. It's easy to find out how your stock has performed, current earnings-to-share ratios, liabilities, assets and profit forecasts. In fact, you can find virtually everything you need to make an informed assessment.

There are many financial news sites listing on-line share price

investment circle

PC as a window on the financial markets

data, enabling you to track shares you may be interested in or have already purchased. You can then paste downloaded data into your portfolio spreadsheet – and even use it to calculate projections for your share dividends.

Once you have decided on your investments, you have to choose an on-line broker and open an account. You can then trade shares on the world markets without getting up from your computer.

If you set up an on-line bank account for your group you can also access your current financial status in a matter of seconds.

With your portfolio in place you can use your PC to administer your investment circle. You could set up

an investors' database to hold relevant information. For example, some members may prefer not to invest in certain industries or countries on ethical grounds.

Create more spreadsheets to monitor members' individual holdings and produce a newsletter to keep everyone informed.

If your group wants to diversify into other areas such as antiques trading, the Internet holds a great deal of useful data. Sites that carry price guides, tips on authenticity, where to buy and what to look for, are easily accessible and will help you make informed choices. You could also try some on-line bidding at some of the world's leading auction houses.

Prepare to invest

- Recruit members and agree aims, level of investment and club rules
- Appoint club officers and outline their responsibilities
- Research and select an on-line broker
- Open a club bank account and agree the signatories
- Set up on-line banking facilities
- Produce copies of initial research material for members

Ideas and inspirations

Adapt the following projects and exercises then apply them to setting up your own investment circle. You may find that you don't need all of them to get things up and running, so include only the documents you need for your own requirements.

94 Searching the Internet
Use search engines to locate on-line brokers, share price and stock performance information.

268 Build a shares portfolio
Set up a spreadsheet for your investment circle to keep track of your portfolio's performance.

272 Keep your accounts
Use separate worksheets in a spreadsheet to keep track of individual and group holdings.

162 Create a newsletter
Produce performance updates for your group. If other members are on-line, e-mail it to them.

148 Write a formal letter
Keep it professional, if you need to send a formal letter to, say, request a prospectus.

Also worth considering...

If you've used most of the above to form your investment circle, you may want to refine it further.

314 Membership database
Create a record of members' details and notes on any investment or non-investment preferences.

Family budget planner

Take control of your household's incomings and outgoings

Keeping track of your household budget makes good financial sense. You can keep an eye on day-to-day outgoings and also see when major expenses, such as a family holiday, lie ahead, and so make provision for them in good time.

The best way to take care of your home accounts is with a spreadsheet program. A spreadsheet allows you to set up professional looking accounts that are easy to use because all the calculations are done for you. Once you have set up your household accounts document, you simply type in your income and expenses, and the spreadsheet updates your balances automatically.

This project is geared towards household accounts, but its structure can be used for a business accounts spreadsheet, too.

1 Go to the **Start** menu, select **All Programs** and click on **Microsoft Excel**. Save your new document by going to the **File** menu and selecting **Save As**. In the 'Save in' box select a suitable folder for it to be stored in. Type in a file name, then click on **Save**.

Templates on CD-ROM

You can type in text in capital letters using the Caps Lock key. Press it down before you start typing, then press it again when you have finished.

Balance carried over

Add a 'Balance carried over' row to transfer credits or debits from the previous month.

Short cut
*To style all your section headings in the same way at the same time, hold down the **Ctrl** key and click on each of the headings in turn. Now style as usual.*

Microsoft Excel - Household Accounts

File Edit View Insert Format Tools Data Window Help

Arial ▾ 10 ▾ **B** *I* U

A10 ▾ fx Total

	A	B	C	D	E	F
1				Household Accounts 2002		
2						
3						
4	INCOME					
5	Primary Income					
6	Second Income					
7	Interest Accrued					
8	Balance carried over					
9						
10	Total					
11						
12						
13						
14						

2 Click on cell **D1** and type in the heading of your spreadsheet. Click on cell **A4** and type in 'Income'. Click on the cells below 'Income' in column A and type in your sources. When you have finished, click on the cell two rows below your last entry and type in 'Total'.

4	INCOME
5	Primary Income
6	Second Income
7	Interest Accrued
8	Balance carried over
9	
10	Total
11	
12	EXPENDITURE
13	Mortgage/Rent
14	Car loan
15	Car insurance
16	Petrol/Repairs
17	Other loans
18	Credit cards
19	Telephone
20	Cable TV etc
21	Gas
22	Electric
23	Water

23	Water
24	Food
25	Council tax
26	Childcare
27	House insurance
28	Contents insurance
29	
30	Total Household Expenditure
31	
32	ADDITIONAL EXPENDITURE
33	Entertainment
34	Clothes
35	Holidays
36	Savings & Investment
37	
38	Total Additional Expenditure
39	
40	OUTSTANDING BALANCE

3 Click on the cell two rows below 'Total' and type in 'Expenditure'. Type your areas of expense in the cells below. Where appropriate, type in 'Total Household Expenditure'. You may also want to include an 'Additional Expenditure' section. Finish with 'Outstanding Balance'.

File Edit View Insert Format Tools

Arial ▾ 10 ▾ **B** U Household Accounts 2002

D1 ▾ 8 / 9 / 10 / 11 / 12 / 14 / 16 / 18 / 20 / 22 / 24 / 26

B *I* U
Household A
Bold

	A	B	C	D
1				Hous
2				
3				
4	INCOME			
5	Primary Income			
6	Second Income			
7	Interest Accrued			
8	Balance carried over			
9				
10	Total			
11				
12	EXPENDITURE			
13	Mortgage/Rent			
14	Car loan			
15	Car insurance			
16	Petrol/Repairs			

4 To style your heading, click on cell **D1** then click on the **Bold** toolbar button. Click on the arrow beside the font size box on the toolbar, scroll through and select a font size. Continue to style the rest of your text in the same way.

Changing format

When you enter text into a spreadsheet its style is determined by the format of the cell you are typing it into. Formats can be altered by clicking on the cell, going to the **Format** menu and selecting **Cells**. Click on the **Font** tab, then select a font, font size, style and colour from the lists displayed.

Format Cells

Number | Alignment | Font | Border | Patterns | Protectio

Font:
Arial

Font style:
Regular

Size:
10

Andy
Arial
Arial Black
Arial Narrow

Regular
Italic
Bold
Bold Italic

8
9
10
11

Underline:
None

Color:
Automatic

☑ Normal fo

Effects
☐ Strikethrough

Preview

Inserting new data

To insert a new row of expenses or income, click on the beige numbered box of the row below where you'd like your new one to be placed. Go to the **Insert** menu and click on **Rows**. A new row will appear above the row you clicked on.

Insert | Format | Tools

Cells...
Rows
Columns

11	
12	EXPENDITURE
13	Mortgage/Rent
14	
15	Car loan
16	Car insurance
17	Petrol/Repairs
18	Other loans

To adjust the width of a column, place the mouse pointer over the right-hand edge of the beige column header. When it becomes a double-headed arrow, press the left mouse button and, keeping it pressed down, drag the column edge to the desired width.

H7 ▼ *fx* Width: 18.71

*If the range of cells that AutoSum selects is incorrect, use the mouse to highlight the correct group of cells and press the **Enter** key.*

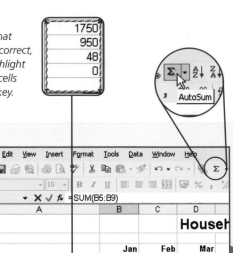

5 Adjust column widths (see above) then type 'Jan' in cell B3. Place the mouse pointer in the lower right-hand corner of B3. When it becomes a cross, click and drag to the right. The months appear in these cells. Select the row then the **Bold** and **Align Right** buttons.

6 Starting in cell B5, and continuing in the cells below, enter the figures for all your income and expenditure for the month of January. In cells where there is no amount to enter, type in a zero.

	Jan	Feb
INCOME		
Primary Income	1750	
Second Income	950	
Interest Accrued	48	
Balance carried over	0	
Total		
EXPENDITURE		
Mortgage/Rent	525	
Car loan	131	
Car insurance	36	
Petrol/Repairs	90	
Other loans	62	
Credit cards	20	
Telephone	0	

7 To calculate January's Total income (then total expenditure and additional expenditure), click on the relevant cell in column B, then click the **AutoSum** toolbar button. A formula appears, indicating the range of cells to add up. If the range is correct, press the **Enter** key.

SUM ▼ ✗ ✓ *fx* =SUM(B5:B9)

Split the screen and freeze panes

Windows allows you to split the screen to make viewing figures across different columns and rows easy. Go to the **Windows** menu and click on **Split**. Place your mouse pointer over the beige 'split' line you want to move. When it changes appearance to a double-headed arrow, hold down the left mouse button and drag the line to the desired position. You can scroll through each part of the split screen separately.

You can also freeze a pane, allowing you to select a section of data that remains static when scrolling in a sheet. For example you may wish to keep the row and column headings visible as you scroll. Experiment with the different ways you can freeze panes by placing your cursor at different points of the spreadsheet then going to the **Windows** menu and selecting **Freeze Panes**. Select **Unfreeze Panes** to undo the action.

	A	E	F	G	H
1		**ehold Accounts 2002**			
2					
3		Apr	May	Jun	Jul
4	**INCOME**				
5	Primary Income	1750	1750	1750	1750
6	Second Income	950	950	950	950
7	Interest Accrued	48	48	53	48
8	Balance carried over	136	242	396	234
9					
10	**Total**	2884	2990	3149	2982
11					
12	**EXPENDITURE**				
24	Food	386	386	466	325
25	Council tax	52	52	52	52

Calculating spreadsheet data can be complicated. Using Works' in-built calculation tools makes it much easier. For further help, see page 31.

► CALCULATING YOUR DATA

Short cut
To save yourself typing in cell references to the formula in the Entry Bar, click on the relevant cell at the appropriate point in the calculation. Excel and Works automatically enter the cell reference into the formula.

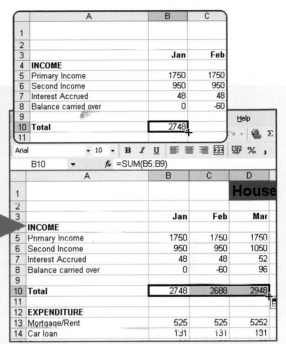

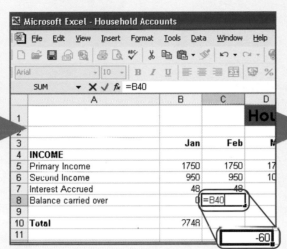

8 To calculate January's Outstanding Balance, click on the relevant cell, then enter the formula shown above in the Entry Bar to subtract Total expenditure from your Total income. Type an '=' sign, then use cell references and minus signs to subtract expenses from income. Press **Enter**.

9 Type in figures for February. To carry over January's balance, click in the relevant cell (here, cell C8) then type an '=' sign, followed by the cell reference for January's Outstanding Balance. Press **Enter**. Now you are ready to calculate totals for the year.

10 Place the mouse pointer over the lower right-hand corner of the cell that holds January's Total income (here, B10). When it becomes a cross, click and drag to the right. The formula is copied to all the other months. Repeat for other totals.

Using your budget planner
Once you have created your spreadsheet, update it every week or so. Where possible, type in expenses you know are due well in advance. That way, you will have a better idea of how much disposable income you will have at the end of every month.

	A	B	C	D
1				House
2				
3		Jan	Feb	Mar
4	**INCOME**			
5	Primary Income	1750	1750	1750
6	Second Income	950	950	1050
7	Interest Accrued	48	48	52
8	Balance carried over	0	-60	96
9				
10	**Total**	2748	2688	2948

Home Contents - Fix&Fittings

Item Type	Description	Value	Where Stored
Electrical	Sharp Microwave 700w	£300.00	Kitchen
Electrical	Panasonic 26" Television	£300.00	Lounge
Electrical	BT Answerphone	£175.00	Hall
Electrical	Zeus Aquarium	£800.00	Bedroom
Electrical	Bose Clock Radio	£27.00	Lounge
Electrical	Sony Video Recorder	£300.00	Kitchen
Electrical	Fridge	£200.00	Kitchen
Electrical	Freezer	£375.00	Kitchen
Electrical	Kenwood Food Processor	£129.00	Kitchen
Electrical	Siebart Cooker	£400.00	Lounge
Electrical	Technic Music System	£900.00	Study
Electrical	Sony Desktop Computer	£1,500.00	Study
Electrical	Digital Camera	£400.00	
		SUM: £5,806.00	
Furniture	Two-seat Sofa	£400.00	Lounge
Furniture	Oak Table & Six Chairs	£600.00	Dining Room
Furniture	Painting - Dali Sketch	£5,000.00	Lounge
Furniture	Grandfather Clock	£6,000.00	Hall
Furniture	Vase	£900.00	Hall
Furniture	Persian Rug	£750.00	Hall
Furniture	Sleepeze Double Bed	£500.00	Bedroom
Furniture	Silent Night Single Bed	£300.00	Bedroom
Furniture	Silent Night Double Bed	£350.00	Bedroom
Furniture	Ikea Dressing Table	£275.00	Bedroom
Furniture	Ikea Coffee Table	£120.00	Lounge
		SUM: £15,195.00	
		SUM: £21,001.00	

Catalogue and value your home contents

Save time and money by keeping a record of your possessions

If you have ever had to look for a receipt or guarantee in order to make a claim on a faulty product, you'll know how frustrating that search can be. Calculating the value of your household possessions when your contents' insurance needs renewing is just as time-consuming. So don't waste your energy sorting through endless old bills, invoices and receipts every time. Instead, create a database to catalogue your home contents. With it you can record, sort, retrieve and update vital information quickly and easily.

Gather together all the information you have about your home contents, such as dates of purchase, values, guarantees, and so on.

▶ **BEFORE YOU START**

Microsoft Works Task Launcher

| Home | Tasks | Programs | History | Customize | ? Help |

PROGRAMS
Type your question and click Search, or click a program.

[Search]

Works Word Processor
Works Spreadsheet
Works Database
Works Calendar
Address Book
Works Portfolio
MSN
Internet Explorer
Outlook Express
Help & Ideas

Works Database
Organize and track household information. The Database stores enables you to create reports showing only the information you nee
Works Database on the Web.

▸ Start a blank database
CD and tape inventory
Home inventory worksheets
Recipe book
Works Web site

▸ **Start a blank database**

1 Go to the **Start** menu, select **All Programs** and then **Microsoft Works**. In the Programs tab of the Task Launcher, select **Works Database**. Then click on **Start a blank Database**.

You can also create a database using Microsoft Excel. Use the spreadsheet to type in your headings, and the Filter feature to create your reports.

▶ **OTHER PROGRAMS**

Templates on CD-ROM

Short cut
When recording items, include a serialised reference field. Your PC will automatically assign a number to each item that you enter, so you won't need to type in the numbers yourself.

Watch out
Don't lose information from your database – save and name it as soon as you have created it. Save it regularly as you work, and immediately after you make any updates.

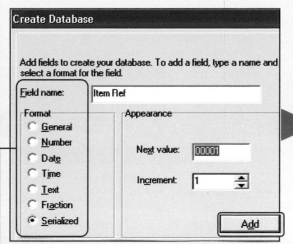

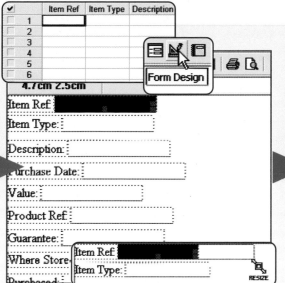

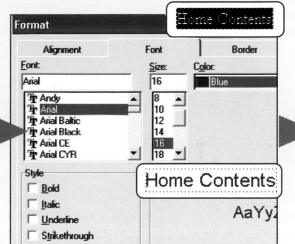

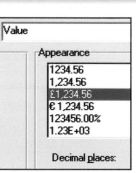

2 In the Create Database dialogue box, input your fields – which are categories of information – and specify a format for each one, such as Text or Number (enter the fields and formats listed below). When you have typed in each field, click on the **Add** button.

3 After creating your fields, click **Done**. The database appears in List form. Click the **Form Design** toolbar button to customise your database. To move text boxes click on them and drag; to resize them, drag the bottom right-hand corner or the handles on the side and bottom.

4 After rearranging your boxes, add a heading. Click at the top of the page and type it in. To style your title, field names or text boxes, click on them, go to the **Format** menu and click on **Font and Style**. Select fonts, sizes, styles and colours. Click the **Alignment** tab and select the Left option.

Fields and formats

Field	Format
Item Ref	Serialized
Item Type	Text
Description	Text
Purchase Date	Date
Value	Number
Product Ref	Text
Guarantee	Text
Where Stored	Text
Purchased	Text

Format style
When you select Number, Date, Time or Fraction as a format, you are given a list of options in the Appearance section. Click on your preferred style.

Different views
There are four ways to view your database:

List View is best for quick reference as it allows you to view lots of entries at the same time.

Form View displays one entry at a time and is the best for entering data.

Form Design doesn't let you enter information; instead it lets you add, delete, move and resize fields, alter font styles and add colours.

Report View allows you to compile selective reports from your database.

Short cut
*To style several text boxes in the same way at once, select them all by holding down the **Ctrl** key and clicking on each box in turn. Any style change will be applied to all boxes.*

It's possible to extract data for specific reasons. An inventory of fixtures and fittings will be useful should you rent out your property.

MAKING A REPORT

Key Word
***Report** This is a printed summary of information stored in a database. From your Home Contents database you could make a report on uninsured and insured household items.*

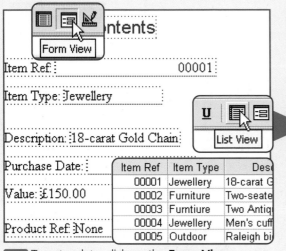

5 To enter data, click on the **Form View** toolbar button. Click on a text box and type in your data. Press the **Tab** key to move to the next field or record, and use the **Shift** and **Tab** keys together to move back a field. Click on the **List View** toolbar button to view your list.

6 To list your furniture and electrical goods, go to the **Tools** menu and select **ReportCreator**. Enter a report name. In the next box click the **Fields** tab. In the 'Fields available' pane, click the fields you want in your report (in the order you want them) then click **Add**. Click **Next** when done.

7 Select the Sorting tab. To sort data into similar types, click in the 'Sort by' box and select **Item Type**. Group the same item type entries by clicking the **Grouping** tab, then clicking in the 'When contents change' and 'Show group heading' boxes.

Finding information

To search for specific data, go to the **Edit** menu and click on **Find**. Type in a key word or words for what you want to search for, select the 'All records' option, then click on **OK**. The database view changes to show only those records that match your search. To return to the full database view, go to the **Record** menu, select **Show** and then select **All Records**.

In Form View you can move through entries fast by clicking on the arrows on either side of the Record counter at the foot of the window.

✔		Item Ref	Item Type	Description	Purchase Date
☐	5	00005	Outdoor	Raleigh bicycle	17/06/1999

Select a report:

Insurance
Claim Items
Fix&Fittings

Preview

Modify

*Microsoft Works automatically saves any report that you create. To print or update an old report, go to the **View** menu and click on **Report**. A list of your reports appears. Click on the relevant one then click on **Preview** or **Modify** as appropriate.*

ReportCreator

The report definition has been created.

Do you wish to preview or modify the report definition?

Preview   Modify

Home Contents - Fix&Fittings

Item Type	Description	Where Stored	Value
Electrical			
Electrical	Sharp Microwave 700w	Kitchen	£300.00
Electrical	Panasonic 26" Television	Lounge	£300.00
Electrical	BT Answerphone	Hall	£175.00
Electrical	Zeus Aquarium	Hall	£800.00
Electrical	Bose Clock Radio	Bedroom	£27.00
Electrical	Sony Video Recorder	Lounge	£300.00
Electrical	Fridge	Kitchen	£200.00
Electrical	Freezer	Kitchen	£375.00
Electrical	Kenwood Food Processor	Kitchen	£129.00
Electrical	Siebart Cooker	Kitchen	£400.00
Electrical	Technics Music System	Lounge	£900.00
Electrical	Sony Desktop Computer	Study	£1,500.00
Electrical	Digital Camera	Study	£400.00
		SUM:	£5,806.00
Furniture			
Furniture	Two-seat Sofa	Lounge	£400.00
Furniture	Oak Table & Six Chairs	Dining Room	£600.00
Furniture	Painting - Dali Sketch	Lounge	£5,000.00
Furniture	Grandfather Clock	Hall	£8,000.00
Furniture	Vase	Hall	£900.00
Furniture	Persian Rug	Hall	£750.00

Filter Name

Type a name for the filter below:

Fix&Fittings

(• Easy Filter

Field name	Comparison
Item Type ▼	contains
or ▼ Item Type ▼	contains
and ▼ (None) ▼	is equal to
and ▼ (None)	
and ▼ (None)	

(• Easy Filter   (Filter using formula

☐ Invert filter

Comparison	Compare To
contains ▼	Furniture
contains ▼	Electrical

ReportCreator - Fix&Fittings

| Title | Fields | Sorting | Grouping |

Select a field:

Item Type
Description
Where Stored
Value

Summaries

☑ Sum
☐ Average
☐ Count
☐ Minimum
☐ Maximum
☐ Standard Deviation
☐ Variance

☑ Show summary name

Done

Display summary information

☑ At end of each group   (• Under each column
☑ At end of report   (Together in rows

8 Click the **Filter** tab and the **Create New Filter** button. Type in a name. Click **OK**. In the 'Field name' box select **Item Type**; in 'Comparison' select **contains**; in 'Compare To' type 'Furniture'. Select **or**, **Item Type**, **contains** and type 'Electrical'. Click **OK**.

9 To add up all the figures in your Value field, click the **Summary** tab, click on **Value** in the 'Select a field' box and click in the 'Sum' box. In the Display summary information section, click the options as shown above. Click on **Done**.

10 A prompt box appears asking whether you want to preview or modify your report. Click **Modify** if you want to add any styling to your report (see below). Click **Preview** to view your report. Click **Print** to print it out.

Reporting in style

To add a professional touch to your reports, adjust the fonts, font sizes and add colour.

Click the **Report View** toolbar button. Click the cell or row you want to style and go to the **Format** menu and click on **Font and Style**. In the Format dialogue box click the various

tabs, selecting fonts, sizes, styles, colours and background patterns as you do so.

If your columns are too close together, adjust their widths. Place the cursor on the right-hand edge of the column heading, hold down the mouse button and drag to the desired width.

Report View

	A	B	C	D
			Home Contents - Fix&F	
	Item Type	Description	Where Stored	Valu
	=Item Type			
	=Item Type	=Description	=Where Stored	=Value
			SUM:	=SUM(Va
			SUM:	=SUM(Va

Calculate your bills

Keep a track of your spending to help predict future bills

A spreadsheet is ideal for keeping track of the amount you spend on household bills and it can help you estimate and plan for future bills. Not only can you enter details about utilities, such as gas and electricity, but you can enter expenses that crop up once a year, such as the television

licence and club subscriptions. These are often the bills that get overlooked.

With the spreadsheet program in Excel you can also create a pie chart to analyse your expenses. This gives a useful visual guide to your spending and can help you spot financial 'black holes' that are eating up your money.

Collect your most recent bills, and make a note of any regular household expenses for which you don't have documentation.

▶ BEFORE YOU START

1 Go to the **Start** menu, select **All Programs** and click on **Microsoft Excel**. Save and name the new spreadsheet by clicking on the **Save** toolbar button. Select a folder to save it in through the 'Save in' box, and type in a name in the 'File name' box. Click on **Save**.

*You can create similar spreadsheets in Microsoft Works. In the Programs tab of the Works Task Launcher, click on **Works Spreadsheet**, then **Start a blank spreadsheet**.*

▶ OTHER PROGRAMS

 Templates on CD-ROM

Short cut
*To style several cells in the same way at the same time, press the **Ctrl** key and, keeping it pressed down, click on each cell in turn. Style as usual.*

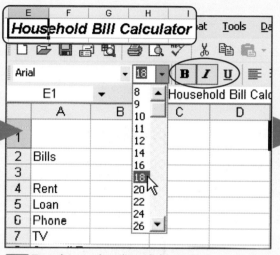

2 Click in cell **E1** and type in your heading. In cell **A2** type in 'Bills'; in cell **A4** type in your first type of bill. Enter the different types of bill in the cells below. When you have finished your list, click in the cell two rows below and type in 'Total'.

3 To style your heading click on **E1** then on the **Bold** and **Italic** toolbar buttons. Click on the arrow beside the font size toolbar box and select a font size. Style the rest of your entries, then adjust the width of column A to fit your text (see below).

4 Type 'Jan' in cell **B2**. Place the cursor in the lower right-hand corner of the cell. When it changes to a black cross, click and drag along row 2 to reveal the other months, until you reach 'Dec'. Release the mouse button, then click on the **Bold** toolbar button to style your months of the year.

Inserting new data

To add a new bill, click on the beige numbered box of the row above where the new one is to be placed. Go to the **Insert** menu and click on **Rows**. A blank row will appear in place. Type in your text as in Step 2.

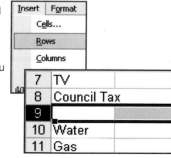

To adjust the width of a column, place the cursor over the right-hand edge of the beige column header. When the cursor becomes a double-headed arrow click and drag the edge to the desired width.

Close-up
When you enter figures into a spreadsheet, they automatically align on the right-hand side of the column. This way, the decimal points align neatly above each other.

	A	B	C
2	**Bills**	**Jan**	**Feb**
3			
4	Rent		350.00
5	Loan		121.00
6	Phone		34.27
7	TV		28.99
8	Council Tax		36.00
9	Water		19.65
10	Gas		0.00
11	Electricity		0.00
12	Credit Card		45.00
13	Car Insurance		37.50

5 Starting in cell **B4**, and continuing in the cells immediately below, enter the amounts paid out in January for each type of expenditure. If you did not pay anything for a particular bill, type '0' into the relevant cell.

	A	B	C	D	E
1					Ho
2	Bills	Jan	Feb	Mar	Apr
3					
4	Rent	350.00			
5	Loan	121.00			
6	Phone	34.27			
7	TV	28.99			
8	Council Tax	36.00			
9	Water	19.65			
10	Gas	0.00			
11	Electricity	0.00			
12	CreditCard	45.00			
13	Car Insurance	37.50			
14					
15	Total	=SUM(B4:B14)			
16		SUM(**number1**, [number2], ...)			

672.41

6 To calculate January's total expenditure on bills, click in the cell to the right of 'Total', then click on the **AutoSum** toolbar button. The cells to be calculated are outlined with a dotted line, and a formula appears in the Total cell. Press **Enter**. The sum of your cells will then appear.

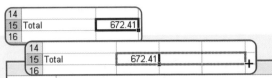

14		
15	Total	672.41
16		

14		
15	Total	672.41
16		

Household Bill Calculato

Mar	Apr	May	Jun	Jul	Aug
350.00	350.00	350.00	350.00	350.00	3
121.00	121.00	121.00	121.00	121.00	1
34.27	34.27	34.27	34.27	34.27	
28.99	28.99	28.99	28.99	28.99	
36.00	36.00	36.00	36.00	36.00	
19.65	19.65	19.65	19.65	19.65	
86.29	0.00	0.00	0.00	0.00	
74.59	0.00	0.00	0.00	0.00	
45.00	45.00	45.00	45.00	45.00	
37.50	37.50	37.50	37.50	37.50	
833.29	672.41	672.41	672.41	672.41	6

7 To copy the formula to add up total expenditure for the other months of the year, first place the cursor in the lower right-hand corner of the cell. When it becomes a cross, click and drag until you reach December's column. Excel will automatically update all cell references.

Decimal places

For financial spreadsheets you need to format your figures so they display two figures after the decimal point. Select the relevant cells, go to the **Format** menu and click on **Cells**. In the Format Cells dialogue box the Number tab is selected. Click on **Number** in the category pane, and set the number of decimal places to '2'. Click **OK**.

Format Cells

Number	Alignment	Font	Border	Patterns

Category:
- General
- Number
- Currency
- Accounting
- Date
- Time

Sample

Decimal places: 2

☐ Use 1000 Separator (,)

To copy and paste a formula, click on the formula cell then click on the **Copy** toolbar button. Highlight all the cells you want the formula to appear in, then click on the **Paste** toolbar button. The cell references automatically update themselves.

To add a background colour, select the cells then click on the arrow next to the **Fill Color** toolbar button. Click on a colour from the options provided.

Household Bill Calculator

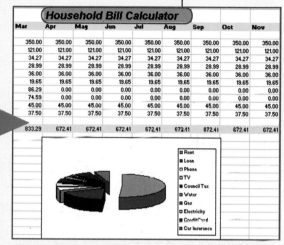

J	K	L	M	N
ep	Oct	Nov	Dec	Totals
350.00	350.00	350.00	350.00	4,200.00
121.00	121.00	121.00	121.00	
34.27	34.27	34.27	34.27	
28.99	28.99	28.99	28.99	
36.00	36.00	36.00	36.00	
19.65	19.65	19.65	19.65	
0.00	0.00	0.00	0.00	
0.00	0.00	0.00	0.00	**Totals**
45.00	45.00			
37.50	37.50			4,200.00
672.41	672.41	672.41	672.41	

8 Type 'Totals' in the cell to the right of 'Dec'. Click on the cell two rows below 'Totals', then double-click on the **AutoSum** toolbar button. The yearly total for your first type of bill will appear. Copy and paste this formula into the cells below to calculate the totals for your other bills.

J	K	L	M	N	O
ep	Oct	Nov	Dec	Totals	
350.00	350.00	350.00	350.00	4,200.00	
121.00	121.00	121.00	121.00	1,452.00	
34.27	34.27	34.27	34.27	411.24	
28.99	28.99	28.99	28.99	347.88	
36.00	36.00	36.00	36.00	432.00	
19.65	19.65	19.65	19.65	235.80	
0.00	0.00	0.00	0.00	86.29	
0.00	0.00	0.00	0.00	74.59	
45.00	45.00	45.00	45.00	540.00	
37.50	37.50	37.50	37.50	450.00	
672.41	672.41	672.41	672.41	8,229.80	

9 Paste the same formula into the cell two rows below the final figure in the 'Totals' column. Press **Enter**. The total amount you have spent on bills in the course of the previous year will appear. This completes the calculation sheet.

Household Bill Calculator

Mar	Apr	May	Jun	Jul	Aug	Sep	Oct	Nov
350.00	350.00	350.00	350.00	350.00	350.00	350.00	350.00	350.00
121.00	121.00	121.00	121.00	121.00	121.00	121.00	121.00	121.00
34.27	34.27	34.27	34.27	34.27	34.27	34.27	34.27	34.27
28.99	28.99	28.99	28.99	28.99	28.99	28.99	28.99	28.99
36.00	36.00	36.00	36.00	36.00	36.00	36.00	36.00	36.00
19.65	19.65	19.65	19.65	19.65	19.65	19.65	19.65	19.65
86.29	0.00	0.00	0.00	0.00	0.00	0.00	0.00	0.00
74.59	0.00	0.00	0.00	0.00	0.00	0.00	0.00	0.00
45.00	45.00	45.00	45.00	45.00	45.00	45.00	45.00	45.00
37.50	37.50	37.50	37.50	37.50	37.50	37.50	37.50	37.50
833.29	672.41	672.41	672.41	672.41	672.41	672.41	672.41	672.41

Legend: Rent, Loan, Phone, TV, Council Tax, Water, Gas, Electricity, CreditCard, Car Insurance

10 To add a pie chart, see below. When you are happy with your spreadsheet go to the **File** menu and click on **Page Setup**. Check your print options then click on **Print**.

Make a pie chart

To make a pie chart, press the **Ctrl** key and select the cells containing your types of bill in column A, and their respective yearly totals in the Totals column (here, column N). Click the **Chart Wizard** toolbar button. In the Chart Wizard dialogue box select **Pie** from the 'Chart type' window, then a style from the 'Chart sub-type' pane. Click **Finish**. Your chart will appear in your spreadsheet. Click on it and drag it into position. To resize it, click and drag one of the corner tabs.

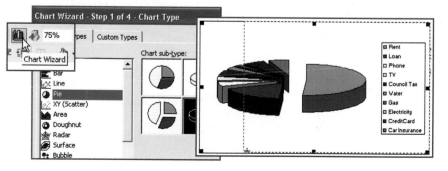

Calculate your car costs

Use your PC to help you get the best mileage for your money

A spreadsheet is ideal for monitoring all sorts of expenditure. As well as creating a budget planner for all your household expenses (see page 252), it's also possible to keep close track of large, individual expenses, such as buying and running a car or building an extension to your house.

By recording all your motoring expenses you can work out your annual costs and build up a comprehensive analysis of your car's value for money. You can also anticipate motoring bills, and so plan a budget to accommodate them. Perhaps you could put away a fixed amount of money every month. Then, if a major expense such as an emergency repair crops up, you will be better prepared.

Once you have set up the car running costs spreadsheet here, all the calculation work will be done for you. All you have to do is enter your monthly figures.

Write down all the costs your car incurs. Include repayments, road tax, insurance, spare parts and servicing, as well as oil and fuel.

BEFORE YOU START

1 Go to the **Start** menu, select **All Programs** then **Microsoft Excel**. A blank spreadsheet will open. Go to the **File** menu and select **Save As**. Select a place to save your spreadsheet, type in a file name and then click on **Save**.

*You can use Microsoft Works to create a spreadsheet. Open Works, then, in the Programs tab of the Works Task Launcher, click on **Works Spreadsheet** in the list on the left.*

OTHER PROGRAMS

Templates on CD-ROM

Short cut

If your columns are not wide enough to accommodate your text, place the cursor over the border between the column headings. When it changes to a double-headed arrow, double-click. The column will automatically resize itself to fit the text.

	A
25	Mileage
26	Month start
27	Month end
28	Monthly Total
29	
30	Cost per mile

Below the cell in which you type 'Mileage' (here, cell A25), type in 'Month start', 'Month end' and 'Monthly Total'. Two cells below that, type in 'Cost per mile'.

Microsoft Excel - Car Costs

File Edit View Insert Format Tools Data Window

Arial   10   B I U

H17

	A	B	C	D	E
1	Car Running Costs				
2					
3					
4	Vehicle Information				
5	Make:	Volkswagen			
6	Model:	Golf GTI			
7	Year:	1997			
8	Reg No:	P714 LYJ			
9	Price:	9700			
10					

Jan

Jan

Jun

1					
2					
3					
4	Vehicle Information				
5	Make:	Volkswagen			
6	Model:	Golf GTI			
7	Year:	1997			
8	Reg No:	P714 LYJ			
	Price:	9700			
10					
11			Jan	Feb	Mar
12	Expenses				
13					
14					
15					
16					
17					
18					

6	Model:	Golf GTI			
7	Year:	1997			
8	Reg No:	P714 LYJ			
9	Price:	9700			
10					
11			Jan	Feb	Mar
12	Expenses				
13	Repayments				
14	Insurance				
15	Road tax				
16	MoT test				
17	Service				
18	Spare parts				
19	Oil				
20	Car valet				
21	Fuel				
22					
23	Total Costs				
24					
25	Mileage				

2 In cell **A1** type in a heading. In cell **A4** type 'Vehicle Information'. Type in the headings as shown above in cells **A5** to **A9** then fill in your car's relevant details in the adjoining cells in column B, starting in cell **B5**.

3 Click on cell **C11** and type in 'Jan'. Place the cursor in the bottom right-hand corner of the cell. When it becomes a cross, click and drag across the spreadsheet until you reach column N, and Microsoft Excel will enter the months of the year. Next, click on cell **A12** and type in 'Expenses'.

4 Starting in cell **A13**, and continuing in the cells below, type in your different types of car cost. Two cells below the final entry (here, **A23**) type in 'Total Costs'. Two cells below that, type in 'Mileage' (see above).

Merge and centre headings

It is possible to merge a number of cells together, then centre the contents within that larger cell. This is particularly useful for headings – use it for your 'Car Running Costs' and 'Vehicle Information'.

To select the cells you wish to merge, click on the first one, then drag the cursor over the others. Now click the **Merge and Center** toolbar button.

	A	B
1	Car Running Costs	
2		
3		

% ,

Merge and Center

F	G	H	I
	Car Running Costs		

Bright idea

You can use your spreadsheet to calculate your fuel consumption. Enter a row for the amount of fuel bought in gallons/litres every month. Then divide the number of gallons/litres by the Total Monthly Mileage to work out how many gallons/litres your car uses per mile.

Copy the formula for the other months of the year. Place the cursor in the lower right-hand corner of a cell. When it becomes a cross, click and drag until you reach column N. Excel will automatically update the cell references.

| Total Costs | | 0 |

Bright idea
To account for annual bills, such as insurance, on a monthly basis, click on the relevant cell in January's column, type '=', the total annual amount, then '/12'. Eg (=515/12). Copy the formula to every month using the technique described left.

Σ ▾ | A↓ Z↓
AutoSum ✕ ✓ fx =SUM(C12:C21)

	A	B	C	D
11			Jan	Feb
12	Expenses			
13	Repayments			
14	Insurance			
15	Road tax			
16	MoT test			
17	Service			
18	Spare parts			
19	Oil			
20	Car valet			
21	Fuel			
22				
23	Total Costs		=SUM(C12:C21)	
24				

SUM(**number1**, [n

SUM ▾ ✕ ✓ fx =C27-C26

	A	B	C	D
17	Service			
18	Spare parts			
19	Oil			
20	Car valet			
21	Fuel			
22				
23	Total Costs		0	
24				
25	Mileage			
26	Month start			
27	Month end			
28	Monthly Total		=C27-C26	
29				
30	Cost per mile			

SUM ▾ ✕ ✓ fx =C23/C28

	A	B	C	D
18	Spare parts			
19	Oil			
20	Car valet			
21	Fuel			
22				
23	Total Costs		0	
24				
25	Mileage			
26	Month start			
27	Month end			
28	Monthly Total		0	
29				
30	Cost per mile		=C23/C28	
31				

5 To set the formula for working out monthly costs, click the Total Costs cell for January (here, **C23**), then the **AutoSum** toolbar button. Click and drag over the cells to be added together then press **Enter**. Copy the formula for other months (see above).

6 To calculate the total monthly mileage for January, click the relevant cell (here, **C28**) and type '='. Click the 'Month end' for January cell (**C27**), type '-', then click the 'Month start' for January cell (**C26**). Press **Enter**. Copy the formula to the other months.

7 To enter a formula for the total cost per mile for January, click the relevant cell (here, **C30**) and type '='. Then click the 'Total Costs' for January cell (**C23**), then '/', then the cell for January's mileage total (**C28**). Press **Enter**. Copy the formula to the other months.

Styling your work

To style the text in your spreadsheet and add some colour, first select the relevant cell or cells. (To style several cells in the same way at the same time, click and drag the cursor over them, or click on the first cell, hold down the **Shift** key, and click on the other cells in turn.)

Now go to the **Format** menu and click on **Cells**. Click on the various tabs and select a

suitable font, size, style, effect and background colour. Click **OK**.

To create a border, select the cells then click on the **Border** tab in the Format Cells dialogue box. Select a style and colour, click **Outline** and then **OK**.

To align text to the left, right or centre, click on the relevant cells then on the appropriate alignment toolbar button.

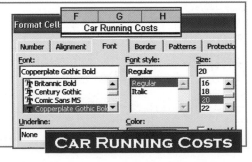

Watch out

Don't be alarmed if you see '#DIV/0!' in any of your cells. It means that Excel is trying to divide a number by zero. This will change when you enter figures for your spreadsheet and AutoSum has something to work with.

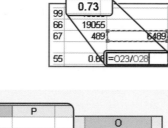

*To calculate your annual cost per mile, click on the cell to the right of December's Cost Per Mile (here, **O30**), type '=', then click on the cell for the Total Annual Costs (**O23**), then type '/' (division sign on the numeric keypad). Now click on the cell for the Total Annual Mileage (**O28**). Press **Enter**.*

	C	D	E	F	G
	Jan	Feb	Mar	Apr	May
	175.25	175.25	175.25	175.25	175.2
	42.76	42.76	42.76	42.76	42.7
	0	0	150	0	
	0	0	22	0	
	0	0	254.26	0	
	25.45	0	12.96	23.55	
	0	12.99	0	0	
	35	35	35	35	
	97.56	79.98	85.07	75.3	89.0
	376.02	345.98	778.10	351.86	342.0

	N	O	P
	Dec	Annual Costs	
.25	175.25	=SUM(O13:N13)	
.76	42.76	SUM(number1, [number2], ...)	
	175.25	175.25	175.25
	42.76	42.76	42.76
	0	0	0
	0	0	0
	0	0	0
	0	17.69	12.51
	0	0	0
	35	35	35
	88.90	91.76	99.67
	341.91	362.46	365.19

O
Annual Costs
2103
78.67

J	K	L	M	N	O
Aug	Sep	Oct	Nov	Dec	Annual Costs
175.25	175.25	175.25	175.25	175.25	2103
42.76	42.76	42.76	42.76	42.76	513.12
0	0	0	0	0	150
0	0	0	0	0	22
135.55	0	0	0	0	389.81
15.44	0	17.69	12.51	0	107.6
0	0	0	0	0	12.99
35	35	35	35	35	420
86.42	88.90	91.76	99.67	78.67	1049.57
					0
490.42	341.91	362.46	365.19	331.68	4768.09
					6499
16618	17110	17566	17899	18566	
17110	17566	17899	18566	19055	
492	456	333	667	=SUM(O28:N28)	
				SUM(number1, nu	
1.00	0.75	1.09	0.55	0.68	

8 Now enter the values into your spreadsheet. Click on the cells and type in the relevant amounts (enter '0' if you do not have a value). For payments that remain the same every month, type the figure in once and copy it to the other months.

9 Click on cell **O11** and type in 'Annual Costs'. To calculate the total annual costs for your first expense, click on cell **O13** then on **AutoSum**. Press **Enter**. Copy the formula into the cells below, stopping at the Total Costs row.

10 To calculate your annual mileage, click on the cell to the right of December's mileage Monthly Total (here, **O28**), then click on the **AutoSum** toolbar button. Press **Enter**. (To calculate your annual cost per mile, see above.) To print, go to the **File** menu and click on **Print**.

Calculating second car costs

You can create a spreadsheet for a second car. Go to the **Edit** menu and select **Move or Copy Sheet**. In the dialogue box, make sure your spreadsheet is selected in the 'To book' box. Click on **Sheet 2** in the 'Before sheet' box, ensure the 'Create a copy' box is ticked, then click **OK**.

Rename the sheet tab by double-clicking on it and typing the new name. All you need do then is highlight any text or figures that need changing.

Move or Copy

Move selected sheets

To book:
Car Costs.xls

Before sheet:
Chart1
Sheet1
Sheet2
Sheet3
(move to end)

Sheet1 \ Sheet1 (2)

Sheet1 \ Car 2 \ Sheet2

Styling numbers

To give your values a uniform format, select all the cells in which you are to enter currency figures (not mileage). Go to the **Format** menu and click on **Cells**. In the Category window click on **Number**, and select **2** in the 'Decimal places' box. Click **OK**.

Format Cells

Number | Alignment | Font | Border | Patterns |

Category:
General
Number
Currency
Accounting
Date

Sample
175.25

Decimal places: 2

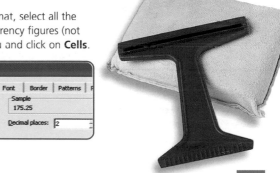

Build a shares portfolio

Follow the stock market with your own monthly guide

A spreadsheet is an excellent tool for taking care of financial calculations, and there's nothing quite as confusing as fluctuating share prices. Because share prices change continually, it's a good idea to assess their performance every month. Your financial adviser or stockbroker will be able to give you detailed advice about the best strategy for buying and selling shares, but using a spreadsheet means you can keep a close watch on the overall trends of all your shareholdings.

The cell references here are correct for those who hold shares in three companies. If you hold shares with fewer or more companies, you must adjust the references accordingly.

► BEFORE YOU START

1 Go to the **Start** menu, select **All Programs**, then **Microsoft Excel**. Save and name your new document by clicking on the **Save** toolbar button. Type in a file name then, in the 'Save in' box, select a folder in which to save it. Click **Save**.

*You can create a similar spreadsheet in Microsoft Works. Open Works then, in the Programs tab of the Works Task Launcher, click on **Works Spreadsheet** in the list on the left.*

► OTHER PROGRAMS

Templates on CD-ROM

To adjust the width of a column to accommodate your text, double-click on the right-hand edge of the beige column heading. The column will adjust to fit the widest piece of text in that column.

To style your text, highlight it then select a font, size and style from the toolbar.

To copy and paste your formula, highlight it then click on the **Copy** toolbar button. Highlight all the cells you want the formula to appear in, then click on the **Paste** toolbar button.

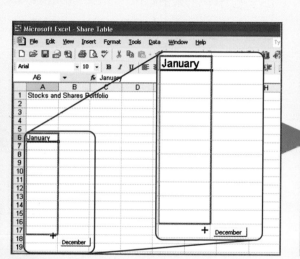

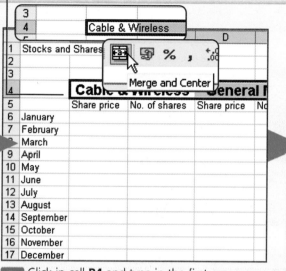

	E	F	G	H
4	Motors	Coca-Cola		Total portfolio value (£)
5	No. of shares	Share price	No. of shares	
6				=(B6*C6+D6*E6+F6*G6)/100

2 Type your heading in cell **A1**. Next, click on cell **A6** and type in 'January'. Place the mouse pointer over the lower right-hand corner of the cell. When it becomes a cross, click and drag down the column until 'December' appears.

3 Click in cell **B4** and type in the first company name. Select **B4** and **C4** then click the **Merge and Center** toolbar button. In cell **B5** type in 'Share price' and in **C5** type in 'No. of shares'. Enter other company names in row 4 as shown.

4 Click in cell **H4** and type 'Total portfolio value (£)'. In cell **H6** (this is the row of your first month) type in '=' then your formula (see below). Press the **Enter** key. Copy and paste the formula into the cells below for subsequent months.

You don't need to start your Shares Portfolio with January. Type in whichever month you want, then click and drag the cursor as described in Step 2. The program will fill in the other months automatically.

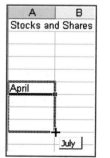

Calculating your shares

The formula for calculating the total value of your share portfolio needs to multiply the current share price by the number of shares for each company and then add them together (place this part of the formula in brackets).

To convert the value into pounds sterling, you must then divide by 100 (share prices are given in pence). Here, the formula is: '(B6*C6+D6*E6+F6*G6)/100'.

You don't need to type cell references into the formula – simply click on the cells at the appropriate point to enter them.

B	C	D	E	F	G	H
Cable & Wireless		General Motors		Coca-Cola		Total portfolio value (£)
Share price	No. of shares	Share price	No. of shares	Share price	No. of shares	=(B6*C6+D6*E6+F6*G6)/100

Cells that contain formulas will display '0' until you enter figures in the relevant share price and share number cells. The calculation cells will update themselves automatically as you enter these figures.

Format	Tools	Data	Window
Cells...		Ctrl+1	
Row			▶
Column			▶
Sheet			▶
AutoFormat...			
Conditional Formatting...			

	H	I
	Total portfolio value (£)	**Monthly change in value (£**
	0	
	0	=H7-H6
	0	
	0	
	0	
	0	
	0	
	0	
	0	
	0	
	0	

	H	I
Initial portfolio value (£)		
	22286.5	
Total portfolio value (£)		**Monthly change in value (£)**
	22276.5	-10
	22247	-29.5
	22221.5	-25.5
	22206	-15.5
	22186	-20
	22896.9	710.9
	22908.2	11.3
	22933.9	25.7
	22387.6	-546.3
	22732	344.4
	22732.5	0.5
	22726.7	-5.8
Yearly change in value (£)		440.2

I22   *fx*

	A	B	C	Share price
1	Stocks and Shares Portfolio			3632
2				3628
3	**Sell now**	3632		3622
4		**Cable & Wireless**		3624
5		Share price	No. of shares	3603
6	January	3632	100	3597
7	February	3628	100	3626
8	March	3622	100	3637
9	April	3624	100	3644
10	May	3603	100	3648
11	June	3597	120	3653
12	July	3626	120	3655
13	August	3637	120	
14	September	3644	120	
15	October	3648	130	

5 Click in cell **I4** and type 'Monthly change in value (£)'. In cell **I7** (the row for your second month) enter a formula that subtracts the Total portfolio value in February (H7) from the Total value in January (H6). Press **Enter**. Copy and paste the formula into the cells below.

6 In **H2** type 'Initial portfolio value (£)'. In **H3** enter the total value of the shares when you bought them. To calculate the change in value for January, click in cell **I6** and type in '=H6-H3'. Type in your share price data and the formulas will update.

7 Now create a warning for when your share value falls below your selling price. In **A3** type in 'Sell now'. In **B3** enter the selling price for the first company. Highlight column B, go to the **Format** menu and click on **Conditional Formatting** (see below).

Yearly change in value (£)	440.2

*Click in cell **H19** and type 'Yearly change in value (£)'. In cell **I19** type in the formula '=H17-H3'.*

Set up a warning

In the Conditional Formatting dialogue box click on the arrow beside the second box and select **less than or equal to**. Click in the third box, then on the cell **B3**.
Click the **Format** button and select a font colour, then click **OK**. Share prices that are less than or equal to your selling price will appear in this colour. Repeat for all your share price columns.

Conditional Formatting

Condition 1
Cell Value Is ▾ | less than ▾ | =B3

Preview of format to use when condition is true: No Format Set   Format...

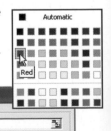

Automatic

Red

*To highlight more than one column at a time, press the **Ctrl** key and click on each beige column heading in turn.*

Stocks and Shares Portfolio

*To style the heading, highlight it, go to the **Format** menu and click on **Cells**. Click on the **Font** tab and select a font, size, style and colour. Click **OK**.*

Fill Color (Violet)

*To centre your heading, select cells **A1** to **I1** and click on the **Merge and Center** button. To add a background colour, click on the arrow beside the Fill Color toolbar button and select a colour from the drop-down palette.*

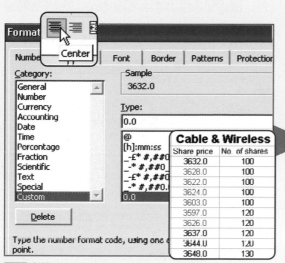

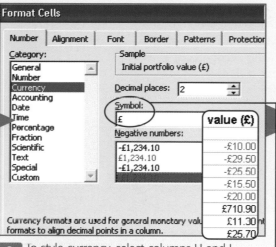

8 Style your share price columns by highlighting them, going to the **Format** menu and clicking on **Cells**. Click on the **Custom** category, then type in '0.0' in the Type box. Click **OK**. To centre columns, highlight them and click on the **Center** toolbar button.

9 To style currency, select columns H and I, right-click your mouse, then select **Format Cells**. Click on the **Currency** category of the Number tab. In the 'Decimal places' box type in '2'. In the 'Negative numbers' box click on your choice of style for negative amounts. Click on **OK**.

10 Create lines to separate your columns so you can read your data more easily. Select the cells in each 'No. of shares' column then click on the arrow beside the Border toolbar button. Click on the button that adds a right border.

In the 'Symbol' box you can choose whether or not to display a currency symbol, such as '£' or '$'.

Printing your table

Your spreadsheet will probably be quite wide, so to make it fit on a sheet of A4 go to the **File** menu and select **Print Preview**. Click on the **Setup** button. The Page tab is selected. Click the Landscape option then, in the Scaling section, select the 'Fit to' option. Click **OK**.

Manage a special event

Learn how to keep track of the budget, and raise money

Managing a budget for, say, a school play or a benefit dinner can be a complex business. Not only must you keep track of a range of expenses, but you also have to weigh up outgoings against projected income to ensure you make a profit. If that profit is earmarked for a particular use – a new computer lab, for instance – you will have a better idea of how much you need to raise, and so be able to budget accordingly.

Using a spreadsheet program on your PC will make light work of budget calculations and projections. Microsoft Excel also allows you to create accounts for specific aspects of a project such as ticket sales, and incorporate these within the accounts for the whole project.

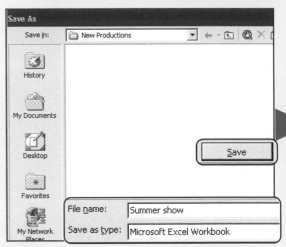

Note each area in which you will have to spend money, and all sources of income. Ask colleagues to provide figures for their projects.

BEFORE YOU START

1 Go to the **Start** menu, select **All Programs** and click on **Microsoft Excel**. Save your document by going to the **File** menu and selecting **Save As**. In the 'Save in' box select a location to store your file, give it a name, then click on **Save**.

You can create a similar spreadsheet in Microsoft Works. However, Works does not have multiple worksheets within the same document, so you must create separate documents for each area of budgeting.

OTHER PROGRAMS

Key word
Format *This refers to the process of setting the appearance of text (font, style, size and colour), and figures (number, currency, date, etc) in cells.*

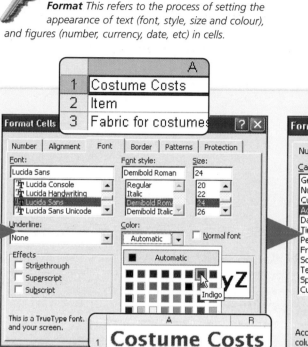

2 In cell **A1** type a heading for your first sheet; in cell **A2** type 'Item'; in cell **B2** 'Estimated costs'; and in cell **C2** 'Actual costs'. In cell **A3** type your first expense. List your expenses in the cells below. Type 'Total' under your list of expenses.

3 To style your text, click on the cell, go to the **Format** menu and click on **Cells**. Click on the **Font** tab in the dialogue box. Select a font, style, size and colour, then click **OK**. To style several adjacent cells in the same way at once, click and then drag your mouse over the cells.

4 Format the cost cells in columns B and C. Click and drag across the cells, go to the **Format** menu and click on **Cells**. Select the **Number** tab and **Accounting** in the Category window. Select **2** in the 'Decimal places' box and **None** in the Symbol box. Click **OK**.

To adjust the width of a column to accommodate your text, double-click on the right-hand edge of the beige column heading. The column will automatically adjust to fit the widest piece of text in that column.

The Accounting format
When you select the Accounting format for cells, the decimal points and currency symbols (if you use them) are aligned directly above each other, making your account-keeping easier.

You should also be aware that when you type '0' into a cell to indicate that there is no cost, it will be expressed as '-' as soon as you click out of that cell.

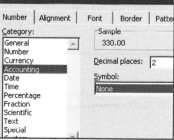

Close-up
*You may need to insert new rows of expenses. Click on the row above where you'd like the new row to appear, go to the **Insert** menu and select **Rows**.*

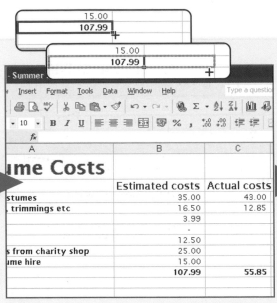

You can keep accounts for various aspects of the same project within one Excel document. Simply create a separate worksheet for each one (see below left).

ADD MORE WORKSHEETS

5 Enter the individual estimates then add up your figures in the Estimated costs column. Click in the Total cell for column B (here, **B10**), then click the **AutoSum** toolbar button. Press **Enter** and the total will appear.

6 Copy the formula for Actual costs. Click the Total cell for Estimated costs (here, **B10**) then place the cursor in its lower right-hand corner. When the cursor turns into a cross, click and drag across to the Actual costs column. The sum will adjust as you enter each cost.

7 To create a second worksheet for, say, income from tickets, click on the **Sheet2** tab at the bottom of the screen. The spreadsheet above has sections for estimated and actual revenue from sales of differently priced seats.

Naming and adding worksheets

To make it easier to navigate between worksheets, rename them. To rename Sheet1 double-click on the **Sheet1** tab at the bottom of the screen and type in a title (here, Costumes), then press the **Enter** key.

To add more worksheets, go to the **Insert** menu and click on **Worksheet**. To re-order the sequence of worksheets, click on the tab of the one you want to move and drag it to its new position.

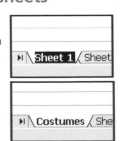

Adding grids

To enclose your worksheet details in a grid, select the relevant cells, go to the **Format** menu and click on **Cells**. In the dialogue box click on the **Border** tab. First, select a Line Style and colour, then, in the Presets section, click on the **Outline** and **Inside** buttons, then click **OK**.

To add a background colour, select the cells, go to the **Format** menu and click on **Cells**. Click on the **Patterns** tab. In the 'Cell shading' section click on your choice of colour, then click **OK**.

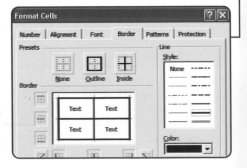

Watch out

If you name your worksheets you must use the new names, rather than Sheet1, 2, etc, when referring to them in cell references. So, you might type "'Costumes'!B10" rather than "'Sheet1'!B10".

Ticket price	Estimated revenue
3.00	=(A3*C3)

SUM ▾ ✗ ✓ fx =SUM(D3:D5)

Ticket sales (estimated)

	No.	Item	Ticket price	Estimated
3	500	Standard seats	3.00	
4	100	Privilege seats	4.00	
5	200	Children's seats		
6			Total	

Estimated revenue

	1,500.00
	400.00
	300.00

=SUM(D3:D5)

SUM(**number1**, [number2], ...)

Ticket sales (actu

	No.	Item	Ticket p
11	389	Standard seats	3.00
12	79	Privilege seats	4.00
13	184	Children's seats	1.50
14			Total

8 To estimate income from standard seat sales, click in the relevant cell (here, **D3**), type '=' then a formula for the total seats multiplied by the price (A3*C3). Repeat for other seats. Click in the Total cell (**D6**), click the **AutoSum** toolbar button and press **Enter**. Repeat for actual sales.

	A	B	
1	**Budget Summary - summer**		
2	**Item**	**Estimated costs**	**Actual c**
3	Costumes	='Sheet1'!B10	
4	Refreshments		
5	Props		
6	Printing/publicity		
7	Total		
8			
10	**Item**	**Estimated revenue**	**Actual r**
11	Refreshments		
12	Tickets		
13	Total		
14			
15	Balance		
16			
17			
18			
19			

107.99

9 Open a worksheet to add up costs and revenue of the individual parts of the project. Create columns as shown. In the costs and revenue columns enter the sheet and cell references of your totals for other worksheets. Eg: "= 'Sheet1'!B10" (total for the Costumes Sheet).

	A	B	
1	**Budget Summary - summer**		
2	**Item**	**Estimated costs**	**Actual**
3	Costumes	107.99	
4	Refreshments	144.24	
5	Props	98.00	
6	Printing/publicity	50.00	
7	Total	400.23	
9			
10	**Item**	**Estimated revenue**	**Actual**
11	Refreshments	330.00	
12	Tickets	2,200.00	
13	Total	2,530.00	
14			
15	Balance		
16			
17			
18			

10 Now calculate total costs and revenue. Click in the Total cell for Estimated costs (here, **B7**) click the **AutoSum** button and press **Enter**. Copy the formula into the Actual costs cell (see Step 6). Repeat for revenue. If you wish to work out balances, see below.

Calculating balances

To calculate Estimated and Actual balances, click in the Estimated Balance cell (here, **B15**), type '=', then a formula that subtracts the total estimated costs from the total estimated revenue (B13-B7). Press **Enter**. Copy and paste the formula into the Actual Balance cell (see Step 6).

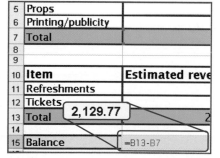

	A	B	
5	Props		
6	Printing/publicity		
7	Total		
8			
9			
10	**Item**	**Estimated reve**	
11	Refreshments		
12	Tickets		
13	Total	2,129.77	2
14			
15	Balance	=B13-B7	

Printing out worksheets

To print a worksheet, first go to the **File** menu and click on **Print Preview** to see how it looks. To make adjustments press the **Esc** key and edit accordingly. When you're happy with how it looks, click **Print**, specify the pages you require then click **OK**.

Form a Neighbourhood

Your PC can make it easier for friends and neighbours

Any community-based project benefits from sound organisation, good communication and a high local profile. Your PC can help make each of these objectives achievable.

Neighbourhood Watch schemes rely on volunteer members keeping an eye on each other's properties, particularly during working hours and holiday periods. Knowing who is available to patrol the area, and which houses are unoccupied, will make your Neighbourhood Watch scheme more efficient.

The ideal starting point is to create a tailored membership form using a database program. Distribute this to prospective members then, when you receive the completed forms, enter the details into a members' database.

Your database will then help in identifying who is at home and who is out, and at what times. By including work and holiday schedules, and using the program's 'sort' facility, you can compile a day-to-day list of unoccupied properties: the ones most at risk. Then, using the information

Watch group

to guard against local crime

on members' availability, you can produce a rota of neighbours who can keep an eye out for suspicious behaviour.

Once you have set up your scheme, your computer can help you to log incidents of crime. Use your database's Form Design feature to create an incident report form on which members can record the date, time, place and type of any incident.

If you set up a separate crime database you will soon be able to build up a profile of the types of crime that occur in your area and when crime is most likely to take place. You can then review your activities and patrols accordingly.

To raise the profile of your scheme, use your PC's graphics capabilities to design a poster for members to display in their windows. You could also design a letterhead for correspondence, and produce a newsletter to keep members informed of any special events and new members, as well as raise awareness of crime trends and home security.

And if you're connected to the Internet, you can take a look at the wide range of Neighbourhood Watch information on the World Wide Web. You'll find messaging forums, details on training, useful contact numbers, home insurance information and lists of the type of items that most appeal to thieves. You can even join a weekly e-mailing list, giving tips on, among other things, home security.

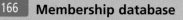

Ideas and inspirations

Below are project ideas to help you set up an effective Neighbourhood Watch group that the local community – and criminals – will take seriously. The projects can be adapted to your own requirements. And using the PC will cut down on paperwork.

166 Membership database
Record members' details, including contact phone numbers and car registration numbers.

162 Create a newsletter
Design an eye-catching publication to keep your neighbours informed of developments.

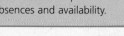

214 Design a poster
Attract attention to a forthcoming meeting or publicise your scheme.

180 Create a diary
Use this handy feature to keep track of members' travel plans, absences and availability.

144 Design a letterhead
Give your scheme's correspondence an official and businesslike appearance.

Also worth considering...

No matter how successful your group is, you may benefit from the experience of others.

94 Search the Internet
Find out more about established Neighbourhood Watch schemes, and correspond by e-mail.

Record a family history

Explore your past with a database of relatives and ancestors

Compiling a family history can be a hugely rewarding exercise. It's amazing how soon knowledge about a family's past is lost if no-one writes it down, but it is equally astonishing how much fascinating detail you can quickly and easily find out about your ancestors, once you start.

The database program in Microsoft Works is ideal for making systematic records of your family's history. Dates of birth, occupations, marriages and so on can all be noted – or left blank until your research bears fruit. You can also make space to record interesting facts about your forebears: the homes where they lived, the medals they won, famous people they met, the traces they left behind. Use your PC to explore your roots – your grandchildren will thank you for it one day.

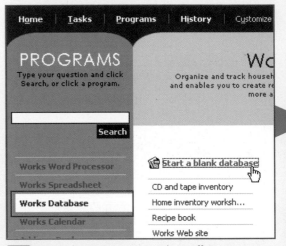

It's quicker to input all your information in one go. But don't worry if you need to do more research as it is easy to amend or add information at any time.

BEFORE YOU START

1 Go to the **Start** menu, select **All Programs** and click on **Microsoft Works**. In the Programs tab of the Works Task Launcher, click on **Works Database** listed on the left. Then click on **Start a blank database** to launch the program.

You can also create a family database in Microsoft Excel. This will let you input and view your data in table form, ready for sorting and styling according to your needs.

OTHER PROGRAMS

Templates on CD-ROM

Bright idea
Create a reference field, in which each record has its own reference number, and give it a 'serialized' format. This way, record numbers will update automatically whenever a new record is added.

*To select more than one field at a time, press the **Ctrl** key and, keeping it pressed down, click on all the boxes you want to alter.*

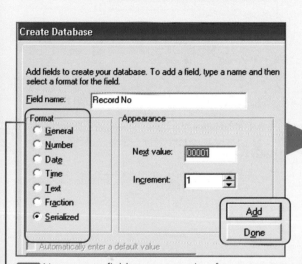

2 Now create fields, or categories, for your database. Type the name of your first field in the 'Field name' box and select a format for it. When you have named and formatted a field, click on **Add**. When you have entered all your database fields, click on the **Done** button.

3 Your database appears in List form. Now name and save it. Then customise the look of it by clicking on the **Form Design** toolbar button. To move a text box, click on it and drag it. (To resize it, see below.) Rearrange your text boxes to leave space at the top of the page for a heading.

4 Click at the top of the page and type in your heading. To style it, highlight it, then go to the **Format** menu and click on **Font and Style**. Select a font, size, colour and style, then click **OK**. Style your field names using the same method.

Fields and formats
Consider using the following fields and formats. For an added sense of history, include a field for biographical facts.

Field	Format	Field	Format
Record No.	Serialized	Married to	Text
Surname	Text	Marriage date	Date
First names	Text	Children	Text
Date of birth	Date	Occupation	Text
Place of birth	Text	Date of death	Date
Mother	Text	Burial place	Text
Father	Text	Notes	Text

Resizing text boxes
To resize a text box, click on it. Place the mouse pointer over the side or bottom or bottom right-hand corner. When the pointer changes to a double-headed arrow, click the mouse and, keeping the button pressed down, drag it across the screen.

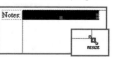

Different views
There are four ways to view your database:

List View is best for quick reference. It lets you view several entries at the same time.

Form View displays one entry at a time and is clearer for entering data.

Form Design lets you add and delete fields and alter their layout.

Report View allows you to compile selective reports from your database.

279

*To move to the next field or record, press the **Tab** key. To move back, press the **Shift** and **Tab** keys.*

Key word

Report *A report extracts designated information from a database. For example, from your family database you could make a report on relatives who emigrated, or who fought in wars.*

Form View

Family Hi

Record No: 00001

Surname: Potts

First names: James B

Date of birth: 11/11/1957

Place of birth: Putney

Mother: Jane Potts (nee West)

Father: Jeffrey Potts

Married to: Gillian West

Marriage date: 08/02

List View

Format   Tools   Help

10

"Grimley Moore Cemetary Leeds"

Date of death	Burial place	Notes
N/A	N/A	Served in Dorset Regim
N/A	N/A	
27/03/1954	Eversham Park Cre	Arrested murderer David
10/12/1971	Eversham Park Cresent	
09/06/1962	Grimley Moore Cer	Drove "The Flying Scots
23/09/1962	Grimley Moore Cer	Worked as domestic so
10/02/1943	Banbury Cemetary	Served under Kitchener
14/07/1940	Du Pont Cemetary	
23/05/1939	Leeds Municipal Cemetary	
17/01/1957	Highgate Cemetary	

Find

Find what: Bertram

Match
○ Next record   ● All records

Help

Bertram

✓		Surname	First names	Date of birth
	13	Bertram	Jim Bruce	29/11/1959
	14	Bertram	Sandra Kim	25/02/1960
	15	Bertram	Jamie Stuart	13/08/1985
	16	Bertram	Hayley Sonia	13/08/1985
	21			
	22			
	23			
	24			
	25			
	26			
	27			
	28			
	29			

5 To enter information, first click on the **Form View** toolbar button. Click on the text boxes adjoining the field names and type in the relevant data. To move to the next field or record, press the **Tab** key. To move back to the previous field, press the **Shift** and **Tab** keys at the same time.

6 When you have entered all your data click on the **List View** toolbar button to view your complete database. To see all the data in a particular cell, click on it. Its contents appear in the Entry bar at the top of the form.

7 To find a record or piece of information – such as everyone who has the same surname – go to the **Edit** menu and click on **Find**. Type a key word in the 'Find what' box, select the 'All records' option, then click **OK**. Works will display all the records containing the key word.

Adding ClipArt

To decorate your 'Family Tree' database, go into 'Form Design' and click in the form. Go to the **Insert** menu and select **ClipArt**. Type 'tree' into the 'type a keyword' box then click **Search**. Click on your choice of image, then on the **Insert** button. Resize and reposition your image in **Form Design** view in the same way as the text and field boxes.

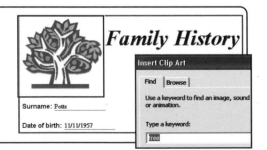

Family History

Surname: Potts

Date of birth: 11/11/1957

Insert Clip Art

Find | Browse

Use a keyword to find an image, sound or animation.

Type a keyword:

tree

Date of birth: 11/29/1959

Mother: Sally Bertram (nee Brown)

Married to: Sandra Potts

Children: Jamie & Hayley

◄◄ ◄ Record 11 ► ►◄ Zoom 100% – + ◄

Scrolling

You can scroll through your records quickly by clicking the arrows either side of the Record counter at the foot of the Form View window.

You may want to create a report – in other words, print out all or parts of your database – for the family to see or to help you in your research.

▶ **CREATING A REPORT**

*If the report's contents are too close together, click on **Modify** and adjust the column widths. Place the mouse pointer on the right-hand edge of the column heading, then click and drag to the right.*

To print all records, select the 'All records' option.

What to Print
- ○ All records
- ⦿ Current record only

OK

Report Name [?][X]

Type a name for the report below:
Family History

Grouping | Filter

Fields available:
- Date of birth
- Place of birth
- Mother
- Father
- Married to
- Marriage date
- Children
- Occupation

Field order:
- Surname
- First names
- Date of birth
- Father
- Mother
- Children

Add >
< Remove
Add All >>
<< Remove All

Display options
- ☑ Show field names at top of each page
- ☐ Show summary information only

Family History

Surname	First names	Date of birth	Father
Potts	James Brian	11/10/57	Jeffrey F
Potts	Gillian	05/09/60	William V
West	Walter	25/09/08	Ernest V
West	Janice	01/01/11	Harold N
Potts	Robert Alfred	06/03/14	Jacob P
Potts	Alice	17/07/14	Henry B
Potts	Jeffrey Francis	17/06/36	Robert F
Potts	Jane	15/10/36	William V
West			
West			
Bertram			
Bertram			
West			
Bertram			

ReportCreator

⚠ The report definition has been created.

Do you wish to preview or modify the report definition?

[Preview] [Modify]

Family History

Record No: 00001

Surname: Potts

Date of birth: 11/11/1957

Mother: Jane Potts (nee West)

Married to: Gillian West

Children: Robert and Emily

First names: James Brian

Place of birth: Putney, London

Father: Jeffrey Potts

Marriage date: 08/02/1982

8 To create a printed record, go to the **Tools** menu and click on **ReportCreator**. Type in a name for your report and click **OK**. Click the **Fields** tab. Click each field you want to print in turn, clicking on **Add** as you do so. When you have finished click on **Done**.

9 A prompt box appears. Press the **Preview** button to see how your report looks. If you are satisfied with it, click on **Print**. To make changes, press **Esc**, click on a section of text, go to the **Format** menu and click on **Font and Style**.

10 To print out a record in Form View, click on the **Print Preview** toolbar button. If you are happy with how it looks, click **Cancel**, go to the **File** menu and select **Print**. Under 'What to Print' select the 'Current record only' option. Click **OK**.

Sorting your records

You can 'sort' or prioritise information within your database. For example, you may want to rank family members from the oldest to the youngest.

In the ReportCreator dialogue box click on the **Sorting** tab. Click on the arrow beside the first 'Sort by' box, scroll through and select the field you want – in this case, 'Date of birth'. Select the Ascending option, then click **Done**.

ReportCreator - Family History

| Title | Fields | Sorting | Grouping |

Sort by
Date of birth
⦿ Ascending
○ Descending

Then by
[None]
⦿ Ascending
○ Descending

Make a recipe collection

Keep all your family's favourites together in a database

Most people keep recipes in different places – in books, written down on bits of paper, or cut out from magazines. Tracking them all down can take time.

Save yourself the trouble by creating a recipe database. This allows you to keep all your recipes together, and lets you sort them to find the right recipe for the occasion. When you've found the recipe you want, you can print it out to use or make copies for friends. Once you've created your database, you can add new recipes as you discover them.

Home Recipe Collection

Recipe type: Chicken

Recipe name: Thai Chicken Curry

...entry: 09/06/02

...620 cals

...erved: 6

...p time: 15 mins

...g time: 30 mins

...ents: 2 garlic cloves 1 medium onion 1 lemon grass stalk 2.5cm/1in piece root ginger 2 small chillies fresh coriander to taste 1 tsp ground coriander grated rind & juice 1 lime 2 tomatoes 6 chicken breast fillets 2 tbsp vegetable oil 2 tbsp fish sauce 1 pint coconut milk salt & pepper.

...hes: Toasted coconut, coriander leaves

...tructions: 1. Peel garlic. Peel and quarter onion. Halve lemon grass. Peel and halve ginger. Put these ingredients in a food processor with ch... lime. Process until they form a paste. 2. Peel and ch... into 3 pieces. Heat oil in a frying pan. Add the sp... high heat for 3 minutes, stirring constantly. Ad... minutes, stirring to coat with spices. 4. Add... milk. Bring to the boil. Cover and simmer... chicken is cooked through. Season to ta...

Recipe ref: 00001

...riations: 100g prawns, defrosted.

BEFORE YOU START

Give some thought to the type of information you want stored in your database. Don't worry if you can't find all your recipes when you start – add them at a later date.

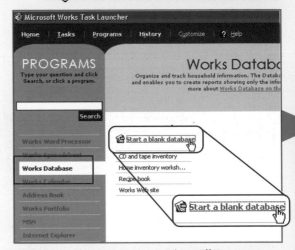

1 Go to the **Start** menu, select **All Programs** and click on **Microsoft Works**. In the Programs tab of the Works Task Launcher, click on **Works Database** listed on the left. Then click on **Start a blank database** to launch the program.

You can also create a recipe collection in Microsoft Excel. This will let you input and view your recipes in table form, ready for sorting according to your needs.

OTHER PROGRAMS

Templates on CD-ROM

Once you have selected a format, select a style for it in the Appearance section.

Bright idea
Always include a serialised reference number field in your database so that each record will have a unique reference number. Works automatically updates the number.

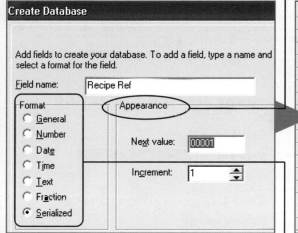

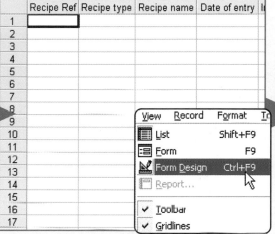

2 In the Create Database dialogue box input your field names. You can specify a format for each field. When you have typed in your field name click on **Add**. When you have entered all your fields click on **Done**. Save your document by clicking on the **Save** toolbar button.

3 Your database appears in List form with the field names appearing at the top of columns. To structure your database go to the **View** menu and select **Form Design**. You can now adjust the position and size of text boxes to make sure your recipe details are visible.

4 Click on the text box adjoining each field name. Keeping the mouse button pressed down, drag it into position. When positioning text boxes, rearrange them so that there is about 8 cm of space at the top of the page for your heading.

Fields can include:

Field	Format
Recipe ref	Serialized
Recipe type	Text
Recipe name	Text
Date of entry	Date
Ingredients	Text
Instructions	Text
Number served	Number
Calories	Number
Cooking time	Time

Sizing field boxes
To increase the size of fields, click on the field box to highlight it then move the mouse pointer over the bottom right-hand corner. When the cursor changes to a double-headed arrow, click the mouse and, keeping the button pressed down, drag the box to the size you require.

Close-up
When you type words into each field they will appear in the Entry Bar above your form. It is here that you correct typing mistakes and edit your text.

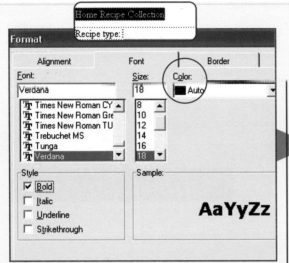

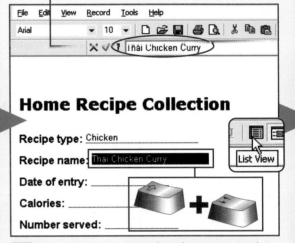

5 Now click at the top of the page, above your first field name, and type your heading. With your heading highlighted go to the **Format** menu and select **Font and Style**. In the dialogue box select a font, font size, colour and style. Click **OK**.

6 Style the field names and the adjoining text boxes, using different fonts for each to make them distinguishable. When you type in text to the empty boxes the text will appear in the style you have set.

7 To input recipes, go to the **View** menu and select **Form**. Type the information into the fields you have made. Press the **Tab** key to go to the next field or record, **Shift** and **Tab** to move back. When you have typed in all your recipes, click on the **List View** toolbar.

*If you have a colour printer, why not add colour to your recipes? In the Format dialogue box select white as your font colour then click on the **Shading** tab. Now select a foreground colour and pattern. Click **OK**.*

Short cut
*To style several field names or text boxes in the same way, click on the first box, press the **Ctrl** key and, keeping the Ctrl key pressed down, click on all the boxes you want to style. Go to the **Format** menu and select **Font and Style**. Now style as you wish.*

Bright idea
You can view your database at different levels of magnification by using the Zoom tool at the bottom of the screen. Simply click on the '+' and '-' buttons.

Recipe type: Duck

Recipe name: Roast Duck with raisin sauce

Date of entry: 12/05/2002

Calories: 650 cals

Number served: 2

Prep time: 15 mins

Cooking time: 45 mins

| |◀| Record 5 |▶|▶| Zoom 100% − + ◀

Sort Records

Sort by
Recipe ref
Instructions
Number served
Calories
Cooking time
● Ascending
○ Descending
● Ascending
○ Descending
OK
Then by
● Ascending
○ Descending

ReportCreator - Low-cal dishes

Title | Fields | Sorting | Grouping

Fields available:
Recipe type
Recipe name
Date of entry
Ingredients
Instructions
Number served
Calories
Cooking time

Add >
< Remove
Add All >>
<< Remove All

Field order:
Recipe ref
Recipe type
Recipe name
Cooking time

Next >
Previous
Done
Cancel

Display options
☑ Show field names at top of each page
☐ Show summary information only

8 When it comes to selecting a particular recipe, click on it in List form then go to the **View** menu and select **Form**. The recipe will then appear in its fully formatted form.

9 To sort recipes by, say, cooking time, go to the **Record** menu and select **Sort Records**. Click on the arrow beside the 'Sort by' box and scroll down to select the field to be sorted. Click **OK**.

10 To list your sorted records, go to the **Tools** menu and select **ReportCreator**. Name your report then select the fields to be included and the order in which they are to appear. Click **Done** to create it. Print your list when you are satisfied.

Scrolling recipes
You can scroll through all the records on your database by clicking on the arrows in the record counter at the foot of the Form View window. This moves you through each formatted recipe to adjacent records or the first or last in the database.

Amending a report
To amend a report go to the **View** menu and select **Report**. Click on the report to be changed then click on **Modify**. To increase space between columns, adjust their width. Click on the right-hand edge of the column header and drag to the right.

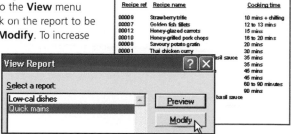

Design a baby book

Keep a special book of memories for all the family to enjoy

Watching children grow up is one of the greatest pleasures in life, and creating a record of their early years allows you to relive the experience time and time again. By designing a baby book on your PC you can use as many photographs as you like, and print copies of the book for your relatives, without needing to make expensive photographic reprints.

Add a few personal design touches, and your baby book will delight your family for generations to come.

Work out which photographs you want to include in your book, and scan them in. For more information on scanning, see page 204.

BEFORE YOU START

1 Go to the **Start** menu, select **All Programs** then click on **Microsoft Word**. A document will open. Go to the **File** menu and select **Page Setup**. Click on the **Margins** tab to set your orientation and the **Paper** tab to select your paper size, click **OK**. Now save and name your document.

You can create a baby book using Microsoft Works. Style your text as normal, but you will need to import scanned photographs through Paint (see page 210 for details).

OTHER PROGRAMS

Templates on CD-ROM

Key word
Styles This describes the text attributes you
set for particular sections of your document.
Styles will add continuity to your book, and will make
it quicker to style new text.

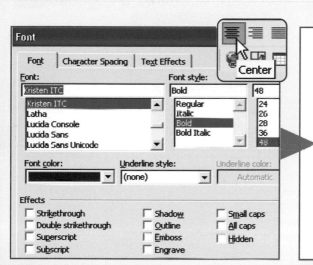

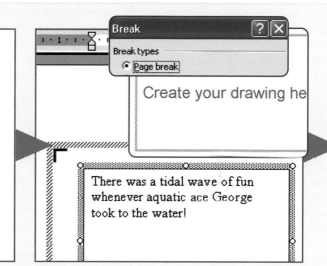

2 First, make a title page. Type in the title then highlight it, go to the **Format** menu and click on **Font**. Select a font, style, size, effect and colour. Click **OK** when you are satisfied. To position it on the page, select it again and click on the **Center** toolbar button.

3 To insert a photo, go to the **Insert** menu, select **Picture** then click on **From File**. Navigate through the 'Look in' box to locate your scan. Files and folders in the My Pictures folder are displayed with thumbnail views of your images. Click on a photo to select it, then click on **Insert**. To position photos, see below.

4 To add a page, go to the **Insert** menu and click on **Break**. Select 'Page break' then click **OK**. You can add text in a text box for easier positioning. Go to **Insert** and select **Text Box**. Click in the box that says 'Create your drawing here' and a text box appears. Move and resize the box in the same way as pictures (see below left).

Placing your pictures

To ensure you can move and resize pictures with ease, click on your image, go to the **Format** menu and select **Picture**. In the Format Picture dialogue box, click on the **Layout** tab. In the Wrapping style section, select the 'In front of text' option, then Click **OK**.

Move a picture or text box by clicking on it and dragging it. Resize a picture by clicking on a corner handle and dragging it diagonally.

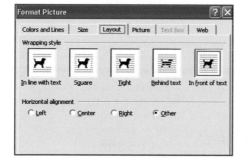

Page and picture borders

To add a border around a page, go to the **Format** menu and click on **Borders and Shading**. Click on the **Page Border** tab and choose the type of border you want. Click on the arrow beside the 'Apply to' box and scroll down to 'This section – First page only'. Then click **OK**.

To put a frame around a photo, click on the photo, go to the **Format** menu and click on **Borders and Shading** again. In the Line section of the Colors and Lines tab, select a colour, style and thickness. Then click **OK**.

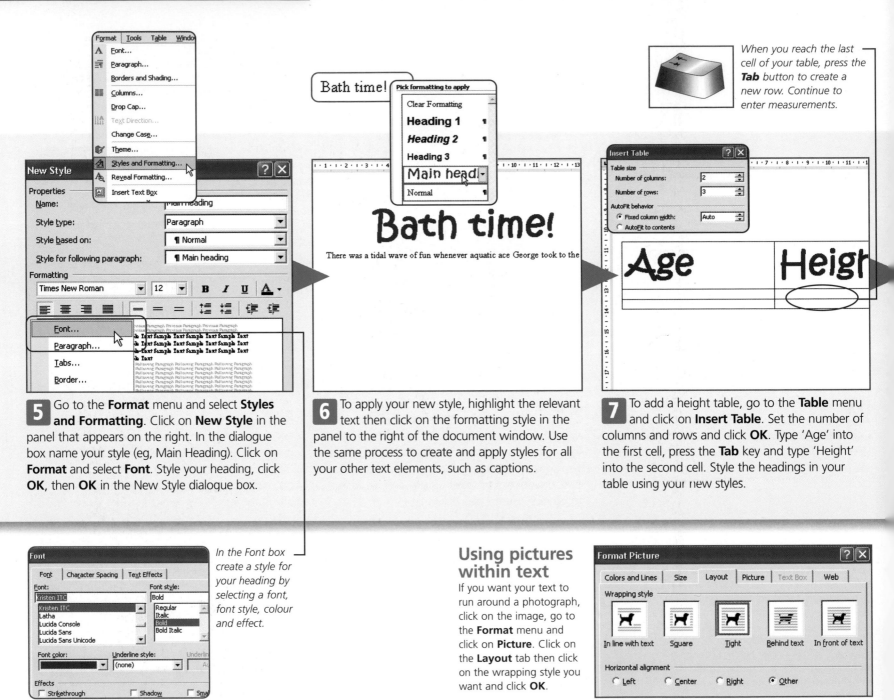

When you reach the last cell of your table, press the **Tab** *button to create a new row. Continue to enter measurements.*

5 Go to the **Format** menu and select **Styles and Formatting**. Click on **New Style** in the panel that appears on the right. In the dialogue box name your style (eg, Main Heading). Click on **Format** and select **Font**. Style your heading, click **OK**, then **OK** in the New Style dialogue box.

In the Font box create a style for your heading by selecting a font, font style, colour and effect.

6 To apply your new style, highlight the relevant text then click on the formatting style in the panel to the right of the document window. Use the same process to create and apply styles for all your other text elements, such as captions.

7 To add a height table, go to the **Table** menu and click on **Insert Table**. Set the number of columns and rows and click **OK**. Type 'Age' into the first cell, press the **Tab** key and type 'Height' into the second cell. Style the headings in your table using your new styles.

Using pictures within text

If you want your text to run around a photograph, click on the image, go to the **Format** menu and click on **Picture**. Click on the **Layout** tab then click on the wrapping style you want and click **OK**.

Bright idea
You could also create a table of milestones, so that you can note down when your baby started smiling, crawling, talking, and so on.

*If you don't want your WordArt to appear on the title page, go to the **File** menu and select **Page Setup**. Select the **Layout** tab and, in the Headers and footers section, click in the 'Different first page' box, then click **OK**.*

8 To style your table with coloured borders, etc, click in the table, go to the **Table** menu and click on **Select Table**. Go to the **Format** menu and click on **Borders and Shading**. Select a setting, line style, colour and width, then click **OK**.

9 Add your baby's name to each page. Using the Zoom facility on the toolbar, view your page at 25% to see all your pages on the screen. Go to the **View** menu and click on **Header and Footer**. Go to the **Insert** menu and select **Picture** then **WordArt**. Click on a style then on **OK**.

10 Type in your baby's name, select a font and size for it, then click **OK**. The WordArt name will appear on the page. Use the alignment toolbar buttons to reposition it. The name will appear in the same place on every page of your baby book.

Print Preview

Once you have added all the elements to your book, go to the **File** menu and click on **Print Preview** to see how the complete pages look. If you are happy, click on the **Print** toolbar button. If you need to make adjustments to the page, press the **Esc** key to return to your page layout.

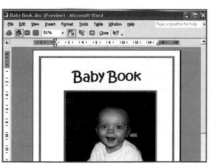

Watch your health

Keep a detailed record of your family's medical history

Everyone values their health, and that of their family, above all things. Yet few people keep accurate records of their own illnesses and treatments.

This information is useful in establishing patterns of illness, in providing up-to-date records for healthcare workers, and in keeping an account of medical and dental expenses.

With your PC, you can create a database that keeps detailed records of your family's health: what medications have been prescribed; dates of inoculations, check-ups and operations; allergies suffered. You can extract specific data when someone gets ill (for example, the name of a medicine that helped last time), and you can print out lists of future appointments.

Family Health Records

Name: Rosie
Consult type: GP
Consult date: 22/02/2002
Appoint time: 11:00 AM
Record ref: 00001
Appoint type: Runny nose
Treatment cost: N/A
Details: Rosie unable to go to playschool today as she was feverish and had a streaming nose
Comments: Dr prescribed antibiotics, advised stay off school for the week and come back if it hadn't cleared up by Sunday

Family Health Records

Name: John
Consult type: Optician
Consult date: 29/07/2002
Appoint time: 11:30 AM
Details: Regular check up

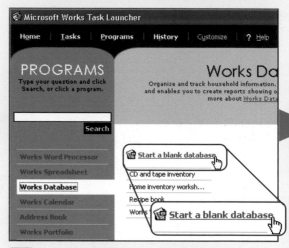

Gather all the information you have about your family's health records, such as dates of check-ups, details of consultations, and so on.

BEFORE YOU START

1 Go to the **Start** menu, select **All Programs** and click on **Microsoft Works**. In the Programs tab of the Works Task Launcher, click on **Works Database** listed on the left. Then click on **Start a blank database** to launch the program.

*You can create a family health database in Excel. Go to the **Start** menu, select **All Programs** and click on **Microsoft Excel**. Enter your data into the grid that appears.*

OTHER PROGRAMS

Templates on CD-ROM

Some formats, such as Number and Date, give a choice of appearance. Click on your choice from the list displayed.

To resize a text box, click on it then place the mouse pointer over the bottom right-hand corner. When the cursor changes to a double-headed arrow, click the mouse and drag the corner until the box is the right size.

Bright idea
When styling your fields and text boxes, use different fonts for each one to make them stand out.

2 In the Create Database dialogue box input your field names. Type the name of your first field in the box, click a format for the field then click the **Add** button. Continue to add all the fields you want, then click **Done**. Your document then appears in List form.

3 Name and save your document. To ensure your details are visible and appear as you wish, adjust the design of your file. Click on the **Form Design** toolbar button. Click and drag on the text boxes to move them. To adjust the size of text boxes, see above.

4 To add a general heading that will appear on each record, click at the top of the form and type it in. Highlight it, go to the **Format** menu and select **Font and Style**. Select a font, size, colour and style. Click **OK**. In the same way, style the field boxes and text boxes.

Fields and formats

For a family health database, you might want to create these fields together with these formats.

Field	Format
Record ref	Serialized
Name	Text
Date of birth	Date
Consult type	Text
Consult date	Date
Appoint time	Time
Appoint type	Text
Details	Text
Comments	Text
Treatment cost	Number

Let the Wizard help

The Microsoft Works Wizard has several health records templates already set up.

Go to the **Start** menu, select **All Programs** then click on **Microsoft Works**. In the Tasks tab of the Works Task Launcher click on **Household Management**, then select **Medical records** from the list that appears. Click **Start this task** then choose from the selection of styles.

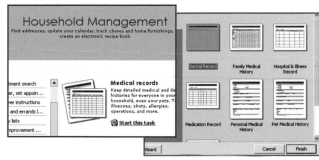

In Form View you can move through entries quickly by clicking on the arrows either side of the Record counter at the foot of the window. To change the magnification of the screen, click on the '+' or '-' signs beside the Zoom tool.

| ◄◄ | ◄ | Record 16 | ► | ►► | Zoom | 100% | − | + |

You can extract and print data from your database. It's a good idea, for example, to print out a list of future appointments to put on display.

► SORTING AND PRINTING

Form View

Family Health Reco

Name: Robert

Consult type: GP   Record Ref: 00017

Consult date: 16/09/2002   Appoint type: Blood t

Appoint time: 03:45 PM   Treatment cost:

Details:

List View

"Rosie unable to go to playscho

	Record Ref	Name	Consult type	Consult dat
1	00001	Rosie	GP	22/02/2002
2	00002	John	GP	01/03/2002
3	00003	John	Dentist	15/03/2002
4	00004	Robert	Dentist	11/04/2002
5	00005	Robert	Dentist	16/04/2002
6	00006	Robert	Dentist	23/04/2002
7	00007	John	Optician	23/04/2002
8	00008	Gill	Dentist	06/05/2002
9	00009	John	GP	09/05/2002
10	00010	Gill	GP	09/05/2002
11	00011	Robert	GP	09/05/2002
12	00012	Rosie	Children's clini	20/06/2002
13	00015	John	Optician	29/07/2002
14	00014	Robert	Dentist	15/08/2002

Name	Consult type	Consult date	Appoint time	Appoint type
Rosie	GP	22/02/2002	11:00 AM	Runny nose
John	GP	01/03/2002	08:30 AM	Vaccinations
John	Dentist	15/03/2002	03:00 PM	Checkup
Robert	Dentist	11/04/2002	08:00 AM	Painful tooth
Robert	Dentist	16/04/2002	12:00 PM	Filling
Robert	Dentist	23/04/2002	09:00 AM	Filling

Find ? ✕

Find what: John   OK   Cancel

Match ○ Next record   ● All records

Record Ref	Name	Consult type	Consult date
00002	John	GP	01/03/2002
00003	John	Dentist	15/03/2002
00007	John	Optician	23/04/2002
00009	John	GP	09/05/2002

5 Change the background colour if you wish (see below) then begin entering your records. Click on the **Form View** toolbar button. Click on the text boxes and type in the data. Press the **Tab** key to move to the next field, and **Shift** and **Tab** at the same time to move back to the previous field.

6 To see all your records at a glance, click on the **List View** toolbar button. If you cannot see all the information in a particular cell, click on it then view the contents in the Entry bar at the top of the screen.

7 To search for specific data in List View, go to the **Edit** menu and click on **Find**. Type in a key word for your search (here, records involving John), select the 'All records' option, then click **OK**. All records concerning John will then appear in a list.

Background colour

You can give the background of your form a colour and pattern. In Form Design click on an area of white space, outside a field or text box, go to the **Format** menu and click on **Shading**. Select a pattern and background colour from the choices available, then click **OK**.

Format

Font   Shading

Shading Pattern: Sample

Colors
Foreground: Background:
Magenta   Auto
Red   Black
Yellow   Blue
Gray   Cyan
White   Green

Showing all

To see all your records after you've done a search or created a Report, go to the **Record** menu, select **Show** then click on **All Records**.

Record	Format	Tools	Help

Insert Record
Delete Record

Insert Field
Delete Field

	ult type	Consult date
	st	15/03/2002
	an	23/04/2002
		09/05/2002
	an	29/07/2002
	st	10/09/2002

Sort Records...

Mark Records
Mark All Records

Show   1 All Records
Hide Record   Displays all records.

Apply Filter

Bright idea
To make an appointments list you probably won't need all your fields. Choose Consult date, Name, Consult type, Appoint time and Appoint type in that order.

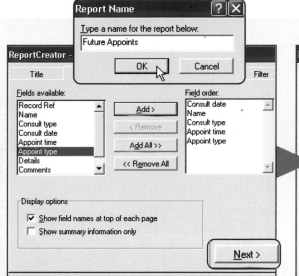

8 To print a list of appointments, go to the **Tools** menu and click on **ReportCreator**. Enter a report name in the dialogue box, click **OK**. In the next box click the **Fields** tab. Click each field you want in turn (in the order you want them) then click **Add**. Click **Next** when done.

9 The Sorting tab is now selected. Scroll through and click on **Consult date** in the first 'Sort by' box. In order to print out future appointments only, now click on the **Filter** tab. Click on the **Create New Filter** button. Type in 'date' as your filter name and click **OK**.

10 In the first 'Field name' box click on **Consult date**. In the Comparison box scroll through and click on **is greater than**. Type today's date in the 'Compare to' box. Click **Done** to see a Summary. You are now ready to print your list.

Printing your list

Once you have sorted your fields and set up a filter system you can print out your document.

Click on **Preview** to see your new report, then click on the **Print** button.

Family Health Records - Future Appoints

Consult date	Name	Consult type	Appoint time	Appoint type
29/07/2002	John	Optician	11:30 AM	Check up
15/08/2002	Robert	Dentist	10:00 AM	Check up
10/09/2002	John	Dentist	09:45 AM	Check up
16/09/2002	Robert	GP	03:45 PM	Blood test
01/10/2002	Gill	Dentist	02:00 PM	Check up

Plan a new kitchen

Try out a variety of room designs to find the one that suits you

Drawing up a plan for your new kitchen helps you decide how best to arrange all the elements for ease of use and optimum storage. You can create a two-dimensional plan on your PC using Microsoft Word. The plan can be easily adjusted as you make new additions, and you can create several alternative versions for comparison.

When you are planning your kitchen think about how you will use it. If you do a lot of cooking, make sure you have plenty of work surfaces and that the three key elements (cooker, fridge and sink) are close to each other and easily accessible.

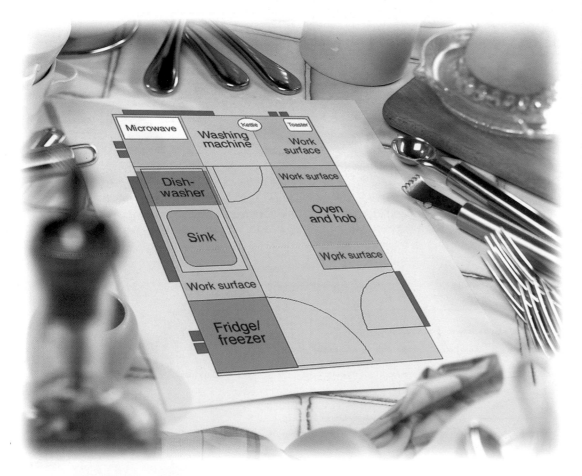

Measure the dimensions of your kitchen, including all doors, windows and appliances. Also note the position of electrical sockets and plumbing outlets.

BEFORE YOU START

Create your drawing

1 Go to the **Start** menu, select **All Programs** then click on **Microsoft Word**. A document opens. Go to the **Insert** menu and select **Text Box**. The words 'Create your drawing here' will appear. Click and drag the mouse diagonally to create a text box that will act as the outline for your kitchen.

It isn't possible to create a detailed plan to scale in Microsoft Works or Windows' accessory program, Paint. However, you can buy specialised interior design programs.

OTHER PROGRAMS

In the Line section select a colour, style and width for your kitchen border.

*As soon as you have opened your new document, save and name it. Click on the **Save** toolbar button and save the document into a suitable folder.*

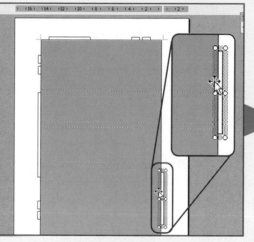

Format Text Box

Colors and Lines | Size | Layout | Picture | Text Box | Web

Size and rotate

Height: 24.45 cm   Width: 14.51 cm

Rotation:

Scale

Height: 100 %

☐ Lock aspect ratio

☐ Relative to original picture size

Original size

Height:

Format Text Box

Colors and Lines | Size | Layout | Picture | Text

Fill

Color:

Transparency:

Line

Color: Style:

Dashed: Weight:

Arrows

Begin style: End style:

Format Text Box

Colors and Lines | Size | Layout | Picture | Text Box | Web

Fill

Color:

Transparency: ◀ ▶ 0 %

Line

Color: Style:

Dashed: Weight: 0.75 p

Arrows

Begin style: End style:

Begin size: End size:

2 To make sure your text box is to scale (see below), go to the **Format** menu and select **Text Box**. Click on the **Size** tab. Specify the height and width of your box. Click on the **Colors and Lines** tab to select a colour for your box in the Fill section, then click **OK**.

3 Now create individual text boxes for all your fixed features, such as doors, windows and electrical sockets in the same way. To move them, click on the edge of the box and drag to the required position.

4 It's a good idea to colour all the fixed features in the same way. To select all the boxes at once, hold down the **Shift** key while clicking on each of them in turn. Go to the **Format** menu and click on **Text Box**. Click on the **Colors and Lines** tab, select a colour and click **OK**.

Drawing to scale

Measure your kitchen, then scale it to fit onto an A4 page. If your kitchen measures 650 cm by 450 cm, divide each figure by the same number to calculate measurements that will fit on the page. Dividing the real measurements by 25, for example, would create a box of 26 cm by 18 cm. Design to real-world standards by scaling down 30, 60 and 90 cm kitchen units and appliances in the same way, and using the same number.

Avoid clashes

To indicate the space needed to open a door, draw an arc. Go to the **Insert** menu, select **Picture**, then click on **AutoShapes**.

Click on the **Basic Shapes** button on the AutoShapes toolbar. Click on the **Arc** icon, then click on your document and draw. Add a straight line to form a complete segment. Adjust the arc's shape and size by clicking on a handle and dragging it.

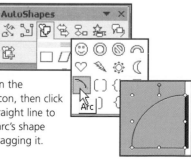

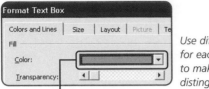

Use different colours for each appliance to make them distinguishable.

Bright idea
Write down some ground rules for planning your kitchen. For example: 'Don't put the sink below electrical sockets' and 'Appliances should be placed in positions where their doors can be opened safely'.

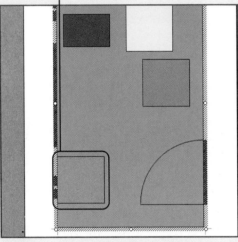

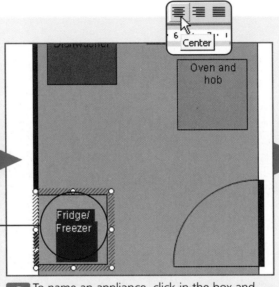

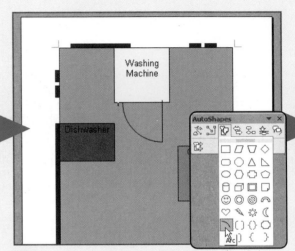

5 You now have the basic structure of your kitchen in place. Create more text boxes to represent your floor-standing appliances, such as a washing machine and cooker. Remember to scale them down in size in the same way as you scaled your kitchen dimensions.

6 To name an appliance, click in the box and type the name. To move the text down, click at the start of the word and press the **Return** key. To position it centrally within the text box, highlight it then click on the **Center** toolbar button.

7 Move your appliances into position by clicking on the edge of the boxes and dragging them. Remember to allow for the space needed to open appliance doors. If you wish, draw arcs to indicate how far they will extend.

Style changes
To change the size and font of your text, highlight it, go to the **Format** menu and click on **Font**. Select a font and size then click **OK**. To rotate text, go to the **Format** menu and click on **Text Direction**. Select an option in the Orientation section then click **OK**.

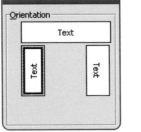

*You may find it easier to position the items on your plan by increasing the magnification of your page. Click on the arrow beside the Zoom tool on the toolbar and click on **Whole Page**.*

Watch out
Although you can 'layer' items in Word, it can be tricky to select the bottom layer, so build your page as you would your kitchen, from the bottom up.

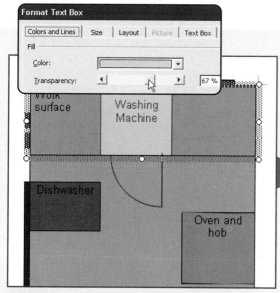

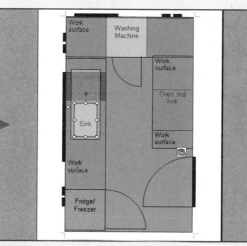

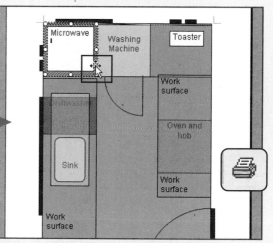

8 Create a semi-transparent text box for your work surface. This will allow you to see the floor-standing items below. Go to the **Format** menu and select **Text Box**. In the Fill section select a colour and choose a transparency value of around 70%. Click **OK**.

9 Continue to add and position as many elements as you need, working with spaces that match standard cupboard sizes. Take into account door spacing and the room needed to move around comfortably. Experiment with several alternative plans.

10 Finally, add smaller items such as the microwave and toaster. They need not be exactly to scale, as this is merely to show you whether your design is feasible in terms of your electric sockets. To print out a copy of your plan, click on the **Print** toolbar button.

Creating different plans

You don't need to start from scratch to create different versions of your plan – you just save them as you go along.

Whenever you want to save a version of what you have done, go to the **File** menu and click on **Save As**. Give the plan a different name from the original (eg, Kitchen plan 2) then click on **Save**.

Save As
Save in: ☐ Household
🔲 Home Insurance
🔲 Kitchen Plan 1
🔲 Kitchen Plan 2

File name: Kitchen Plan 3
Save as type: Word Document

Bright idea
Add wall units to your plan by creating semi-transparent boxes as described in Step 8.

Take the effort and stress out

Finding, buying and moving to a new property is hard work – make sure

Project planner

Create a folder called 'Moving House.' Add folders to cover each part of the process.

- Moving House
  - Mortgage
  - Solicitor
  - House details
  - Correspondence
  - New house
  - Moving out letters

Moving house can be one of the most exciting events of your life, but also one of the most stressful. Big decisions and large amounts of money are involved, and you will need all the help you can get to make the process go smoothly.

You can get your PC involved as soon as you start looking for a new home. Use the Internet to look for property, gather information about mortgages, find a solicitor, and investigate the local amenities in the place you want to move to.

Before deciding which is the best mortgage for you, you could input the details of different packages into a spreadsheet program and compare the costs. All the various and confusing factors such as cashback offers, varying interest rates, compulsory

# of moving house

your computer is the last thing you pack

life cover and indemnity guarantee premiums can be built into the equation, so you can see the best deal at a glance. Keep another spreadsheet for outgoings such as search fees, deposit and estate agent's fees.

When you find the house you want, you can create folders for all the correspondence with solicitors, lenders, estate agents and surveyors. There is no need even to print off a copy for yourself: the file on the PC is your record.

And once the deal is complete, you have the whole matter of moving to deal with. The key to a successful move is sound budgeting and effective planning, and here too you should make the most of your PC. Make a spreadsheet to track the cost of a removal van and other moving expenses. You might also make a checklist of appointments – have you cancelled the milk, transferred the TV licence, arranged to have the utility meters read?

Before moving day you can print off labels for packing boxes. Then, once you are safely installed in your new home, remember to send a card (which you have designed yourself) or an e-mail to all your friends, to let them know your new address.

Countdown to moving

- Book time off work for the move
- Inform friends, bank, work and schools of your move
- Re-catalogue and value home contents
- Set up a budget document for the move
- Source removal firms and insurance (request quotes)
- Purchase or hire packing boxes and materials
- Plan packing schedule
- Arrange final readings and closing accounts for utilities: gas, electricity, telephone and water
- Arrange house clearance for unwanted items
- Design invitations for new house-warming party

Ideas and inspirations

Below are some suggestions to get your house move started. The projects can be adapted to your particular circumstances. You may want to give various tasks to different family members. Plan early to avoid the last-minute rush that plagues most home-moves.

260 Calculate your bills
Use a spreadsheet to budget for your move (don't forget to include any house sale profit).

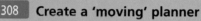

256 Catalogue home contents
Create a database to keep a record of how much each of your possessions is worth.

308 Create a 'moving' planner
Use the principles of a travel planner to set out all aspects of the move and allot various tasks.

194 Change-of-address slips
Produce eye-catching cards to inform friends and colleagues of your new contact details.

170 Packing labels
If your boxes are clearly marked you'll be able to unpack items at your own pace, as you need them.

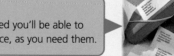

Also worth considering...

Once you've moved into your new house, put your own stamp on it by designing your dream kitchen.

294 Plan a new kitchen
Create a simple, overhead 2D plan of your new kitchen and organise your space effectively.

Create a gardening diary

Timetable your gardening tasks all year round

It might seem that computers and gardens have very little to do with each other. In fact, a PC can be an invaluable tool for the gardener. Database programs can help with keeping track of seed and plant types. Design programs allow you to plan a garden and then view the results as a 3-D animation that shows how the garden will change with the seasons.

One of the most important things for the green-fingered is knowing what needs to be done each month. Using the diary in Windows XP, you can set-up and maintain your own special gardening calendar that reminds you when crucial outdoor tasks need to be done.

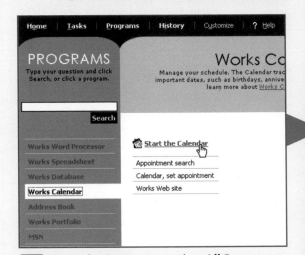

> Make a list of all the regular gardening tasks you perform, and find out the correct time of year for planting any new flowers or plants you'd like to add to your garden.

> **BEFORE YOU START**

1 Go to the **Start** menu, select **All Programs**, then select **Microsoft Works**. The Works Task Launcher opens. Click on **Programs**, then **Works Calendar**, then **Start the Calendar**.

> Microsoft Outlook also has a calendar function you can use to plan your gardening tasks. Go to the **Start** menu and select **All Programs**. Select **Microsoft Outlook** then click on the **Calendar** icon.

> **OTHER PROGRAMS**

Watch out
If you use your calendar for more than just gardening tasks, make sure you use the category filter to show appointments in all categories to avoid double booking your time.

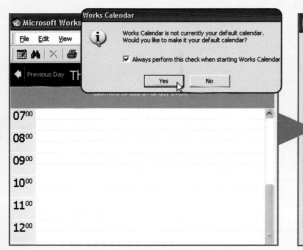

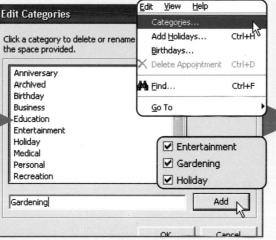

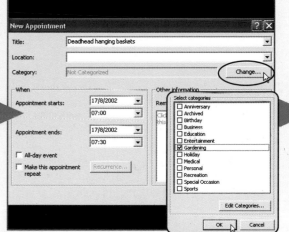

2 If the Works Calendar is not your default calendar, a dialogue box appears giving you the option to make it your default calendar. If you wish to make it your default calendar, click on **Yes**. The program then opens. You can view your calendar in a number of different ways, see below for how to change the view.

3 If the Category Filter is not displayed, go to the **View** menu and select **Show Category Filter**. To create a new gardening category, go to the **Edit** menu and select **Categories**. Type 'Gardening' in the dialogue box and click on **Add**. Click **OK** and Gardening appears listed alongside your other categories.

4 To enter a task into your diary, go to the **File** menu and select **New Appointment**. In the 'Title' pane of the dialogue box, type in a short description of the task. To categorise the appointment as a Gardening task, click on the **Change** button and click in the box next to the Gardening category, then click **OK**.

*You can change the way you view your calendar by clicking on the view buttons on the toolbar. Click on **1** to see just one day, click on **7** to display one week and click on **31** to see the whole month. The view you're in when you quit the program will be the view that's displayed when you next open the calendar.*

Works help

When you first open the Works Calendar a Works Help pane is displayed on the right. Click on a link in the column to display information about different functions of the Works Calendar, or type in a keyword search in the 'Answer Wizard' box and click on **Search**. To close Works Help, click on the cross at the top-right of the pane. If you need to open it again, go to the **Help** menu and select **Works Help**.

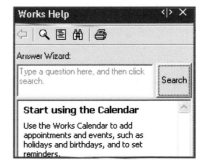

If your task is likely to last all day, you can click in the box next to 'All-day event'. All-day events are displayed in a beige bar, in the 1 day view, this is at the top of the calendar.

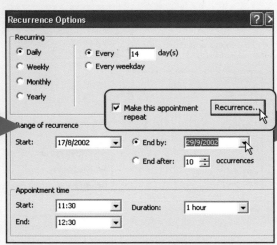

5 Now assign the correct date and time for your task. Click on the arrows in the When section of the dialogue box and scroll down to set the start and end date and time.

6 If it is a task you do regularly, set it up as a recurring appointment. To do so, click in the box next to 'Make this appointment repeat', then click on the **Recurrence** button. Set the frequency of the task in the Recurrence Options dialogue box. Click **OK** when you have finished.

7 You can set up a reminder that will alert you to a task you have to do. Click on the arrow in the Other Information section and scroll down to select how far in advance of the task you'd like to be reminded, then click **OK**. The View Reminders window will pop up on screen at the correct time with the reminder.

Getting around the Calendar

You can navigate around your calendar by using the arrows at either end of the black date bar. Depending on the view you're in, these will take you to the previous or next day, week or month. Wherever you are in your calendar, clicking on the **Go to Today** toolbar button, you will bring you back to today's date.

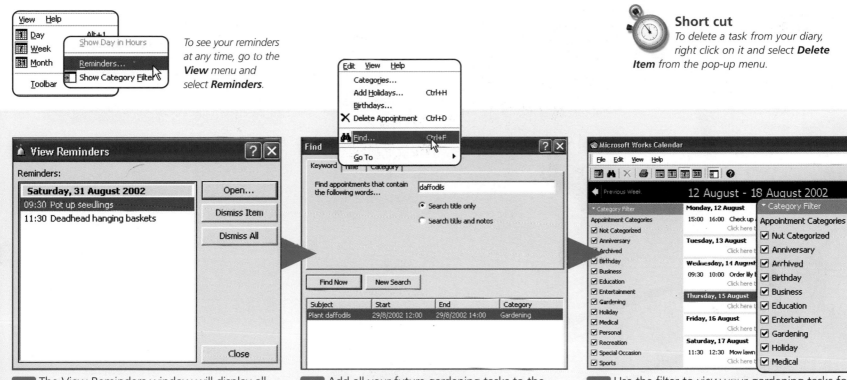

To see your reminders at any time, go to the **View** menu and select **Reminders**.

Short cut
To delete a task from your diary, right click on it and select **Delete Item** from the pop-up menu.

8 The View Reminders window will display all the tasks you have set and have not yet dismissed. If you have completed a task, highlight it and click on **Dismiss Item**. Click on **Dismiss All** if all your tasks have been carried out. Click **Close** to close the window

9 Add all your future gardening tasks to the diary, and set up their recurrence, you can input annual, monthly, weekly and seasonal tasks. To search for a task, go to the **Edit** menu and select **Find**. In the keyword tab, type in search term and click on **Find Now**. The results are listed below. See below left for searching by category.

10 Use the filter to view your gardening tasks for a certain day, week or month. Display the Category Filter (see Step 3). Click in the boxes next to all the other categories to un-tick them, leaving the Gardening box ticked. This will leave only the Gardening tasks displayed in your calendar. To print it, go to the **File** menu and select **Print**.

Gardening tasks at a glance

To see a list of all your upcoming gardening tasks, go to the **Edit** menu and select **Find**. Click on the **Category** tab, then click in the boxes next to all your other categories to un-tick them, leaving only the Gardening box ticked. Click on **Find Now**. All your gardening tasks then appear listed below. To delete a task in the list, click on it to highlight it and click on **Delete Item**.

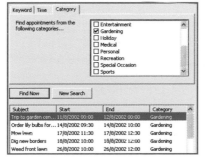

Devise a fitness plan

A simple spreadsheet can help you schedule regular exercise

Along with your training shoes, stop watch and sheer determination, your computer can play an integral part in devising and maintaining an effective fitness plan. Using a spreadsheet program, such as the one in Microsoft Works, you can create a fitness log to keep track of your progress, using both figures and written comments.

Getting in shape can involve many forms of exercise. These pages show you how to put together a jogging schedule, but you can adapt the project to suit any fitness plan.

Keeping a log of your progress can help you to see how well you are doing, or how far you have to go to achieve your goals, and allows you to make changes if you've overestimated or underestimated your time and abilities. It also allows for breaks for illness or injury.

It's important that the schedule you devise is appropriate for your level of fitness. If you do not exercise regularly, consult your doctor first.

▶ BEFORE YOU START

1 Go to the **Start** menu, select **All Programs** and click on **Microsoft Works**. In the Works Task Launcher click on **Programs**, then **Works Spreadsheet** and **Start a blank spreadsheet**. In the **File** menu click on **Save**. Save the document into an appropriate folder.

You can create a similar fitness schedule using Microsoft Excel and Lotus 1-2-3.

▶ OTHER PROGRAMS

Templates on CD-ROM

Key word
Formatting *This term describes the collection of style elements – including fonts, colours, effects and alignment – that determine how a cell looks.*

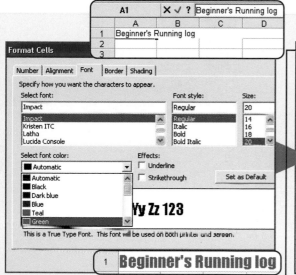

2 Cell A1 is automatically selected in your spreadsheet. Type a title for your plan into this cell. Highlight it, go to the **Format** menu and click on **Font**. Select a font, size and colour. The row height will automatically adjust to include your text.

3 Starting in cell **A2**, and continuing in the cells along the same row, type in headings as shown. In cell **A3** type in 'Monday'. Drag the bottom right-hand corner of the cell down so that the rest of the days of the week appear in the cells below. In cell **A10** type in 'Total'.

4 To change the position of text within cells, select a cell or block of cells with the mouse, then click on your choice of alignment toolbar button. Click **OK**.

Adjusting column widths

Some of the text that you enter into cells may not be visible. To adjust the width of cells in a single column to accommodate your text, place the mouse pointer on the right-hand edge of the beige lettered column header. When the mouse pointer changes to a double-headed arrow, hold down the left mouse button and drag the column edge to the required width. Or double-click on the column header and it will resize automatically.

Your jogging schedule

When you start your schedule, concentrate on running continuously for a certain time, rather than covering a certain distance. Don't push yourself too hard. In the early sessions, alternate between brisk walking and running.

Before each jogging session warm up by walking briskly for 10 minutes. Cool down afterwards by walking for 5 minutes then stretching. Hamstring stretches are especially important.

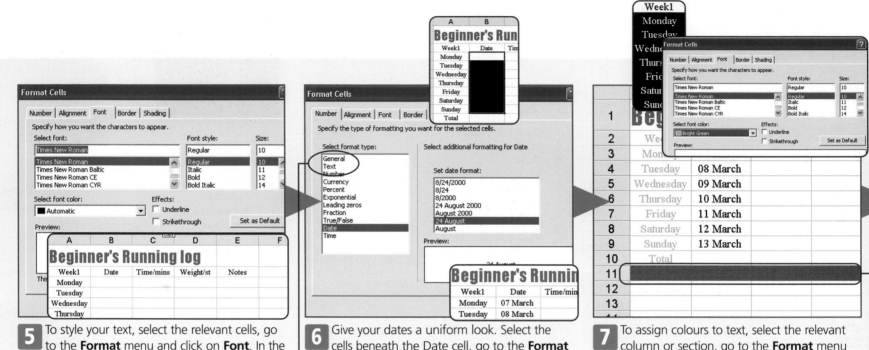

5 To style your text, select the relevant cells, go to the **Format** menu and click on **Font**. In the Font tab of the Format Cells dialogue box, select a font, size, colour and style. Click **OK**.

6 Give your dates a uniform look. Select the cells beneath the Date cell, go to the **Format** menu and click on **Number**. Select the **Date** option in the 'Select format type' box and a style from the 'Set date format' box. Click **OK**.

7 To assign colours to text, select the relevant column or section, go to the **Format** menu and click on **Font**. Select a colour then click **OK**. Mark the end of your plan by adding a bar below the last row (see below).

Number formats

You need to select a format for the 'Time/mins' column. Go to the **Format** menu and select **Number**. Click on the **Number** option in the 'Select format type' box. Select a style from the additional formatting section – here, two decimal places.

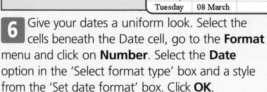

Adding a divider

To add a divider beneath your weekly schedule, click and drag your cursor along the required number of cells in the row below the Total row. Go to the **Format** menu and click on **Shading** then, in the Shading section, click on your choice of colour and pattern. Click **OK**.

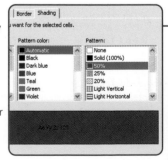

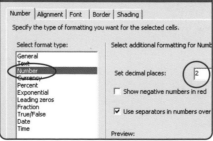

Key word

Template *A template is created to use as the basis for further documents which share the same basic features. A template is opened, edited, then saved under a different file name.*

When you paste your fitness plan in this way, you need to clear the information in the pasted log and change the weekly heading.

Beginner's Running log

Week1	Date	Time/mins	Weight/st
Monday	07 March	20.00	12st 11lb
Tuesday	08 March	0.00	
Wednesday	09 March	21.00	12st 11lb
Thursday	10 March	0.00	
Friday	11 March	0.00	

Number | Alignment | Font | Border | Shading

Specify how you want the border lines to appear.

Select border color: Line type: Border location:

- Automatic
- Black
- Dark blue
- Blue
- Teal
- Green
- Violet
- Dark Red
- Red
- Turquoise

None | None | Outline | Inside

Text

		D	
1			**log**
2			Weigh
3	Monday	07 March	
4	Tuesday	08 March	
5	Wednesday	09 March	
6	Thursday	10 March	
7	Friday	11 March	
8	Saturday	12 March	
9	Sunday	13 March	
10	Total		
11			
12	Week2	Date	Time/mins	Weigh

Beginner's Running log

Week1	Date	Time/mins	Weight/st	No
Monday	07 March	20.00	12st 11lb	Walk/run - started
Tuesday	08 March	0.00		Rest day
Wednesday	09 March	21.00	12st 11lb	Walk/run - found
Thursday	10 March	0.00		Rest day
Friday	11 March	0.00		Had a brisk walk
Saturday	12 March	0.00		Rest day
Sunday	13 March	21.00	12st 10lb	Walk/run - thorou
Total				

Notes
Walk/run - started too fast
Rest day
Walk/run - found it hard going
Rest day
Had a brisk walk at lunch
Rest day

	D	E
Beginner's Running log		

Week1	Date	Time/mins	Weight/st	Notes
Monday	07 March	20.00	12st 11lb	Walk/run - started too
Tuesday	08 March	0.00		Rest day
Wednesday	09 March	21.00	12st 11lb	Walk/run - found it ha
Thursday	10 March	0.00		Rest day
Friday	11 March	0.00		Had a brisk walk at lu
Saturday	12 March	0.00		Rest day
Sunday	13 March	21.00	12st 10lb	Walk/run - thoroughl
Total		62.00		
Week2	Date	Time/mins	Weight/st	Notes
Monday	14 March			
Tuesday	15 March			
Wednesday	16 March			
Thursday	17 March			
Friday	18 March			
Saturday	19 March			

8 To place lines between sections, select a section, go to the **Format** menu and click on **Border**. Select where you want the border and choose a line style. Click **OK**. To remove gridlines, go to the **View** menu and click on **Gridlines**.

9 Your fitness schedule is finished – now the hard work really starts. Fill in the relevant data every day and monitor your progress. Remember to build in rest days.

10 Use your plan as a template for subsequent weeks. Starting in row 2, select the cells in the plan then click on the **Copy** toolbar button. Place your cursor at the start of the row beneath the divider under Week 1. Go to the **Edit** menu and click on **Paste**.

Adding up totals

To calculate, say, the total number of minutes you have run in a single week, use the Works AutoSum facility.

Click in the cell below the cells containing your times, then click on the **AutoSum** toolbar button. Press the **Enter** key. For AutoSum to work, you must enter times into all the cells in the week, even if that time is zero.

Σ AutoSum

1	**Beginner's Ru**		
2	Week1	Date	Time/mins
3	Monday	07 March	20.00
4	Tuesday	08 March	0.00
5	Wednesday	09 March	21.00
6	Thursday	10 March	0.00
7	Friday	11 March	0.00
8	Saturday	12 March	0.00
9	Sunday	13 March	21.00
10	Total		=SUM(C3:C9)

=SUM(C3:C9)

Make a holiday planner

Keep all your family's travel details up to date and in order

Holidays are a time to relax and forget the stresses and strains of everyday life. But even relaxation has to be planned if you are to get the most out of it.

There are some things you need to plan in advance, especially if you are going abroad. Do you have the right visas? Is your passport still valid? Have you had the immunisations you need? Are there important articles you must remember to pack?

Your computer can help here. Spreadsheets are ideal for preparing lists of things that need to be done, and checking them off as they are completed. You may find that several separate spreadsheets are helpful when planning your annual holiday.

1 Go to the **Start** menu, select **All Programs** then click on **Microsoft Excel**. A new spreadsheet opens. Click on the **Save** toolbar button and save and name your document. Cell A1 is automatically selected. Type your heading and checklist into column A as above.

To adjust the width of a column, place the mouse pointer over the right-hand edge of the beige column header. When it becomes a double-headed arrow drag the edge to the desired width.

A1	Width: 16.00 (117 pixels)

	A	B
1	HOLIDAY PLANNER	

Watch out
The currency converter does not take into account the commission you will be charged when you exchange cash or buy travellers' cheques.

=E9*E10

*To enter a multiplication sign, press the **Shift** key and '**8**' simultaneously.*

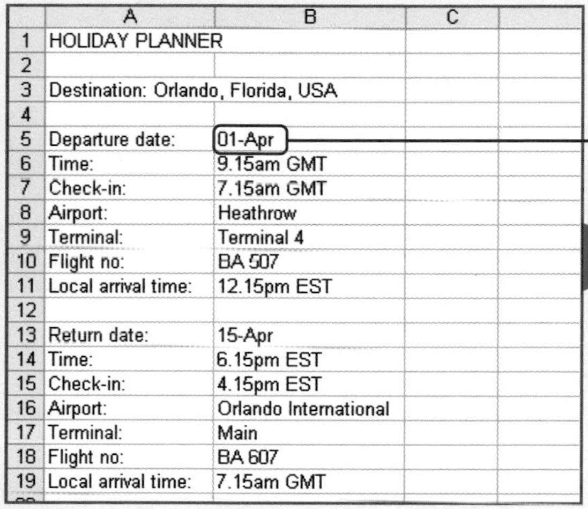

	A	B	C
1	HOLIDAY PLANNER		
2			
3	Destination: Orlando, Florida, USA		
4			
5	Departure date:	01-Apr	
6	Time:	9.15am GMT	
7	Check-in:	7.15am GMT	
8	Airport:	Heathrow	
9	Terminal:	Terminal 4	
10	Flight no:	BA 507	
11	Local arrival time:	12.15pm EST	
12			
13	Return date:	15-Apr	
14	Time:	6.15pm EST	
15	Check-in:	4.15pm EST	
16	Airport:	Orlando International	
17	Terminal:	Main	
18	Flight no:	BA 607	
19	Local arrival time:	7.15am GMT	

	A	B	C	D
1	HOLIDAY PLANNER			
2				
3	Destination: Orlando, Florida, USA			
4				
5	Departure date:	01-Apr		
6	Time:	9.15am GMT		
7	Check-in:	7.15am GMT		Currency converter
8	Airport:	Heathrow		
9	Terminal:	Terminal 4		Sterling:
10	Flight no:	BA 507		Exchange rate:
11	Local arrival time:	12.15pm EST		Foreign currency =
12				
13	Return date:	15-Apr		Foreign currency:
14	Time:	6.15pm EST		Exchange rate:
15	Check-in:	4.15pm EST		Sterling value =
16	Airport:	Orlando International		
17	Terminal:	Main		
18	Flight no:	BA 607		
19	Local arrival time:	7.15am GMT		
20				
21				
22				
23				
24				

	B	C	D	E
	R			
	, Florida, USA			
	01-Apr			
	9.15am GMT			
	7.15am GMT		Currency converter	
	Heathrow			
	Terminal 4		Sterling:	1000.00
	BA 507		Exchange rate:	1.57
	12.15pm EST		Foreign currency =	=E9*E10
	15-Apr		Foreign currency:	
	6.15pm EST		Exchange rate:	
	4.15pm EST		Sterling value =	
	Orlando International			
	Main			
	BA 607			
	7.15am GMT			

2 Adjust the width of column A so that your text, except for your title and subtitle, fits neatly within the column (see above). Type your travel details into the relevant cells in column B. If necessary, adjust the width of this column, too.

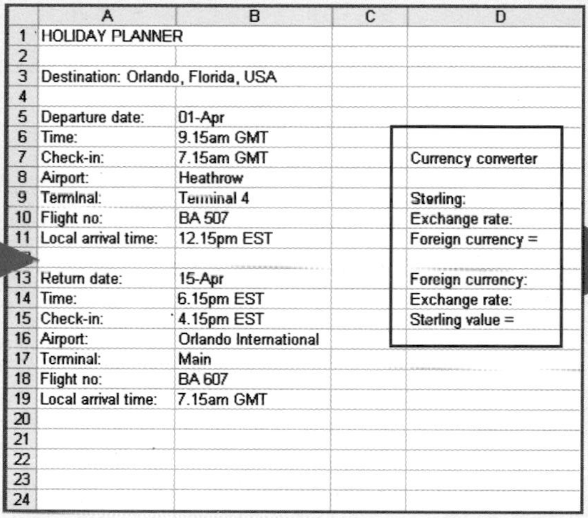

3 You can now create a currency converter. This will automatically work out how much foreign currency your sterling buys, and vice versa. Type the text shown above into column D, starting in cell D7 and continuing in the cells immediately below.

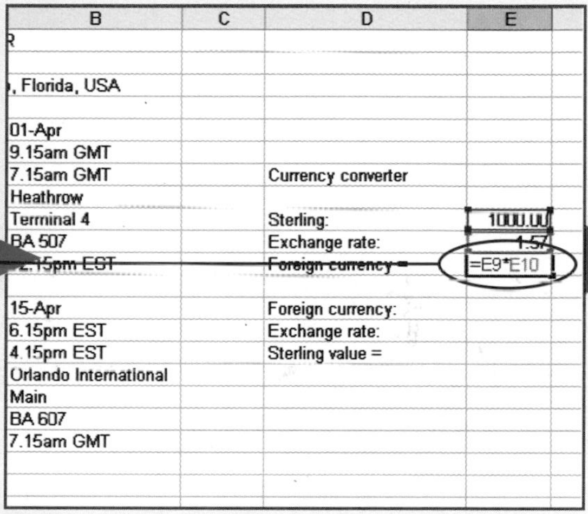

4 To calculate the foreign currency you can buy, click in **E11** then type in '=E9*E10'. Press **Enter**. To convert into sterling, click in **E15** and type in '=E13/E14'. Press **Enter**.

Formatting your cells

You will be entering different types of data into column B, including dates and times. You can select a style for each by clicking on the cell in question then going to the **Format** menu and selecting **Cells**. The **Number** tab is selected.

In the Category pane click on the type of information to be entered, or chose the **Custom** option. In the Type pane, click on your preferred style. Click **OK**.

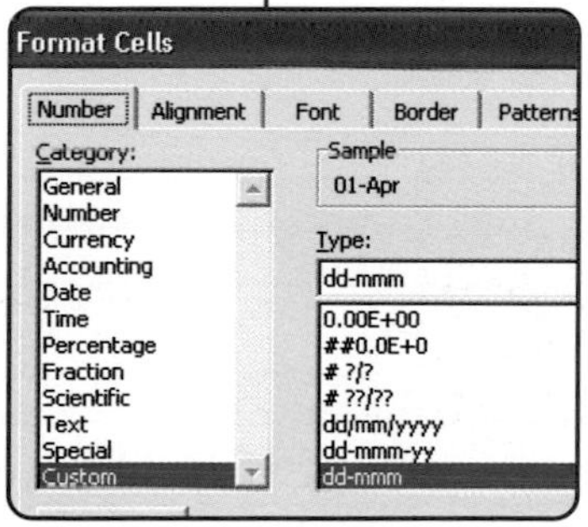

Format Cells

Number	Alignment	Font	Border	Patterns

Category:
General
Number
Currency
Accounting
Date
Time
Percentage
Fraction
Scientific
Text
Special
Custom

Sample
01-Apr

Type:
dd-mmm
0.00E+00
##0.0E+0
?/?
??/??
dd/mm/yyyy
dd-mmm-yy
dd-mmm

Let the Wizard help

Microsoft Works has a Wizard that can help you plan your holiday. When you open Works the Works Task Launcher appears. Click on the Tasks tab, then click on the **Travel Information** option in the left-hand list. Select **Travel Planning Tools**, then click **Start this task**. Now choose from a selection of different document templates.

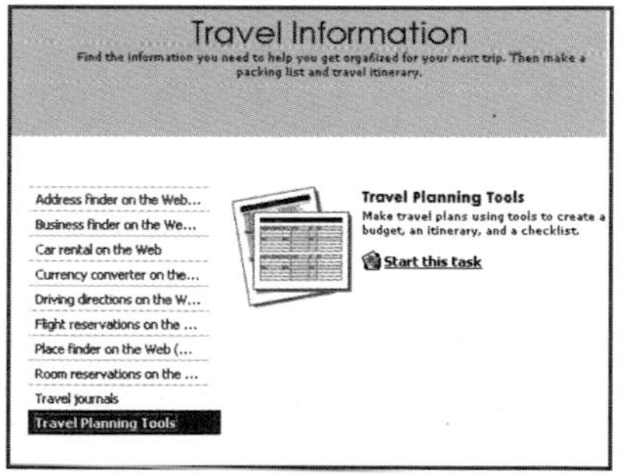

Travel Information
Find the information you need to help you get organized for your next trip. Then make a packing list and travel itinerary.

Address finder on the Web...
Business finder on the We...
Car rental on the Web
Currency converter on the...
Driving directions on the W...
Flight reservations on the ...
Place finder on the Web...
Room reservations on the...
Travel journals
Travel Planning Tools

Travel Planning Tools
Make travel plans using tools to create a budget, an itinerary, and a checklist.
Start this task

Close up

*When you choose a large font size
for text, the spreadsheet row
automatically adjusts to accommodate it.*

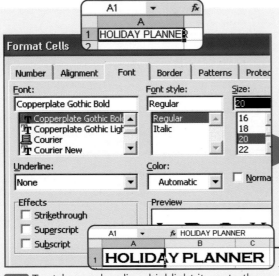

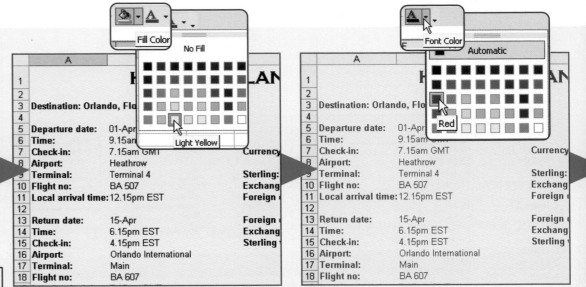

5 To style your heading, highlight it, go to the **Format** menu and select **Cells**. Choose a font, style, size and effect, then click **OK**. Style the rest of your text in the same way. To select a number of adjacent cells in one go, click on the top cell then drag over the others.

6 To add a background colour, select the cells and click on the arrow beside the Fill Color toolbar button. A drop-down colour palette appears. Click on your chosen colour to apply it. (If you cannot see the Fill Color button, go to the **View** menu, select **Toolbars** then **Formatting**.)

7 To colour all your text with the same colour, select the cells and click on the arrow beside the Font Color toolbar button. As before, a colour palette appears. Click on a colour to apply it.

Centre your heading

To position the heading in the centre
of your page, click on cell **A1** and
drag your cursor
along the top row
of cells until the full
width of your form
is covered (here, to
column F). Then click the
Merge and Center
toolbar button.

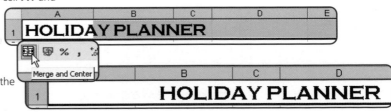

Bright idea
*If you want to add another page to your spreadsheet, go to the **Insert** menu and click on **Worksheet**. Another sheet tab will appear at the bottom of your screen.*

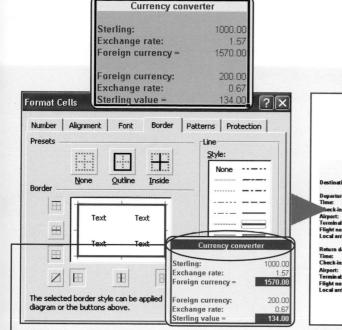

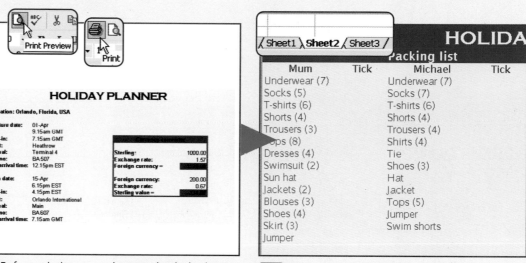

HOLIDAY PLANNER

Destination: Orlando, Florida, USA

Departure date:	01-Apr
Time:	9.15am GMT
Check-in:	7.15am GMT
Airport:	Heathrow
Terminal:	Terminal 4
Flight no:	BA 507
Local arrival time:	12.15pm EST

Return date:	15-Apr
Time:	6.15pm EST
Check-in:	4.15pm EST
Airport:	Orlando International
Terminal:	Main
Flight no:	BA 607
Local arrival time:	7.15am GMT

HOLIDA

Packing list

Mum	Tick	Michael	Tick
Underwear (7)		Underwear (7)	
Socks (5)		Socks (7)	
T-shirts (6)		T-shirts (6)	
Shorts (4)		Shorts (4)	
Trousers (3)		Trousers (4)	
Tops (8)		Shirts (4)	
Dresses (4)		Tie	
Swimsuit (2)		Shoes (3)	
Sun hat		Hat	
Jackets (2)		Jacket	
Blouses (3)		Tops (5)	
Shoes (4)		Jumper	
Skirt (3)		Swim shorts	
Jumper			

8 To separate your currency converter from the rest of your travel details, place a border around it. Select the relevant cells, go to the **Format** menu and click on **Cells**. Click on the **Border** tab. Select a line style, colour and outline for your border, then click **OK**.

9 Before printing your planner, check the layout by clicking on the **Print Preview** toolbar button. If it needs adjusting, press the **Esc** key and edit the layout accordingly. When you are happy with it, click on the **Print** toolbar button to print it.

10 Using the same process, it is possible to create a packing list and a list of tasks to complete before going on holiday. At the bottom of the page you will see a series of tabs. Click on the **Sheet2** tab. A blank spreadsheet page appears.

Currency converter

To make your headings really stand out, reverse your 'fill' and 'font' colours. In this case, the background has been coloured red, and the text light yellow.

Setting up your page

You may need to adjust the page settings of your document prior to printing if, for example, it is wider than 210mm.

Go to the **File** menu and click on **Page Setup**. Click on the **Page** tab, then select the Landscape option in the Orientation section. Ensure **A4** is selected in the 'Paper size' box. Now click the **Margins** tab and centre your printout **Horizontally** and **Vertically**. Click **OK**.

Plan a holiday you'll

Don't leave your holiday enjoyment to chance –

Project planner

Create a folder for the entire project, called 'Holiday'. Add sub-folders for each element.

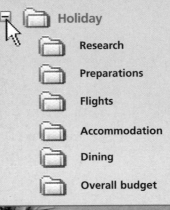

- **Holiday**
  - **Research**
  - **Preparations**
  - **Flights**
  - **Accommodation**
  - **Dining**
  - **Overall budget**

Everyone dreams of escaping from their day-to-day routine. For some, the ideal escape is a beach and a book on a desert island; for others it is a hectic round of entertainment and shopping in a big, cosmopolitan city. Your computer can help you achieve your dream.

With your PC you can access Web sites on the Internet to check out national, regional and resort destinations. You can look up weather forecasts to help you decide which clothes to pack. You can even find out about wider weather patterns to ensure your visit doesn't coincide with monsoons or hurricanes. You may also be able to read about local

remember forever

your PC can help it go smoothly

events listings such as carnivals or exhibitions, scheduled to happen during your stay.

Through the Internet you can purchase travel guides, order brochures, check which inoculations or other health precautions, if any, are needed, and book flights, hire cars and organise excursions and accommodation. You may even be able to check train timetables, ferry services and bus routes for destinations on the other side of the world, and pick up tips from fellow travellers.

In short, every aspect of your holiday arrangements can be researched, sourced and paid for via your computer.

Your computer is the ideal tool for precision planning. You can create a database to organise all the essential tasks that need completing before your departure, and set up a spreadsheet to project costs and a budget for your holiday. You can then create a diary to organise your trip day by day and take it away with you in printed form.

On your return you'll be able to scan in your holiday pictures and produce your own photo album, which you can either display on a Web site for your friends to see or e-mail/post to them. You could even send a holiday newsletter to friends with stories and pictures from your trip!

The adventure starts here

- 6 months: book time off work
- 5 months: check whether inoculations are required
- 4 months: budget for holiday
- 3 months: confirm booking/itinerary
- 1 month: organise travel insurance
- 2 weeks: buy currency/travellers' cheques

Ideas and inspirations

Below are project ideas to make your holiday run as smoothly, and be as memorable, as possible. All the projects can be adapted to your own circumstances and will give you further ideas of your own. Just alter the wording, layout or search details of each exercise as you work.

94 **Find information on the Net**
Research destinations and weather conditions, and book accommodation and tickets on-line.

252 **Travel budget planner**
Spreadsheet software on your PC helps you plan the finances for any purchase or project.

308 **Make a holiday planner**
Produce a document containing all the practical details of your trip, from time zones to car hire.

82 **Use your PC as a fax**
Confirm bookings and itineraries with hotels and tour operators by fax.

218 **Create an on-line photo album**
Make sure your trip is one you'll remember with a pictorial souvenir created on the Internet.

Also worth considering...

Once you've finished, don't let your research go to waste. You can use information again and again.

166 **Create a contact database**
You can produce address and contact lists specific to transport, accommodation and new friends.

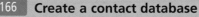

A collector's database

Keep a detailed record on every addition to your collection

Whatever you collect, whether it's stamps, coins or wine, or music albums or CDs, it is useful to keep a log of each item you own. As your collection grows, it becomes necessary to keep a check on its contents, its value and even the whereabouts of each item. You can use a database program on your PC to keep such records.

Creating a database is straightforward, and once you have entered all your details you can find any information you need quickly and simply. Not only do you have all the information about your collection in one place, but a database is also a way of spotting 'gaps' in your collection and can help you to plan future purchases.

Classical CDs

CD ref: 00003

Composer: Bach

Title: Preludes and Fugues

Musician(s): Academy of St. Martin-in-the-Fields

Venue: St Paul's Cathedral, London

Conductor: Marriner

Date: 05/96

Label: Philips

Catalogue No: 7458929722

Purchased: 02/97

Price: 14.45

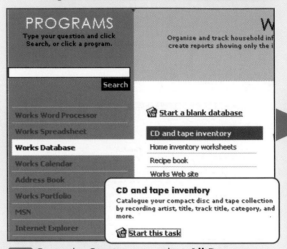

For a music database, gather together all your CDs, records and cassettes. If you have kept receipts for them, have these to hand, too.

► BEFORE YOU START

PROGRAMS
Type your question and click Search, or click a program.

[Search]

Works Word Processor
Works Spreadsheet
Works Database
Works Calendar
Address Book
Works Portfolio
MSN
Internet Explorer

Organise and track household inf create reports showing only the i

🏠 **Start a blank database**

CD and tape inventory
Home inventory worksheets
Recipe book
Works Web site

CD and tape inventory
Catalogue your compact disc and tape collection by recording artist, title, track title, category, and more.

📖 Start this task

1 Go to the **Start** menu, select **All Programs**, then **Microsoft Works**. In the Works Task Launcher click on **Programs**, then **Works Database** in the left-hand column. Click on **CD and tape inventory**, then **Start this task**.

You can also make a record of your collection using Microsoft Excel. Use the spreadsheet to type in your headings and data, then the Filter feature to create your reports

► OTHER PROGRAMS

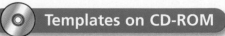

Templates on CD-ROM

Key word

Fields A field is a category of information. Fields appear as columns of data in a database. The combination of several fields about a single subject make up a record.

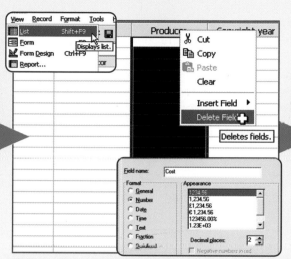

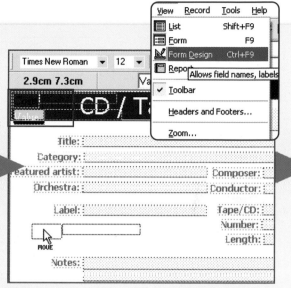

2 The CD/Tape Collection database opens up. It is quite comprehensive, but you may want to change some fields to suit your needs. For instance, changing 'Producer' and 'Copyright' to include instead the purchase cost of your item, and its estimated collector's value now.

3 To delete fields and add new ones, go to the **View** menu and click on **List**. Click on the beige column header entitled 'Producer', then right-click and select **Delete Field**, then **OK**. Right click again and select **Insert Field**, then **Before**. Name your new field 'Cost' and select **Number** in the Format section. Click on **Add**, then **Done**.

4 Repeat the actions in Step 3 to delete the 'Copyright year' field and add a 'Value' field. Go to the **View** menu and select **Form Design**. The new fields appear in the top right-hand corner of the window. Click on them and drag them into position. ('Copyright' may still appear in this view, click on it then hit the **Delete** key.)

Fields and formats

Before you build a database, take some time to familiarise yourself with the various field formats.

You can preset data fields to style numbers, dates and text; applying font characteristics, rounding decimal places and so on. It is a good idea to include a serialised reference number to automatically update each record with a new number.

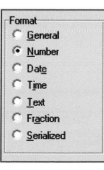

Styling fields

You can assign fonts, colours, effects and styles to your fields and their adjoining text boxes. Click on the **Form Design** toolbar button, then on a field name or adjoining text box.

Go to the **Format** menu and click on **Font and Style**. Select a font, size, style and colour, then click **OK**. Click on the alignment toolbar buttons to position the text within the text boxes. To style several text boxes in the same way at once, press the **Ctrl** key and, keeping it pressed down, click on the boxes in turn, then style them.

Fields that have been formatted as 'serialized' will automatically update themselves as you enter new records. Set this option before you enter any data.

Field name:
Format
- General
- Number
- Date
- Time
- Text
- Fraction
- ● Serialized

*To move to the next field or record, press the **Tab** key. To move back, press the **Shift** and **Tab** keys.*

To extract and display specific information from your database – for an insurance valuation, perhaps – you need to create a report.

► CREATE A REPORT

Format Tab Order

Format   Tools   Help

Field…

Alignment…
Font and Style…
Border…
Shading…
Protection…

Insert Page Break
Delete Page Break

Snap To Grid
Send To Back
Bring To Front

Field Size…
✓ Show Field Name

Tab Order…

Set tab order

Title
Category
Featured artist
Orchestra
Label
Cost
Copyright year
Composer
Conductor

Reset

Title: Symphony no.5 in C
Category: Classical
...red artist: _____   Composer: _____
...Orchestra: CBSO   Conductor: _____

Label: Decca   Tape/CD: _____
Cost: £14.99   Number: _____
Value: £5.00   Length: ▮

Notes: _____

I◄ ◄ Record 5 ► ►I Zoom 150% – + ◄
ALT for commands; F2 to edit; CTRL+PGDN/UP for next record.

ReportCreator - Insura...

Title   Field...

Fields available:

Conductor
Label
Cost
Copyright year
Tape/CD
Length
Notes
01

< Remove

Add All >>

<< Remove All

Display options
☑ Show field names at top of each page
☐ Show summary information only

Report Name

Type a name for the report below:

Insurance

Notes

---

5 Once your form is designed, go to the **Format** menu and down to **Tab Order**. When you type in records you can move from field to field using the tab key – setting a logical order will speed up data entry. To change the order, click on a field name to highlight it then on the Up or Down buttons to move it along the list.

6 To enter data, go to the **View** menu and click on **Form**. Enter the data for the first item and when it is complete, click on the next record arrow in the bottom left-hand corner or hold down the Control key and hit the Page Down key. To see all your entries at once, go to the **View** menu and click on **List**.

7 Go to the **Tools** menu and click on **ReportCreator**. Give your report a title then click **OK**. In the next box click on the **Fields** tab. In the 'Fields available:' pane click each field you want to print in turn, clicking on **Add** as you do so. Click **Next** when you finish.

You can move through your records quickly in Form View by clicking on the arrows on either side of the Record counter at the bottom of the window.

I◄ ◄ Record 5 ► ►I Zoom 150% – + ◄
ALT for commands; F2 to edit; CTRL+PGDN/UP for next record.

Searching for information

To search for specific data – say, all the music you have by a particular composer – go to the **Edit** menu and click on **Find**. Type in a key word, or words, for what you want to search for, select the 'All records' option, then click on **OK**.

The database changes to show only those records that match your search. To return to the full database view, go to the **Record** menu, select **Show** and then click on **All Records**.

Find

Find what: CBSO

Match
○ Next record   ● All records

✓		Category	Featured artist	Orchestra	Composer
☐	5	Classical		CBSO	Beeth...
☐	10	Classical		CBSO	H...
☐	14	Classical		CBSO	Tchaiko...

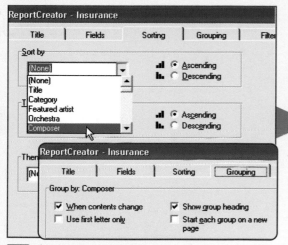

*Works automatically saves all reports. To print or update an old report, go to the **View** menu and click on **Report**. A list of reports appears. Click on the relevant one then click on **Preview** to view it (then go to the **File** menu and select **Print** to print it), or **Modify** to update it.*

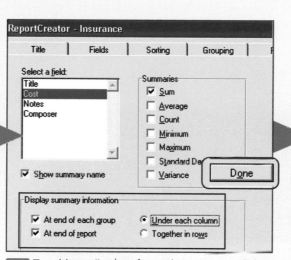

8 The Sorting tab is selected. To organise your data in order of, say, composer, click in the 'Sort by' box and select **Composer**. Click the **Grouping** tab, then click in the 'When contents change' and 'Show group heading' boxes.

9 To add up all prices for each composer, click the **Summary** tab. In the 'Select a field' pane click on **Cost**; in the Summaries section click in the Sum box; in the 'Display summary information' section select the options as shown above. Finally, click on **Done**.

10 A prompt box appears asking whether you want to preview or modify your report. Click **Modify** if you want to add any styling to your report (see below). Click **Preview** to view your report. When you're happy with it, click **Print** to print it out.

Styling a report

In the same way that it's possible to style forms, you can also adjust the fonts and sizes, and add colour and effects in your reports.

Click the **Report View** toolbar button. Select the cell or row you want to style and go to the **Format** menu and click on **Font and Style**. In the Format dialogue box click the

various tabs, selecting your fonts, sizes, styles, colours and background patterns as you do so.

To adjust column widths, place your cursor on the right-hand edge of the column heading. When the cursor changes appearance, click and drag to the desired width.

Record your golf scores

Keep track of your rounds and calculate your handicap

A spreadsheet is a great way of keeping records of your sporting achievements. Here, we create a golf scorecard but you could design a spreadsheet for any sport. With it, you can record every course and round played. Each time you input a score-card, your playing handicap will be updated.

There are two handicap calculators: one is an overall handicap, based on every scorecard entered into the system; the second calculates your current handicap by taking an average of your last three rounds.

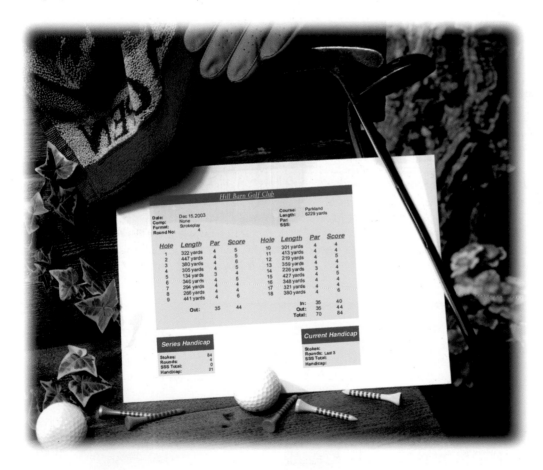

Collect at least three of your recent scorecards to provide scores and the course data you need to set up your spreadsheet.

BEFORE YOU START

1 Go to the **Start** menu, select **All Programs** and click on **Microsoft Excel**. To name and save your new document, click on the **Save** toolbar button. Select a suitable folder in which to save it in the 'Save in' box, type in a file name then click on **Save**.

*You can also record your golf scores in Microsoft Works. In the Works Task Launcher, click on **Programs**, then **Works Spreadsheet** and **Start a blank spreadsheet**.*

OTHER PROGRAMS

Templates on CD-ROM

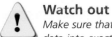

Watch out
Make sure that you enter the headings and data into exactly the same cells as used below. If you do not, the cell references used later in the handicap calculation formulas will not be correct.

Close-up
Unless directed otherwise, AutoSum adds figures immediately above the selected AutoSum cell. To adjust the formula, include new cell references (simply click on the cells themselves to do this) and appropriate calculation symbols, such as '+', '-', '/' and ''.*

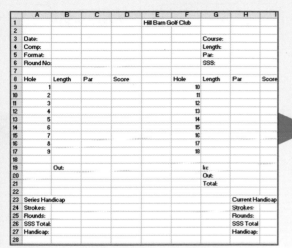

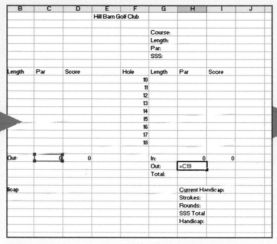

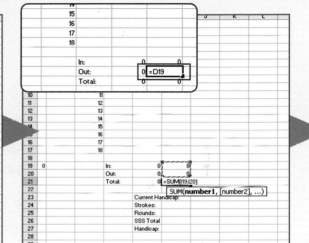

2 Click on cell **E1** and type in the course name. Type in the text for the rest of the spreadsheet as shown above. It is important that you use the same cells as here, otherwise your formulas won't work. Now you are ready to add your Score and Par totals.

3 Click on cell **C19**, then on the **AutoSum** button. Select cells **C9** to **C17** and press **Enter**. When course data is entered, AutoSum will add it up. Repeat for all Par and Score columns. Then click **H20** and type '=C19' and press **Enter** to carry over par from the front nine.

4 Click on **I20** and type '=D19' to carry over the front nine score. To calculate total par for the round, click **H21**, then the **AutoSum** button. Highlight cells **H19** and **H20**. Press **Enter**. For total score, click **I21**, then **AutoSum**. Select cells **I19** and **I20**. Press **Enter**.

Working out handicaps

A handicap is the number of strokes a golfer takes, on average, to play a course, over and above Standard Scratch Score (SSS). SSS is the score a scratch golfer, with a handicap of '0', should take to play the course.

SSS can differ from par for the course as it takes account of the difficulty of the course, while par for each hole is dictated by length. The handicap calculators in this project are 'Series' and 'Current'.

Series is calculated by subtracting the SSS total for all rounds played from the total number of strokes for those rounds, and then dividing the remainder by the number of rounds played.

The Current Handicap is calculated by taking the SSS total for the last three rounds only from the strokes played in the last three rounds, and then dividing the remainder by three.

Series Handicap = (B24 [total number of strokes played] minus B26 [SSS total for all rounds]) divided by B25 [number of rounds played].

=(B24-B26)/B25

Format the cell to ensure your handicap is rounded to a whole number. Click on the cells showing your Current and Series handicaps, go to the **Format** *menu and click on* **Cells***. The Number tab is selected. Click on* **Number** *in the Category pane, and set 'Decimal places' to '0'. Click* **OK***.*

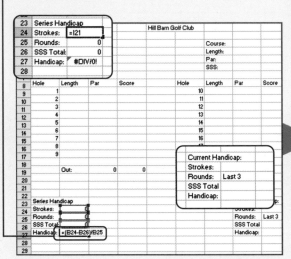

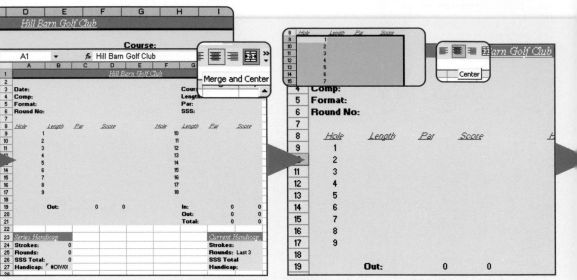

5 To set up the Series Handicap calculator, click on cell **B24** and type in '=I21'. Click on **B25** and type '=B6'. Click on **B26** and type '=H6'. Then click **B27** and type in the formula '=(B24-B26)/B25'. For the Current Handicap, click in **I25** and type 'Last 3'.

6 To centre your heading, select cells **A1** to **I1**. Click the **Merge and Center** button on your **Formatting** toolbar. Style your document (see below). To widen a column to fit all the text, place the mouse pointer on the right edge of the column heading and double-click.

7 To centre the hole numbers and other data at the same time, click and drag the cursor over the relevant cells then click on the **Center** toolbar button. Now enter all the course, length, par and score data. Excel will automatically calculate your formulas.

Using the toolbar to add style

You can style text and colour through the toolbar. To change cells, select them then use the toolbar's drop-down lists for font and font size. Click on the **Bold**, **Underline** and **Italic** toolbar buttons to further enhance the text. To alter text colour, click the arrow beside the Font Color toolbar button and select from the colour palette. To add a background colour click the arrow beside the Fill Color toolbar button and choose a colour.

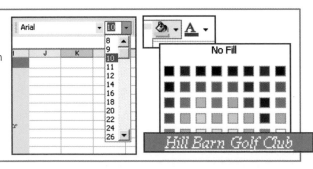

Adding worksheets

When you open an Excel document, the default settings give you three sheets to work with (tabs for each sheet appear at the bottom of each page). To add more sheets for new rounds, click on the **Insert** menu and select **Worksheet**.

Apply the same formulas each time, but don't forget to add in another value for each sheet, for example: =H6+Sheet1!B26 +Sheet2!B26.

Current Handicap = (I24 [total number of strokes played in last three rounds] minus I26 [SSS total for last three rounds]) divided by 3 [number of rounds played].

Handicap	=(I24-I26)/3

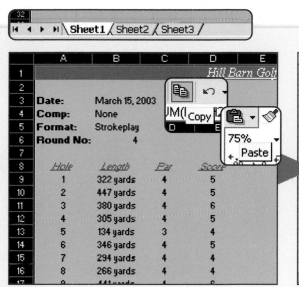

	A	B	C	D	E
1					*Hill Barn Golf*
2					
3	**Date:**	March 15, 2003			
4	**Comp:**	None			
5	**Format:**	Strokeplay			
6	**Round No:**	4			
7					
8	*Hole*	*Length*	*Par*		*Score*
9	1	322 yards	4		5
10	2	447 yards	4		5
11	3	380 yards	4		6
12	4	305 yards	4		5
13	5	134 yards	3		4
14	6	346 yards	4		4
15	7	294 yards	4		4
16	8	266 yards	4		4

Copy / Paste / 75%

23	*Series Handicap*	
24	**Strokes:**	0
25	**Rounds:**	0
26	**SSS Total:**	0
27	**Handic.**	

8					
9	1	322 yards			301
10	2	447 yards			413
11	3	380 yards			
12	4	305 yards			
13	5	134 yards			228
14	6	346 yards			427
15	7	294 yards	4	4	16	348
16	8	266 yards	4	4	17	321
17	9	441 yards	4	6	18	380
18					
19	**Out:**		35	44	In:
20					Ou
21					To
22					

23	*Series Handicap*		
24	**Strokes:**	=I21+Sheet1!B24	
25	**Rounds:**	4	
26	**SSS Total:**	140	
27	**Handicap:**	#VALUE!	

23	*Series Handicap*		
24	**Strokes:**	182	
25	**Rounds:**	4	
26	**SSS Total:**	140	
27	**Handicap:**	10.5	

	F	G	H	I
	18	380 yards	5	5
	In:		34	46
	Out:		35	44
	Total:		69	90

Current Handicap:	
Strokes:	272
Rounds:	3
SSS Total	210
Handicap	=(I24-I26)/3

8 To create a second scorecard, copy and paste the document. Highlight cells **A1** to **I27** and click on the **Copy** toolbar button. Click on the **Sheet 2** tab and then the **Paste** button. Adjust column widths and fill in the new scorecard, overwriting data where it is different.

9 For each new scorecard, carry over total strokes and SSS from the previous card. On Sheet 2, click **B24** then type '=I21+Sheet1!B24'. Click **B26** and type '=H6+Sheet1!B26'. After three rounds, and three sheets, set the Current Handicap calculator.

10 Click on cell **I24** and type '=I21+Sheet1!I21+ Sheet2!I21'. Click **I26** and type '=H6+Sheet1!H6+Sheet2!H6'. To work out the Current Handicap, click on **I27**, then type in '=(I24-I26)/3'. To print, click on the **Print** button.

Current Handicap

For the Current Handicap calculation you must total up the strokes and SSS for the last three rounds:

● **Strokes:** to add the last two rounds to the current score, click **I24** and type '=I21+Sheet1!I21+Sheet2!I21'.

● **SSS:** to add SSS for the last two rounds to current SSS, click **I26** and type '=H6+Sheet1!H6+Sheet2!IH6'.

When you play a new round, adjust the sheet references in the formula. After 50 rounds, for example the formula for the SSS for the last three rounds would be '=SUM(H6+Sheet48!H6+Sheet49!H6)'.

f_x	=I21+Sheet1!I21+Sheet2!I21

Current sheet total score

Sheet 2 total score

Sheet 1 total score

Design your own cross-stitch pattern

Use your computer to create your own embroidery projects

You can use your computer to enhance your enjoyment of any hobby or interest. Designing patterns for cross-stitch on your PC is just one example. Not only can you use your imagination to the full, but any errors can be corrected and amendments made in a matter of seconds.

By using the Windows' accessory program Paint, you can design the most intricate of patterns. The program allows you to construct your design stitch by stitch and experiment with colours. Our design fits on an A4 sheet and is for a 38cm (15in) square cushion, with each square representing a cross-stitch.

Make a rough sketch of your cross-stitch design on squared paper, experimenting with colour and ensuring you get the scale of the objects correct.

▶ BEFORE YOU START

1 Go to the **Start** menu, select **All Programs**, then **Accessories**, then **Paint**. Paint launches with a blank page open. Go to the **File** menu and select **Save As**. Find a location for your file in the 'Save in' box and type in a file name. Click **Save**. Leave the file type as 24-bit Bitmap.

You can also design a cross-stitch pattern using other, more advanced graphics packages such as Adobe Illustrator and CorelDraw for PCs. Ask at your local PC store for details.

▶ OTHER PROGRAMS

 Templates on CD-ROM

Close-up

It's a good idea to start your design at the centre of the grid and work your way out. This way, you can copy and paste items and keep your design well balanced. Use the scroll bars to find your way to the centre.

*To colour in half the house, click on the **Brush** tool, select a style option for it, then a colour, then click on the part of the house you wish to colour.*

*To draw straight lines with the Pencil tool, click on the grid, press the **Shift** key then, keeping it pressed down, drag the cursor. This eliminates any shaky hand movement.*

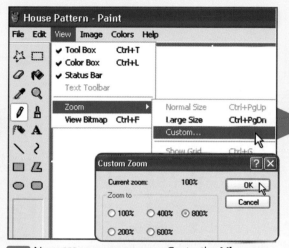

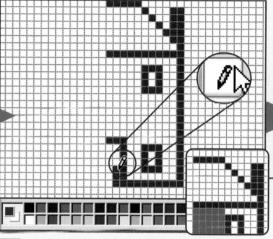

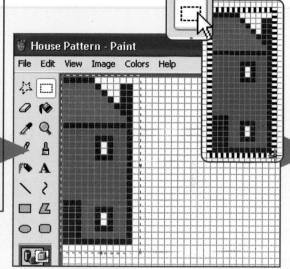

2 Now set up your canvas. Go to the **View** menu, select **Zoom** then **Custom**. In the dialogue box click the **800%** option then **OK**. Go to the **View** menu again, select **Zoom** then **Show Grid**. This brings up a square-by-square grid to represent your fabric.

3 For the outline of your first item (here, a house), click on a colour from the Color box at the bottom of the screen. Click the **Pencil** tool then click on the canvas and drag to draw the outline of one half of the house.

4 Now copy and paste your 'half house'. Click the **Select** tool then click and drag over the house. Go to the **Edit** menu and select **Copy**. Go to the **Edit** menu again and select **Paste**. The copied house now appears in the top left-hand corner of your screen.

Using the Tool box
Some tools, such as the brush and eraser tools, have a variety of styles which appear below the tool panel. Click on a style before using the tool.

The functions of the most popular tools are described here. To find out what other tools do, place your mouse pointer over the relevant tool button – a description will pop up.

Free-Form Select Selects an irregular-shaped area. Click and drag the pointer to select.

Select Selects a rectangular area. Click on the canvas and drag diagonally.

Eraser/Color Eraser Acts just like a rubber. Click and drag the pointer over the area to erase it.

Fill With Color Colours in a specific area with the colour of your choice. Click on the relevant area.

Pick Color Picks up a colour from the canvas. Apply the colour elsewhere by selecting another tool.

Magnifier Shows an area in close-up. Just click on the area. Also demagnifies magnified areas.

Pencil Draws a thin freehand line. Click and drag the pointer to draw.

Brush Used to draw a brushstroke style line. Select a brush then click and drag the pointer.

Airbrush Gives a textured paint effect. Choose a spray radius then click and drag the pointer.

Line Draws a straight line. Select a thickness then click and drag the pointer.

Curve Used to draw a curve. You draw a line first then click on the line and drag it to make a curve.

To ensure your side borders are mirror images of each other, it may be necessary to rotate the top border by 270° for the second side border.

To make your border corners, click on the **Pencil** tool, then on the appropriate colour from the Color box, and do it manually.

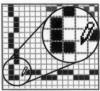

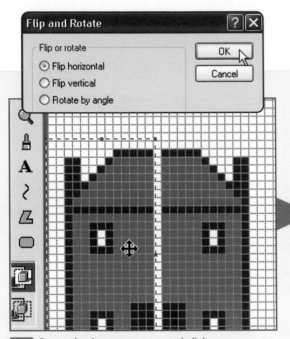

Flip and Rotate

Flip or rotate
- ⦿ Flip horizontal
- ○ Flip vertical
- ○ Rotate by angle

OK

Cancel

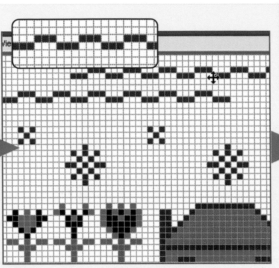

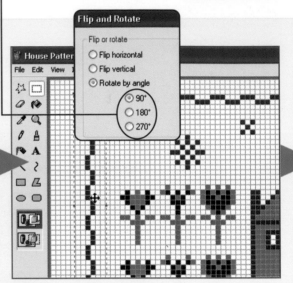

Flip and Rotate

Flip or rotate
- ○ Flip horizontal
- ○ Flip vertical
- ⦿ Rotate by angle
  - ⦿ 90°
  - ○ 180°
  - ○ 270°

House Patter

File   Edit   View

5 Go to the **Image** menu and click on **Flip/Rotate**. In the dialogue box click the 'Flip horizontal' option, then **OK**. Click on the image and drag it into position. Draw one each of the other items in your design, and copy and paste them into position in the same way.

6 To add a uniform border around your design, draw a small section of it at the top of your page. Select it, then copy, paste and reposition it to complete the top and bottom borders.

7 To add the side borders, select, copy and paste the top border. Go to the **Image** menu and click on **Flip/Rotate**. Select the 'Rotate by angle' option, then 90°. Click **OK**, then move the side border into position.

Customise colours

To create a new shade, customise an existing colour. Double-click on the colour in the Color box. In the Edit Colors dialogue box click on the **Define Custom Colors** button. To create your colour, move the slider on the right up or down until you get the right tone in the Color/Solid window. To save your new colour, click on the **Add to Custom Colors** button, then **OK**.

When you want to use it again, double-click on the Color box colour you customised. In the Edit Colors dialogue box your new shade appears in the 'Custom colors' section. Click on it to select it.

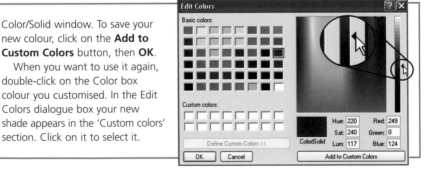

Edit Colors

Basic colors:

Custom colors:

Define Custom Colors >>

ColorSolid

Hue: 220   Red: 249
Sat: 240   Green: 0
Lum: 117   Blue: 124

OK   Cancel   Add to Custom Colors

You need to print your design with the grid in place. Paint does not allow this, but it can be done using other built-in features of your PC.

When you press the Alt and the Print Screen keys a snapshot of the current window is taken and stored. The Print Screen key is to the right of the F12 key.

Watch out
When you paste an item, click on it immediately to move it. If you click on something else, the pasted item becomes de-selected, and you will need to select it again by dragging the cursor over it.

▶ PRINTING YOUR DESIGN

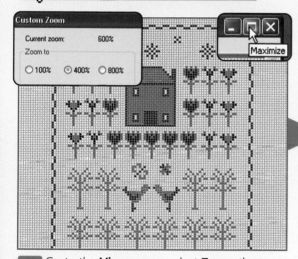

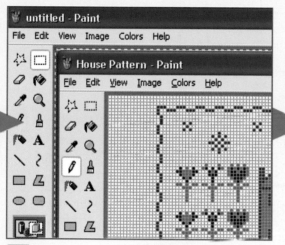

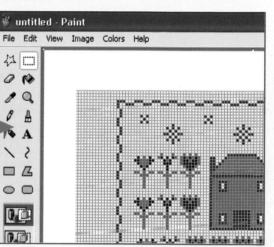

8 Go to the **View** menu, select **Zoom** then **Custom**. In the dialogue box select the 400% option. (If you can't see all your design, click on the **Maximize** button.) If the grid isn't visible go to the **View** menu, select **Zoom** and then **Show Grid**.

9 Press **Alt** and the **Print Screen** keys (see above). Now save your file then go to the **File** menu and click on **New**. Go to the **Edit** menu and select **Paste**. A snapshot of your Paint window now appears on your new page.

10 Select the areas of the snapshot you don't need – the Paint window's Tool box, for example – and press the **Delete** key. Go to the **File** menu and click on **Save As**. Name and save your file. Go to the **File** menu and select **Print**.

Correcting mistakes

 If you make a mistake when drawing, go to the Color box and click on the colour white. Then click on the affected squares to make them white again.

 To correct larger mistakes, click on the **Eraser** tool, select a size of eraser then drag it across the affected area.

Now that you are familiar with Paint, use it to edit photographs and other images, or to paint an original picture. See pages 210 and 222 for more ideas.

▶ OTHER IDEAS TO TRY

Organise a reunion and relive

Whether bringing distant family members together, or catching up with

It is all too easy to lose touch with the people who used to be part of our lives. All of us have friends we would like to see more often. That is why a reunion is so special – and your PC can help bring together people separated by the years and the continents.

Start by setting up an event planner database. Record what tasks need to be taken care of, by when and by whom. Add guest details, such as address, e-mail address and phone or fax numbers, as well as contact information for caterers and other professionals you may need to recruit to make the reunion a success.

The increasing popularity of the Friends Reunited Web site (www.friendsreunited.co.uk) means old school chums can be easy to trace. There are also worldwide e-mail directories of people who are on-line.

Once you have compiled your initial guest list, try searching

the good old days

old schoolfriends, your PC can help you

on-line for those you haven't yet been able to trace. Some people – as well as your old school or workplace – might be easier to contact using your PC as a fax. For letters, faxes and e-mails, you could create an attention-grabbing 'reunion' letterhead, then adapt it for subsequent gatherings.

Use your word processing program to produce a newsletter to keep everyone updated on the arrangements.

This could be a 'missing persons bulletin', to encourage others to help you trace 'lost' invitees.

When you have a rough idea of how many people will be attending the event, book the venue and arrange catering and entertainment, at the same time as keeping track of expenses through a spreadsheet.

One item you won't have to pay for is the invitations. Just design and print them on your PC – personalise the design and create a stir from the start.

Ideas and inspirations

Co-ordinating guests, possibly from all over the world, requires military-style planning. Make sure you dip into your armoury of PC-based skills to reduce as much of the hard work as possible. Adapt the following projects as desired, then prepare for a truly memorable occasion.

94 Searching the Internet
Locate people anywhere in the world via e-mail address databases and make contact with them.

308 Event planner database
Set up a document to handle the logistics of your reunion and delegate jobs to others.

166 Compile a guest list
Make a database to incorporate people's address, phone, fax and e-mail details.

162 Create a newsletter
If the timescale for planning your event is long, you may wish to update guests on your progress.

198 Create an invitation
It may be the first or the last task you carry out, but it's sure to be distinctive with your PC's help.

Also worth considering...

You can adapt virtually any communications skill you have learned to help you plan the reunion.

82 Use your PC as a fax
Make sure overseas guests receive updates if they don't have e-mail.

Get old friends together

- Contact your old company or college for a list of previous employees or students
- Conduct research over the Internet
- Draw up a guest list
- Mail, fax or e-mail a proposal to potential guests
- Start to compile a reunion database
- Design and send final invitations
- Scan in and e-mail photos of the event

TROUBLE

Frozen screens, printing errors, corrupt programs and malevolent computer **viruses** can befall any PC user. But in most cases these and many other problems are **easy** to solve. Wherever the fault lies – in Windows, in any application or in the computer hardware – this section will help you to **identify** the symptoms, **diagnose** the problem and come up with a **remedy**.

SHOOTING

My computer won't start up

There are steps you can take when you can't get your PC to start working

A start-up problem is the most serious and worrying of hardware hiccups. It is hard to cure the sickness if the patient cannot tell you what is wrong and it is difficult to assess how serious the problem might be. But there are a number of steps you can take to diagnose the problem if your computer will not start at all. Then, even if you cannot solve the problem yourself, you can at least give some useful leads to a specialist PC repairer.

Usually, when your computer won't start, it is due to problems with the hard disk. This vital part stores Windows files and all your documents. If the Windows files get damaged, your PC may not be able to start. A hard disk failure of this type is difficult to solve and should only be attempted once all other possible causes have been addressed.

The hard disk consists of a 'read/write' head which hovers over magnitised disks. The distance between the head and the disks is less than the thickness of a human hair. If the read/write head touches the disk the result is a 'head crash' – a damaging collision between the head and the fast spinning platters. A head crash can destroy large amounts of data on the hard disc, including the data needed to make Windows operate.

Are you connected?

If your computer doesn't react at all when you turn it on, check whether the power lights on the system unit and monitor are on. If not, check that both units are plugged into the mains, that the sockets are working and turned on and that the fuses in the plugs haven't blown. Also, check that the brightness control on the monitor hasn't been turned down. Finally, check the cable that connects the monitor to the PC.

Try resetting

If none of this helps, turn your computer off, leave it for a minute, then switch it back on again. If the screen remains blank, note down the number of beeps given out by the computer during the start-up routine as this might help a PC specialist diagnose the problem.

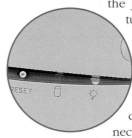

Key word

POST *The POST (Power On Self Test) routine checks that your most vital hardware components are working correctly. If the POST messages move up the screen too fast for you to read them, press the **Pause** key in the top right of your keyboard. Press **Enter** to continue*

What does your computer think is wrong?

Make a note of any error messages displayed after you turn on your PC. Some common messages are listed below; others may be explained in your PC's manual. At the very least, this information may help a service desk to analyse the fault.

`201 Memory error`

`Parity error`

These messages probably denote a faulty memory chip which might need replacing. You need to get the right type for your PC so consult the manufacturer or get a local PC dealer to fit it for you. Parity error could also indicate problems with the motherboard, the main circuit board of your computer, or even a computer virus.

`Non-system disk`

`Diskette boot failure`

Both these messages indicate that there is a floppy disk in the [A:] drive and that your PC is trying to use it to start up. You may get the supplementary message 'Replace and press any key when ready', in which case eject the floppy disk and press any key. Otherwise, eject the disk, turn off the PC, then switch it on again. Always eject CDs and floppy disks before you shut down your PC.

`CMOS checksum failure`

This indicates that your CMOS (Complimentary Metal Oxide Semiconductor) battery has run down and needs replacing by a repairer. Your PC will then work as before, with no data loss. The CMOS stores data for your system set-up and uses a small battery that recharges when your PC is switched on – make sure you turn it on at least once a month for an hour or so.

`Operating system not found`

`Boot disk failure`

If you get either of these, you have a problem with your hard disk. Start from your XP CD-ROM.

`Operating system found`

If you get as far as the Windows XP start-up screen before your system freezes, then you will probably find that the problem is a Windows Configuration Problem.

Start with your XP CD-ROM

If all else fails, you may need to use the Windows XP CD-ROM to start up the computer.

If you've checked the connections and power supply and Windows still won't start up, locate your Windows XP CD-ROM. Insert it into your CD-ROM drive and switch your PC off. Then switch it back on again to start your system from the Windows XP CD-ROM. You can then go to the installation menu and select the 'Repair' option to try and correct the fault.

Some older PCs may not support start-up from the CD-ROM, in which case you will not be able to use the XP CD-ROM as a rescue disk and will need to consult with an expert.

Older systems

Users of Windows 95, 98 and Me should have a rescue disk created when you first installed the system. Start up your PC with the disk in the floppy drive. At the prompt **[A:\>]** type 'c:' then press the **Return** key. Your computer will attempt to access the hard disk. If you get a C:> prompt then the hard disk is working, at least to a limited extent. A specialist should be able to save your data.

Watch out

Don't move your system unit, which houses the hard disk, when it is switched on. This can cause the hard disk's read/write head to touch the disk platters, in turn causing a head crash and destroying a great deal of data. When the computer is turned off, the head moves away from the platters and you can move your PC in safety.

My printer isn't working

Check your hardware and software to solve printing problems

Nothing is more frustrating than to put the finishing touches to a document, only to find that you can't print it out. But don't worry. While printing problems are the most common of hardware hiccups, they are also amongst the easiest to solve.

Nowadays printers are usually very good at telling you what's gone wrong. Sometimes it is simple: is there paper in the tray? Has the ink (or the toner) run out? Otherwise, there is a limited number of things that can go wrong: paper jams, loose connections, and mistaken set-up commands cover most difficulties. The steps on this page should lead you to the root of any problem. After a while, you will develop a feel for what has gone wrong with your own printer. In the meantime you can use the excellent Help and Support files in Windows XP.

In the hardware

If you send a document to print, and it fails to do so, the first thing you should check is that the printer is switched on – is the power light on? Check that it is switched on at the mains socket too.

Next, make sure there is paper in the printer paper tray, and that none of it has become jammed as it has been fed through. If the printer runs out of paper you should get an error message on your computer screen. If your printer is quite old and is jamming frequently, getting the rollers replaced may help. Otherwise, you may need to buy a new printer.

When your computer recognises that you have a printing problem, Windows will alert you by bringing up an error message suggesting certain action that you can take.

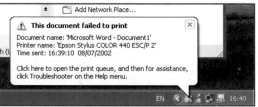

Is the printer connected?

Depending on the model, your printer connects to your PC through a USB, parallel or serial connection. With the latter two types of cable, make sure all connections are secure and screwed in firmly. USB cables plug into a free USB socket. Problems with USB printers can often be cleared simply by unplugging and then reconnecting the cable from the socket on the computer.

Start again

One way of quickly solving a printer problem is to try resetting the printer. To do this, just turn it off, wait a few seconds, then turn it on again.

Getting ready to print

The first step to successful printing is making sure you have made the correct settings.

Page Setup

Occasionally, a page will fail to print, or will print out wrongly, if your page isn't 'set up' correctly. Get into the habit of checking your Page Setup before you print. To do this, go to the **File** menu and click on **Page Setup.**

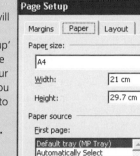

In the Page Setup dialogue box you set the parameters for the way the document will print – its physical size and orientation. If you want A4 size, click on the **Paper Size** tab and select **A4** in the 'Paper size' box. Check you have the correct orientation, too. With Portrait the page's width is the shorter dimension. With Landscape, the page's height is the shorter.

Print Preview

In many programs you can look at how the page appears before printing by going to the **File** menu and clicking on **Print Preview**. You will be able to see any set-up problems, such as if text runs over to other pages because the orientation is wrong.

Paper source

Your printer may have more than one feeder tray for paper, such as a manual feed tray needed to print envelopes. If so, make sure that you have selected the right tray to print from. In the **Page Setup** dialogue box click on the **Paper Source** tab and select the appropriate tray. Then check that the tray you want to print from has the right size paper in it.

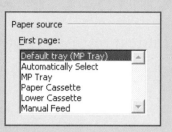

Troubleshooters

If none of the above solutions works, you may have a software problem. Windows XP has an extensive set of help files that help solve problems with your printer.

Go to the **Start** menu and click on **Help and Support**.

Fixing a printing problem

Fix a problem:
Printing Troubleshooter
Fixing connection problems

Pick a task:
Install new or updated printer drivers
Ensure that complex pages print properly
Print a test page
Cancel printing all documents
Pause or resume printing of a document

Click on **Printing and faxing**, then on **Fixing a printing problem**, then **Printing Troubleshooter**. Work through the options on screen to find a solution to your problem. The Troubleshooter is good at identifying whether problems with printing are being caused by the printer itself or by a piece of software.

Printer tools

Many printers come with a set of tools on a disk or CD-ROM that check for common printer faults and may even try to fix them. If you do not have the original CD-ROM, try downloading the utility from the manufacturer's website.

Reinstalling your printer

If all else fails, you could try reinstalling your printer. Go to the **Start** menu, select **Control Panel** then **Printers and Other Hardware**. Click on **View installed printers or fax printers**. Click on your printer's icon and press the **Delete** key to uninstall the printer. Confirm your choice. Double-click on **Add a printer** and follow the on-screen instructions to identify the type of printer you are installing and install its driver.

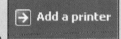

Checking ink levels

If the printer is printing your work but the printed text is faint or invisible, check that the ink or toner has not run out. Most printers will have a light on the front that will indicate if either is running out, and may also have software that warns you when levels are getting low. Sometimes with colour inkjet printers, the cartridge for one colour gets blocked or runs out sooner than the others. This can lead to strange colours being printed. It may be possible to clear a temporary blockage – check the printer's manual for details. If this doesn't work out, you'll have to replace the cartridge.

My keyboard isn't working

Hardware or software may be at fault if your keyboard is playing up

Your keyboard is perhaps the most vulnerable part of your computer. It gets the heaviest wear and tear; it is more likely to be moved and dropped; it takes a physical pounding every single time you key in a letter; and it is also exposed to dust, dirt and the occasional spillage. Fortunately, most modern keyboards are hardwearing and can take a lot of punishment before they start malfunctioning.

The best way to avoid problems in the first place is to look after your keyboard (see page 62). But even if you take good care of your equipment, you may find keys start to stick or fail to respond when you press them. The problem may be due to a faulty connection or (more rarely) to a software error. You need to check every possibility before you rush out and buy a new keyboard: the remedy could be as simple as giving the keys a quick clean.

If the whole keyboard fails

If none of the keys on your keyboard is responding, check whether your PC has crashed. Try using your mouse to move the mouse pointer on screen. If it moves as usual and the PC responds, the problem must lie with your keyboard.

First check the connections. Make sure it is plugged in properly and into the right socket in the system unit (it is possible to plug the keyboard into the mouse port by mistake). It is also possible that the lead itself has been damaged in some way – check for signs of damage.

If you are using a keyboard that connects via a USB socket try unplugging and plugging it in again. This can sometimes restore a lost connection.

If a key won't respond

If one of the keys on your keyboard isn't working properly check whether dirt has built up between the keys. Use a dust spray, or work cleaning cards dipped in cleaning solution between the keys, to solve the problem. As a final measure, gently lever off the offending key and check for debris trapped underneath.

If this doesn't work, and you know the software isn't to blame (see opposite), it is often less expensive to buy a new keyboard than to have the current one repaired.

Dealing with a spillage

If you spill a drink on your keyboard, unplug the keyboard, wash it using a clean sponge and a bowl of soapy water and leave for a day or two to dry thoroughly. Modern keyboards can be washed without suffering ill-effects.

Solving keyboard software problems

Windows has several settings that can affect the use of your keyboard. Check these if you are having problems with the keyboard or if the settings don't suit your special needs.

Select the correct language

Sometimes, a new PC will be set up for a different country, so that keyboard letters produce unexpected symbols on screen. Also dates and numbers may appear with unfamiliar formats.

To check this, go to the **Start** menu, click on **Control Panel**, then on **Date, Time, Language, and Regional Options**. Now click **Regional and Language Options** and select the **Regional Options** tab in the dialogue box. Ensure the correct country is selected in the

dropdown box. Next, click on the **Languages** tab and then on the **Details** button. If the correct language is not displayed in the pane – English (United Kingdom) for the UK; English (United States) for the US – click on the **Add** button. Click the arrow to the right of the 'Input language' box, scroll down and select the correct language. If you have changed any of the settings, click **Apply** then **OK**. You will need to restart your computer before the settings can take effect.

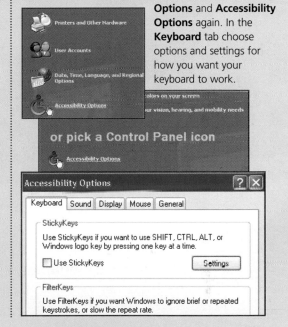

Make your keyboard easier to use

If you have difficulty using your keyboard because of a disability, Windows XP has a special Accessibility function that will make it easier. You can set up your PC so that you don't have to press more than one key at a time (StickyKeys). You can also set it up to ignore multiple presses of the same key (FilterKeys), or to warn you when you have pressed an important key, such as the Caps Lock (ToggleKeys).

To customise the keyboard in this way, go to the **Start** menu click on **Control Panel**, then **Accessibility Options** and **Accessibility Options** again. In the **Keyboard** tab choose options and settings for how you want your keyboard to work.

Watch out

If you press a key and an unexpected character appears, it may not necessarily mean the language your PC is using is incorrect. You may simply be using the wrong font. Some fonts, such as Zapf Dingbats and Wingdings, are entirely composed of unusual characters. Highlight the character then look at the font box on the toolbar to view the font used.

My mouse isn't working

If your mouse stops responding, it isn't necessarily broken

Don't be alarmed if something seems to go wrong with your mouse. As with most hardware difficulties, there are ways of working out where the problem lies.

If your cursor starts to move in a jerky way, or stops moving altogether, there are three likely causes. The two most common reasons are that the inside of your mouse needs to be cleaned (see page 63) or that your mouse is not properly connected (see opposite). When you open up your mouse to clean it, you can also check for a third possible problem – that one or other of the mouse rollers has worn out. If this is the case, buying a new mouse is the best remedy.

If you do have to buy a new mouse, you may never have these sort of problems again. The most recent types of mouse have no ball and rollers to get dusty or sticky. Instead they track your hand's movement using infrared light. The only maintenance an 'optical' mouse like this needs is gentle cleaning of its lenses.

Different types of mouse

Most computers use a conventional mouse connected directly to the system unit. However, other styles of mouse are available.

● Trackballs contain a ball and rollers on top of the mouse, and need maintenance and cleaning just like conventional mice.

● Touchpads and tiny joysticks, used mainly with laptop computers, do not plug into the computer and so cannot be cleaned easily. If you experience problems with these, and your computer is still under guarantee, take it back to the shop where you bought it. If it is not under guarantee, take your computer to a specialist repair shop.

Trackball

Touchpad

Bright idea
*If you want to shut down your computer but your mouse isn't working, press one of the **Windows** keys on your keyboard (to either side of the space bar). This will bring up the Start menu. Now press the **U** key twice to shut down.*

Watch out
If your mouse isn't plugged in properly when you turn on your computer, Windows will give you a warning message and you will find that the mouse will not respond to your hand movements.

Pointing you in the right direction

If you are having problems with your mouse, first check that the hardware is connected and in working order, then check for software trouble.

Check your connection

If your mouse stops responding while you are working, first check that the cable is plugged in properly to the system unit, and that it's in the correct port. Most modern mice plug into the PS/2 port or a USB socket. However, it's possible to plug a 'PS/2' mouse into the keyboard port by mistake. If you have to plug the cable back in, re-start the computer to get the mouse working again.

USB pointing devices

Many input devices connect to a computer using a USB port. Such devices include tablets – touch sensitive pads that you write or draw on with a pen-like tool, and a wide variety of joysticks. Most problems with USB devices can be solved by simply unplugging and then reconnecting the device in the socket.

The serial port

Not all computers have USB or PS/2 ports for the mouse and keyboard. You may find that your mouse has a larger plug that fits into a different socket – the serial port (also called the communications port). Switch off the PC then disconnect and reconnect the mouse in its serial port. Then switch the PC back on.

Cleaning your mouse

If your mouse isn't responding as it should, you may need to clean it. For instructions on cleaning your mouse, see page 63.

If all else fails...

If none of the above works, try borrowing a mouse that definitely works from another computer. Make sure the mouse has the same connector as yours. If the borrowed mouse works on your computer, there must be something wrong with the mechanics of your mouse. If you are sure your mouse is broken and it is not under guarantee, then you will have to buy a new one.

Check your mouse properties

Strange mouse behaviour may be caused by settings in the Mouse Properties dialogue box. To open it, go to the **Start** menu, click on **Control Panel**, then on **Printers and Other Hardware**. Clicking on **Mouse** brings up the Mouse Properties dialogue box.

The Buttons tab lets you choose to switch the functions of the left and right buttons (to suit a left-handed user, for example). You can also set the interval between the two clicks of a double-click.

If you have a scroll wheel you can change the way it works in the Wheel tab. To investigate other mouse problems, click on the **Hardware** tab, and then on **Troubleshoot**. Follow the steps to discover where the trouble lies.

My speakers don't work

What to do if the only sound coming from your PC is silence

Computer speakers will generally give many years of use without any need for maintenance, apart from regular cleaning. Over time – years, in fact – the sound computer speakers generate may become increasingly crackly. This is merely a sign of wear and tear, and the most economical solution is to replace them.

So seldom do computer speakers malfunction that, if you're using your computer and no sound comes out of them, the likelihood is that the problem lies not with the speakers but with the way they have been connected to the PC, or with the software you are using.

A little knowledge of how speakers connect to your computer and interact with your software should help you get to the bottom of the problem fast.

Some sound advice

It may seem obvious, but first check that the volume control is turned up. Next, check that the speakers are plugged into a mains socket and switched on – is there a power light? Also check that they're plugged into the correct socket on your sound card in the system unit. There are usually a number of connectors, for microphones as well as speakers. Sometimes these are colour-coded – the speaker socket is often green. Swap the speaker plug around until you hear the speakers. If you have stereo speakers, you need to make sure they are connected to each other.

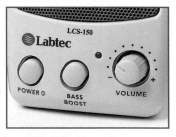

Software options

Another user may have disabled the sound facility on the piece of software you are using. Many games allow you to turn off the sound, out of consideration to those who share your space. If you can find no reference to sound in the program, check that sound is actually supposed to come from the software you are using (look in the manual).

Watch out
The sockets on a sound card can be very difficult to tell apart so it's easy to plug your speakers into the wrong one. This could be the cause if your speakers don't appear to be working but make sure the volume is turned down when you connect them to the correct socket.

Volume Control — EN 16:28

Options Help

Volume Control	Wave	SW Synth	Line In	CD Audio
Balance:	Balance:	Balance:	Balance:	Balance:
Volume:	Volume:	Volume:	Volume:	Volume:
☐ Mute all	☐ Mute	☐ Mute	☑ Mute	☐ Mute

Creative Sound Blaster PCI

Checking your volume control

If none of the checks to your connections and external controls reveals the fault, then you probably have a software problem. First of all check that the speaker volumes are not turned off.

Locate the small speaker icon that appears on the right-hand side of the Windows Taskbar. (If you cannot see it, click on the white **Show hidden icons**

arrow.) Double-click on it to reveal the Volume Control dialogue box. Check that none of the Mute boxes is ticked (if any are, click in them to untick the option), and that the volume sliders are near the top of their respective scales.

If you have stereo speakers check that the Balance options are even before closing the dialogue box.

Extra help

Remember that Windows has its own built-in help and support pages which explain how it works and what to do when things go wrong. Go to the **Start** menu and click on **Help and Support**. Click on **Music, video, games, and photos** then on **Music and sounds**. Now click on **Fixing a music or sound problem** and finally **Sound Troubleshooter**. You will be presented with a list of options describing common sound problems. Choose the one that applies then click on the **Next** button.

Search

Set search options

☑ Search only Music, video, games, and

Music, video, games, and photos

☐ Music and sounds
  ☐ Playing and copying music
  ☐ Using Windows Media Player
  ☐ Understanding digital media conc
  ☐ Music on the Web
  ☐ Recording and using computer so
  ☐ Fixing a music or sound problem
☐ Video
☐ Games
☐ Photos and other digital images

Sound Troubleshooter

What problem are you having?

○ I do not hear sound from my
○ A sound appears to play, but
○ A sound plays, but then stops
○ The sound skips or misses in
○ The sound is distorted or scra
○ The computer stops respondi
○ The computer restarts when i
○ I receive a sound-related err

Next >

Types of speakers

Most PCs emit sound through their own separate, free-standing speakers. However, it's possible that your PC's speakers are built into the monitor, one on either side of the screen. These speakers also connect by cables to the main system unit.

Ensure your speakers are part of your regular cleaning routine (see page 62), and that their cables are kept clear of any obstruction.

If all else fails...

Borrow a pair of speakers from a friend and connect them to your PC. If these work (keep the volume low to avoid damage), then you need to get your own speakers repaired or replaced.

Bright idea
If you can't borrow a pair of speakers to check the connection, you may be able to use your Hi-Fi speakers. Use a cable to connect between the speakers port on your system unit and the auxiliary jack socket of your amplifier (you may need to get a special cable). Do not place your Hi-Fi speakers too close to your PC as they are magnetic and may corrupt your hard disk and affect the picture quality on your monitor. Proper computer speakers are magnetically shielded to avoid these problems.

My modem isn't working

How to solve problems linking to the Internet or sending e-mail

On some occasions, a piece of software or hardware that has been functioning well for months can suddenly go wrong or stop working altogether. If something like that happens with your modem, don't panic. There are a number of reasons why your modem might not be working, and most of the problems are easily resolved.

Problems with your ISP

You should first check whether the problem is at your end. Try to connect to your Internet Service Provider (ISP) to see if the modem starts to dial. If you hear a series of loud, high-pitched tones (the sort you hear when you connect to a fax machine) then you know your modem is trying to make a connection. If the connection process does not complete, the cause could well be with the service provider's equipment rather than yours. In this case, call your ISP to find out if other customers are having problems and, if so, when the fault will be fixed.

Modem checks

If, when you try to make a connection, your modem does not emit the usual high-pitched tones, the problem may be with the modem set-up on your computer – the modem might not be properly installed, for example. Sometimes, if you add a new piece of hardware or software to your computer, it can affect the way your modem is set up. Run through the

set-up procedure in the modem manual to check that everything is arranged correctly. Alternatively, Windows XP has a number or helpful tools to diagnose and repair problems, including an interactive Modem Troubleshooter (see opposite).

Plugs and switches

Although it may seem obvious, check that the modem is properly connected. If you have an internal modem, check that the cable that connects it to the phone socket is plugged in at both ends. If you have an external modem, check that all its cables are firmly plugged in, and that the right  cables are plugged into both the PC and the mains supply. Check that the modem and the mains power are switched on.

If you are sure that your modem is set up correctly, that your phone line is working and that all your cables are correctly fitted, but you still can't make a connection, it's possible that the delicate head of the modem cable that connects the modem to the phone line is damaged. This is a standard cable, so simply buy a new one from a computer shop and reconnect your modem (see opposite).

Key word

Troubleshooter *This is a special facility in Windows that diagnoses and helps you to fix problems. The modem troubleshooter takes you through possible faults step by step until you find out what is causing the breakdown. It then shows you how to make the necessary repairs.*

The Modem Troubleshooter

If your ISP and your connections seem to be OK, try using the help available in Windows XP.

Before troubleshooting

Go to the **Start** menu and then **Control Panel**. Select **Printers and other hardware**, then **Phone and Modem Options**. Click on the **Modems** tab and check that your modem is listed (this means your computer recognises it as installed).

If your modem is not listed, it may have been accidentally removed by another installation. Reinstall it by clicking on **Add** to bring up the Add Hardware Wizard. Work through the simple steps suggested by the Wizard to reinstall your modem.

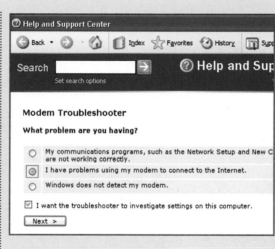

Windows XP Troubleshooter

Go to the **Start** menu and click on **Help and Support**. In the Help and Support Center dialogue box click on **Hardware** then scroll down in the left hand panel and click on **Fixing a hardware problem**. Choose **Modem Troubleshooter** (*not* **Troubleshooting modems**) from the list on the right and a list of symptoms will appear. Click the button next to a symptom that's relevant to your problem, then click the **Next** button. Now work through

the series of questions and possible symptoms the troubleshooter displays. Try to ensure you have all the information you might need to hand, such as your ISP's telephone number, your connection for dial up, your username and passwords.

You can also access the troubleshooter and other diagnostic tools through the **Start** menu. Go to the **Control Panel** then click on **Printers and Other Hardware**, then **Phone and Modem Options**. Now click on the **Modems** tab, select your modem from the list if there is a choice and click on **Properties**. Then click on the **General** tab and click on **Troubleshoot**.

Coping with call minding

Most users can now set up 'call minding' services, which allow callers to leave messages when the phone is not answered or the line is engaged. However, the service alerts users that they have a message by interrupting the telephone dialling tone, and this stuttering tone can cause a modem to drop its connection.

To work around the problem, go to the **Start** menu, click on **Control Panel**, **Printers and Other Hardware** and then **Phone and Modem Options**. Then click on the **Modems** tab, select your modem and click on the

Properties button. Choose the **Modem** tab. At the bottom of the panel click in the box next to 'Wait for dial tone before dialing' so that it is unticked. If you have more than one modem repeat this for each one.

A **Speaker volume** slider is on the same panel. The slider is set to On by default, so you can hear if the modem is dialling correctly. Once your modem is working well you might prefer silence; simply drag the slider all the way to **Off**, although this may not work for some external models.

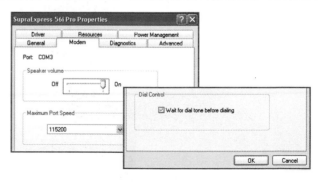

Upgrading your hardware

Improve the capabilities of your PC by adding or replacing a component

As your computer gets older you may find that it does not run as quickly as you would like, particularly when you add new software applications. The easiest way to resolve this problem is often to add more RAM (Random Access Memory). RAM is the place where your PC stores the program you have open and the data you are currently working on.

Installing more RAM will help your computer to function better, but it will not get the best performance from newer programs. If, for example, you load the latest computer game onto an old machine, you may find that the quality of graphics and sound effects is not what you were hoping for.

While it is possible to upgrade individual components you may find that if there are several items requiring replacement it might be more cost-effective to buy a new PC. As time passes it will become more expensive to 'match' upgrades to the capabilities of your old PC.

Before installing new components, be sure to create a System Restore Point (See page 350) and back up your hard disc (See page 357 for advice), so you can revert to a proven system should something go wrong.

Watch out

As with all mains powered devices, treat your PC with caution. Switch the electricity off at the wall and then pull the plug out of the wall in case the switch is faulty. If your PC is an 'all-in-one' take care – components in your monitor can give you a painful shock, even if the machine is unplugged.

Bright idea

Computer developments come thick and fast. It's hard to know whether this month's hot new item will be next month's white elephant. Wait for new products to establish themselves before you buy; successful devices will improve in quality and fall in price.

The basics of upgrading

Upgrading your PC will often involve opening up the system unit. Here we show you how to fit a graphics card – use it as a guide to fitting a sound card or internal modem.

Fitting a new graphics card

A graphics card generates the picture signal and sends it to the computer monitor. The latest graphics cards generate faster and smoother 3D graphics, and many support DVD and television playback. These cards will be designed to fit into a PCI or AGP slot at the rear of your system unit (Older PCs are unlikely to have AGP slots). To make sure you buy the appropriate card for your PC, consult your PC's manual or contact the manufacturer.

Switch off the PC, remove the power cables from the back of the system unit, then take the cover off (consult your PC's manual to find out how to do this). Locate your existing graphics card – this is the card your monitor cable will be attached to at the rear of the unit.

Unplug the monitor cable and then remove the screw that holds the card in place and put it to one side. Carefully but firmly ease the card out of the slot, then gently insert the new card in its place, making sure the socket for the monitor cable is facing outward from the

back of the unit. Secure the card by replacing the screw, then replace the system unit's cover.

Replace all the cables and turn on your PC. Windows XP will automatically detect the change to your components and, if it can, will install drivers for the device and configure it for use.

If Windows does not have the required drivers it will run the Add New Hardware wizard so you can tell Windows where to find them (see below).

If you have an Internet connection Windows XP will automatically search the Windows Update Internet site for an up-to-date driver. If all else fails you may find a suitable driver on the manufacturer's web site.

Remove the existing graphics card to make space for the new one

Gently insert the new card, pushing it firmly if necessary to make sure it is in place

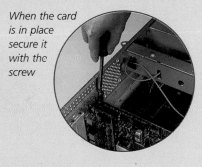

When the card is in place secure it with the screw

The Add New Hardware Wizard

Windows will usually detect new items of hardware when you start your PC and automatically run the Add New Hardware Wizard. If Windows does not, you will need to start the Add New Hardware Wizard yourself. To do this, go to the **Start** menu and click on **Control Panel**. Click again on the **Printers and other hardware** option and then select **Add Hardware** from the

See Also menu to run the Wizard.

The Wizard will begin by looking for new hardware. If it finds any it will check to see whether it already has a driver available. A driver is the piece of software that Windows uses to run or access the device, and many drivers come pre-installed with XP.

If the New Hardware Wizard cannot find appropriate drivers it will prompt you to insert the hardware supplier's CD or disk with the files required.

Add Hardware Wizard

Welcome to the Add Hardware Wizard

This wizard helps you:

- Install software to support the hardware you add to your computer.
- Troubleshoot problems you may be having with your hardware.

⚠ **If your hardware came with an installation CD, it is recommended that you click Cancel to close this wizard and use the manufacturer's CD to install this hardware.**

Watch out
Modern PCs use RIMMs or DIMMs (dual inline memory modules), older ones use SIMMs (single inline memory modules). They each have different size and pin configurations and SIMMs need to be fitted in pairs of the same capacity.

What to get and why
Think carefully before you upgrade. Be sure the new hardware will make a real difference.

Upgrading memory
Installing extra RAM in your PC is one of the most cost-effective upgrades you can make. Windows XP needs at least 128MB of RAM, but will perform much better with 256MB. If you find that your PC operates very slowly, or that your hard disk light flickers constantly as you use your PC, you will almost certainly benefit from additional RAM.

Fitting memory is easy. Remove the cover from the system unit and 'clip' the chip into the appropriate slot (your PC's manual will show you the exact location). Make sure you fit the correct type of memory for your machine (see above). If in doubt, take your PC to a dealer to have your RAM fitted correctly.

Sound cards
Although PCs have come equipped with perfectly adequate stereo sound cards for some time, the higher quality devices now available provide a richer audio experience. High definition digital sound cards can provide a surround sound environment for the latest computer games or for setting up a digital home cinema. Some cards also create realistic instrument sounds and 'acoustic environments' that make it seem as though sounds are coming from some distance away. They may also allow recording from several sources to enable mixing, which is useful for video editing, as well as for musicians.

Fitting a sound card is almost the same procedure as replacing your graphics card (see page 343). The sound card is easy to identify – it's the card your speakers are attached to at the rear of the system unit.

Graphics cards
Modern computers are sold with a graphics card that will handle most programs with ease. But if you work on very large scanned images, or if you want to run 3D games at top speed and high resolution, you might find that you need to upgrade to a faster graphics card.

Some graphics cards will also improve the picture when viewing DVD movies on your computer screen (see below), and may allow the use of a second monitor.

Shaping up for DVD
Digital Versatile Disks (DVDs) are now an established format for storing video as well as audio and computer data. A DVD can store over two hours of high quality film footage; a CD-ROM can only accommodate just over one hour of low quality video.

As well as the ability to play DVD films and software, a DVD-ROM drive will also play existing audio CDs and CD-ROMs. There are a number of competing formats of writeable DVD that will allow the recording of between 4 and 17 Gigabytes of data, much more than a recordable CD.

If you want to fit a DVD-ROM drive to an older system you should consider buying an 'all-in-one' kit. This adds an MPEG-2 decoder which is required for DVD movies, unless you already have a suitable card. Check the manufacturer's specifications for your graphics card if you are unsure.

Adding a DVD-ROM player will expose any weaknesses in your current graphics and sound cards and you may need to make further upgrades to get the most out of the system.

Bright idea
Software manufacturers have a vested interest in encouraging you to buy products that might mean having to upgrade hardware. So, if in doubt, read product reviews in computer magazines for impartial advice on whether such an item is worth buying.

CD-RW Drive

The standard 1.44MB floppy disk isn't adequate for loading or copying the large amounts of data required by many of today's applications. If you work with graphics or video on your desktop you're going to want a device capable of holding hundreds of megabytes. A CD-RW (Re-Writeable) disk can be used over and over again, just like a floppy disk, except it can hold up to 750MB of data. Get your dealer to fit and configure the new drive for you.

Monitors

Buying a bigger or better quality monitor won't make your PC run any faster, but in conjunction with a modern graphics card it will improve the quality of images you see on the screen. Most PCs are sold with 15 or 17-inch monitors. Buying a 19 or 21-inch monitor will make using your PC more fun, especially for games and DVD movies.

Another option that might be attractive is the replacement of your bulky screen with a new flat-screen panel – this will free up huge amounts of desk space as well as providing an improved image.

Hard disks

Modern programs take up a lot of hard disk space, especially if they use graphics, sound or videos. If your hard disk is nearly full your PC will run more slowly (for guidance on how to check its capacity and available space, see page 52). Adding a new hard disk, and keeping your current one for extra storage, is one solution. Installing a new hard disk and making the necessary adjustments to the old hard disk is a job for a PC dealer.

New processors

You can even upgrade the central processing unit (CPU) of your PC. This is the main chip on the motherboard, through which signals between all the other circuit boards are routed. The latest Pentium 4 processor chips work at speeds of up to 2.5 GHz, which mean they 'think' up to 2,500 million times a second. A faster processor will improve the speed of computer games and other processor-intensive activities such as video editing

as well as making your computer simply 'feel' faster.

Buying a new processor can be expensive, and there may be a variety of options to consider. Your motherboard may also need upgrading to maintain compatibility. Your PC dealer will advise on the best match with your current set up and will be able to install it for you. If your PC is old, you may well be better off buying a whole new system.

Speakers

The standard speakers supplied with most PCs are adequate for normal use. However, if you want the loudest, Hi-Fi quality sounds, and you have a new sound card, you may want to upgrade your speakers. Changing speakers is easy – simply plug the new speakers into the sound card at the rear of the system unit.

Only buy speakers intended for a PC – they are specially shielded to stop their magnetic components from damaging your computer.

Problems after upgrading

Here's how to solve hitches encountered with new hardware

Upgrading your system with new hardware will rarely present you with a problem. Usually, after you connect additional hardware to your computer, Windows automatically detects it and installs the relevant software files for operating it. The process is designed to be straightforward and you should be able to complete it yourself. However, if you are concerned, you can ask a dealer to carry out the upgrade for you.

If problems do arise, they can often stem from using incorrect or outdated drivers, and Windows XP can resolve these with very little fuss. Faulty connections or incorrectly fitted cards also cause difficulties – don't be brutal, but fit all components and cables firmly, and ensure they are plugged into the correct socket.

Troubleshooting new hardware

Take some precautions to help things run smoothly when you tackle problems with new hardware.

Before you begin

In most cases installing new hardware is a relatively straightforward process. But there are some important preparations you can make.
● Make a System Restore point (See page 350 for details)
● Always check the requirements of your new hardware. Are you running the correct version of Windows? Do you have enough RAM? Do you need any other components?
● For example, if you want to use a new large screen monitor, can your graphics card drive it? If you want to use new surround sound speakers, does your sound card actually support them?

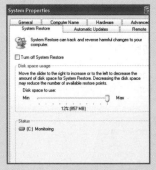

● Always check the manufacturer's Web site to see if there are any updated drivers you should download. New software may have been tweaked soon after its release to improve compatability.

Why upgrades can be a problem

Both hardware and software upgrades can cause difficulties. With hardware you may have been supplied with an incorrect part – for instance, the wrong kind of RAM. Software glitches are more common, and fall into two camps: adding software that is incompatible with your existing set up and simply doesn't work – for instance, installing a graphics program designed to work with earlier version of Windows, that may not be compatible with Windows XP; and adding software that conflicts with existing programs, causing a system crash.

Key word

Expansion card *This is a circuit board that adds certain functions to a computer. Expansion cards can be installed for improved or additional features. For example, a sound card gives a PC the ability to record and play sound.*

System Properties

System Restore | Automatic Updates | Remote
General | Computer Name | Hardware | Advanced

System:
Microsoft Windows XP
Home Edition
Version 2002

Registered to:
Tom Ruppel

55285-011-7602706-21459

Computer:
Intel Pentium III processor
863 MHz
256 MB of RAM

Memory problems

If your computer is unable to locate a new memory chip, it may be because it is not plugged in properly. To check the memory, go to the **Start** menu, right-click on **My Computer** and click on **Properties** in the pop-up menu. With the **General** tab selected, the dialogue box will tell you how much memory your PC thinks it has. If your RAM memory has increased, your memory card is fitted correctly.

If a series of error messages mentioning memory problems and 'parity errors' are displayed, your memory may be of the wrong type. In that case, check with your PC manufacturer to discover the correct specification.

Hard drives

Your PC may not recognise a new hard drive. If so, take the computer back to your dealer. There are several possible solutions, but they require specialist knowledge.

External drives

If a new external drive – such as a hard disk, CD writer or Zip drive – is not recognised by your PC, first check that cables are properly connected. Then ensure that any new driver card, such as a SCSI card, is correctly seated in its slot. If the problem persists, you may be using the wrong driver or have a hardware conflict (see page 349).

Sound cards

If you're not hearing any sounds from your PC after fitting a new sound card, first check that the card has been fitted properly, that your speakers are plugged in, and that all the connections have been made, including the cable from the CD-ROM to the sound card. If this doesn't solve the problem, or the sound from the speakers is very poor, you may have a driver problem.

Monitor problems

If your new monitor does not work, first check that it is properly plugged into the power supply and the graphics card. Check the settings by turning up the brightness and contrast controls. If it still doesn't work, connect another monitor that you know works (this may be your old one). If this one works, then the new monitor is faulty and should be taken back to your dealer. If the other monitor doesn't work either, the fault lies with the graphics card.

Graphics cards

If the graphics card is not working at all, you won't see anything on your screen. But you should still hear your hard disk 'whirring' when you turn on your PC. The most likely explanation is that the card is not connected properly. Switch the PC off at the mains, open the system unit and make sure the card is seated along its full length.

If your screen is 'snowy' or your Windows display looks strange, you have a graphic driver problem. Make sure you use the latest driver – you can visit the card manufacturer's Web site to obtain the latest version.

This may also be the case if the only screen resolution available is the standard 640 by 480 with 16 colours. To view the resolution settings, go to **Start**, click on **Control Panel**, then click on **Appearance and Themes**, then on **Change the screen resolution**. The current resolution and colour depth is displayed on the **Settings** tab.

Screen resolution
Less ——— More
800 by 600 pixels

Color quality
Highest (32 bit)

Troubleshoot... | Advanced

OK | Cancel | Apply

Why most upgrades are flawless

Most new hardware is described as 'Plug and Play' and installs automatically, or with minimum involvement from you. Most Plug and Play devices are external and have a USB type connector: you just plug them in, and let Windows do the rest.

USB connection has replaced most earlier peripheral connections, and appears to be immune to the kind of hardware conflicts that plagued older systems. However, to ensure future Plug and Play compatability it is essential to keep your system up to date.

Bright idea
Always install the software supplied with your new device. XP will probably find functioning drivers, either after a restart or by using the Add Hardware Wizard, but the manufacturer's software may have better features and compatability than basic Windows drivers.

Key word

USB *(Universal Serial Bus) This is the standard way of linking external devices – such as disks, cameras or microphones – to your PC. In theory you can connect up to 127 USB devices at once.*

Watch out

*When you click on the **Device Manager** tab in the System Properties dialogue box, devices should appear just once in the list (unless you have more than one installed). If any appear twice, remove them, then reinstall the relevant device by running the Add New Hardware Wizard.*

Troubleshoot hardware conflicts

If you install lots of hardware, particularly devices that are not Plug and Play, you may encounter problems such as a piece of hardware that has functioned very well for a long time suddenly refusing to work.

You can check to see what hardware you have, and its

settings, in the Device Manager. Go to **Start**, then **Control Panel** and click on **Printers and Other Hardware**, then **System**. Select the **Hardware** tab, then **Device Manager**.

Click the plus signs to see more detail about any of the devices attached to your PC, and double click any particular item to troubleshoot it.

An exclamation mark indicates some kind of a problem – perhaps the device is not fitted correctly, or your driver is out of date.

```
File   Action   View   Help
┌─────────────────────────────────────┐
│ □─🖳 AGENDASI                         │
│   ⊞─ 🔋 Batteries                     │
│   ⊞─ 💻 Computer                      │
│   ⊞─ 💾 Disk drives                   │
│   ⊞─ 🖥 Display adapters              │
│   ⊞─ 💿 DVD/CD-ROM drives            │
│   ⊞─ 🔌 Floppy disk controllers      │
│   ⊞─ 🖴 Floppy disk drives           │
│   ⊞─ 🔌 IDE ATA/ATAPI controllers    │
│   □─ 📡 Infrared devices              │
│       📡 VIA Fast Infrared Controller │
│   ⊞─ ⌨ Keyboards                     │
│   ⊞─ 🖱 Mice and other pointing devices│
│   □─ 📞 Modems                        │
│       📞 HSP56 MR                     │
│   ⊞─ 🖥 Monitors                      │
│   ⊞─ 🖧 Network adapters             │
│   ⊞─ 📇 PCMCIA adapters              │
│   ⊞─ 🖨 Ports (COM & LPT)            │
└─────────────────────────────────────┘
```

```
┌─────────────────────────────────────┐
│ ⊞─ ⌨ Keyboards                      │
│ ⊞─ 🖱 Mice and other pointing devices│
│ ⊞─ 📞 Modems                        │
│ ⊞─ 🖥 Monitors                      │
│ ⊞─ 🖧 Network adapters              │
│ ⊞─ 🖨 Ports (COM & LPT)             │
│ ⊞─ 🖳 Processors                    │
└─────────────────────────────────────┘
```

Click on the '+' sign beside individual device types to view the drivers installed for the device you are upgrading. To hide the drivers, click the '-' sign.

System Information

You may also find it useful to use System Information to help resolve persistent problems. From the **Start** button choose **All Programs**, **Accessories**, **System Tools** then **System Information**. Now click on the plus sign next to **Hardware Resources**, then **Conflicts/Sharing**. The information here looks quite complex, but it can help you quickly identify hardware that is sharing important system resources. Factory-fitted items that share resources – such as your central processor and video card – are unlikely to cause problems, but devices you have fitted yourself might be at the root of any difficulties. If you discover a particular item is conflicting, contact its manufacturer's technical support department for advice.

```
┌──────────────────────────┬────────────────────────────────────┐
│ System Summary           │ Resource                           │
│ □─ Hardware Resources    │ I/O Port 0x00000000-0x00000CF7     │
│     Conflicts/Sharing    │ I/O Port 0x00000000-0x00000CF7     │
│     DMA                  │                                    │
│     Forced Hardware      │ I/O Port 0x000003C0-0x000003DF     │
│     I/O                  │ I/O Port 0x000003C0-0x000003DF     │
│     IRQs                 │                                    │
│     Memory               │ IRQ 10                             │
│ ⊞─ Components            │ IRQ 10                             │
│ ⊞─ Software Environment  │ IRQ 10                             │
│ ⊞─ Internet Settings     │ IRQ 10                             │
│ ⊞─ Applications          │                                    │
│                          │ Memory Address 0x90000000-0x9FFFFFFF│
│                          │ Memory Address 0x90000000-0x9FFFFFFF│
└──────────────────────────┴────────────────────────────────────┘
```

Upgrade in stages

It's a good idea to upgrade a number of items of equipment in stages. Add each part as a separate exercise, checking that each has been installed properly before installing the next. If a problem arises, it is then easier to tell which part is responsible.

Keep your system up to date

It is not only owners of newer computers who can experience problems. If your computer is a little old and you buy new hardware for it, there may be problems. The cause might include existing software or hardware, or even the operating system itself.

It is a good idea to try and keep your operating system and all your hardware drivers as up to date as possible, in order to avoid any problems.

Windows Update

Windows XP has a feature called Windows Update that keeps your operating system up to date. It automatically finds on-line software updates for your computer whenever you launch it.

Go to **Start** and select **Help and Support**. Under **Pick a task** choose **Keep your computer up-to-date with Windows Update**. When Windows Update has connected to the Internet choose **Scan for Updates**.

Key word

Hardware conflict *This occurs when your PC is unable to recognise a piece of hardware. This can happen when the hardware is set up incorrectly, or because it is incompatible with your particular PC or the software you are attempting to use it with.*

Welcome to Windows Update

Get the latest updates available for your computer's operating

Windows Update scans your computer and provides you with for you.

▸ Scan for updates

New! Let Windows manage critical updates for you.
Tell me about automatic updating

Note Windows Update does not collect any form of personal computer.
Read our privacy statement ▸ Scan for updates

Wait while a list is gathered – this may take some time if you have a dial-up connection. The first time you run the program it will ask if you are happy to trust Microsoft updates. Click on **Yes** and also click in the check box next to **Always trust files from**

Microsoft Corporation. You can then choose which updates to install. The simplest option is to accept all the updates. Many updates will be designed to fix security lapses. Because software developers and computer hackers are engaged in a continual battle it makes sense to use each security advance as it becomes available.

You may need to authorise downloads if they are not Microsoft Certificated, and you might also need to reboot your computer after installations are completed – but you will be informed of this by on-screen messages.

Automatic Updates

You can also set XP to search for updates by itself. Go to **Start**, **Control Panel**, **Performance and Maintenance**, **System** and click on the **Automatic Updates** tab. Then click on the button next to **Download the updates automatically**. This option is particularly handy if you have an always-on Internet connection such as an ADSL or cable line. If you leave your computer running all the time (something most computers are designed for), you will always be right up to date.

Manufacturers' Web sites

Visit manufacturers' Web sites, and check them for new information or updates for your hardware and software.

Generally, new drivers will be located in a section of the site known as Support, Software Updates or Downloads. Work systematically through the options available to find the right driver for your operating system and hardware device, and don't forget to check the version of your existing driver first. You can find out what driver you already have by right-clicking on the device in **Device Manager**, and then choosing the **Driver** tab.

If you do encounter a problem after installing new hardware and software, go straight to the manufacturer's Web site. It is likely you will not be the only person to have encountered the problem, so a 'patch' to fix it or suggestions of things to try may have been posted on the Web.

Your consumer rights

In Britain you have a number of legal rights that a UK-based retailer must abide by. One example given by the government's Office of Fair Trading is that if you specifically request products for one particular computer system, and are supplied with goods that only work with a different set up, you are entitled to return the goods and ask for your money back. You may also be entitled to compensation if the goods cause damage to your machine that costs more than several hundred pounds to put right.

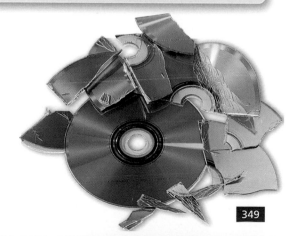

Troubleshoot using System Restore

If an upgrade results in a problem, here's one way of solving it

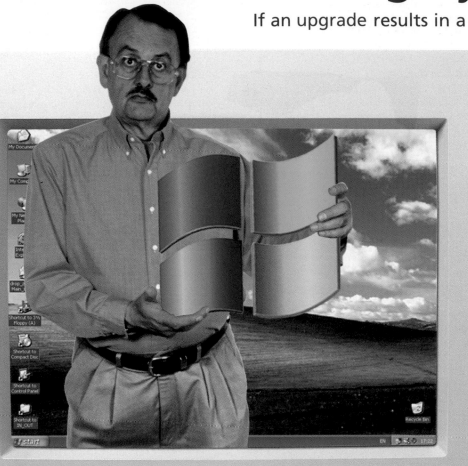

Windows XP is designed to be user-friendly, versatile and robust. Even professional users making complex videos or animations find crashes are rare. But this doesn't mean that XP leaves you on your own, should a crash occur. Instead it has one of the most reliable and comprehensive recovery and diagnosis tools available: System Restore.

Use 'time travel' to fix problems

System Restore is a clever utility that lets you take 'snapshots' of the state of your system at regular intervals. If something goes wrong when you install new software or hardware, you can use System Restore to quickly put your machine back into a working condition – effectively stepping back in time to a point before your PC became unstable.

System Restore can be used for much more; however. With a little logical thought you can diagnose and track down the source of problems – repairing, not just recovering.

The process involves trial and error: starting from a point where you know your PC works, add in suspect software and devices, making System Restore Points as you go, until your PC crashes again. Then roll back to your last Restore Point. The chances are that the last piece of software or hardware you added caused the crash. Often problems are cause by a conflict between two programs, and that is where using an additional system tool, Conflicts/Sharing, can help.

Using System Restore to diagnose a conflict

Your computer might crash for a variety of reasons, such as a power surge or cut. System Restore gets you up and running again very quickly. Persistent failures, however, may have deeper roots.

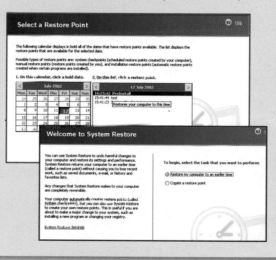

First steps

Before you install new hardware, use System Restore to create a Restore Point.

Go to **Start**, then click on **Help and Support**, then **Performance and Maintenance** in the left hand column, then click on **Using System Restore to undo changes**. Scroll down in the right hand panel to click on **Run the System Restore Wizard**. Then next to 'Create a restore point', then on the **Next** button, then name your point. In this example, we called ours 'Pre-Install'. All your Restore Points automatically have a date attached for ease of use.

Then install your new items. A subsequent crash indicates that one or more items, or their drivers, are causing problems.

Reverting to an earlier state

After a crash you can jump back to your pre-install point where the PC worked well. Navigate to **Run the System Restore Wizard** as before, then click on **Restore my computer to an earlier time**, then on **Next**, and then choose the Restore Point you prefer – we used our PreInstall. Keep in mind that XP will also create Restore Points whenever you install files or hardware, so you will have a wide choice.

Then use the System Restore Wizard to move through subsequent Restore Points, rebooting each time, to locate the point at which problems develop

Focusing on the suspects

Once you have established the point at which your system became unstable, you can find out why. For hardware, check that all cards are firmly seated in their slots and that cables are securely attached. Then check that you have the latest drivers – either by visiting the manufacturer's website or by using the **Hardware Update Wizard**.

Go to the **Start** Menu, click on **Control Panel**, then on **Performance and Maintenance** then **System** at the bottom of the window. Click on the **Hardware** tab, then on **Device manager**. Click on the plus sign next to the category matching your new device. Right-click on your device and choose **Update Driver** from the drop-down list. The Hardware Update Wizard will launch. Follow the steps to search for an up-to-date driver for your device (you may need to connect to the internet during the process). If these measure fail to remove the instability then got to **All Programs**, **Accessories**, **System Tools**, **System Information** then click on the plus sign next to **Hardware Resources**, then **Conflicts/Sharing** to see if your suspect device is clashing with any others. If it is clashing with a device you can do without, then remove that item. If it is clashing with a built-in system component then contact the device's manufacturer for advice.

What System Restore doesn't do

System Restore is a clever piece of software. If you tried to do manually what it manages automatically you'd be in for long hours of detailed work.

But it gets better. A basic piece of software would simply take a snapshot of your system and, when a failure occured, would revert to exactly that. System Restore doesn't. It recognises that there will be many files that you *don't* want to dispense with – such as your recent Outlook emails and Word documents.

System Restore will not affect items like documents, e-mail messages, your web browsing history, and passwords. All these are saved when you revert to an earlier state.

Furthermore, you can ensure that System Restore protects all your personal files, no matter what type they might be, by keeping them in the My Documents folder. By default, System Restore leaves that untouched. Also, it does not restore any files created with everyday programs such as Microsoft Word or Excel.

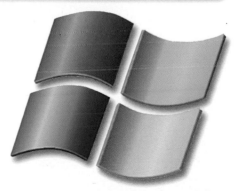

Windows won't close down

This is what to do when your operating system freezes

Occasionally, Windows XP will appear to freeze on screen – a condition known as 'hanging'. You'll realise this has happened when the cursor doesn't respond to your mouse movements, and you can't issue any keyboard commands.

If your computer has these symptoms but you're still not sure whether Windows has hung,

press the **Num Lock** key (found above the numeric keypad on the right of the keyboard) on your keyboard a few times. If the Num Lock light above the key doesn't go on and off, then you know the system is definitely frozen.

Whereas the remedy for a hung program is fairly straightforward because you can still access help facilities in Windows itself, having Windows

hang on you can be a bit more tricky. This is because Windows governs everything you do on your PC, including accessing help facilities, and once it seizes up you will find you cannot carry out any of your normal actions.

First steps to closing Windows

When Windows hangs, you won't be able to restart by going to the Start menu as usual. Instead, press the **Ctrl + Alt + Del** keys together. You then have several choices – either click **Shut Down** immediately or, if you had programs running when Windows hung, shut them down and save any changes you made by selecting each in turn in the **Applications** panel then clicking **End Task**. A dialogue box will appear asking if you want to save changes. Click **Save**. If you had Internet Explorer open, close this last as it doesn't have active documents.

Sometimes, closing programs in this manner can unfreeze Windows. If it doesn't, then restarting Windows usually does the trick. But if the problem persists, run through the Startup and Shutdown Troubleshooter to diagnose and solve your problem.

Bright idea
If you cannot solve the problem using Windows troubleshooters you should consider reinstalling Windows. This is not as daunting a process as it sounds. See page 354 for more details.

Close up
Whenever possible, make sure you restart or shut down your computer through the Start menu. This will mean that all current information is saved and that each program closes before Windows.

Using the Troubleshooter to diagnose problems

If you often experience problems when you try to close Windows down, its own step-by-step Help facility will be able to give you guidance.

Use the Troubleshooter

Windows XP is at the heart of your PC, underlying all the other programs you use. Because of this, the Startup and Shutdown Troubleshooter may need to shut down your PC in order to examine and correct the files that govern your system's operation.

It makes sense to familiarise yourself with the troubleshooting steps in advance, before beginning the real process. You will probably find that you want to print out the troubleshooting steps for later reference when the PC is restarting. If you have another PC available, also running Windows XP, you could follow the instructions on that system as you examine your problem computer.

Don't Panic

As with many XP Troubleshooters, this process covers quite complex areas and may at first appear too technical. Don't be put off; the troubleshooters and related utilities are designed to give even a novice the help needed to repair their system, step-by-step. It is vitally important that you follow the Troubleshooter's instructions accurately, and also complete fully any process you begin.

What the Troubleshooter does

The path taken by the Troubleshooter will depend on your particular problem, but generally it will use the System Configuration Utility to launch XP in different ways, aiming to detect damaged or conflicting software as it does. It is a 'trial and error' process that will involve several restarts, each time loading or unloading particular batches of system software.

Naturally, a process like this can be quite time consuming, but it is also a comprehensive and effective method, so don't try to rush things. If you find yourself confused at any stage, or realise you have not printed out the

necessary troubleshooting guidance in advance, don't guess! Just go back a stage, or even begin the process again – a stab in the dark at this level could cripple your machine and might force a complete system reinstall.

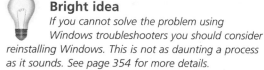

*If you cannot shut down Windows by pressing the **Ctrl** + **Alt** + **Del** keys, use the **Reset** button on your system unit. If your PC has no Reset button, switch the PC off, wait 30 seconds and switch on again.*

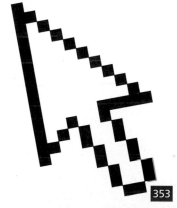

Reinstalling Windows

If you can't repair a fault with the operating system, reload it

Reinstallation is the last resort for solving problems with Windows. The process leaves almost all your work unaffected, and returns Windows to its original state.

Complete reinstallation may be necessary if, for example, you keep experiencing serious crashes. All you need to begin reinstallation is your Windows XP CD-ROM. For safety, back up your work before you start (see page 357).

Reinstalling Windows does have risks and should be tackled only after you have tried all other remedies, and only when you are sure that problems you are having relate to the Windows operating system, rather than an individual application. Windows XP should reinstall without losing critical system data, such as Internet settings, but take note of these first, just in case.

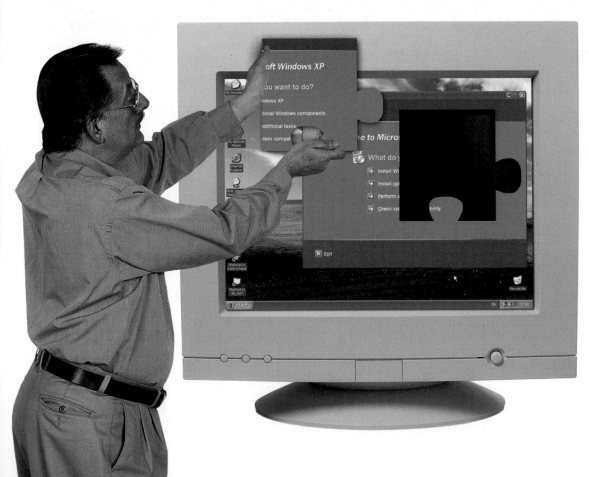

Generally you will be able to reinstall from within Windows as shown here. However, if Windows won't start up, you must boot from your XP installer CD (see overleaf).

IF REINSTALLATION FAILS

1 Put your Windows XP CD-ROM into the CD drive. The CD will run automatically, and begin leading you through the install process. When asked what kind of an install you require – Upgrade or New – choose **New Install** to completely replace your copy of Windows XP.

Getting expert help

If you are worried about the reinstallation process, consider getting expert guidance. For extra help during reinstallation, call the Microsoft technical support line or, if Windows came preinstalled, your PC's manufacturer.

Bright idea

*Making screen grabs is a good way to note system settings. Open the relevent panels, for instance, ISP settings. On your keyboard press **Print Screen**, then open a graphics program such as Paint and **Paste** in the grab. Print it out as a permanent record.*

Watch out

During the set-up procedure you will be asked to enter your Windows XP product key or serial number (you'll find this on your Windows CD sleeve or manual cover). Be careful to input the number correctly and not to lose it.

2 The installer program examines your computer to determine the best configuration for it. If you have an Internet connection, it will be used to check for Microsoft updates to Windows XP – this means that you should get a newer system than the one on your original CD.

3 Most of the reinstallation time is taken up by the process of copying the important Windows files from the installation CD-ROM to your PC. The time this takes depends on how fast your CD drive and hard drives are, and on the speed of the computer.

4 During the final stage of installation Windows XP will ask you for the names of all system users, and whether you wish to 'activate' Windows XP online. Activation can sometimes cause problems – call Microsoft if you have trouble with the process.

Explorer favourites

Internet Explorer is tightly integrated into Windows XP, so much so that it is reinstalled at the same time as the operating system. Losing your Explorer favourites can be frustrating, so don't be caught out, and preserve your data first. In Explorer go to **File**, **Import/Export** to open the Import/Export Wizard. Follow the onscreen instructions to export your favourites. For added safety, export them to a file on a floppy disc. After your system reinstall simply insert the floppy disc, open Internet Explorer and go to the Import/Export Wizard again and this time Import the file. Your favourites will appear as before.

⚠️ **Watch out**
If, after following the procedure below, Windows still won't load, it may be that your hard disk isn't working properly. For more information on how to diagnose and deal with hard disk problems see page 330.

How to reinstall when Windows won't load

If Windows won't start up, you need to start from your Windows XP installer disk and deal with any problems from there. Here's how.

Boot from your installer CD

If Windows doesn't load normally when you switch on your PC you should be able to start your system using the original Windows XP installer CD-ROM.

If you are faced with a blank or blue screen, perhaps a message that you have an **'Invalid Boot Diskette'**, insert your CD. It may load automatically. If it doesn't, switch off the PC and then switch it on again, leaving the CD inside the machine.

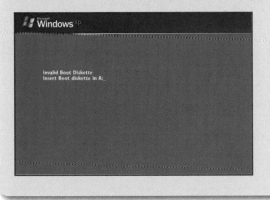

When your machine recognises the CD and starts from it, it begins by examining your system. If it cannot find a viable copy of Windows XP it will give you three options: setting up Windows XP, repairing Windows XP with Recovery Console, or quitting. You will need Administrator level access, and Administrator passwords, to run the Recovery Console – and if Windows is damaged it may be wiser to proceed with a full reinstall rather than a partial repair, so click **Enter** to begin installation. With luck a fresh install will solve your problems.

However, if you receive a message saying 'Setup did not find any hard disk drives installed on your computer' you may have a severe hardware failure, rather than a software problem. This could have several causes – most often a hard disk crash. If a hard disk has failed it does not make enonomic sense to repair it, as replacement will cost less than a hundred pounds. Recovering data from a broken hard disk is job for an expert, and will not be cheap. That's why it is always a good idea to back up important data regularly.

Backing up your work

Before reinstalling Windows it's a good idea to make a back-up, or copy, of your files.

Install Backup

Backup is a program included on the Windows XP CD-ROM, used to maintain an insurance copy of all the data on your hard disk in case of failure. Not all of its features work in Windows XP Home – it's really aimed at business users – and for this reason it isn't installed with the Home Edition by default.

Even so, Backup is a useful program. To install it, insert your Windows XP installer CD. In the **Start** menu, click on **My Computer**, then right-click the installer CD and select **Open**. Double click **VALUEADD**, double click **MSFT**, double click

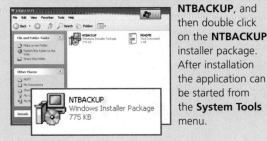

NTBACKUP, and then double click on the **NTBACKUP** installer package. After installation the application can be started from the **System Tools** menu.

Give your hard disk a check-up

If your computer is having difficulties loading Windows you might have a hard disk problem. Use Windows XP's built-in disk utility to examine and repair any flaws.

Go to the **Start** menu, click on **My Computer**, and then right-click your hard disk drive, normally **C:**. Click **Properties**, and then click on **Tools**. Under **Error-checking**, click **Check Now**. In the next panel click in the boxes next to 'Automatically fix file system errors' and

'Scan for and attempt recovery of bad sectors', then click on **Start**. The utility will ask if you wish to schedule the disk examination for the next time you start your computer – click on **Yes**. Then restart your machine and let the utility check your disk.

A full check will take some time – do not cancel the examination half way through. If it does find errors, follow the on-screen instructions and you should be able to make repairs.

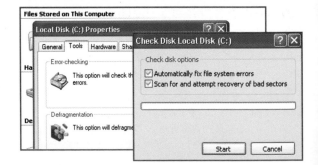

Close-up

For the first PCs, floppy disks were suitable for backing-up data. Now Zip disks or recordable CDs have taken on their role because they have a larger storage capacity. For large networks fast tape drives or banks of hard disks store data.

Making and storing back-ups

Once you have Backup installed you need to tell it where to place your copied files and schedule it to do its work automatically

Configuring Backup

Click on **Start**, then on **All Programs**, **Accessories**, **System Tools**, and then **Backup**. The **Backup or Restore Wizard** will open – click on **Next**. On the next panel choose **Back up files and settings** then click **Next**. Choose 'My documents and settings' then click on **Next**. Choose the files or disks you want to back up on the next panel, then click on **Next** again. Use **Browse** to navigate to your new drive (see below) where the data will be stored – make sure you have a disk installed if it is a removeable media drive such as a Zip. Click on **Next**, then on the next panel click on **Advanced**. Choose a style of back-up. **Normal** simply duplicates all your files every time you back up – this can be slow. The other options back up all your files the first time you run the process, thereafter only files that have been

changed. These methods are faster, and should give you the same result – **Differential** is a popular choice. Choose, then click on **Next**. On the next window you have the option of replacing your back-up files each time the program runs. This saves storage space but means you won't be able to restore files after they have been changed several times.

Set a schedule

Backing up can be a slow process, so many people leave their PC running all the time and set it to back up during the night. Start Backup as previously described, then click on **Advanced Mode** in the Backup Wizard. Click on the **Schedule jobs** tab and then on the date on which you want the back-up to take place. The Backup Wizard will launch, allowing you to choose the data that you want to save and the drive that you want to save it to as described previously.

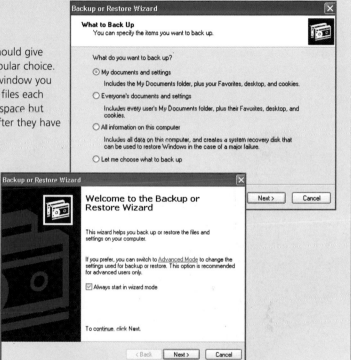

Choose a back up medium

Before you back up you need to decide what you want to save and how often. It's worth planning in advance because you might need to buy new hardware or storage media. Your circumstances will probably govern your choices; for instance, how critical is your data? If you're running a small business it is vital to protect accounts on a day by day basis. If, on the other hand, you use your PC for creating a quarterly newsletter, then a weekly back-up might be adequate. Also, how much time do you wish to devote to this? Floppy disks are too small and slow for

most people's needs. Because of their slow writing speed, CD-RW drives are not suitable either. To run an automated back-up you will need either a separate internal hard drive, an external hard drive or a Zip drive.

Zip drives are available in three capacities – 100MB, 250MB or the very latest version that fits in 750MB. However, this still is not large enough to be able to back up even the basic files installed by Windows, so it makes most sense to invest in an external hard disk. These are now available with capacities of more than 100GB – large enough to keep multiple back-ups on if necessary.

My program has crashed

If an application stops responding to your commands, here's what to do

When a program crashes, your mouse pointer will appear as an hourglass and you will not be able to type or to access menus. It may seem that your PC has stopped working – but if the hourglass pointer changes back to an arrow when you move it onto your Desktop, this means Windows is still working. Windows runs each program in its own protected memory space, so problems with one active program do not usually affect the others.

It is possible to exit the crashed program using keyboard commands, and then to open it again. If you have not saved changes in the document you were working on before the crash, you will lose some of your work when you exit the program. This is why it is vital to make a habit of saving your work regularly, and why it's also worth remembering to save work in other programs that are running.

Closing a crashed program

When a program crashes you won't be able to close it in the usual way – for example, by going to the **File** menu and clicking on **Close**. The best way to proceed is to press the **Ctrl + Alt + Del** keys simultaneously.

This brings up Windows Task Manager, which lists all the programs currently running on your PC in the Applications tab. It also shows Processes – system programs that run invisibly on your computer. In the Applications tab, scroll down the list until you see the name of the program that's crashed – it will be labelled 'Not Responding' – then click the **End Task** button.

The crashed program window should then close. If it doesn't, another dialogue window will open, giving you the option of either waiting for the program to close by itself or terminating it immediately by clicking the **End Task** button. Windows XP, unlike some older versions of the operating system, usually does not require you to restart your machine. However, if more than one program has crashed it is probably a wise precaution to start up again.

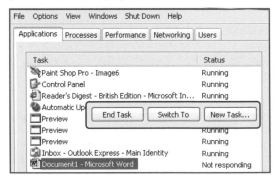

Close-up
If you cannot exit from the crashed program by pressing the **Ctrl + Alt + Del** *keys, you must press the* **Reset** *button on your system unit.*

Bright idea
Some programs allow you to save data automatically at set intervals. In Word, for example, go to the **Tools** *menu and click on* **Options**. *Click on the* **Save** *tab and select an interval time – say, 15 minutes – from the 'Save AutoRecover info every:' box. Click* **OK**.

What to do when a program crashes

Some programs let you recover lost work after a crash. When you restart, check your PC for problems, and maybe reinstall troublesome programs.

Document Recovery in Office XP

Microsoft Office XP, which includes Word, Excel and Powerpoint, works hard to ensure that you don't lose valuable data and work when a program crashes (see the 'Bright Idea' panel above).

If an Office XP program stops working, go to the Start menu, point to **All Programs**, then **Microsoft Office Tools** and then **Microsoft Office Application Recovery**. Choose the program that has crashed and click on **End Application**.

When you restart the program after a crash you will see the Document Recovery pane in the left-hand side of the window. It will list files that are available for recovery, giving details about when they were last saved. If you're not sure which file to open, click on **Which file do I want to save?** for guidance. Most of the time files marked '[Recovered]' will be the ones that are most up to date.

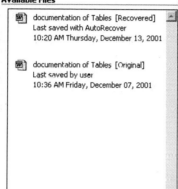

Document Recovery

Word has recovered the following files. Save the ones you wish to keep.

Available Files

documentation of Tables [Recovered]
Last saved with AutoRecover
10:20 AM Thursday, December 13, 2001

documentation of Tables [Original]
Last saved by user
10:36 AM Friday, December 07, 2001

[?] Which file do I want to save?

Close

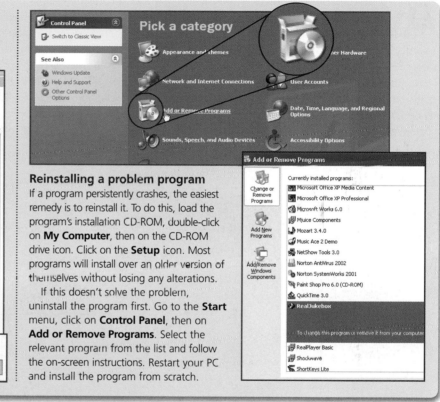

Reinstalling a problem program

If a program persistently crashes, the easiest remedy is to reinstall it. To do this, load the program's installation CD-ROM, double-click on **My Computer**, then on the CD-ROM drive icon. Click on the **Setup** icon. Most programs will install over an older version of themselves without losing any alterations.

If this doesn't solve the problem, uninstall the program first. Go to the **Start** menu, click on **Control Panel**, then on **Add or Remove Programs**. Select the relevant program from the list and follow the on-screen instructions. Restart your PC and install the program from scratch.

Automatic clean-up

When a program crashes it can leave behind temporary files (with filenames ending in '.TMP') that are usually deleted when you exit the program normally. Windows XP comes with 'Disk Cleanup' that is designed to remove unwanted (TMP) files.

To access it, go to the **Start** menu and select **All Programs**, then **Accessories**, then **System Tools** and then **Disk Cleanup**. In the dialogue box that appears, with the Disk Cleanup tab selected, select **Temporary files** from the 'Files to delete' window. Make sure only the items you want to delete are checked, then click **OK**.

Disk Cleanup for SYSTEM (C:)

Disk Cleanup | More Options

You can use Disk Cleanup to free up to 556,243 KB of disk space on SYSTEM (C:).

Files to delete:

Downloaded Program Files	0 KB
Temporary Internet Files	74,172 KB
Offline Web Pages	13 KB
Recycle Bin	7,538 KB
Setup Log Files	775 KB

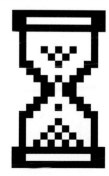

I can't read a document

Find out how to open and read seemingly impenetrable files

As a rule, if you receive a file from another source, such as the Internet, and you do not have the program in which it was created, then you will not be able to open the file.

But there are ways around this problem. Your software may recognise the type of document and be able to convert it. If not, you can ask the sender to supply it in a 'neutral format'. So, for example, a text document saved as 'Text Only' should be readable in any word-processing program (though you cannot retain text styling in this 'no-frills' format). Here are some other ways you can access 'unreadable' documents.

1 If Windows doesn't know how to open a particular file, it displays it as a plain icon. When you double click on the icon you will see a dialogue box asking whether you want to look online to find out which program created the file or if you want to try selecting a program from a list of the ones installed on your computer.

A quick guide to file extensions

File extensions are letter combinations (usually three) that indicate which program created a file. To display the extensions on your files, go to the **Start** menu, then **My Documents**. In the **Tools** menu select **Folder Options**. In the **View** tab, untick the **Hide extensions for known file types** box. Some common extensions are:
● **Text file** .asc .doc .htm .html .msg .txt .wpd
● **Image file** .bmp .eps .gif .jpg .pict .png .tif
● **Sound file** .au .mid .ra .snd .wav

Just as Windows sometimes cannot open a document created on another operating system, other systems can have difficulty reading files created in Windows. To almost guarantee that this does not occur, save documents as 'Plain Text' or 'Rich Text' format. To do this, scroll down the 'Save as type' menu of the Save As dialogue box. Note that this will mean you will lose any complex formatting

2 Windows lists all the programs you have on your PC and asks you which one you want to open the file with. If you know what type of content is in the file – a word processing document, for example – try opening it with a relevant program, such as Microsoft Word.

3 If the file won't open with the program you have selected, try another one. Notepad is able to open most files, but you will often see only an unreadable mass of code and symbols (above). If this happens, close the file without saving.

4 Another option is to launch a program such as Microsoft Word and try to open the file by going to the **File** menu and clicking **Open**. Navigate to the folder containing the file, then choose **All Files** from the 'Files of type' list. Select the file and click **Open**. If this works, go to **Save As** and save the file in the appropriate format.

Opening compressed documents

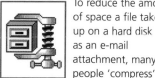

To reduce the amount of space a file takes up on a hard disk or as an e-mail attachment, many people 'compress' them. If you receive a compressed file (often with the file extension '.zip')

you will need the same compression program in order to decompress it and then open it. WinZip is a common compression program. You can download it from the Internet (www.winzip.com) free of charge.

If you don't have the relevant program to decompress a file, ask the sender to mail it again in an uncompressed version.

I'm getting error messages

What to do when your computer warns you there's a problem

When your PC has difficulty carrying out one of your commands it will display an error message. Generally, error messages include a description of the error, a possible reason for it and, if appropriate, a way to resolve the problem. Some error messages are easier to understand than others.

Do not ignore error messages. If you do, you may lose your work or, at worse, make your computer unusable. Follow the on-screen advice, which may mean exiting from the program you are using or restarting your computer. There are many error messages – the ones described here are the most common.

Storage problems

One of the most common error messages appears when Windows detects that your hard disk is getting full and storage space is becoming limited. This can seriously affect the performance of your PC, and may prevent you saving files. It will also limit the amount of space System Restore can use to back up critical data and will disable Virtual Memory.

If 'Not enough disk space' messages appear, use **Disk Cleanup** to delete unnecessary files and create more space. Go to the Start menu, click on **All Programs**, **Accessories**, then **System Tools** and **Disk Cleanup**. In the scroll box and click next to the items you want to delete. Click on **OK** then **Yes** to confirm your choice.

Understanding error messages

Although the wording may vary, most error messages will fall into one of these catagories

Error messages caused by hardware

● Hardware conflict

Many error messages arise from a hardware 'conflict'. This is when two devices try to use the same part of your PC at the same time.

If your hardware seems to be working properly but you still get error messages, a defective or conflicting driver may be the cause. (See page 351 for possible solutions).

If your computer freezes – or 'hangs' – when you try to use a particular device, or if a device refuses to work, this, too, can be the result of a hardware conflict.

● Parity Error, Fatal Exception, or Illegal Operation

These messages usually appear on a screen with a bright blue background. They can be caused by a software error or, especially if you see a Parity Error message, may indicate problems with your PC's memory. If you have just installed new hardware or software that could be the cause too.

Recovery from a blue screen error is an easy task with Windows XP. Simply restart your PC, and as soon as you see the message **Please select the operating system to start**, press **F8** on your keyboard. Then you will be presented with a number of options. Choose **Last Known Good**. This will roll back the system's configuration to a point before it became unstable – for instance, before a conflicting driver or incorrect memory was installed.

Error messages caused by software

● This file is being used by another user

This occurs when you try to open the same document in different programs at the same time. You can either close down the document before opening it in a second program, let Windows tell you when the file is available for editing, or to open a Read-only copy – one that you cannot make changes to.

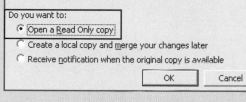

● This file is write protected

You cannot delete, rename or sometimes copy write-protected files. To remove the protection, right-click on the file's icon, go to **Properties** and uncheck the box next to **Read-only** in the General tab.

● Error Deleting File

This happens when you try to delete a file that is open on your Desktop or Taskbar.

● Sharing Violation/You don't have permission to open this file.

This can be caused by having a file open in two programs at the same time, or by a program trying to open a file that is either corrupted or missing.

● File Corruption

Sometimes, a file gets 'mangled' by Windows. The best solution is to replace it from your back-up copy.

● Missing or Out-of-Date Files

This message appears if somebody deletes a file by mistake, or if a program overwrites, deletes or renames a file as it is installed or uninstalled. If the problem is with a program, you need to reinstall it.

Special Windows files – DLLs (Dynamic Link Libraries) are shared by many programs to provide special functions. Unfortunately they can occasionally be deleted or overwritten when you uninstall a program or update it.

What to do if you cannot understand messages

● Windows XP's Help and Support Center will explain most error messages, and suggest solutions.
● Save any opened files. Shut down the program that prompted the message, then restart it.
● If the message reappears, shut down the program (and any others running) and restart your computer (go to the **Start** button, select **Shut Down** then **Restart**).
● If the message occurs again, make a note of what it says and seek expert advice. If the error is prompted by Windows rather than a program, contact your PC dealer. If a program is causing the problem, contact the software manufacturer.

Use Event Logs

Error messages and blue screen reports are saved to documents called Events logs, and can be invaluable to an engineer trying to diagnose problems with your PC. However, left to default settings the logs may miss out crucial information. You can configure them to record much more.

Go to the **Start** menu, then **My Computer**, your **C:** drive, **WINDOWS**, **system32** (take care navigating sytem folders), then look for and double-click on **eventvwr**. Right click **Application**, bring up **Properties** and raise the **Maximum log size** to around 5120KB. Repeat this for the **Security** and **System** logs.

Using anti-virus software

Run specialist packages to preserve or restore your PC's health

Although the spread of computer viruses is often reported in the media, the problem is not as widespread or difficult to deal with as most people think. Simple preventative steps (see page 56), will help you reduce the risk of getting a virus and put you in a better position to eradicate any that you do get.

Anti-virus software

There are many packages available. In general, they detect viruses on storage disks, such as floppies, and files that have been downloaded from the Internet. Such programs stop viruses infecting your PC in the first place.

Most anti-virus packages can be set up to scan every item downloaded to your system, but it's also a good idea to run the program every week or so to examine your whole system.

If a virus does make its way onto your computer, the software will alert you by bringing up a warning on screen. At this point you must use the disinfecting function in the anti-virus program, which will attempt to repair the infected file. This is normally a straightforward process, performed by following the on-screen instructions given by the program. Sometimes, the infected item cannot be repaired. In this case you should delete the file or, in the case of a program, uninstall, then replace it.

Keeping up to date

It is vital to keep your software defences up to date. This doesn't mean having to buy new software. The best anti-virus packages allow you to stay up-to-date by downloading new information from their Web sites. Check your software for details on how to do this.

> *A good anti-virus package such as McAfee VirusScan or Norton AntiVirus is essential. Ask at a local computer store for advice on which package is best for your needs.*

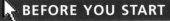

BEFORE YOU START

Bright idea
There are several useful Web sites that offer information about viruses. Some also provide software updates to help you defend your PC from infection. Try www.symantec.com/avcenter/ for news and downloads.

Key word
***Virus** A virus is a computer program whose sole purpose is to get into your PC and cause unwanted and unexpected behaviour, such as erasing files, displaying messages and attacking your PC's set-up.*

Make the software do the work
Without the right software you might never know your PC is infected until it's too late.

The main types of viruses that are likely to infect your computer are 'file viruses', 'macro viruses' and 'boot and partition sector viruses'. Each one attacks different parts of your computer, including your hard disk, programs and document files. Some Web sites may also place small applets (mini-programs) on your system that can have similar highly destructive effects.

Stopping viruses at source
Norton AntiVirus is typical of the effective anti-virus programs now available. You can configure AntiVirus to examine every file downloaded or read from floppy disks

and CDs. It continually checks for known viruses and other harmful software on your system. You can also set the software to regularly check on the Internet for software updates, so you will always be protected quickly against new viruses. If an infected file is located it is 'quarantined' on your system and you will be notified of the best steps to take.

Disinfecting your system once a virus is found

```
KEYB       COM      14986  09/04/91    5:00
KEYBOARD   SYS      34697  09/04/91    5:00
NLSFUNC    EXE       7052  09/04/91    5:00
DISPLAY    SYS      15792  09/04/91    5:00
EGA        CPI      58873  09/04/91    5:00
HIMEM      SYS      11552  09/04/91    5:00
                     8169  09/04/91    5:00
                     5873  09/04/91    5:00
                     0912  09/04/91    5:00
                     8335  09/04/91    5:00
                  2058566 bytes
                 11087872 bytes  free
```

If your software detects a virus you should use the disinfecting or cleaning function in the software to remove or isolate it. If it is a new virus, some anti-virus programs may even send the file to their laboratory for examination.

If an infected file cannot be repaired then it will generally be renamed to prevent it being used again. You will then have the option of deleting it. Files that you delete may need to be replaced. If these are system files

(the files that make up Windows) then you will definitely need to do so. To reinstall program software, see page 359; to reinstall Windows, see page 354.

Worst-case scenario
With proper use of an anti-virus program, you should be able to detect and remove any viruses before they cause really serious damage. Without taking such precautions it is possible, although not likely, that a virus could destroy the contents of your hard disk.

In such a case you will have to restore the hard disk from your original system disks. This is like restoring your computer to its original state, as it was on the day you bought it. The original settings for it will be restored, but you will probably have lost all your documents and data files.

Viruses affect computers in different ways. Some contain messages that appear automatically on screen.

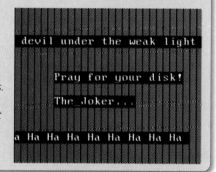

Norton AntiVirus (screenshot)

1 Scan Progress	Scan Progress: Scan for Viruses	
2 Repair Wizard	Scanning for viruses:	
Repair	Current Item	
Quarantine	C:\WINDOWS\system32\drivers\disdn	
Delete	Action	Files
3 Summary	Scanned	202
	Infected	0
	Repaired	0

Hit back at hackers
Top level security packages like Norton's and McAfee's also protect your computer against the threat of hacking – unauthorised entry to your machine using the Internet. With the spread of 'always on' connections hacking has become much easier and more widespread. Setting up a 'firewall' – a barrier to hackers – is simple with these two products. Persistent attackers can also be tracked, providing evidence for possible prosecution.

My text doesn't look right

If your fonts look odd on screen or when printed, the solution is easy

Font problems are rare nowadays, largely because the leading software developers have come together to create new user-friendly technologies such as TrueType and OpenType. Windows XP's default fonts should display and print faultlessly.

Difficulties only arise when additional fonts are installed either by other software programs, or manually, from a free CD for instance. You may find that a font that looks fine on screen prints badly, or not at all. Alternatively your screen display could be terrible, but a document might print superbly.

Don't worry – using Windows XP's troubleshooters and utilities you can solve most typographical problems with ease.

Do you have a problem?

If a font looks strange on screen or when printed, first check whether there really is a problem. Some fonts are specifically designed to look unusual. Wingdings and Zapf Dingbats are made up entirely of quirky characters.

To check how a font should look, go to the **Start** menu, then **Control Panel**, click on **Appearance and Themes** and then on **Fonts** in the left-hand panel. All the fonts installed on your PC will be listed. Double-click on the font in question to bring up a sample of what it should look like. If the sample text shown looks the same as the text in your document, you have simply chosen an unusual-looking font.

The fonts folder icon view indicates what kind of fonts you have; OpenType and TrueType should predominate, but you may also have some PostScript fonts. PostScript fonts need special software – Adobe Type Manager (ATM) – to display correctly. If a PostScript font's screen appearance is irregular or jagged, check www.adobe.com/support/downloads/ for the latest version.

Bright idea
*If you only use TrueType fonts you should never have trouble with text appearing strange. Go to **Start**, click on **Control Panel**, then **Appearance and Themes**, then **Fonts** in the left-hand column. The Fonts window will open. In the **Tools** menu, go to **Folder Options** and click on the **TrueType Fonts** tab. Click in the box next to 'Show only TrueType fonts in the programs on my computer' and then **OK**.*

Bright idea
*Windows XP has a great Printing Troubleshooter. Go to **Start**, **Help and Support**, **Printing and Faxing**, **Fixing a printing problem** and then **Printing Troubleshooter**. Follow the steps to get back on track.*

Solving font software problems
Understanding what different font files do and where they are located is the first stage of problem-solving.

Types of font
The type of font you are using may affect the way it appears on screen or when printed. TrueType fonts are designed to print the same way as they look on-screen, as are OpenType fonts, which are in fact a newer kind of TrueType file.

WST_Engl

abcdefghijklmnopqrstuvwxyz
ABCDEFGHIJKLMNOPQRSTUVWXYZ
123456789.:,;(:*!?')
12 Jackdaws love my big sphinx of quartz. 123456
18 Jackdaws love my big sphinx of quartz. 123456
24 Jackdaws love my big sphinx of quartz. 123456
36 Jackdaws love my big sp
48 Jackdaws

O Latha	**TT** Copperplate Gothic Bold	**A** Modern
OpenType	TrueType	PostScript

PostScript and printer-only fonts can look slightly different on screen to how they appear when printed. PostScript fonts used without ATM typically display jagged edges, particularly at larger point sizes. Some printers (notably laser printers) use printer fonts, which are stored on the printer itself, to speed up the print process. Problems can develop when the font you are using on screen, and its equivalent on the printer, don't match. Most printer driver options will allow you to over-ride printer fonts.

Click on **Start**, then **Control Panel**, **Printers and Other Hardware**, **Printers and Faxes**. Right-click on your printer driver icon and select **Printing Preferences**. All printers are different but you should find an option marked **Download as softfont**. Select that, or check the box next to it, and from that point on your printer will only use the same fonts as in your documents.

Common difficulties

You have been e-mailed a Word document that prints badly
Check in the font box on the toolbar to find the name of the font that prints incorrectly. Then click a section of text that doesn't use that font, or add a few words in a system font such as 'Arial'. Return to the font box, click in it and scroll down to check whether the name of the problem font appears. If it doesn't, then the font is not installed on your system. Either install the font on your system (see right) or highlight the text and select a new font from the font box.

You can't print the Euro symbol
Some older fonts may not have the Euro symbol. Call it up on a standard European keyboard by pressing **Alt Gr** (to the right of the space bar) and typing **4**. For US PCs, hold down the **ALT** key and type **0128** using the number key pad. Non-EU machines can use free fonts available from www.adobe.com/type/eurofont.html that consist entirely of the Euro symbol.

Managing fonts

Removing fonts
Fonts may become damaged, or non-standard fonts may have been incorrectly constructed in the first place. If every document using a particular typeface has problems you may wish to remove the suspect font. Go to **Start**, **Control Panel**, **Appearance and Themes**, **Fonts**. Click on the font you want to remove. In the **File** menu, click **Delete**. You system will ask 'Are you sure you want to delete these fonts?' Click **Yes**.

Installing fonts
To install or reinstall a font, first insert the disk or CD-ROM containing it. Go to **Start**, **Control Panel**, **Appearance and Themes**, **Fonts**. On the **File** menu click **Install New Font**. In the **Add Fonts** dialogue box click on the arrow beside the **Drives** box and select the drive containing new fonts. In the **Folders** section, scroll through and double-click on the folder that contains the font. Then click on your chosen font, then on **OK**.

Viewing foreign text
Multilingual users will probably want to view foreign Web sites – in the past any language using unusual characters or pictograms, such as Russian or Japanese, could cause problems. Nowadays, Internet Explorer, used in conjunction with Windows XP, will breeze through any linguistic complexities, even right-to-left reading languages.

In most cases Windows XP will have already set up your system to view international texts such as Russian and Hebrew – if not, when you load a web page with unusual characters Explorer will prompt you to insert the Windows XP installer disk, to automatically install the correct files. If the files are not available on your CD, Explorer may suggest downloading material from the Microsoft Web site.

Problems with passwords

You can unlock your computer even if you forget your password

In Windows XP it's easy to let several different people use the same PC, each with their own set of files and folders, and preferences for Windows' appearance. You can set a password to protect your files, but the level of security is not so great that forgetting a password is a disaster. As long as the user with administration rights knows their password, they can get you back in. You can also create a special password reset disk that gives you access. Even if you have not created the reset disk, technical support helplines can talk you through relatively simple ways to get back into your PC.

If you need real security for your work, there are plenty of reasonably-priced programs you can buy that offer much stronger password protection. However, they are not as forgiving if you forget your password!

Create a password reset disk
Use Windows XP's utilities to create this handy backup device.

Getting started
Once you have started a new user account, and chosen a password, you can create a password reset disk. This floppy disk can be used at a later stage if your forget your log-in password.

Go to **Start**, **Control Panel**, **User Accounts** then click on your account name. On the next panel you will see **Prevent a forgotten password** in the left hand column. If you don't see it, you may have clicked on the wrong user – you can only create a disk for the user currently logged in. Shut down your PC and log in again if necessary.

Clicking on **Prevent a forgotten password** brings up the **Forgotten Password Wizard**. Insert a blank floppy disk, follow the Wizard's instructions, and you will soon have a disk that you can use as a 'key' to unlock your PC.

Bright idea
If you need tighter security check out the utilities at www.tucows.com/system/usermanage95.html. However, take care. If you forget a password for a high-security program you risk being locked out of your PC.

Watch out
Using one password for many applications is convenient, but it means that a single breach of security could render all your protection useless.

What to do if you forget your password

There is no need to panic if you forget your password. Load your password reset disk and you'll be up and running in no time.

If you have a reset disk
Simply start your PC as usual and when asked for your password type in a few random letters, then click on the **green arrow**. You will be asked if you have forgotten your password, if you want to see your password 'hint', and also if you want to use your password reset disk. If your hint does not remind you of

your password, click on the link **use your password reset disk** and follow the instructions on screen.

If you don't have a reset disk
There are other ways to enter a password-protected system. If another user has an account set up on the machine you use, ask them to log on then go to **Start**, **Run**, and enter 'control userpasswords2', then click **OK**. Click on your User Name, and then click on **Reset Password** and choose a new password. The user that does this, however, must have administrator rights to be able to change passwords.

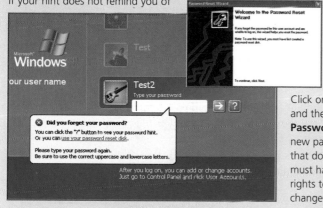

Forget your passwords safely
Even a relatively light user of a computer and the Internet soon finds that they build up a difficult-to-remember list of passwords and usernames for banking, shopping and logging on to websites. However, there are shareware programs (ones you can download and try before you buy) that can help out. The programs store all your passwords for you, and are activated by one single password – the only one that you will have to remember.

Two of the best known utilities are Password Tracker, available from www.clrpc.com and Password Agent from www.moonsoftware.com. Both programs are modestly priced and each is approved by Microsoft.

Shortcut	User ID	Password
http://www.chicagot... C:\Program Files\In...	lindasman	cubs&sox
http://www.irnet.co... C:\Program Files\M... C:\Program Files\M...	david87	Gv4z?%W
http://edit.my.yaho... C:\QUICKENW\QW...	dave	linda457 mYfinancE
http://www.digits.co... C:\WINNT\Profiles...	dave@t... davidsp	gFtCwo4I dave-linda

Beef up security
If you want to hide your files and applications from prying eyes, at home or in the office, there are a number of programs which give differing levels of protection.

User management systems replicate Windows XP's own password-protected log in system, but add much tougher controls. Passwords are non-recoverable, different levels of access can be permitted for different users, system use can be monitored and recorded.

File and folder encryption systems do not block users out – they simply allow you to encrypt specific parts of your disk so that no one can read your personal files and folders. Different levels of encryption are available – the strongest is practically unbreakable, so be sure to remember your password. Travellers please note: The possession and use of strong encryption software is lawful throughout the EU and North America, but is strictly controlled in much of the Middle East, the former USSR, China and other countries.

Tips for effective passwords
An effective password is one that cannot be easily guessed. For this reason make sure your password adheres to several of the following:
● It is at least six characters long.
● It contains a mix of capital letters and lowercase letters.
● It contains at least one digit or special character such as a punctuation mark.
● It cannot easily be guessed (for example, do not use your child's, spouse's or pet's name).
● It is changed frequently.

A

A: The floppy disk drive on a PC. In speech it is referred to as the 'A drive'. See *Floppy disk*.

Accessories Mini-programs, such as Calculator, Notepad or Wordpad, built into Windows to perform simple tasks.

Active window The window you are working in. To activate a window, click on it and it will jump to the front of your screen, in front of any other open windows. See *Window*.

ADSL Asymmetric Digital Subscriber Line. A way of getting broadband Internet access through a normal telephone line. See *Broadband*

Alt key A key on the keyboard which gives commands when pressed in combination with other keys.

Application program A piece of software that performs specific kinds of tasks. For example, Microsoft Word is a word processing application program. See *Program*, *Software*.

Archive To transfer files to a separate storage system, such as a Zip disk.

Attachment A file such as a picture or spreadsheet that is sent with an e-mail message.

Audio file A file containing a digital recording of sound. In Windows, audio files usually have '.wav' after their file name. See *Digital*.

B

Back-up A duplicate copy of a file, made in case of accidental loss or damage to the original. Back-ups can be made onto a second hard drive fitted to the computer, or on to removeable media like Zip disks.

Benchmark software Standard, most widely used program packages. This book uses Microsoft® Office XP and Microsoft® Works 6 as its benchmark software. One or other of the two packages comes preinstalled on many PCs.

BIOS Basic Input/Output System. Instructions that control the computer's hardware at the most basic level. The BIOS tells the operating system which hardware to expect to come into operation and how it is arranged.

Bit The smallest unit of computer memory, Bit is a contraction of 'binary digit'. Its value can be only 0 or 1. All computers use the binary system to process data.

Bitmap An on-screen image made up of tiny dots, or pixels. See *Pixel*.

Bits per second (bps) A measurement for the speed with which data can be sent to or from a computer via a modem.

Boot or boot up To switch on the computer.

Broadband High-speed Internet access via either an ADSL, Cable or Satellite connection.

Bug An accidental error or fault in a computer program. Bugs may cause programs to crash, which can lead to data loss.

Button An on-screen image that can be clicked on using the mouse. Clicking on a button performs a function, such as opening a dialogue box or confirming an action.

Byte A unit of computer memory, made up of eight bits. It takes one byte of memory to store a single character, such as a letter of the alphabet.

C

C: The hard drive of a PC, where programs and documents are stored. In speech it is referred to as the 'C drive'.

Cable Broadband Internet access that is delivered via a cable television network.

Cache A section of high-speed memory that stores data recently used by the PC's processor, thereby increasing the speed at which that data can be accessed again.

CD-ROM Compact Disc Read Only Memory. A storage device, identical in appearance to a normal CD, containing up to 650 MB of data. Most software programs come on CD-ROM. CD-ROMs are usually inserted into and accessed from the 'D drive' on the PC.

CD-R/CD-RW Compact Disc Recordable/Rewritable. CDs that can be written to in a special type of disc drive (sometimes called a 'burner'). CD-Rs can only be written to once, CD-RWs can be rewritten many times over.

Cell A small rectangular section of a spreadsheet or database, into which text or figures are entered. Click on a cell to make it active, ready for entering data.

Chip A device that processes information at the most basic level within a computer. A processor chip carries out calculations and a memory chip stores data.

Click To press and release the left mouse button once. Used to select menu and dialogue box options and toolbar buttons. See also *Right Click*.

Clip Art Graphic images that can be inserted into text-based documents from the Clip Art gallery and then resized and manipulated.

Clipboard When text is cut or copied from a document it is stored on the Clipboard. The Clipboard has a viewer option which enables you to store several pieces of cut or copied data at once. You can put the current Clipboard material back into as many documents as you like using the paste command. See *Copy*, *Cut*, and *Paste*.

Close A menu option, usually found under the File menu, that shuts the active document, but not the program. A document can also be closed by clicking the close button in its top right-hand corner.

CMOS Complementary Metal Oxide Semiconductor. A type of memory chip that stores the computer's configuration settings and the date and time. To protect its data, this memory is maintained by battery. See *Configuration*.

Compressed files Files that have been temporarily condensed so they use less memory and can be copied or downloaded in a fraction of the time it would take for the full-sized version.

Configuration The settings used to ensure hardware or software runs as the user requires.

Control Panel Any adjustments made to your system or its settings are made via the Control Panel. In the Control Panel you change the way your Desktop looks, add new hardware or alter your PC's sound output.

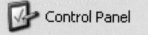

Copy To make a duplicate of a file, folder, image or section of text.

CPU Central Processing Unit. The brain of your PC which carries out millions of arithmetic and control functions every second.

Crash Your PC has crashed if it has stopped working, the screen has 'frozen' and there is no response to keyboard or mouse commands. A crash usually requires you to restart the computer.

Cursor A marker, usually a flashing vertical line, that indicates where the next letter or digit typed in will appear in the document.

Cut To remove selected text and/or images to the Clipboard, where they are stored for later use.

D

D: The CD-ROM drive on a PC. In speech it is referred to as the 'D drive'. See *CD-ROM*.

Data Any information processed by, or stored on, a computer.

Database A program used for storing, organising and sorting

information. Each entry is called a record and each category of information held in a record is called a field.

Default Settings and preferences automatically adopted by your PC for any program when none are specified by the user.

Defragmenter A program which 'tidies' files on the hard disk. When a file is saved to the hard disk, Windows may not be able to save all parts of it in the same place, so its elements become fragmented. This makes the retrieval of the file much slower. The 'defrag' program solves this problem by regrouping all related data in the same place.

Delete To remove a file, folder, image or piece of text completely. If you accidentally delete something from a document you can undelete it using the Edit/Undo function or the Undo toolbar button.

Desktop When Windows has finished starting up, it presents you with a set of icons on screen. The icons represent the items you would find in an office, such as files, a wastebin and a briefcase. These icons, together with the Taskbar and Start button are known collectively as the Desktop. See *Icon* and *Taskbar*.

Dialogue box A window that appears on screen displaying a message from the program currently in use. This usually asks for preferences or information to be input by the user.

Dial-up connection The process of accessing another computer via a telephone line.

Digital Data that exists in binary number form as '0's and '1's. Computers process digital data.

Digital image An image stored in number format, that can be transferred to hard disks or removable storage disks, displayed on screen or printed.

Disk A device for storing digital data. A hard disk is composed of a stack of rigid disks; a floppy disk has just one flexible plastic disk.

Disk tools Programs that manage and maintain the hard disk, ensuring data is stored efficiently and that the hard disk runs at optimum speed.

Document A single piece of work created in a program. Also referred to as a file. See *File*.

DOS Disk Operating System. The standard operating system for PCs before the advent of *Windows*.

Dots per inch (dpi) The number of dots that a printer can print on one square inch of paper. The more dots, the greater the detail and the better quality the printout.

Double-click To press and release the left mouse button twice in quick succession.

Download To copy a file or program from another computer to your own. For example, when you collect e-mail from an Internet Service Provider, you are downloading it.

Drag A mouse action used to highlight text, reshape objects or move an object or file. To move an object with the mouse pointer, for instance, click on it and keep the left mouse button held down. Move the mouse pointer and the object moves with it.

Drive A device that holds a disk. The drive has a motor that spins the disk, and a head that reads it – like the stylus on a record player.

Driver Software that translates instructions from Windows into a form that can be understood by a hardware device such as a printer.

DVD Digital Versatile Disc. A CD-like disc that can store 4.7 GB or more of information – several times more data than a CD-ROM.

E

E-mail Electronic Mail. Messages sent from one computer to another through the Internet.

Error message A small window that appears on screen warning the user that a fault has occurred and, where appropriate, suggesting action to remedy it.

Expansion card An add-on piece of hardware that fits into the system unit and expands the functions of the PC – for example, a sound card.

External hardware Additional computer equipment, such as a printer or scanner, attached by cable to the system unit.

F

Field A category of information in a database, such as Name, Address or Telephone Number.

▶

File Any item stored on a computer, for example, a program, a document or an image.

File extension A code, usually of three letters, that appears at the end of a file name to indicate its format (what type of file it is).

File format The way in which files created by different programs are saved. This differs from program to program, so that one program may have difficulty reading files created by another. Common file formats are listed below:

Text	.asc .doc .htm .html .msg .txt .wpd
Image	.bmp .eps .gif .jpg .pict .png .tif
Sound	.au .mid .ra .snd .wav
Video	.avi .mov .mpg .qt
Compressed	.arc .arj .gz .hqx .sit .tar .z .zip
Program	.bat .com .exe

Flash A plug-in that enables animations and games to play within a browser window.

Floppy disk A portable data storage device. Each 3.5 inch disk can hold up to 1.44 MB of information. Often used to back up data from the hard disk. See *Hard disk*.

Folder An electronic storage compartment used to keep related files and relevant documents in the same place on the hard disk.

Font A particular style of type, such as Helvetica, Arial or Times New Roman. Most fonts can be displayed and printed in different sizes. They can also be styled in bold or italic, or with other effects.

Format To alter the appearance of a document – for example, its typography, layout, and so on.

Freeware Programs, usually produced by hobby programmers, for which users do not pay a fee. Freeware can often be downloaded from the Internet.

Function keys The 12 keys (labelled F1, F2, and so on) at the top of the keyboard. Their function depends on which program is in use. So, for instance, Shift + F7 in Word will call up the Thesaurus, and F12 will call up the Save As dialogue box.

G

.GIF file Graphics Interchange Format. This is a commonly used format for storing images and bitmapped colour graphics, especially on the Internet.

Gigabyte (GB) A unit of memory capacity. A single gigabyte is 1000 megabytes which is equivalent to about 200 copies of the Bible.

Graphics Pictures, photographs, illustrations, Clip Art and any other type of image.

H

Hard disk A computer's high-speed storage device. It contains the operating system, the programs and all created files. The hard disk is referred to as the 'C drive'.

Hardware The physical parts of a computer, including the system unit, monitor, keyboard, mouse and other devices such as the printer, scanner and speakers.

Header The area at the top of a page in a document. Text entered in the header (such as a title) appears on every page of the document.

Help key Usually the F1 key. Pressed to access advice and information on how to perform the task the user is currently engaged in.

Highlight To select a word, a section of text or a group of cells, by clicking and dragging over them using the mouse.

I

Icon A graphic representation of a file or a function, which is designed to be easily recognisable as the item it represents. For example the printer icon on the toolbar accesses the print function.

Import To bring an element from another file, such as a photograph, illustration or Clip Art image, into the active document.

Inkjet printer A printer that works by squirting tiny drops of ink onto the surface of the paper.

Install To copy a program on to the hard disk and then set it up so it is ready for use. Programs are usually installed from a CD-ROM.

Internet Millions of computers throughout the world linked together via telephone and cable lines. Computer users can communicate with each other and exchange information over the Internet for the price of a local telephone call.

ISP Internet Service Provider. A company that provides connection to the Internet (compare *OSP*).

J

JPEG Joint Photographics Experts Group. A compressed format for storing images so that they take up less space on a computer.

K

Keyboard shortcut A method of issuing a command using a combination of keystrokes. To the practised user, this is quicker than manipulating the mouse.

Kilobyte (KB) A unit of memory capacity. A single kilobyte is equivalent to 1000 bytes. A short letter created in Word uses about 20 KB. See *Gigabyte, Megabyte*.

L

Landscape See *Orientation*.

Laptop A portable computer.

Laser printer A printer that uses a laser beam to etch images onto a drum and then transfers the image to paper. The reproduction quality is usually higher than with an inkjet printer. See *Inkjet printer*.

Launcher A window in some software suites, such as Microsoft Works, through which the suite's various programs and 'mini programs' can be opened.

Logging on The process of accessing computers or files using a username and password or other instructions. Some web sites also require users to log on.

M

Maximise To increase the size of a window so that it fills the entire screen. The Maximise button is the middle button in the set of three in the top right-hand corner of a window. Once used, this button becomes a Restore button. Click on it to restore the window to its original size.

Megabyte (MB) A unit of memory capacity. A single megabyte is 1000 kilobytes, which is equivalent to a 400 page novel.

Memory A computer's capacity for storing information. See also *RAM* and *ROM*.

Menu bar The line of menu options that runs along the top of a window. When a menu is selected, you can access its entire list of options through a drop-down menu.

MIDI Musical Instrument Digital Interface. A universal standard language by which specially adapted musical instruments communicate with computers. MIDI cable leads are required to connect the instrument to the computer.

Minimise To reduce a window to a button on the Taskbar. The Minimise button is the left button in the set of three in the top right-hand corner of a window. To restore the window to the screen, click on its button on the Taskbar.

Modem A device that converts electronic signals from a computer into sound signals that can be transmitted by phone then reconverted by another modem into the original electronic data. An ADSL 'modem' is misnamed: it really works as a router. See *router.*

Monitor The viewing screen on which you see your computer's files. Images are made up of thousands of tiny red, green and blue dots called pixels that combine to form colours.

Motherboard The circuit board which houses a PC's central processing unit (see *CPU*), some memory and slots into which expansion cards can be fitted. See *Chip, Expansion card* and *Memory.*

Mouse pointer A small arrow on screen that moves when the mouse is moved. Other representations of the pointer, depending on the program being used and the type of action being carried out, include a pointing hand, a pen, a cross and a double-headed arrow. When you click in a text document, the cursor will appear. See *Cursor.*

My Computer An icon found in the Start menu of a PC running Windows XP. Click on the icon to access everything stored in the system on the hard drive, floppy drive and CD-ROM drive. See *Icon.*

My Documents A folder icon found in the Start menu. Each user has a My Documents folder for his or her files. See *Icon.*

My Music The default folder for storing music files in Windows XP.

My Pictures The default folder in Windows XP for storing photographs and other images.

N

Network The connection of several computers and printers so that they can share files and messages.

O

On-line The status of a computer that is actively connected via a modem to the Internet. Also used as a general term for people who are able to connect to the Internet. See *Internet.*

Open To look inside a file or folder to view its contents. To open a file or folder, either double-click on it, right-click on it and select Open from the pop-up menu, or select it, go to the File menu and click Open

Operating system The software that controls the running of a computer, allowing, for example, programs to communicate with hardware devices such as printers. Windows is now the most popular operating system for PCs.

Orientation An option available when creating a document. Users can choose to set up a page as either Landscape (of greater width than height) or Portrait (of greater height than width), depending on how they want the final version of the document to appear.

OSP Online Service Provider. A company that provides not only Internet access (compare *ISP*), but also additional content, such as shopping, entertainment and leisure channels, chat rooms and newsgroups. OSPs include AOL, Compuserve and MSN.

P

Page break The point at which one page ends and another begins. Insert a page break into a Microsoft Word document by pressing the Ctrl key and, keeping it pressed down, pressing the Enter key.

Parallel port A socket at the rear of a system unit that allows you to connect a peripheral device.

Paste The insertion into a document of text or other data that has previously been cut or copied.

PC-compatible Software or hardware that will work on a standard PC.

PCI slot A spare space inside a PC for extra expansion cards, such as a sound or graphics card.

Peripheral A device such as a scanner that can be connected to a PC, but is not vital to its function.

Pixel An individual dot on a computer screen. The number of pixels horizontally and vertically on the screen determines the level of detail and quality of image that can be displayed. This can be set and altered by the user.

Plug-ins Programs that are needed to open and run certain files, such as video clips or sound files. Web sites often provide plug-ins for visitors to download, so that they are able to view the entire site. See *Download.*

Point size Measurement used to describe the size of fonts. For example, this page is in 9 point; newspaper headlines are usually between 36 and 72 point. ▶

Port A socket at the rear of the system unit that allows users to connect a peripheral device to the PC.

Portrait See *Orientation*.

Printer driver A piece of software that helps Windows to communicate with the printer. See *Driver*.

Print Preview On-screen display that shows users exactly how the active document will look when printed.

Processor The central processing unit (CPU) of a PC. See *Chip, CPU*.

Program A product that allows the user to interact with the computer's hardware to perform a specific type of task. For instance, a word processing program allows the user to direct the computer in all aspects of handling and presenting text. See *Application, Software*.

Prompt A window that appears on screen to remind users that additional information is required before an action can proceed.

Properties The attributes of a file or folder, such as its creation date and format. Some Properties, such as the author's name, can be altered.

R

RAM Random Access Memory. The memory used for the temporary storage of information on active documents and programs.

Record An individual entry in a database comprising several categories of information. For example, an address book database comprises entries – or records – each of which has a name, address and telephone number.

Recycle Bin A Desktop feature that allows you to delete files. To rescue or 'recycle' a file, drag it back out of the bin. To delete a file completely, right-click and select Empty Recycle Bin.

Right click To press and release the right mouse button once. Right clicking often calls up a pop up menu and is often a shortcut to various actions. See also *Click*.

Resolution The degree of detail on a screen or a printed document. It is measured in dots per inch (dpi). The more dots per square inch, the greater the detail.

ROM Read Only Memory. Memory chips used by the computer for storing basic details about the PC, such as *BIOS*.

Router Device that links a local or home network of computers to a remote network, such as the Internet. See *Internet*.

Run command A Windows feature that allows you to type in the name of the program you wish to use, or the DOS command you wish to execute. To enter a command, go to the Start menu and click on Run.

S

Save To commit a document to the computer's memory. To do so, press the Ctrl + 'S' keys, or click on the Save toolbar button or go to the File menu and click on Save.

Save As A way of saving a file under a different name or format. If the file was previously saved under a different name or format, that version will remain unchanged. This

is useful for saving an edited file, while still keeping the original.

Scanner A device for converting images on paper into electronic images that can then be manipulated and reproduced by a PC. See *Digital, Digital image*.

Screensaver A picture that appears on-screen when the PC is left idle for a specified time.

Scroll To move through the contents of a window or menu vertically or horizontally.

Search A program that searches a PC for a file, if given information such as the file name or creation date.

Search engines Huge databases on the World Wide Web that are used to locate information on the Internet. They can look for either key words or phrases, or for categories, then sub-categories.

Select To choose a file, folder, image, piece of text or any other item, by clicking on it or highlighting it, before manipulating it in some way. For example, selecting some text before styling it.

Serial port A socket at the rear of the system unit where peripheral devices are connected. Some PCs have two serial ports, identified as COM1 and COM2. Compare *Parallel port*.

Shareware Programs, or reduced versions of programs, that can be sampled for free for a limited period. Users must then purchase the program to continue to use it.

Shortcut An icon on the Desktop that links to a file, folder or program stored on the hard disk. It is created to provide quicker access

to the file, and looks identical to the icon of the linked item, except that it has a small arrow in the bottom left-hand corner.

Software Programs that allow users to perform specific functions, such as to draw up accounts. Microsoft Excel and Microsoft Outlook are examples of software. See *Application, Program*.

Software suite A collection of programs that come in a single package, often supplied when a PC is bought. For example, Microsoft Works is a software suite that includes word processing, database and spreadsheet programs.

Sound card A device that lets users record, play and edit sound files. Fits into an expansion slot within the system unit. See *Sound file*.

Sound file A file containing audio data. To hear the sound, double-click on the file (you will need speakers and a sound card).

Spreadsheet A document for storing and calculating numerical data. Spreadsheets are used mainly for financial planning and accounting.

Start button The button on the left of the Taskbar through which users can access the Start menu and its options, which include Programs or Help. It is sometimes referred to as the Windows button.

Status bar A bar that appears along the bottom of program windows, giving users information about the document being worked on.

Styling Altering the appearance of the content of a file. For example, by making text bold (heavier-looking and more distinct) or italic (slanting to the right), or by changing its colour and size. See *Format*.

Super disk A portable storage device similar in appearance to a floppy disk. Each disk can store up to 240MB of data. A super-disk drive can also read floppy disks. See also *Floppy disk, Jaz disk, Zip disk*.

System software The software that operates the PC, managing its hardware and programs. Windows is the system software for PCs.

System unit The rectangular box-shaped part of the PC that contains the hard disk, the CPU, memory and sockets for connections to peripheral devices.

T

Tab A function used for setting and pre-setting the position of text.

Tab key A key on the keyboard

used to tabulate text, to move between cells in spreadsheets, or to move from one database field to the next.

Taskbar A bar usually situated along the bottom of the screen in Windows that displays the Start button and buttons for all the programs and documents that are currently open. The Taskbar can be moved to any of the four sides of the screen by clicking on it and dragging it to a new location.

Task Wizard See *Wizard*.

Template A format for saving a document, such as a letterhead, the basic elements of which you regularly want to use. When you open a template, a copy of it appears for you to work on, while the template itself remains unaltered for further use.

TFT (Thin Film Transistor) A type of LCD (Liquid Crystal Display) screen used on laptop computers and flat screen monitors. TFT screens are brighter and crisper than earlier types of LCDs.

Tile To reduce in size a group of open windows and then arrange them so that they can all be seen on screen at once.

Toolbar A bar or window containing clickable buttons used to issue commands or access functions. For example, spreadsheet programs have a toolbar that contains buttons that are clicked on to perform calculations or add decimal places. Other toolbars include ones for dealing with pictures or drawing. See *Taskbar*.

U

Undo A function in some programs that allows you to reverse tasks. Word, for example, also has a Redo option.

Uninstall To remove programs from the PC's hard disk. Software is available for uninstalling programs that do not contain an inbuilt uninstall option.

Upgrade To improve the performance or specification of a PC by adding new hardware, such

as a higher capacity disk drive, or software. See *Hardware, Software*.

URL Uniform Resource Locator. A standard style used for all Internet addresses on the World Wide Web. The first part of the URL, such as www.yahoo.com, indicates the location of a computer on the Internet. Anything that follows, such as /myhome/mypage.htm, gives a location of a particular file on that computer.

USB Universal Serial Bus. A hardware connector that allows users to plug a wide range of USB devices into a computer without having to restart. See *Hardware*.

Utilities Software that assists in certain computer functions, such as uninstalling and virus-scanning.

V

View A menu through which users can change the way a file is displayed on screen. For example, in a Works database users can choose to see a document in List, Form or Form Design View.

Virus A program designed to damage a computer system. Viruses can be 'caught' through floppy disks or through programs downloaded from the Internet.

W

WiFi Popular name for IEEE 802.11b, a standard for wireless networks suitable for use in the home.

Window Each program or file on your PC can be viewed and worked on in its own self-contained area of

screen called a Window. All windows have their own menu bar, through which users can issue commands. Several windows can be open at once on the Desktop.

Windows The most popular operating system for PCs, which allows users to run many programs at once and open files on screen in windows. See *Operating system*.

Windows Explorer A program that allows users to view the contents of a PC in a single window.

Wizard A tool within a program which guides users through the process of customising a pre-designed document.

WordArt A graphic text image that can be customised and imported into a document.

Word processing Text-based tasks on the PC, such as writing letters.

World Wide Web The part of the Internet, composed of millions of linked web pages, that can be viewed using web browsing software. Other functions of the Internet such as e-mail do not count as part of the World Wide Web. See *Internet*.

Z

Zip disk A portable storage device that is capable of storing up to 250MB of information. Zip disks require a separate drive.

Zip file A file that has been compressed with the WinZip compression program. The term is not related to Zip drives or disks. ∎

►

▶

W

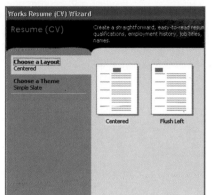

END USER LICENCE AGREEMENT FOR THE CD-ROM

IMPORTANT: CAREFULLY READ THIS LICENCE BEFORE USING THIS PRODUCT. INSTALLING, COPYING, OR OTHERWISE USING THIS PRODUCT INDICATES YOUR ACKNOWLEDGMENT THAT YOU HAVE READ THIS LICENCE AND AGREE TO BE BOUND BY AND COMPLY WITH ITS TERMS. IF YOU DO NOT AGREE, RETURN THE PRODUCT TO THE READER'S DIGEST ASSOCIATION LTD, WITHIN 14 DAYS OF THE DATE YOU ACQUIRED IT FOR A FULL REFUND. THIS LICENCE AGREEMENT IS YOUR PROOF OF LICENCE. PLEASE TREAT IT AS VALUABLE PROPERTY.

A. LICENCE:

The Reader's Digest Association Ltd provides you with storage media containing a computer program, computer software, including its code, objects including their API's as well as any images, photographs, templates, animations, video, audio, music, text and "applets" incorporated into the software, the accompanying printed materials, a Licence, and "on-line" or electronic documentation (together called the "Product") and we grant you a licence to use the Product in accordance with the terms of this Licence. Any supplemental supporting materials provided to you as part of support services provided by The Reader's Digest Association Ltd for the Product shall be considered part of the Product and subject to the terms and conditions of this Licence. The copyright and all other rights to the Product shall remain with the Reader's Digest Association Ltd or the licensors. You must reproduce any copyright or other notice marked on the Product on all copies you make.

B. YOU MAY:

1. install and use one copy of the Product on a single computer. You may also make and use a second copy of the Product on a home or portable computer provided that copy is never loaded in the RAM of the home or portable computer at the same time as it is loaded in the RAM of the primary computer.
2. store or install a copy of the Product on a storage device, such as a network server, used only to install or run the Product on your other computers over an internal network; however, you must acquire and dedicate a licence for each separate computer on which the Product is installed or run from the storage device.
3. make one copy of the Product for archive or backup purposes.
4 use the ClipArt and or Photo Images only if you comply with the terms set out in the Guidelines for the Use of ClipArt and Professional Photo Images below.
5. transfer the Product to someone else only if you assign all of your rights under this Licence, cease all use of the Product, erase or destroy any copy (including the hard disk copy) made in support of your use of the Product, and ensure that the person to whom you wish to transfer the Product agrees to the terms of this Licence.

C. YOU MAY NOT:

1. use the Product or make copies of it except as permitted in this Licence.
2. translate, reverse engineer, decompile, or disassemble the Product except to the extent the foregoing restriction is expressly prohibited by applicable law.
3. rent, lease, assign, or transfer the Product except as set out in paragraph B above.
4. modify the Product or merge all or any part of the Product with another program.
5. redistribute the fonts or sound files included with the Product.
6. separate the component parts of the Product for use on more than one computer.

D. TERM:

This Licence shall remain in effect only for so long as you are in compliance with the terms and conditions of this agreement. This Licence will terminate if you fail to comply with any of its terms or conditions. You agree, upon termination, to destroy all copies of the Product. The Limitations of Warranties and Liability set out below shall continue in force even after any termination.

E. LIMITATION OF WARRANTIES AND LIABILITY:

EXCEPT FOR THE EXPRESS WARRANTY ABOVE, THE PRODUCT IS PROVIDED ON AN "AS IS" BASIS, WITHOUT ANY OTHER WARRANTIES OR CONDITIONS, EXPRESS OR IMPLIED, INCLUDING, BUT NOT LIMITED TO, WARRANTIES OF MERCHANTABLE QUALITY, SATISFACTORY QUALITY, MERCHANTABILITY OR FITNESS FOR A PARTICULAR PURPOSE, OR THOSE ARISING BY LAW, STATUTE, USAGE OF TRADE, COURSE OF DEALING OR OTHERWISE. THE ENTIRE RISK AS TO THE RESULTS AND PERFORMANCE OF THE PRODUCT IS ASSUMED BY YOU. NEITHER WE NOR OUR DEALERS OR SUPPLIERS SHALL HAVE ANY LIABILITY TO YOU OR ANY OTHER PERSON OR ENTITY FOR ANY INDIRECT, INCIDENTAL, SPECIAL, OR CONSEQUENTIAL DAMAGES WHATSOEVER, INCLUDING, BUT NOT LIMITED TO, LOSS OF REVENUE OR PROFIT, LOST OR DAMAGED DATA OR OTHER COMMERCIAL OR ECONOMIC LOSS, EVEN IF WE HAVE BEEN ADVISED OF THE POSSIBILITY OF SUCH DAMAGES, OR THEY ARE FORESEEABLE. WE ARE ALSO NOT RESPONSIBLE FOR CLAIMS BY A THIRD PARTY. OUR MAXIMUM AGGREGATE LIABILITY TO YOU AND THAT OF OUR DEALERS AND SUPPLIERS SHALL NOT EXCEED THE AMOUNT PAID BY YOU FOR THE PRODUCT. THE LIMITATIONS IN THIS SECTION SHALL APPLY WHETHER OR NOT THE ALLEGED BREACH OR DEFAULT IS A BREACH OF A FUNDAMENTAL CONDITION OR TERM OR A FUNDAMENTAL BREACH.

F. GENERAL:

This Licence is the entire agreement superseding any other agreement or discussions, oral or written, and may not be changed except by a signed agreement. This Licence shall be governed by and construed in accordance with the laws of England, excluding that body of law applicable to choice of law and excluding the United Nations Convention on Contracts for the International Sale of Goods and any legislation implementing such Convention, if otherwise applicable. If any provision of this Licence is declared by a Court of competent jurisdiction to be invalid, illegal, or unenforceable, such a provision shall be severed from the Licence and the other provisions shall remain in full force and effect.

GUIDELINES FOR THE USE OF CLIPART, PHOTO OBJECTS AND PHOTOGRAPHIC IMAGES

This product contains numerous ClipArt and Photo Images (collectively referred to as the "Images") which are licenced from a third-party. As a user of this product you are free to use, modify and publish the Images as you wish subject to the restrictions set out below. If you are uncertain as to whether your intended use is in compliance with the Guidelines set out below, we recommend that you seek legal advice.

A. YOU MAY, subject to any restrictions set out below:

1. incorporate any Image(s) into your own original work and publish, display and distribute your work in any media. You may not, however, resell, sublicence or otherwise make available the Image(s) for use or distribution separately or detached from a product or Web page. For example, the Image(s) may be used as part of a Web page design, but may not be made available for downloading separately or in a format designed or intended for permanent storage or re-use by others. Similarly, clients may be provided with copies of the Image(s) (including digital files) as an integral part of a work product, but may not be provided with the Image(s) or permitted to use the Image(s) separately or as part of any other product.
2. make one (1) copy of the Image(s) for backup or archival purposes.

B. YOU MAY NOT:

1. create scandalous, obscene, defamatory or immoral works using the Image(s) nor use the Image(s) for any other purpose which is prohibited by law.
2. use or permit the use of the Image(s) or any part thereof as a trademark or service mark, or claim any proprietary rights of any sort in the Image(s) or any part thereof.
3. use the Image(s) in electronic format, on-line or in multimedia applications unless the Image(s) are incorporated for viewing purposes only and no permission is given to download and/or save the Image(s) for any reason.
4. rent, lease, sublicence or lend the Image(s), or a copy thereof, to another person or legal entity. You may, however, transfer all your licence to use the Image(s) to another person or legal entity, provided that (i) you transfer the Image(s) and this Licence, including all copies (except copies incorporated into your work product as permitted under this Licence), to such person or entity, (ii) that you retain no copies, including copies stored on a computer or other storage device, and (iii) the receiving party agrees to be bound by the terms and conditions of this Licence.
5. use any Image(s) except as expressly permitted by this Licence.
6. use the Image(s) related to identifiable individuals, products or entities in a manner which suggests their association with or endorsement of any product or service unless you clearly print a statement which indicates that in the case of an individual or recognisable product, the person/product is used for illustrative purposes only.

ACKNOWLEDGMENTS

We would like to thank the following individuals and organisations for their assistance in producing this book.

Photography: Steven Bartholomew, Steve Tanner and Karl Adamson.

Styling: Mary Wadsworth.

Picture agencies: 152-3 Pictor International Ltd/Carl Yarbrough. **174** The Stock Market/ Jim Erickson. **184** Gettyone Stone/Frans Lanting. **202** Comstock Photofile Limited/ Michael Stuckey. **204** Associated Sports Photography/Stuart Franklin, **TL**; Associated Sports Photography/George Herringshaw, **BL**; Colorsport/Andrew Cowie, **BC**; Associated Sports Photography/Nigel French, **BR**. **205** Colorsport/Andrew Cowie. **206-7** Colorsport/ Andrew Cowie. **208** Colorsport/Michael Stuckey. **208-9** Colorsport/Andrew Cowie. **209** Associated Sports Photography/Ed Lacey. **228** Hulton Getty Images, **BC**; Hulton Getty Images, (rest). **235** Hulton Getty Images, **BR**; Hulton Getty Images, **BR**; Hulton Getty Images, BR (rest). **250-1** Gettyone Stone/ Mark Harwood. **276-7** The Stock Market/ Al Francekevich. **298-9** The Stock Market/ Gary D Landsman. **312-13** Pictor International Ltd/Ethel Davies. **326-7** Gettyone Stone/ Lonny Kalfus.

Equipment and Photographs Courtesy of: Microsoft Corporation, Epson Corporation, Fujifilm, Dell Computer Corporation, Canon (UK) Ltd, D-Link Systems Inc., Alcatel, Nokia, Carrera Technology Ltd, Logitech, Iomega, Yamaha Kemble Music Ltd, Bite, KYE Systems UK Ltd, PMC Electronics Ltd.

Software: Microsoft Corporation, Steinberg Media Technologies AG, Guildsoft Ltd, Focus.

PLANET THREE PUBLISHING NETWORK

Edited, designed and produced by

Planet Three Publishing Network
Northburgh House,
10 Northburgh Street, London EC1V 0AT
Phone +44 (0) 20 7251 3300
Fax +44 (0) 20 7251 3399
ISDN +44 (0) 20 7253 0298
E-mail postmaster@planet3.co.uk

Windows XP Edition

Editor Tom Ruppel

Deputy Editor Jennifer Banks

Art Editor Kate Painter

Designer Yuen Ching Lam

Associate Editor Frank Fisher

Illustrator Nancy Dunkerley

Producer Paul Southcombe

Contributors
Susannah Hall
Hugh Livingstone
Steven Dunsthorne
Roger Gann
Steve Malyan
Sandra Vogel

For Reader's Digest

Editor Alison Candlin

Art Editor Jane McKenna

Technical Consultant Tony Rilett

Editorial Assistant Rachel Weaver

Pre-press Accounts Manager Penny Grose

Production Controller Nikola Hughes

Reader's Digest General Books

Editor Cortina Butler

Art Director Nick Clark

Executive Editor Julian Browne

Development Editor Ruth Binney

Managing Editor Alastair Holmes

Picture Resource Manager Martin Smith

Style Editor Ron Pankhurst

Book Production Manager Fiona McIntosh

Pre-press Manager Howard Reynolds

How to do *just about* anything on a computer Microsoft® Windows® XP Edition

was edited and designed by
The Reader's Digest Association Limited, London.

Based on *How To Do Just About Anything
On A Computer* (first published 2000)

First edition Copyright © 2002
The Reader's Digest Association Limited,
11 Westferry Circus, Canary Wharf, London E14 4HE.

We are committed to both the quality of our products and the service we provide to our customers. We value your comments, so please feel free to contact us on 08705 113366, or via our web site at www.readersdigest.co.uk
If you have any comments about the content of our books, you can e-mail us at: gbeditorial@readersdigest.co.uk

Reprinted 2003 (twice)

Copyright © 2002 Reader's Digest Association Far East Limited.
Philippines Copyright © 2002 Reader's Digest Association Far East Limited.

Web site addresses and the contents of Web sites change constantly; Web sites may disappear without warning. The publisher accepts no responsibility for the accuracy of any of the information given in this book concerning Web sites, their contents, or any of the views expressed in them.

Every effort has been made to establish ownership of copyright material depicted in this book. All queries regarding copyright issues should be directed to Martin Smith at: martin_smith@readersdigest.co.uk

Origination: Colour Systems Limited, London

Printing and binding: Mateu Cromo, Madrid

CD-ROM replication: Sonopress

CD packaging production: St Ives Multimedia Limited

Concept Code IE 0055/G
Book Code 400-149-04
ISBN 0 276 42749 1